And the WORD *Became Flesh*

And the WORD Became Flesh

Studies in History, Communication, and Scripture

in Memory of Michael W. Casey

◆ EDITED BY

THOMAS H. OLBRICHT and DAVID FLEER

PICKWICK *Publications* · Eugene, Oregon

AND THE WORD BECAME FLESH
Studies in History, Communication, and Scripture in Memory of Michael W. Casey

Pickwick Publications
A Division of Wipf and Stock Publishers
199 W. 8th Ave., Suite 3
Eugene, OR 97401

www.wipfandstock.com

ISBN 13: 978-1-60608-516-5

Cataloging-in-Publication data:

And the word became flesh : studies in history, communication and scripture in memory of Michael W. Casey / edited by Thomas H. Olbricht and David Fleer.

Eugene, Ore.: Pickwick Publications, 2009

xxii + 318 p. ; 23 cm.

Includes bibliographic references and index.

ISBN 13: 978-1-60608-516-5

1. Casey, Michael W. 2. Restoration movement (Christianity)—History.
3. Preaching. 4. Pacificism. 5. Just war doctrine. I. Olbricht, Thomas H.
II. Fleer, David. III. Title.

BX 7315 A4 2009

Manufactured in the U.S.A.

Contents

PART III: Pacifism, Just War, and Areas of Related Inquiry

Contributors

W. DAVID BAIRD
Pepperdine University
Malibu California

CARISSE MICKEY BERRYHILL
Abilene Christian University
Abilene, Texas

DAVE BLAND
Harding University Graduate School
of Religion
Memphis, Tennessee

LEE C. CAMP
Lipscomb University
Nashville, Tennessee

SHAUN A. CASEY
Wesley Theological Seminary
Washington, DC

ROBERT C. CHANDLER
University of Central Florida
Orlando, Florida

DAVID FLEER
Lipscomb University
Nashville, Tennessee

DOUGLAS A. FOSTER
Abilene Christian University
Abilene, Texas

MARK W. HAMILTON
Abilene Christian University
Abilene, Texas

JOHN MARK HICKS
Lipscomb University
Nashville, Tennessee

JEFFREY DALE HOBBS
University of Texas at Tyler
Tyler, Texas

RICHARD T. HUGHES
Messiah College
Grantham, Pennsylvania

JOHN M. JONES
Pepperdine University
Malibu, California

MARTIN J. MEDHURST
Baylor University
Waco, Texas

THOMAS H. OLBRICHT
Pepperdine University (Emeritus)
Malibu, California

ROBERT STEPHEN REID
University of Dubuque
Dubuque, Iowa

HANS ROLLMANN
Memorial University of
Newfoundland
St John's, Newfoundland

JERRY RUSHFORD
Pepperdine University
Malibu, California

GARY S. SELBY
Pepperdine University
Malibu, California

BOBBY VALENTINE
Palo Verde Church of Christ
Tucson, Arizona

Introduction

THOMAS H. OLBRICHT and DAVID FLEER

Almost immediately upon hearing of Michael Casey's death in October 2007, we concluded we must do something to memorialize our departed friend. Among many options that surfaced we chose to publish a book of essays written by Mike's academic friends and colleagues. We were even more convinced of our decision upon discovering the readiness of many scholars to submit essays in tribute. Mike's interests were varied so we assembled a list of possible authors from a broad spectrum of disciplines. We sent our list to Mike's wife Judy Jordan Casey and his brother Shaun Casey and invited their input and recommended additions. From the resulting slate we contacted prospective authors and were elated by the response. It is therefore our privilege to present this volume as an enduring *memoriam* for our distinguished friend.

In his fifty-three years Mike Casey made an indelible impact upon all his academic friends in the United States, Great Britain, and elsewhere in the world. His thirty some years of research and publications were multinational. Mike was especially adept at looking into archival details on the numerous subjects that interested him in communication, Scripture, and history, especially as they focused upon Churches of Christ and the Stone-Campbell Movement. If a scholar ever believed that the grandest project depends on the accuracy of the smallest component, it was Mike Casey. He was interested in the human employment of words for affirming, persuading, and defending. He believed that words were enfleshed in concrete persons. All his studies recognized the persuasive powers of committed humans. It is for this reason that we have selected as the title for this volume *And the Word Became Flesh*.

When we heard the disturbing news that Mike was diagnosed with cancer, we contacted him by e-mail to express our concern. Mike, in his inimitable manner, was eager to comment on his situation regardless of how difficult that might be for some. He had researched the characteristics for his specific type of cancer, the treatments normally pursued and the prognostication for achieving remission. He clearly knew the dangers but was optimistic for a cure. We exchanged several e-mail posts regarding his illness and appreciated his openness and acceptance of whatever awaited. He was a person who relished life but trusted his future to the Lord Jesus Christ.

❧

Mike was born on May 14, 1954, in Kennett, Missouri, to Paul and Melba Casey. The family moved to Paducah, Kentucky, in 1961 where Mike was baptized and the Caseys attended the Broadway Church of Christ.

Mike's father taught school as a young adult before he entered the Navy in WWII. His mother was a teacher before marriage, and then went back to the classroom when her youngest child reached adolescence. She became an administrator, spending several years as Executive Director of the West Kentucky Educational Cooperative. Mike's paternal grandmother taught for many years in a one-room schoolhouse and three grandparents of varying "greats" attended and then taught at the same college.[1] With this heritage Mike and his siblings naturally pursued careers in education.[2] Paul and Melba Casey nurtured their children's curiosity about the world, and encouraged Mike's aptitude for rhetoric, research, and history.[3] Deep into their professional lives the Casey kids continued to stimulate one another through their strong family tradition of debate.[4]

1. Email correspondence with Rita J. Casey, January 11, 2009, in possession of the editors.

2. Rita J. Casey is Associate Professor of Psychology at Wayne State University. Shaun A. Casey is Associate Professor of Christian Ethics at Wesley Theological Seminary. Neil Casey teaches music and is Band Director at Cape Central High School in Cape Girardeau, Missouri. Karen, Mike's oldest sister, passed away in 1979, and had been a teacher.

3. Based on email correspondence with Neil Casey, December 3, 2008, in possession of the editors.

4. Mike's sister, Rita recalls, "There was almost no topic in American or European intellectual history that he didn't know well . . . [T]here's a good deal of overlap in the theories of communication and psychology. It was always valuable to describe some theory that informs psychology, and have him dissect it. These discussions generated many ideas, at least for me, and also generated some great arguments—I think two of our family's strongest

We first became acquainted with Mike when he matriculated at Abilene Christian University. Tom first met him either at ACU, where Mike enrolled in both undergraduate and graduate courses under Tom's instruction, or at the Minter Lane Church of Christ, where Tom served as an elder. Early on Mike was of a serious demeanor, but not opposed at all to a bit of fun. His intellectual curiosity took him in all sorts of directions ranging from deep philosophical and theological questions to brotherhood journals and politics. He was active among the college students at Minter Lane and could normally be counted upon to participate in whatever activities were held from devotionals to helping persons who lived in the vicinity of the Minter building. As a Kentuckian he was especially interested in basketball and he and Shaun wrote a column on national intercollegiate basketball in the ACU *Optimist*.

We talked often on matters having to do with Scripture, Restoration History and communication. When Mike decided to pursue a PhD in Speech Communication, Tom encouraged him and wrote recommendations. Upon receiving an invitation to work on his doctorate at the University of Pittsburgh Mike decided to accept their offer. Tom knew his major advisor, Robert P. Newman, from his years as a Professor at the Pennsylvania State University and when Mike defended his dissertation Newman invited Tom to be an external examiner on the committee. Mike, of course, was an excellent scholar and the exam proceeded smoothly.[5]

In the summer of 1986 Mike returned to Abilene to finish his Old Testament thesis. That August the Olbrichts moved to Malibu where Tom took a position as chair of the Religion Division at Pepperdine University. When they put their house on the market, Mike lived in it until it sold in the spring of 1987. Meanwhile, Tom and Dorothy had come to know Judy Jordan who lived on country acreage out of Abilene and to whom they entrusted the family's pet upon their move. Mike married Judy Jordan on November 27, 1987, in Abilene, Texas, at the Minter Lane Church of Christ. Their son, Neil Jordan Casey, was born on May 9, 1989.

---

traditions are the study of history, and debating." Email correspondence with Rita J. Casey, December 4, 2008, in possession of the editors.

5. "The Development of Necessary Inference in the Hermeneutics of the Disciples of Christ/Churches of Christ" (PhD dissertation, University of Pittsburgh, 1986). A decade later he published the dissertation with some revision, Michael W. Casey, *The Battle over Hermeneutics in the Stone-Campbell Movement*, 1800-1870 (Lewiston, NY: Mellen, 1998).

In the mid 1980s Mike got wind of a volume on American orators[6] and asked Tom to co-author two essays with him.[7] After Tom's retirement and move to Maine, he and Mike corresponded regularly, especially regarding Mike's research on pacifism in Churches of Christ. Mike did fundamental sleuthing in regard to people who took conscientious objector status during WWII and interviewed several persons to gather details that have now been preserved, but would no longer exist had not Mike ferreted them out. Both Mike and Tom were among the founders of the Stone-Campbell List, launched in 1994, when Mike served as the first moderator.

Mike was an active participant and tireless leader in the Christian Scholars' Conference. His research and writing represented quality scholarship and his loyalty to the Churches of Christ modeled for young scholars and peers the highest levels of academic achievement. At the inaugural conference, in 1981, Mike was the youngest participant, reviewing *Journey in Faith: A History of the Christian Church (Disciples of Christ)*.[8] Soon, Mike's presentations reflected the breadth of his growing scholarly interests. For example, "Rhetoric and Induction: The Baconian Ideal in the Disciples Movement" (CSC, 1982), "J. S. Lamar: From Exegesis to Theology, A Response to Leonard Allen" (CSC, 1984), and "Scripture as Narrative: The Church as a Story-Form People" (CSC, 1989) showed skills in a variety of disciplines. Mike quickly assumed leadership roles and promoted the conference amongst colleagues and students, often organizing panel reviews and inviting speakers.[9] He proved a generous fellow researcher and historian who shared both insights and encouragement.[10] At the 1998 conference, for example, Mike joined Hans Rollmann

---

6. *American Orators Before 1900: Critical Studies and Sources*, eds. Bernard K. Duffy and Halford R. Ryan (New York: Greenwood, 1987).

7. Michael Casey and Thomas H. Olbricht, "Thomas Hart Benton" and Thomas H. Olbricht and Michael Casey, "Phillips Brooks." The order of the authors indicates who took the lead in each essay.

8. Lester G. McAllister and William Eldon Tucker, *Journey in Faith: A History of the Christian Church (Disciples of Christ)*, 1975. The paper was presented July 20, 1981 at ACU.

9. Mike encouraged David's interest in rhetoric and homiletics, evidenced in David's CSC presentations on public apology (1989), a medieval preacher, Peter Chyrsologus (1994), and a panel review of Stephen H. Webb's *The Divine Voice* (2004). In fact, Mike took a central role in bringing Stephen H. Webb to the 2004 conference, hosted by Pepperdine University.

10. Hans Rollmann, email correspondence, January 12, 2009, in possession of the editors.

to organize and chair a session on Robert H. Boll and Premillennialism.[11] While this particular collection of papers did not make it to publication, the effort demonstrated his collegiality and vision of the conference as a venue for nurturing scholarship. Mike, like his mentor Tom Olbricht before him,[12] had become the face of the Christian Scholars' Conference.[13]

One pivotal session at the 2007 conference in Rochester featured a panel review of Mike's last volume, *The Rhetoric of Sir Garfield Todd*.[14] Mike, too ill at the time to attend, was on hand via telephone conference call to listen and respond to the panelists' prepared critique. The Christian Scholars' conference thus framed Mike's professional life, beginning with his 1981 review of the McAllister and Tucker history of the Restoration Movement and ending with a scholarly review of his final one volume contribution to the broad spectrum of academic disciplines that characterized his career.

It is, therefore, altogether appropriate that this *memoriam* be presented to Mike's family and colleagues at the gathering of the Christian Scholars' Conference on June 26, 2009. Farewell faithful friend. We anticipate meeting again in far more auspicious circumstances.

We wish to express our appreciation for all those involved in the making of this book, both those who have submitted essays and those who have helped in editing and production. We are especially indebted to the budget of recently retired Dean W. David Baird of Seaver College, Pepperdine University, for help in publishing the book and to Lipscomb University and the Christian Scholars' Conference for making it available to the 2009 conference attendees.

---

11. Doug Foster, Steve Wolfgang, Mike Casey, Paul Clarke, Alex Wilson, and Hans Rollmann presented papers. Don Haymes and Richard Hughes responded.

12. Rita Casey articulates well what so many of us have respected, "Tom Olbricht as Mike's true mentor in his scholarly work, had such a strong influence on Mike's life, helping Mike find a direction for his talents and interests." Email Correspondence, December 3, 2008, in possession of the editors.

13. When the conference left Abilene for Malibu and subsequently to a variety of locations, Mike continued to present his research. For example, July 23, 1993 at Harding University, "Government Surveillance of the Churches of Christ in World War I."

14. Michael W. Casey, *The Rhetoric of Sir Garfield Todd: Christian Imagination and the Dream of an African Democracy* (Waco, TX: Baylor University Press, 2007). The session was convened by Robert Stephen Reid and included Evrett Huffard, Val Prill (reading the remarks from Paul Prill), and Pepperdine student, Mushambi Mutuma. See http://www.rc.edu/csc/session_update.php.

Michael W. Casey's Scholarship

DOUGLAS A. FOSTER

I make no pretense that this is an "objective" or "scholarly" article. Mike was my friend and brother, a colleague and co-laborer in Christian higher education, and a co-lover of our religious heritage. From the time Neil was a pre-schooler I have been privileged to be one of the Casey's Pepperdine Lectures houseguests—always a time to catch up on current projects, to share stories from Stone-Campbell history, and to envision and collaborate on shared projects. Mike's exuberance for his work and studies was a constant encouragement.

We worked together for three years identifying and gathering important articles on Stone-Campbell history and theology originally published in journals not easily accessible to students and scholars that was published as *The Stone-Campbell Movement: An International Religious Tradition* in 2002. We co-wrote the introductory chapter on the state of Stone-Campbell scholarship and trajectories for the future. It was a shock to both of us when several months after publication a colleague offhandedly commented about how upset we must have been over the misspelling of "Campbell" on the book cover. We immediately rushed to look and discovered that neither of us had noticed that "Stone-Campbell Movement" had become "Stone-Campell Movement" on the book's spine.

Mike loved our heritage in Churches of Christ. As is the case with many of us, there have been times when we wondered whether we could or should stay. In his 2005 tenure review portfolio that Judy shared with me, Mike wrote about this.

> I am a fifth generation member of Churches of Christ, but my loyalty to Churches of Christ goes beyond mere family ties. As a young adult I had to make a choice on whether to stay within Churches of Christ or to leave. Despite a lack of support at times

for my educational goals, I believe that the church's idea that one can study the scripture for one's self gave me intellectual freedom that is unrivalled by any other religious tradition. Admittedly the Churches of Christ often do not live up to that lofty ideal, but the ideal is still there.[15]

He went on to talk about the focus he saw in Churches of Christ on biblical Christianity, that is, on trying to identify what is central to scripture, and the essential role of the community of faith. These things were at the center of his Christian commitments, and Mike lived them out in his devotion to family, students, church and school.

Throughout his career Mike continued to develop his courses in ways that reflected his own scholarly maturation process. He was excited about his increasing effectiveness in bringing Christian perspectives to his classes. In his Interpersonal Communication class, for example, he combined rigorous scholarship with an unashamed inclusion of Christian perspectives through books like Ron Arnett's *Dwell in Peace: Applying Nonviolence to Everyday Relationships*. In his course on Rhetorical Theory he introduced significant readings from the journal *Rhetoric and Public Affairs* dealing with the relationship of rhetorical invention and religious traditions.[16]

Yet the thing that Mike felt best about, and which he believed had improved his teaching more than anything else, was the practice begun in 2002 of having one-on-one interviews with each of his students outside of class at the beginning of each semester. He visited with them about why they came to Pepperdine, other schools they had considered, and their academic major and vocational choices. It was easy to pick up from the conversation whether they were Christians or not, he said. It broke down barriers and began to build relationships that helped him identify students who would benefit from special encouragement and mentoring.[17] This reflects the heart of the man—his commitments were to people, not simply to a subject.

In September 2007, the month before Mike died, I had scheduled him to speak at the Restoration Lectures as part of the ACU annual Bible Lectures (now Summit). He had been very ill and in the hospital just days

15. Michael W. Casey, Faculty Data Form, Five-Year Evaluation of Tenured Faculty (January 10, 2005) 20. Copy in possession of author.

16. Ibid., 4–5.

17. Ibid., 2.

before he was to come to Abilene. I contacted him and insisted that he did not need to come—it would be asking too much for him to do so. Yet he persisted and came anyway. His lectures focused on the significance of the Stone-Campbell Movement on the political formation of Sir Garfield Todd, the anti-apartheid leader of Zimbabwe—the subject of his 2007 Baylor University Press book. He had lost his hair, he was thin and tired easily. Yet when he got up to speak he was energized and told the story of Todd's life with enthusiasm and vigor.

Mike loved our story; he loved telling the parts of it that he knew especially well. And he was doing it to the end of his life.

The bibliography that follows this essay does not claim absolute comprehensiveness, though I hope it is very close. When I began to make inquiries with Judy and with Robert Chandler, chair of the Pepperdine Communication Division, I found that Mike had not turned in the yearly Faculty Update Form for several years, explaining that since he had tenure, he didn't need to turn in "busywork reports."[18] This further endears Mike to me as a resister of bureaucratic institutional requirements. Yet as a historian, it also strikes fear into my heart that important things can too easily slip through the cracks. Between material from Judy, who found computer files with some of Mike's information, and a thorough search this Fall with the help of my graduate assistant Rosten Callarman, the bibliography that appears below is close to complete.

Mike's scholarly work began with his undergraduate studies at Abilene Christian University where he graduated summa cum laude in 1976 with a B.A. in communication and biblical studies. He completed course work for an MA degree in Old Testament and church history from ACU over the following three years, a combination reflected in the title of his 1989 thesis, "The Interpretation of Genesis One in the Churches of Christ: The Origins of Fundamentalist Reactions to Evolution and Biblical Criticism in the 1920s." This research would give Mike insight into American Fundamentalism and its relationship to Churches of Christ that would inform much of his subsequent scholarly work. His insights are especially reflected in his essay on Fundamentalism and Churches of Christ in the *Christian Chronicle* "Decades of Destiny" series in 2000 and two articles in *Restoration Quarterly* in 2002, examining the earliest attempts at graduate education in Churches of Christ.

18. E-mail note, Robert C. Chandler to Douglas A. Foster (October 30, 2008).

In the meantime, Mike entered the University of Pittsburgh, inspired by ACU church history professor LeMoine Lewis to pursue a PhD and prepare to teach in a Christian school. He earned an MA in Rhetorical Theory and Religious Communication in 1981, and a PhD in Rhetorical Theory and Criticism in 1986. His dissertation, titled "The Development of Necessary Inference in the Hermeneutics of the Disciples of Christ/ Churches of Christ," would inform two seminal articles on hermeneutics in *Restoration Quarterly* in 1989 and would be published by Edwin Mellen Press in 1998 as *The Battle Over Hermeneutics in the Stone-Campbell Movement, 1800–1870.*

In Fall 1987 Peppeprdine University extended an invitation to Mike to join its communication faculty, which he did and where he served with distinction for twenty years. He became a full professor in 1997, and was awarded the Carl P. Miller Endowed Chair of Communication in 2000, which he occupied at the time of his death. During the academic year 2002-3 Mike received a fellowship from Baylor University's Institute for Faith and Learning to bring together his long-time research on primitivist pacifism and to work with Baylor faculty on issues of integrating faith and learning.

In looking at Mike's scholarly work, several things become evident. First, the topic about which he was most passionate and which forms the largest corpus of his published materials was that of pacifism in Churches of Christ, including how that history related to pacifism in other primitivist bodies. He published widely in this field during his career, both in academic publications and in the *Gospel Advocate* and *Leaven* journal. This was groundbreaking work, and though he published no less than ten significant scholarly articles on this subject, his planned book on the topic was not completed. He clearly set the agenda for studies in this area, providing vital insights and ample material for others to carry on.

Mike's training and teaching in communication and rhetoric, coupled with his intense interest in Stone-Campbell history and American and British Christianity, led to a number of important projects in these areas. His 1995 book *Saddlebags, City Streets and Cyberspace* looked at major historical and theological trends in the preaching of Churches of Christ in the twentieth century. Two articles co-written with Aimee Rowe in 1996 and 1997 examined the rhetoric of the anti-Semitic "radio priest" Charles E. Coughlin. His article "The First Female Speakers in America (1630–1840): Searching for Egalitarian Christian Primitivism," published in the *Journal of Communication and Religion* in 2000 won the Religious Communication Association's article of the year award and was nominated for three other awards by the RCA and the National Communication Association. In that study Mike challenged standard accounts concerning the earliest women public speakers in America and proposed an innovative theoretical grounding for their role.

Further contributions to the study of religious rhetoric continued to reflect Mike's interest in serious examination of the Stone-Campbell Movement. A 2001 article in *Southern Communication Journal* used Alexander Campbell as a case study of the shift in rhetorical theory, and he investigated rhetorical invention in Churches of Christ in a 2004 *Rhetoric and Public Affairs* study. Finally, he brought his training to bear on the rhetoric of an African missionary from the New Zealand Churches of Christ, Sir Garfield Todd, who became Prime Minister of Southern Rhodesia and championed black majority rule in what would become Zimbabwe. His 2007 volume by Baylor University Press titled *The Rhetoric of Sir Garfield Todd*, in the words of one reviewer, "provides undisputed evidence that . . . Todd's democratic ethos emanated from his religious heritage within the Churches of Christ" and not from the British liberal political tradition.[19]

What more can I say about this friend and colleague? He served his profession in countless ways, including his work on the editorial board of the *Journal of Communication and Religion* which he helped build, and on the editorial board of the Baylor University Press series on Studies in Religion and Rhetoric. He served his university through committees on academic affairs, admissions and scholarships, curriculum and research. He served the University Church of Christ in Malibu through teaching Bible classes, and serving on education, body life and campus ministry committees. When away from home he taught a Bible class at the Crestview Church of Christ in Waco during his Baylor Fellowship in 2003. He served Churches of Christ through his founding work with *Leaven* journal and his service on its editorial board. He spoke widely in our colleges and congregations helping people learn more about and appreciate our heritage.

No short essay can capture the fullness of a life. It is my hope that this brief account does just a bit to honor the life and continuing legacy of Michael W. Casey, our brother, colleague and friend.

---

19. Jairos Kangira, *Rhetoric & Public Affairs* 11 (2008) 350–52.

A Bibliography of the Published Work of Michael Wilson Casey

BOOKS

Saddlebags, City Streets and Cyberspace: A History of Preaching in the Churches of Christ. Abilene, TX: ACU Press, 1995.

The Battle Over Hermeneutics in the Stone-Campbell Movement, 1800-1870. Studies in American Religion 67. Lewiston, NY: Mellen, 1998.

And Douglas A. Foster, editors. *The Stone-Campbell Movement: An International Religious Tradition.* Knoxville: University of Tennessee Press, 2002.

The Rhetoric of Sir Garfield Todd: Christian Imagination and the Dream of an African Democracy. Waco, TX: Baylor University Press, 2007.

CONTRIBUTIONS TO ENCYCLOPEDIAS AND REFERENCE WORKS

With Thomas H. Olbricht. "Thomas Hart Benton." In *American Orators Before* 1900: *Critical Studies and Sources,* edited by Bernard Duffy and Halford Ryan, 47–57. Westport, CT: Greenwood, 1987.

With Thomas H. Olbricht. "Phillips Brooks." In *American Orators Before* 1900: *Critical Studies and Sources,* ed. by Bernard Duffy and Halford Ryan, 58–67. Westport, CT: Greenwood, 1987.

Encyclopedia of the Stone Campbell Movement, edited by Douglas A. Foster, Paul M. Blowers, Anthony L. Dunnavant, and D. Newell Williams. Grand Rapids: Eerdmans, 2004.

> "Bible, Authority and Inspiration of Scripture."
> "Campus Ministry: Churches of Christ."
> "*Christian Leader.*"
> "Cordell Christian College."
> "Pacifism."
> "Preaching, Twentieth Century: Churches of Christ."
> "Todd, Sir Garfield (1908–2002) and Lady Grace (1911–2001)."

"Restorationist Christianity." In *The New Encyclopedia of Southern Culture,* Volume 1: *Religion,* edited by Samuel S. Hill. Chapel Hill: University of North Carolina Press, 2006.

"Primitivism." In *Encyclopedia of Religious Revivals in America,* edited by Michael W Clymond, 344–45. Westport, CT: Greenwood Press, 2007.

"Disciples of Christ." In *Women in American History: An Encyclopedia.* New York: Facts on File, forthcoming.

"Kate Richards O'Hare." In *Women in American History: An Encyclopedia.* New York: Facts on File, forthcoming.

ARTICLES IN SCHOLARLY JOURNALS AND BOOKS

"An Era of Controversy and Division: The Origins of the Broadway Church of Christ, Paducah, Kentucky." *Restoration Quarterly* 27.1 (1984) 3–22.

"The Origins of the Hermeneutics of the Churches of Christ, Part One: The Reformed Tradition." *Restoration Quarterly* 31.2 (1989) 75–91.

"The Origins of the Hermeneutics of the Churches of Christ, Part Two: The Philosophical Background." *Restoration Quarterly* 31.4 (1989) 193–206.

"The Use of Narrative in a Public Speaking Assignment." In *Narrativity and Community: Proceedings of the Second Conference on Christianity and Communication*. Malibu, CA: Conference on Christianity and Communication, 1991.

"From Pacifism to Patriotism: The Emergence of Civil Religion in the Churches of Christ During World War I." *Mennonite Quarterly Review* 66 (1992) 376–90.

"New Information on Conscientious Objectors of World War I and the Churches of Christ." *Restoration Quarterly* 34.2 (1992) 83–96.

"Warriors Against War: The Pacifists of the Churches of Christ in World War II." *Restoration Quarterly* 35.3 (1993) 159–74.

With Aimee Rowe. "Driving Out the Money Changers: Radio Priest Charles E. Coughlin's Rhetorical Vision." *Journal of Communication and Religion* 19 (1996) 37–47.

With Michael W Jordan. "Government Surveillance of the Churches of Christ in World War I: An Episode of Free Speech Suppression." *Free Speech Yearbook* 34 (1996) 102–11.

"Churches of Christ and World War II Civilian Public Service : A Pacifist Remnant." In *Proclaim Peace: Christian Pacifism from Unexpected Quarters*, edited by Theron F. Schlabach and Richard T. Hughes, 97–114. Urbana, IL: Snow Lion, 1997.

With Aimee Rowe. "Villains and Heroes of the Great Depression: The Evolution of Father Charles E. Coughlin's Fantasy Themes." *Journal of Radio Studies* 4 (1997) 112–33.

"The Closing of Cordell Christian College: A Microcosm of American Intolerance During World War I." *Chronicles of Oklahoma* 76 (1998) 20–37.

"Pacifism and Nonviolence: The Prophetic Voice of the African-American Churches of Christ." *Discipliana* 59.2 (1999) 35–49.

"The First Female Public Speakers in America (1630–1840): Searching for Egalitarian Christian Primitivism." *Journal of Communication and Religion* 23 (March 2000) 1–28.

"The Theory of Logic and Inference in the Declaration and address." In *Quest for Christian Unity, Peace, and Purity in Thomas Campbell's Declaration and Address*, edited by Thomas H. Olbricht and Hans Rollmann, 223–42. Lanham, MD: Snow Lion, 2000.

"Walter Scott: A 19th-Century Evangelical." *Restoration Quarterly* 42.1 (2000) 58–59.

"The Overlooked Pacifist Tradition of the Old Paths Churches of Christ: Part I—The Great War and the Old Paths Division." *Journal of the United Reform Church History Society* 6 (2000) 446–60.

"The Overlooked Pacifist Tradition of the Old Paths Churches of Christ: Part II – Labour and Pacifist Ties from the 1920s to the Present." *Journal of the United Reform Church History Society* 6 (2000) 517–28.

With Peter Ackers. "The Enigma of the Young Arthur Horner: From Churches of Christ Preacher to Communist Militant (1894–1920)." *Labour History Review* 66 (Spring 2001) 3–23.

"From British Ciceronianism to American Baconianism: Alexander Campbell as a Case Study of a Shift in Rhetorical Theory." *Southern Communication Journal* 66 (Winter 2001) 151–67.

"The First Graduate Theological Education in the Churches of Christ. Part 1, Jesse Sewell's and George Klingman's Audacious Synthesis of Spirituality and Academic Excellence at Abilene Christian College." *Restoration Quarterly* 44.2 (2002) 73–92.

"The First Graduate Theological Education in the Churches of Christ. Part 2: The Controversy over William Webb Freeman's 'Modernism' and the Resulting Collapse of Sewell's Dream." *Restoration Quarterly* 44.3 (2002) 139–57.

"From Religious Outsiders to Insiders: The Rise and Fall of Pacifism in the Churches of Christ." *Journal of Church and State* 44 (2002) 455–75.

"From Patriotism to Pacifism: The Emergence of Civil Religion in the Churches of Christ in World War One." In *The Stone Campbell Movement: An International Religious Tradition*, ed. by Michael W. Casey and Douglas A. Foster, 466–80. Knoxville: University of Tennessee Press, 2002.

With Douglas A. Foster. "The Renaissance of Stone-Campbell Studies: An Assessment and Directions." In *The Stone Campbell Movement: An International Religious Tradition*, edited by Michael W. Casey and Douglas A. Foster, 1–65. Knoxville: University of Tennessee Press, 2002.

"The Fundamentalist Controversy, 1920–1930." In *Decades of Destiny: A History of Churches of Christ from 1900–2000*, edited by Lindy Adams and Scott LaMascus, 51–57. Abilene, TX: Abilene Christian University Press, 2004.

"'Come Let Us Reason Together': The Heritage of the Churches of Christ as a Source for Rhetorical Invention." *Rhetoric & Public Affairs* 7 (2004) 487–98.

"Mastered by the Word: Print Culture, Modernization, and 'The Priesthood of all Readers' in the Churches of Christ." In *Restoring the First-Century Church in the Twenty-First Century: Essays on the Stone-Campbell Restoration Movement in Honor of Don Haymes*, edited by Warren Lewis and Hans Rollmann, 311-322. Studies in the History and Culture of World Christianities 1. Eugene, OR: Wipf & Stock, 2005.

ARTICLES IN CHURCH PUBLICATIONS

"Looking Back and Looking Forward . . ." *Mission* 15 (May 1, 1982) 21.

"Church Growth: New Information (1)." *Image* 3 (May 1, 1987) 14.

"Church Growth: New Information (2)." *Image* 3 (May 15, 1987) 20.

"Preaching in the Worldly Church." *Leaven* 1 (July 1, 1990) 17.

"Our Cloud of Witnesses." *Leaven* 2 (April 1, 1992) 41.

"Pacifism in the Restoration Movement." *Gospel Advocate* 135 (November 1, 1993) 57.

"Pacifism and David Lipscomb." *Gospel Advocate* 135 (December 1, 1993) 46.

"Pacifism in the Restoration: WWI." *Gospel Advocate* 136 (January 1, 1994) 46.

"Between the World Wars." *Gospel Advocate* 136 (March 1, 1994) 30.

"Corbett Bishop." *Gospel Advocate* 136 (April 1, 1994) 45.

"World War II." *Gospel Advocate* 136 (May 1, 1994) 46.

"1945 to the Present." *Gospel Advocate* 136 (December 1, 1994) 28.

"Kingdoms of This World: The Rise of the Political Pulpit." *Leaven* 6 (July 1, 1998) 151.

"Churches of Christ Scholars Network Formed." *Christian Chronicle* 55 (1998) 6.

"Ethics of War: Pacifism and Militarism in the American Restoration Movement." *Leaven* 7 (October 1, 1999) 194–98, 211.

"Restoration Retrospective: 1920–1930 (Third in a Series)." *Christian Chronicle* 57 (March 1, 2000) 20.

PART I

Restoration History

R. W. Officer and the Indian Mission

The Foundational Years (1880–1886)

W. DAVID BAIRD

In 1880, Robert Wallace Officer launched a mission effort among the Native peoples of Indian Territory, now the eastern one-half of the State of Oklahoma. As a well-connected minister in the Stone-Campbell movement, Officer's enterprise was widely welcomed by journal editors, church leaders, and evangelists. Conservative and southern elements in the movement were especially enthusiastic, for Officer announced that he would accept support for his mission only from individuals and congregations rather than from the American Christian Missionary Society (ACMS), a para-church organization underwritten by the more progressive and northern congregations.

Scholars of the Stone-Campbell movement have seen Officer and the Indian Mission as pivotal in the late-nineteenth century controversy over whether the church should conduct mission work through "human societies" rather than the local church. It may also be true, as the scholars argue, that the Indian Mission was the most successful mission effort conducted according to the "Lord's plan," as David Lipscomb termed it.[1] But it does not follow that Officer's twenty years of labor in Indian

---

1. See David Edwin Harrell, Jr., *The Social Sources of Division in the Disciples of Christ, 1865–1900: A Social History of the Disciples of Christ, Vol. II* (Atlanta: Publishing Systems, Inc., 1973) 271–74; Robert E. Hooper, *Crying in the Wilderness: A Biography of David Lipscomb* (Nashville: David Lipscomb College, 1979) 289; and Richard T. Hughes and R. L. Roberts, *The Churches of Christ* (Westport, CT: Greenwood, 2001) 273–74. For additional insights to Officer's work in Indian Territory see: Earl Irvin West, *The Search for*

Territory was a success when measured against his original expectations, or those of his supporters. By those standards, the Indian mission was a failure, although that failure had more to do with circumstances unique to Indian Territory than whether the methodology of mission work was Bible-based or not. This essay, however, focuses upon the foundational years of the mission, when calling was certain, vision was clear and hopes were high. The frustrations, disappointments and defeats of later years will be addressed in subsequent essays.

Born in August 1845, R. W. Officer was one of Alexander and Francis Officer's ten children. The family lived in Murray County, northern Georgia, and farmed land only recently taken from Cherokee Indians. In the late 1850s and for undetermined reasons, the family moved to Polk County, Tennessee.[2] Little is known about Officer's formal education as a teenager other than it was interrupted by the Civil War. At the age of sixteen he and an older brother enlisted with other Polk County men in Company A of the 43rd (Mounted) Tennessee Infantry Regiment, CSA, in April 1862. He was assigned the rank of private, while his brother was commissioned 3rd Lieutenant. Barely a year later, his unit saw action at Vicksburg, where then Corporal Officer was wounded and on July 4, 1863, taken captive by Union troops. Eleven days later he was paroled after he swore "not [to] take up arms again against the United States . . . ." A prisoner exchange some three months later returned him to Confederate authority, whereupon he promptly joined the Army of East Tennessee, then commanded by General John H. Morgan, where he served as a scout until the end of the war. On May 21, 1865, at Chattanooga, Tennessee, Officer put the war behind him, when he gave his oath of allegiance to the United States. He was almost twenty years old, five feet, eight inches tall, with blue eyes, dark hair, and a fair complexion.[3]

---

the Ancient Order: A History of the Restoration Movement, 1800–1918, Vol. 3, 1900–1918 (Indianapolis: Religious Book Service, 1979) 132–34; Michael D. Slate, "R. W. Officer: An Example of Frontier Individualism," Restoration Quarterly 22 (1979) 144–58; and Paul Goddard, "Robert Wallace Officer, 1845–1930," from "A Study of James Jenkins Trott and Robert Wallace Officer and Their Work in Indian Territory," Research Paper, Harding University Graduate School of Religion, 1982 (http://www. therestorationmovement.com/officer2.htm; accessed Dec. 2, 2008).

2. U.S. Census for 1840, Murray County, GA, District 824 (Roll 47, p. 265); U.S. Census for 1850, Murray County, GA, (Roll 78, p. 191b); U.S. Census, Polk County, TN, 10th Judicial District, Benton, Household #1287.

3 Robert W. Officer, Service Records, Compiled Service Records of Confederate Soldiers Who Served in Organizations from the State of Tennessee, RG 109, National Archives,

In the immediate five years after his military discharge, Officer pursued various educational opportunities, changed residences, and found a bride. Of his education, we know only that he attended school at London, Cocke County, in eastern Tennessee, and at Oak Hill Seminary just east of Tullahoma, Coffee County, in middle Tennessee.[4] Virtually nothing is known about these experiences, other than it left him with a good knowledge of history, a grasp of biblical languages, a love of rational thinking, and an ability to express himself well on paper or in the pulpit. In addition to an educational benefit, his move to Middle Tennessee made it possible for him to meet Lota, the charming, refined and well-educated daughter of William and Jane Curle Venable in nearby Winchester, in Franklin County. She became his wife on December 26, 1871.

Just twenty years old when she married, Lota Venable was one of the five daughters and two sons born to William and Jane Venable. Her father was a respected Winchester attorney and politician, having served in the State Senate (1847–49), the Nashville Convention (1850), as a founder of Mary Sharp College in Winchester, and as "minister resident" of the United States in Guatemala (1857). He died in Guatemala of cholera before he was able to present his credentials.[5] William Venable left his family with interest in a considerable amount of property, including the family home in Winchester, some 600 acres of land, a number of slaves, and prospective legal fees from clients he and his partner represented. Adjudication of the estate was interrupted by the Civil War, complicated by dishonesty on the part of the executor, and litigated before the Tennessee Supreme Court. Settlement did not occur until the late 1870s.[6]

Washington, DC. See also H. F. O'Beirne, *Leaders and Leading Men of Indian Territory . . . Vol. 1: Choctaws and Chickasaws . . .* (Chicago: American Publishers' Association, 1891) 187, and Donn Patton Brooks, *East Tennessee's Forgotten Soldiers: The Forty-Third Tennessee Infantry Regiment, Confederate States of America* (Kyle, TX: Westpump, 1995). See R. W. Officer [Lynnville, TN] to Bro. Lynn, np, nd, *Gospel Advocate* (hereinafter *GA*) 27 (Sept. 23, 1885) 604, c. 1–2, for his brooding reflection on the Civil War, speaking of a "dark damp shadow," "shivered hopes," "crushed prospects," and a "huge iron pen in my mother's heart."

4. O'Beirne, *Leaders and Leading Men*, 187.

5. "Venable, William Edward, 1804–1857," Vertical File, Franklin County Historical Society, Franklin County Library, Winchester, TN; Beatrice Alexander Collins, "The Venable Homestead," *The Franklin County Historical Review* 20 (1989) 15–19.

6. Deed Record T, p. 184, Records of the County Clerk, Franklin County, Winchester, TN; Jane E. Venable, et. al. vs. Wm. Edw. Venable, Loose File #1860–1302 and "The Separate Answer of F. J. Estill," Jan. 23, 1873, Loose File #1870–1632, Records of the County Court (microfilm), Franklin County Historical Society, City Library, Winchester, TN.

Lota's inheritance from her father's and mother's estates did not make her wealthy, but it did provide her with financial resources well beyond what would be generally associated with a missionary's wife located in a destitute place. Subsequently, Officer estimated that her inheritance amounted to somewhat less than $3,000, an amount large enough to cause friends and foe alike to mark him down as rich and without any need for "fellowship," or financial support from the churches.[7]

If his biographer, F. D. Srygley, was right, R. W. Officer accepted his Christian faith in 1870 under the preaching of a Methodist minister. He announced, however, that he wanted to be baptized like the Ethiopian eunuch. When the minister declined to accommodate him, he found, taught, and converted a Mr. Burris, who then baptized him. Thereafter, Officer considered himself a Baptist. He shortly accepted a call to preach from the Liberty Baptist Association, which sent him as a missionary to northern Mississippi and Alabama, where he served for six years.[8]

But Officer and the Baptist leadership often found themselves in disagreement. According to Srygley, who knew him well, "Officer was a constant and careful student of the Bible, an original and independent thinker, and a fluent and vigorous speaker."[9] He adhered tenaciously to the Bible as the source for all things divine, and the energy with which he attacked the work and worship of Christian communities whose practices he did not find in the New Testament attracted a lot of interest, and opposition. Many individuals and some entire Baptist congregations embraced his advocacy of "undenominational, New Testament Christianity." The result, according to one Baptist partisan, was that "[e]very Baptist church where Officer [had] preached [had] broken up."[10]

Concerned about the consequences of Officer's dynamic and effective preaching, the Baptist leadership summonsed him to an open meet-

7. R. W. Officer, Atoka, IT, to Bro. Lipscomb, [Nashville, TN], Mar. 16, 1892, *GA* 34 (Mar. 21, 1892) 204, c. 3; "Indian Territory," R. W. Officer, Atoka, to Bro. Somers, [Indianapolis], Nov. 5, 1890, *Octographic Review,* 33 (Nov. 27, 1890) 2, c. 4.

8. F. D. Srygley, *Biographies and Sermons: A Collection of Original Sermons by Different Men, with a Biographical Sketch of Each Man Accompanying His Sermon; Illustrated by Halftone Cuts* (Nashville: n.p.: c. 1898) 309. Officer seems to have been based in Luka, Mississippi, where both of his sons were born, Raymond in 1874 and Leon in 1877, but his circuit extended into Cherokee, Lauderdale, and Limestone counties, Alabama, and across the state line into southern Tennessee. See Faye Acton Axford, *The Scintillating Seventies* (Athens, AL: n.p., 1996) 75, 98, and 123.

9. Srygley, *Biographies and Sermons*, 311.

10. Ibid., 326.

ing at the Popular Creek Baptist Church in western Limestone County, Alabama, about 1876. The purpose was to demonstrate that Officer was not sound in the faith or loyal to Baptist doctrine. According to the transcript of the "heresy trial" published some twenty years or more afterwards, the well-known editor of the *Tennessee Baptist*, James R. Graves, questioned Officer on issues of human depravity, baptism and grace. Graves quickly concluded that Officer's answers, or non answers, were more in harmony with "Campbellite" doctrine than Baptist. And what was true theologically was also true practically, or so Elder Wininger charged. Officer was in the company of the Campbellites more than the Baptists.[11]

Wininger was probably correct, but Officer's identification with the Stone-Campbell movement did not occur suddenly. Through 1876, the occasional reports of the *Athens (Alabama) Weekly Post* on Officer's preaching appointments consistently identified him with the Baptists.[12] The so-called heresy trial did not change that relationship inasmuch as Officer continued to preach for the Temperance Oak (Baptist) Church in Limestone County, Alabama, a connection that galled James Graves and the *Tennessee Baptist*.[13] But under the influence of mentors and colleagues like N.B. Wallace, whom Officer considered his "father in the faith," Murrell Askew, a preaching co-worker of Choctaw Indian descent, and T. B. Larimore, the accomplished president of Mars Hill College in Florence, Alabama, he found himself increasingly comfortable in the company of Stone-Campbell congregations.[14] After 1876, Officer often spoke in churches associated with that movement (Tullahoma and

11. Ibid., 311, 321–37. Unfortunately, Srygley failed to tell us just exactly when this trial took place, although it must have been in 1876 or 1877. See also Andrew B. Ellis, "The Power of the Gospel in a War-Torn Town, Athens, Alabama, 1860–1862," Dec. 15, 2000, p. 9, http://drewellisfamily.tripod.com/restmov2.htm (March 1, 2003).

12. "Notices," *Athens (Alabama) Weekly Post*, March 28, 1873; January 16, 1874; August 27, 1875; and May 26, 1876, in Axford, comp., *The Scintillating Seventies*, 75, 98, 123.

13. "Defense of Bro. R. W. Officer," R. W. Officer to Brethren L[ipscomb] and S[ewell], [May 1882], and L. R. Sewell to Bro. L. & S., Franklin, Ky., Jan. 24, 1879, *GA* 23 (Apr. 13, 1882) 229, c. 1–2. My attempt to confirm Baptist irritation with Officer in the the *Tennessee Baptist* and the *Alabama Baptist* was unsuccessful.

14. "Indian Territory," R. W. Officer, Atoka, I. T., Mar. 11, 1889, *GA* 31 (May 1, 1889) 288, c. 1; "Letter To Bro. Officer," N. B. Wallace, np, nd, *GA* 25 (Dec. 26, 1883), p. 823, c. 2–3; and Askew. My conclusion about the influence of Larimore is an inference drawn from the fact that Larimore was an active evangelist in Lauderdale County at the same time Officer was there, and because the two subsequently worked together on multiple occasions in Indian Territory.

Lewisburg, Tennessee, for example), and wrote for at least one of the movement's journals (the *Gospel Advocate*) even while he served as minister for the Temperance Oak Church.[15]

The controversy with the Baptists wearied Officer. To be in the dock, to be misunderstood and then maligned, troubled him greatly, not so much because of his own ego but because it inhibited his preaching the gospel message and breeched the peace of the Kingdom. His response to the controversy revealed much of his own personality, and became precedent for action that he took on three different occasions over the next two decades. So, in the Spring 1880, Officer packed up his wife and son, loaded the family's household goods in a wagon, and moved to Texas, where he would serve the Christian church at Gainesville as city evangelist.

No more than five miles south of Red River and Indian Territory, Gainesville was a prosperous border town. The church had been organized six years before, and, like the town, its prospects were strong. Although committed to local work, Officer preached widely in North Texas, seldom failing to report to the *Gospel Advocate* on the success of his "meetings."[16] He also went north into Indian Territory, specifically the Chickasaw Nation, nowthe south central part of Oklahoma.

Officer did little more in Indian Territory than make acquaintances of its residents, learn something of Indian culture, familiarize himself with geography, and distribute religious tracts. He did not preach his first sermon until February 1881, and that in English to an audience of thirty Chickasaws gathered around a campfire near present Madill. At this service, Officer met the second-term Governor of the Chickasaws, B. F. Overton, a talented statesman who sought the economic, educational and spiritual improvement of his people. He was impressed with Officer, and encouraged him to focus his preaching, when he was among the

15. "Letter to the Church at New Hope, Ala," R. Wallace Officer to Brethren at New Hope, Athens, Ala., Nov. 7, 1877, *GA* 20 (July 14, 1878) 104, c. 1; "Defense of Bro. R. W. Officer," L.R. Sewell to Bro. L[ipscomb]. & S[ewell]., Franklin, Ky., Jan. 24, 1879, *GA* 24 (Apr. 13, 1882) 229, c. 1; US Census Records, 1880, Marshall County, Tennessee.

16. "Texas Work and Workers," R. Wallace Officer, Paris, TX, to Bro. Poe, np., July 28, 1883, *GA* 25 (Aug. 8, 1883), 507, c. 1. See also "History," First Christian Church (Disciples of Christ), Gainesville, Texas, nd. (http://www.firstchristiangainesville.com/history.html; accessed Dec. 6, 2008).

Indians, on the Chickasaws. Officer agreed to do so, a promise that gave birth to what he would soon describe as "our Indian Mission."[17]

Officer was not the first evangelist from Stone-Campbell churches to minister in Indian Territory. That honor belonged to James J. Trott who reported organizing congregations among the Cherokees near present Westville, Oklahoma, in 1857. The Civil War terminated his activity and dispersed his churches so completely that thirty years later no evidence of them could be found.[18] In the post-War era, other Stone-Campbell preachers passed through Indian Territory, but so far as is known, none left congregations that functioned for more than a very brief period of time.[19]

When Officer promised Governor Overton that he would focus his mission activity among the Chickasaws, he had not thought so much of himself as Murrell Askew, his revered friend with whom he had fought the Baptist wars in Alabama. Initially, the seventy year-old Askew was not interested in making the long trek west with his seven-member family.[20] But Officer was able to persuade him, reminding Askew that his Choctaw blood made him and other adult members of his family eligible for tribal citizenship, including land use, and promising him financial assistance if necessary. Officer was true to his word. Finding the Askews virtually destitute when they stopped at Denton, Texas, on their way to the Chickasaw Nation, Officer, without thought of repayment, loaned them $378. One-half of that amount would underwrite establishing Askew's citizenship and land rights in the Choctaw-Chickasaw Nations. Subsequently, Governor Overton gave Askew a horse and appointed

17. "Work Among the Indians," R. W. Officer, Atoka, Jan. 7, 1887, *GA* 29 (Jan. 26, 1887) 55, c. 3; "Correspondence," R. W. Officer, [Paris, TX], n.d., ibid., 26 (July 16, 1884) 453, c. 2.

18. Stephen J. England, *Oklahoma Christians: A History of Christian Churches and of the start of the Christian Church (Disciples of Christ) in Oklahoma* (Christian Church in Oklahoma, 1975) 35–40. In his various reports, Trott placed the site of his work as twenty-six miles east of Fayetteville, AR, near Westville, OK. Officer, however, located it near what is now Vinita, OK, probably for no other reason than that descendents of Trott lived there. See *Northwest Christian Magazine* (April 1858) 110–12, quoted in ibid., 39, and "Indian Territory," R. W. Officer, Atoka, IT, Dec. 12, 1891, *GA* 34 (Jan. 14, 1892) 22, c. 2–3. William G. McLoughlin, *Cherokees and Missionaries, 1789–1839* (New Haven: Yale University Press, 1984) provides an excellent analysis of Trott's missionary trials among the Cherokees before they removed to Oklahoma.

19. A partial listing of these preachers is found in England, *Oklahoma Christian*, 40–42.

20. If his son is to be believed, Askew had reservations about Officer's plans, especially his decision not to take support from the ACMS. See "Mission Work," A. Askew to Christian Review, np., nd., *Octagraphic Review*, 30 (Jan. 6, 1887) 8, c. 3.

him teacher at Burney Institute, a tribal school near present Lebanon, Oklahoma, with a salary of $100 per year.[21]

Askew was an effective missionary among his Choctaw and Chickasaw relatives. In less than thirty months, he established fifty-three active churches. Among his converts was Governor Overton.[22] In September 1883, Askew and Officer attended the annual meeting of the Chickasaw National Council at Tishomingo. He took the occasion to preach, to submit credentials endorsed by the elders of the churches at Gainesville and Paris, Texas, and to propose that Stone-Campbell churches organize an institution of learning for the Chickasaws. The council did not endorse the school proposal, but it did grant Officer and Askew the privilege of "locating a preacher of the faith" in the Chickasaw Nation.[23] Officer could have asked for more, but for the moment what he got was enough. The council's action affirmed the reality and sanctioned the work of the Indian Mission.

With Askew hard at work and a full-time co-worker anticipated among the Chickasaws, Officer made some personal adjustments that facilitated his own work in Indian Territory. In late 1883, he moved his family to Paris, Texas, some ninety-five miles east of Gainesville, to become city evangelist for the Christian Church. Organized in 1856, the congregation was a stable, healthy church, and its leadership had agreed to sponsor the Indian Mission according to the "Lord's plan." The elders were also willing to release Officer from his preaching so that he could devote one-half of his time to mission work. A residence in Paris was also helpful because it would give him easier access to Indian Territory. The community was a stop on the MK&T Railroad, a line that traversed Indian country from north to south. Paris, moreover, seemed to provide a

21. "Correspondence," R. W. Officer to Bro. Poe, Paris, TX, nd, GA 26 (Mar. 12, 1884) 164, c. 1–2; and "Our Indian Mission," James D. Elliott report, [Paris, TX], nd., ibid., 26 (Mar. 26, 1884) 194, c. 1–2; see also Wayne Kilpatrick, "Murrell Askew, The Reluctant Baptist," nd. (http://www.therestorationmovement. com/ askew.htm; accessed Dec. 2, 2008), and D. C. Gideon, Indian Territory, Descriptive, Biographical and Genealogical . . . (New York: Lewis, 1801) 541.

22. "Correspondence," R. W. Officer, Gainesville, TX, to Brethren, [Nashville, TN], nd., GA 23 (June 23, 1881) 392, c. 2–3; D.C. Gideon, History of Indian Territory (New York: Lewis, 1901), quoted in England, Oklahoma Christians, 42.

23. "Our Indian Mission," E.L. Dohoney and W.H. Sluder, Paris, TX, to Brethren, [Nashville, TN], nd., GA, 25 (Nov. 7, 1883) 708, c. 3.

healthier environment and a more stable living arrangement for Officer's family; eighteen months earlier their home in Gainesville had burned.[24]

The Indian Mission may have been appropriately and scripturally organized, but it still lacked the means to operate successfully. After the Chickasaw Council meeting, the Paris elders proposed to Stone-Campbell churches through the pages of the *Gospel Advocate* that they dedicate one Lord's Day contribution to help fund construction of a small church building in the Chickasaw Nation. That appeal netted less than $40.[25] Officer did not find the response too disturbing, because at the time he was using his personal resources to cover his and part of Murrell Askew's expenses. Later, after the work of the mission expanded and contributions did not improve, it troubled him greatly.

Just as Officer opened a new phase of his mission work, the first ended dramatically. Murrell Askew died in early January 1884. Governor B. F. Overton died six weeks later. In the passing of these two co-workers, Officer felt a deep sense of loss. Askew's death, he wrote, left him lonely and sad, with a heart that bled and eyes that could not be dried. Askew was "a true and tried soldier of the cross, who died the death of the righteous." Overton, a dear friend who had wept with him at Askew's funeral, was a ruler with a "bold, liberal spirit" who did right "because it was right."[26] But the deaths of his co-workers did not leave Officer disconsolate or with a lack of resolve. His friends were at rest in the hands of God, and he had work to do in the Choctaw Nation.

After his relocation to Paris and for several months each year, Officer went by train and/or wagon north into Indian Territory. On these excursions he always took with him a supply of religious books and pamphlets, generously provided by the readers of the *Gospel Advocate*. One of his more generous suppliers was the venerable Jacob Creath, who on one occasion had sent out several boxes of material that among other things

24. "Letter from Bro. Officer," R. W. Officer, Paris, TX, to Brother Lipscomb, [Nashville, TN], Aug. 12, 1884, *GA* 26 (Aug. 27, 1884) 546, c. 2–3; "Defense of Bro. R. W. Officer," R. W. Officer, [Paris, TX], to Brethren L. & S., [Nashville, TN], nd., ibid, 24 (Apr. 13, 1882) 229, c. 1.

25. "Our Indian Mission," R. W.O., Paris, TX, to Bro. Poe, Oct. 7, 1883, *GA* 25 (Nov. 7, 1883) 708, c. 3; "Letter from Bro. Officer," R. Wallace Officer, Paris, TX, to [Advocate, Nashville, TN], Nov. 19, 1883, ibid., 25 (Dec. 12, 1883) 788, c. 3–4.

26. "Letter to N.B. Wallace," R. W. Officer, Paris, TX, to Father in the Gospel, np, nd., *GA* 26 (Jan. 23, 1884) 55, c. 1; "Correspondence," R. W. Officer, Paris, TX, to Bro. Poe, np, nd., ibid., 26 (Mar. 12, 1884) 164, c. 1–2; ibid., 26 (July 16, 1884) 453, c. 2.

contained most of the issues of the *Advocate* published since 1861. Officer believed that the distribution of Christian literature was an effective and inexpensive way to introduce the gospel in any mission field.[27]

On his frequent trips into the Choctaw Nation, Officer was touched by the number of orphaned or fatherless children he encountered. He fairly quickly devised a plan to place such children in a Christian home in one of the United States, where they would get care for their physical, educational, and spiritual needs. One of the first to take advantage of the program was a ten-year old Choctaw girl, Phoebe Anderson, who was placed in a home in Springfield, Illinois. Over a period of time, some thirty-six boys and girls took advantage of this program, often spending weeks or months in the Officer home before joining their "adopted" families. Over time, Officer stayed in touch with all of these children who found homes in one of seven states plus Indian Territory and considered each to be a member of his family. Unfortunately, we know the names of only a few.[28]

In Indian Territory, Officer also preached. Although he spoke in English, and at times with the aid of an interpreter, he spoke generally with great effect. His sermons, according to one observer, were "practical discourses" that abounded with "glittering gems of truth . . ." and were presented with "logic and purity."[29] Among his listeners in the territory, however, he seldom found individuals who knew of or identified with the Stone-Campbell movement. But the circumstance was different in Atoka, a county seat town for the Choctaw Nation and a stop on the MK&T Railroad line. There he found James S. Standley and his family, widely recognized as one of Atoka's most prominently families. A direct descendant of Chief Apukshunnubbee, Standley was Mississippi born, privately educated, a Confederate veteran, and an attorney by profession. In 1872,

27. "A Mistake," R. W. Officer, [Paris, TX], to Bro. Poe, np., nd., *GA* 26 (May 28, 1884) 346, c.3; "Books for the Indian Mission," Jacob Creath, np., to Bros. Lipscomb & Sewell, [Nashville, TN]., nd., ibid., 26 (Aug. 20, 1884) 530, c. 2.

28. "Correspondence," R. W. Officer, [Tushka-Homma, IT], to [Editors, Nashville, TN], Oct. 28, 1886, *GA*, 28 (Nov. 10, 1886) 713, c. 1; Chas. H. Lord, per W. N. Jones [np.] to Bro. Officer, Atoka, IT, Nov. 1, 1886, ibid., 28 (Nov. 10, 1886) 707, c. 3; "Mission Work," A. Askew, [I.T.], to Christian Review, np., nd., *Octagraphic Review* 30 (Jan. 6, 1887) 3, c. 2–3.

29. "Correspondence," Justice, Honey Grove, TX, July 4, 1885, *GA* 27 (July 22, 1885) 456, c 3–4. There is little evidence beyond his ownership of a Choctaw-English dictionary that Officer tried to master the Choctaw–Chickasaw language. Nat Purkins assisted him as a translator on appropriate occasions.

he had emigrated to the Choctaw Nation, established his citizenship, and made his permanent home in Atoka.[30] On frequent occasions he represented the tribe in Washington, D.C. Of most importance, Stanley was a long-time member of the Christian Church, having been baptized in the late 1860s. Upon meeting Officer, he invited the missionary to preach in his home. Subsequently he convinced him to spend every fourth Sunday in Atoka, an appointment that he seldom failed to keep after 1883.[31]

Primarily through the agency of Standley, Officer made the acquaintance of a large number of Choctaw dignitaries. These included former chiefs, the then current chief, jurists, lawmen, ranchers, and merchants. His circle of high-placed friends even included the chiefs of the Cherokees and the Seminoles.[32] No doubt it was the influence of these men, and the success Officer had enjoyed the previous year speaking at the Chickasaw council, that caused the Choctaw National Council to invite him to preach at its annual meeting scheduled for Tuskahoma in October 1844. The invitation was historic, as the Choctaws would meet in a new and architecturally impressive capitol building.

For Officer, the invitation was a rare opportunity to draw attention to the Indian Mission, the work of which had become increasingly ambitious. Rather than continue to send orphan children to foster parents in the States, he now envisioned enrolling them in an Industrial Boarding School situated near Atoka. The institution would provide Choctaw students both liberal and vocational educations, and it would be staffed by members of the Indian Mission and built by the donations of Churches of Christ. Indeed, Officer had already sent out Katie Price, a talented Choctaw linguist and business woman, to solicit funds for the school from among the congregations. Of the Choctaw council, he expected to ask only for a small grant of land and a tuition subsidy of $2 per student per month.[33]

30. O'Beirne, *Leaders and Leading Men of the Indian Territory . . . Choctaws and Chickasaws*, 92.

31. Ibid.

32. "Trip to the Choctaw Nation," R. W. Officer, Paris, TX, nd., *GA* 26 (June 11, 1884) 372, c. 2; "Correspondence," R. W. Officer, [Paris, TX], to Bro. Poe, [np.], nd., ibid., 26 (June 11, 1884) 373, c. 1; "Correspondence," R. W. Officer, [Paris, TX], to Bros. Lipscomb & Sewell, [Nashville, TN], nd., ibid., 26 (Oct. 29, 1884) 691, c. 1–2; and "Correspondence," R. W.O., Paris, TX, to [Advocate, Nashville, TN], July 4, 1885, ibid., 272 (July 22, 1885) 455, c. 3.

33. "Letter from Bro. Officer," R. W. Officer, Paris, TX, to Brother Lipscomb, [Nashville, TN], Aug. 12, 1884, *GA* 26 (Aug. 27, 1884) 546, c. 2–3; "Correspondence," R. W. Officer, [Paris, TX] to Bro. Poe, np, nd., ibid., 26 (Aug. 6, 1884) 500, c. 1–2.

Another evolving component of the Indian Mission was its neighborhood school initiative. The Choctaw government itself funded day schools in tribal neighborhoods at $2 per month per scholar. It made no provisions, however, for buildings or for non-Indian students. Officer and his associates saw this as an unusual opportunity to share the gospel. They envisioned constructing "houses" in the neighborhoods where traditional schools would meet, as well as a Sunday school and a church. The success of the plan required teachers who had a strong Christian commitment and pedagogical competency, but it also required teachers who were self-confident women. Men need not apply, wrote Officer, for "women work with more earnestness than men, and as a rule, are more honest and unselfish in their efforts." Besides, the Choctaws wanted women teaching in their neighborhood schools.[34]

The Choctaw National Council was willing to hear from Officer, but it wanted assurances that he represented the "denomination" he claimed to. The council had learned from cruel experience that some of the missionaries among them asserted relationships that they did not possess, including individuals that identified themselves as being part of the Stone-Campbell movement. The rogues were more interested in themselves than the Choctaws, and generated significant prejudice in the Indian and broader missionary communities against legitimate representatives of the movement. The endorsement desired by the council was fairly simple for Methodists, Presbyterians, Baptists and Catholics to secure. But the congregational polity of Stone-Campbell churches made denominational endorsements of that kind problematic. Officer resolved that particular issue by asking the Texas state convention of the Stone-Campbell churches meeting in Bryan, Texas, to affirm his qualifications as a legitimate representative to the Choctaw Nation. The request was granted, but only after an uncivil if not unchristian debate.[35]

34. "Texas," R. W. Officer, Paris, TX, Mar. 3, 1886, *Christian Standard*, 21 (Mar. 27, 1886) 102, c. 2; "Correspondence," R. W. Officer, Paris, TX, Advocate, [Nashville, TN], nd., *GA* 27 (Nov. 18, 1885) 726, c3; L.W. Oakes, Longview, IT, to R. W. Officer, Paris, TX., Nov. 26, 1885, ibid., 27 (Dec. 16, 1885), p. 792. c. 3; "Notes from Indian Territory," R. W. Officer, [Paris, TX], nd., ibid., 27 (July 22, 1885) 455, c. 3. See also "Correspondence," R. W. Officer, Paris, TX, to Advocate, [Nashville, TN], nd., ibid., 27 (Nov. 18, 1885) 726, c. 3; "Correspondence, " R. W. Officer, Paris, TX, to Advocate, [Nashville, TN], Jan. 22, 1886, ibid. 8 (Feb. 17, 1886) 107, c. 2; R. W. Officer, [Paris, TX] to Bro. L[ipscomb], [Nashville, TN] nd., ibid., 8 (Apr. 14, 1886) 236, c.2.

35. "Letter from Bro. Officer," R. W. Officer, Paris, TX, Aug. 12, 1884, *GA* 26 (Aug. 27, 1884) 546, c. 2; "Correspondence," R. W. Officer, [Paris, TX] to Bros. Lipscomb & Sewell, [Nashville, TN], nd., ibid., 26 (Oct. 29, 1884) 691, c. 1–2.

With three companions, Officer travelled by wagon from Atoka to Tuskahoma. The Choctaw council itself, he discovered, was filled with "novel, big-hearted . . . men, whom one could learn to love without much effort." For three evenings he preached to them and their guests. During one of the council's formal sessions, he submitted his credentials as provided by the Texas convention and shared his vision of Stone-Campbell churches supporting a mission that would not only share the gospel, but would care for orphan children, construct an industrial boarding school and create neighborhood and Sunday schools. Presumably, he also spoke of the financial supplement that the mission would require from the Choctaws themselves.[36]

Officer's written reports suggest that the Choctaws embraced his vision of an Indian Mission. No known official record of the Choctaw Nation confirms as much, although anecdotal evidence does; the records of the Choctaw tribal government itself are in Oklahoma City. There is nothing in them about Officer or the Indian Mission. George W. Harkins, a former chief of the Choctaws who was present, was sufficiently impressed that he pledged $50 a year for three years to help implement the dream.[37] Doubtless the Choctaw delegates also affirmed his credentials, and it certainly flattered him by reacting positively to his preaching. The responses were all encouraging save two: the council allocated no land and appropriated no money for the Industrial Boarding School.

Officer's appearance before the Chickasaw and Choctaw councils and his many reports of the ongoing work of the mission stirred the imagination and interest of members of Stone-Campbell churches and especially editors of its periodicals. Dramatic work was occurring without the aid of any para-church group. For editors like David Lipscomb of the *Gospel Advocate* and Daniel Sommer of the *Octographic Review* that was mission work according to the "Lord's plan" and deserved the support of the churches. "Brethren," Lipscomb wrote of Officer, "help him. He is a self-sacrificing brother, working for the upbuilding and exaltation of a race long lost in ignorance of the gospel." Moreover, it was "church work" as opposed to "State meeting" work.[38] Sommer picked up on the same theme, noting that Officer had never been "under the auspices of

36. "Correspondence," R. W. Officer, [Paris, TX] to Bros. Lipscomb & Sewell, [Nashville, TN], nd., *GA* 26 (Oct. 29, 1884) 691, c. 1–2.

37. Ibid.

38. Editorial Comment, *GA* 26 (Nov. 26, 1884) 756, c. 3.

any man-made society" and was laboring with a people "whose manners [were] simple . . . ." He commended the Indian Mission "wholeheartedly" and hoped that his readers would say "Amen" by sending a contribution to the Paris church elders.[39]

Officer, of course, hoped they would do the same thing. Finding support for the mission was critical. Through his reports and sermons in the *Advocate* and *Review,* and other church-related journals,[40] he encouraged his readers to take "fellowship" with him in the Indian Mission, meaning make a free-will gift. He often suggested that the congregations dedicate the offering of a particular Lord's Day or divide a regular contribution, or that Sunday schools take up a special collection. Whatever the source of the contribution, it should be sent to the elders of the Paris church, to the editorial offices of the periodical publishing the report, or directly to him. All gifts would be reported in the periodicals and distributed only by the elders of the Paris church. Additionally, Officer dispatched co-workers, generally women, to solicit churches for contributions to carry on the work of the mission, especially as it related to orphans and neighborhood schools.[41]

The appeals generated just enough interest and gifts for Officer to remain positive about the future of the Indian Mission. At least five young women agreed to take charge of different neighborhood and Sunday schools. By late 1885, one of the schools was operational with twenty scholars.[42] A possible grant of 640 acres from the Choctaw Nation made the construction of the Industrial Boarding School less problematic, especially if it were placed near Atoka. And some 300 residents of Indian Territory had signed a petition requesting that Officer make his home and full-time work in the Choctaw Nation.

39. Editorial Comment, *Octographic Review* 30 (Dec. 29, 1887) 8, c. 3.

40. For example, the *Christian Leader, Christian Standard, Firm Foundation*, and *Primitive Christian*, among others.

41. "Texas," R. W. Officer, Paris, TX, May 2, 1885, *Christian Standard* 20 (May 16, 1885) 158, c. 2; "Indian Territory," R. W. Officer, [Paris, TX], nd., ibid., 20 (Nov. 11, 1885) 336, c. 3; "Texas," R. W. Officer, Paris, TX, Mar. 3, 1886, ibid., 21 (Mar. 27, 1886) 102, c. 2; "Indian Mission," R. W. Officer to V. M. Metcalf, Paris, TX, Mar. 26, 1886, *GA* 28 (Apr. 21, 1886) 252, c. 2–3; R. W. Officer to Advocate, Paris, TX, Oct. 23, 1885, ibid., 27 (Nov. 4, 1885) 696, c. 3.

42. "Correspondence," The Church of Christ at Paris, Texas to the Christian Brotherhood, Oct. 26, 1885, *GA* 27 (Nov. 4, 1885) 699, c. 1; "Correspondence," R.W.O., np. to [Advocate], nd., ibid., 26 (Dec. 23, 1885) 811, c. 3.

The continuing interest of the Choctaw National Council also encouraged Officer. In April, 1885, he had received another invitation to preach at its next annual meeting. He recalled that at the previous meeting he "was first to thrust . . . the sword of the spirit in . . . [Tuskhoma]" and, with the help of the brethren, would build there "the first house of worship in the name of the Lord Jesus . . ."[43] The reception he actually received at the council when it met in October was gratifying. He stayed in the new McCurtain Hotel, and when he preached each evening, "all" came to hear him. More important, six turned to the Lord, and on the last Sunday the newly ordered congregation celebrated the Lord's Supper, "for the first time in the history of the world."[44]

Whether Officer used the occasion of the 1885 council meeting to broach the idea of an industrial boarding school for orphan children is unknown, although it is fair to assume that he did. It is also reasonable to assume that, as in the previous year, the council neither committed itself to support the school financially nor to help it with a grant of land. But surely the prospect of assistance remained, for Officer did not abandon his plans, he only recast them. He would have to look elsewhere for property and financial support.[45]

Given the warm receptions of two National Council meetings, Officer could no longer resist the call of his heart to move to Indian Territory and give the Indian Mission his full time and attention. But how could he sustain his family in a destitute field? After prayer and discussion, he and Lota decided that they would use the inheritance she received from her father's estate plus what the two had been able to save over the previous six years of ministry to get them established in Indian Territory. By the time those "means" ran out, they had faith that the mission would have produced congregations in Indian Territory that could sustain them. To supplement and extend their own resources, they would continue to call upon the churches in the States to "divide" their means with them. And if that were not enough, Officer, like the apostle Paul, could work with

43. R. W. Officer, Paris, TX, to Bro. Poe, [Nashville, TN] April 15, 1885, *GA* 27 (May 13, 1885) 292, c. 2.

44. "Correspondence," R. W. Officer, Paris, TX, to Advocate, [Nashville, TN] Oct. 22, 1885, *GA* 27 (Nov. 4, 1885) 699, c. 1.

45. "Letter from Bro. Officer," R. W. Officer, Tuska-Homa, CN, to Advocate, [Nashville, TN], Oct. 17, 1885, *GA* 27 (Oct. 28, 1885) 674, c. 3.

his hands to support his family. It was a leap of faith to leave Texas, but Officer and Lota had faith to spare.[46]

That faith was shaken and then restored in the winter of 1885–1886. Because of Lota's health, Officer took his family back to Winchester, Tennessee, where she could get additional care and help. In December, he learned from the Paris church that the response to their pleas for "fellowship" in the work of the Indian Mission had been "feeble." He was dismayed. "I have thought a majority of the brethren who read the *Gospel Advocate*," he wrote to David Lipscomb, "believed as I do [about the ways and means of Christianizing the world] and that they were only waiting for an opportunity to show their faith by their works." Is the "Lord's plan to fail?" he asked. Officer reminded Lipscomb that "the brethren who [were] in sympathy with the society suggested years ago that [he] consign the work to them, with the promise that it would be supported." He respectfully declined that opportunity. Yet in the present case, unless the brethren respond more liberally, he would be "compelled to turn the work over to the first man who [came] recommended by the Church of Christ." With irony and a touch of bitterness, he concluded: "I have never called upon one of the brethren who endorsed the society, that I know of, who did not respond; but the rule is, in almost every community, where the brethren endorse God's plan, I am turned away empty. What I have said is true, and it bleeds my heart."[47]

Officer's despair caused David Lipscomb to publish a ringing call to arms. If "we claim to be a missionary people on God's plan," he said, "let us all see [to it] that this mission is supported by the church of God. The church of God is Missionary Society enough, if we will only work." Substantial support now will "show skeptical brethren that the church can evangelize foreign lands without doing it through the Society."[48] Three months later Lipscomb wrote another strong editorial in support of the neighborhood school program, endorsing the call for committed Christian women to serve as teachers.[49] For him, supporting the Indian Mission became a virtual test of fellowship.

46. R. W. Officer, Atoka, IT, to Bro. Lipscomb, [Nashville, TN], Mar. 16, 1892, *GA* 34 (Mar. 21, 1892) 204, c. 3.

47. R. W. Officer, [Paris, TX], to Advocate [Nashville, TN], nd., *GA* 27 (Dec. 23, 1885) 803, c. 3.

48. [David Lipscomb], Editorial comment, *GA* 27 (Dec. 23, 1885) 811, c. 3.

49. "The Indian Mission," D[avid] L[lipscomb], *GA*, 28 (March 31, 1886) 198, c. 1–2.

Lipscomb's endorsement restored Officer's hope and rekindled his faith in the Stone-Campbell churches. There would yet be support for the mission, enough to supplement his own "means" and to sustain other evangelists, not to mention neighborhood school teachers, an orphan's program, and an industrial boarding school. Joyfully and expectantly he would relocate to Atoka and trust that the Lord and the churches would provide. If contributions were limited, he was not above working with his hands. Either way, he and his family were casting their lots with Indian Territory.

But it was not just the "pull" of Indian Territory that caused Officer to leave Paris. There were significant "push" factors too. Most important was that the Texas churches were wrangling over the so-called innovations in work and worship, especially whether mission activity was to be conducted through the local church or a para-church organization. Officer clearly had strong feelings on the matter, although he was not inclined to see the innovations as salvation related. Yet they did impinge upon the peace and harmony of the church, which he believed *was* a salvation issue. In 1884, he experienced the passion of the controversy first hand at the time he had asked the mass meeting of the Texas churches at Bryan to commend him officially to the Choctaws. He had no interest in being part of such dissension.[50] He would prefer working in a destitute field like Indian Territory where such controversies did not exist. Some years before, that same preference had caused him to leave Alabama and move to Texas.

Both pulled and pushed to Indian Territory, Officer and his family left Paris, Texas, and relocated in Atoka, Choctaw Nation, in July 1886. He had bright hopes for the future of the Indian Mission, not only because of his faith in God and confidence in the Lord's plan of evangelization, but because of the foundation that had been built over the previous six years. The Indian Mission was not a figment of the imagination, but a reality involving evangelism, a program to place orphan children in Christian foster homes, and a series of neighborhood and Sunday schools taught by dedicated Christian women. Its ambitious plans for an Industrial Boarding School were ready for execution. Moreover, Officer knew the power-brokers of the Choctaw Nation, who had welcomed him to Indian

50. Stephen Daniel Eckstein, *History of the Churches of Christ in Texas, 1824–1950* (Austin, TX: Firm Foundation, 1963) 237. The focus of the dissension was not Officer's request but the proposal to charter a Christian Women's Board of Missions.

Territory, listened to him preach, and blessed the work of the Indian Mission. And he was especially encouraged by the vote of confidence he had received from David Lipscomb and the *Gospel Advocate*, an endorsement that would result in contributions sufficient to fund the Mission in the years ahead.

Clearly, Officer had laid a remarkable foundation for the Indian Mission by 1886. Four years later that groundwork would yield an impressive harvest, especially in number of churches and members. Ten years later, however, the Indian Mission as it had been planned and executed no longer existed, and Officer had left Indian Territory as he had come, in a vain effort to escape the controversy that swirled about him and his work. Why and how that happened is the subject of another essay.

2

From Facts to Feeling

The Rhetoric of Moral Formation in Alexander Campbell's Morning Lectures at Bethany College

CARISSE MICKEY BERRYHILL

The "Old Man Eloquent"[1]

Two young men blinked and waited as students filed into the college chapel in Western Virginia early in the morning on October 2, 1855.[2] H. Pangburn, from Ohio,[3] prepared to make some notes so he could record the substance of them in the journal he had begun a week before. W. T. Moore, 23, had come to Bethany after attending preparatory school in Newcastle, Kentucky, and teaching for a year, saving money for the move.[4] As the last youths came in and took their seats, the college bell ceased. There was a step and the room quieted as a tall, distinguished

1. This phrase is used by editor W. T. Moore on the dedication page of Alexander Campbell's *Familiar Lectures on the Pentateuch: Delivered before the Morning Class of Bethany College During the Session of 1859–60* (St. Louis: Christian Publishing, 1867). References to the *Familiar Lectures* come from this edition.

2. H. Pangburn's manuscript journal has a flyleaf date of Sept. 24, 1855, and dates the first lecture as October 2, 1855. The journal is held at the Center for Restoration Studies, Brown Library, Abilene Christian University, Abilene, Texas.

3. Pangburn and W. T. Moore and their states are listed in the 1858 graduating class. *Millennial Harbinger* 1863:378.

4. John T. Brown, "W. T. Moore," *Churches of Christ: A Historical, Biographical, and Pictorial History of Churches of Christ in the United States, Australasia, England, and Canada* (Louisville, KY: John P. Morton, 1904): 467.

man in his sixties strode to the front of the room and surveyed his students. His face was craggy but kindly, with a prominent aquiline nose, sharp blue eyes, and a shock of grey hair. This was Alexander Campbell, the President of Bethany College.

The fifteenth session of Bethany College had begun. Campbell stood on a short platform that ran across the front of the room, with a small table beside him, and an armchair behind him. He called the roll. Then he called the first student on the roll to come to the front to read the first chapter of Genesis from the Bible on the small table.

While the reading was going on, the president sat in his armchair and listened intently, almost motionless. When the reading was done, he thanked the reader, stood, and said, "Let us pray."

His prayer was fervent, extemporaneous, and clear. He spoke humbly and yet as if to someone well known and loved.

Then Campbell took his seat in the armchair and looked out at the hundred and thirty young men before him.[5] His eyes traveled across the room. Most of them were not much older than his son Wickliffe would have been by now. Someone shuffled his feet and then was still. Campbell's hand lay still on the table. There were no notes.

"Young gentlemen," he began, "This morning we commence the consideration of a superlative work of transcendent value and importance. It spans the whole arch of time, leans upon eternity past and eternity to come, and comprehends time in its history and in its prophecy. It gives to man a knowledge paramount to all knowledge of the sciences of the earth; yea, it involves his whole destiny, and is, therefore, the superlative study of life."[6]

The president's voice was clear and light but carried well, a brogue from his Scots-Irish childhood still noticeable.

"There is a beginning of all things; and this book commences at the beginning of man's career. It is the beginning of the universe as far as man is concerned. It begins at the foundation of man's history. Therefore Moses began his history correctly when he said, 'In the beginning . . .'"[7]

Pangburn made a note: "The most important lesson for man and the most difficult for him to learn is to know himself." He jotted down,

---

5. Alexander Campbell, "Bethany College," *Millennial Harbinger* 1855: 657.

6. Adapted from *Familiar Lectures*, 67. In this vignette I blend excerpts from Pangburn's 1855 notes and the 1859 printed lectures.

7. Pangburn journal, entry for October 2, 1855.

"This book begins at the right place to teach man to know himself—it begins with man's origin."[8]

Campbell explained to them that the Bible is the essential textbook for any curriculum because it reveals who humans are, and what place they have in the grand scheme of God's creation, governance, and redemption of the world. Campbell seldom gestured, nor did he rise from his seat. About thirty minutes went by, but eons seemed to roll before their minds as he spoke. Moore sat entranced. Pangburn forgot to make notes.

"The word is the power of God," Campbell was saying. "It manifests his power by words. We communicate our ideas by words; God manifests his power."[9]

The bell outside began to clang. The students' attention snapped. It was time for their various classes to begin. The president stood and with a gesture dismissed them. They stretched, gathered up their books, and filed out.

For the next nine months, Pangburn and Moore attended the Morning Class daily, as all Bethany students did. Whenever Campbell was in Bethany, he presided and took up whatever biblical chapter was assigned for the day as the source of his reflections. Sometimes students placed slips of paper on his table with a question for him to answer. Sometimes he spent a day calling on them to stand and deliver. By January 1856 they had worked their way through all fifty chapters of Genesis. January and February were devoted to Exodus. In March and early April Campbell reflected on the gospel of Matthew, then for the remainder of the spring and summer on chapters from Acts, Psalms, Proverbs, and I Corinthians. Pangburn recorded their progress in his journal, sometimes just noting the day's topic, other times writing out something of substance.

By the time both young men graduated from Bethany in the summer of 1858,[10] they had followed the annual cycle three times. During his enrollment, Moore became convinced that "If a faithful report of his Lectures to his pupils could be obtained, much good might be accomplished by its publication."[11] Someday, he thought, he would try to publish them.

---

8. Ibid.

9. Ibid.

10. *Millennial Harbinger* 1863: 378.

11. *Familiar Lectures,* 57.

Publication of the *Familiar Lectures*

So in 1859 Moore hired an expert "phonographer," or shorthand reporter, Charles V. Segar, to attend Campbell's morning lectures and transcribe them word for word.[12] It was an opportune moment, for the 1859-60 session was the last during which Campbell conducted the morning Bible study. Moore edited Segar's transcripts with the help of his friend J. Sprigg Chambers; Segar compiled a biographical sketch of Campbell from several print sources. They intended to publish a first volume, *Familiar Lectures on the Pentateuch*, in 1862. But in 1861 their plans to ask Campbell to correct the manuscript were stalled by Campbell's poor health. The project ground to a halt during the war years. When Campbell died in 1866, Moore resolved to resume the effort to publish the manuscript not only for its content but as a memorial. Although Segar died during the final preparations, the volume finally came out in 1867. No further volumes were published. The whereabouts of Segar's transcripts is unknown.

Familiar Lectures on the Pentateuch; Delivered Before the Morning Class of Bethany College, During the Session of 1859–60 was published in 1867 by both H. S. Bosworth in Cincinnati and Christian Publishing in St. Louis. It included a title page, title page verso, a two-page preface, a 42-page biographical sketch compiled by Segar, a ten-page introduction written by Moore, thirty-four lectures, a reprint of the "Sermon on the Law," and 102 sermon extracts, anywhere from a sentence to several pages in length. It was reprinted in 1871 (Bosworth), 1887 (Christian Publishing), 1901 (Christian Publishing), and—with the "Sermon on the Law" deleted—in 1958 (Old Paths Book Club). The 1867 St. Louis edition was reproduced in 1993 in microfiche in the ATLA Monograph Preservation Program series by the American Theological Library Association, from which it is available.

The intended second volume comprising the New Testament lectures never appeared. W. T. Moore notes that he inserted the "Sermon on the Law" "as a proper sequel to the preceding Lectures on the Pentateuch, and as, in some respects, supplying the omission of Mr. Campbell's Lectures on the New Testament, which always occupied the latter portion of the session, but which we did not think proper to give in this volume."[13] Moore explains in his Preface that "the Lectures on the New

---

12. Ibid., v, 57–58 tell the story of their efforts to publish the lectures.

13. Ibid., 266.

Testament and incidental subjects, delivered during the session, are reserved for another volume, should there be such a demand for it as will
justify its publication."[14] The following year Moore published his *Living
Pulpit of the Christian Church* while carrying out ministerial duties in
Cincinnati and teaching occasionally at the University of Kentucky.[15] By
the time the Pentateuch lectures reached their second and third print-
ings, Moore was organizing mission efforts and even worked as a missionary in England, where he edited the *Christian Commonwealth*.[16] The
New Testament lectures were never published.

The Contents of the Lectures

When Campbell met with the Bethany students, he took his lecture topic
from the scripture for that day's reading. When returning from preaching or fundraising trips, he would simply pick up the narrative from that
day's reading. This practice may account for many omissions, but comparing the 1855 notes and the 1859 published lectures makes it clear that
the schedule of daily readings was selectively focused on two "historical"
books from each Testament, for reasons rooted (as we shall see in the
next section) in Campbell's educational intent for the morning sessions,
which were usually referred to as Sacred History.

Pangburn's journal from October 2, 1855, to June 25, 1856, records
the topics of more than 110 lectures. The list shows that Campbell's attention in the lectures lay in Genesis (26 entries), Exodus (27 entries),
Matthew (20 entries), Acts (37 lectures), with a few chapters from Psalms,
Proverbs, and I Corinthians scattered in the late weeks. Pangburn documents no discussion of Numbers, Deuteronomy, the prophets, Mark,
Luke, John, the other epistles, or Revelation.

As Table 1 (below) indicates, the first ten *Familiar Lectures* are from
Genesis 1 and 2. In all, twenty of the thirty-four lectures are from Genesis.
There are seven lectures from Exodus and five from Leviticus, concluding
with two from Hebrews 8 and 9. No lectures are taken from Numbers or
Deuteronomy.

Campbell's great theme is that the Bible reveals God's loving purposes for his creation through its record of God's actions. In laying out

14. Ibid., vi.

15. Brown, 468.

16. Ibid.

his vision for biblical instruction at Bethany, Campbell lists five divine "dramas" depicted by God's actions in history: "creation, legislation, providence, moral government, and redemption."[17] Campbell envisions no bare recital of atomized facts from Scripture. The actions of God recorded in Scripture depict, or dramatize, God's nature and work in the world. Campbell's thematic analysis of the biblical account is designed to develop a narrative framework for moral reflection, similar to Tom Olbricht's development in the recent *He Loves Forever*.

The Genesis lectures focus repeatedly on the themes of creation and providence. Campbell contemplates the nature of humans, their relation to God and to the created order. He depicts the redemptive intent in God's providence in the lives of the patriarchs. The Exodus-Leviticus lectures are devoted to the "remedial system," that is, the drama of redemption, as typologically represented in the tabernacle and worship practices ordained at Sinai.

Table 1: Topics of Familiar Lectures (given 1859–60; published 1867)

Lecture Number	Biblical Topic	Lecture Number	Biblical Topic
1	Introductory	18	Genesis 40
2	Genesis 1	19	Genesis 49
3	Genesis 1	20	Genesis 49
4	Genesis 1	21	Exodus 24, 25:16
5	Genesis 1	22	Exodus 25:17
6	Genesis 2	23	Exodus 26
7	Genesis 2	24	Exodus 38
8	Genesis 2	25	Exodus 38
9	Genesis 2	26	Exodus 38
10	Review	27	On types
11	Genesis 21	28	Leviticus 11
12	Genesis 20	29	Leviticus 11
13	Genesis 23	30	Leviticus 3
14	Genesis 22	31	Leviticus 16
15	Genesis 27	32	Leviticus 17
16	Genesis 27	33	Hebrews 8, 9:8
17	Genesis 39	34	Hebrews 9

17. Alexander Campbell, "Address: The Corner-Stone of Bethany College: Delivered May 31, 1858," in *Popular Lectures and Addresses* (Philadelphia: Challen, 1866): 491.

Moral Education and the Bible: The Purpose of the Lectures

Duane Cummins describes Campbell's view of education as emphasizing "wholeness of person, moral formation of character, biblical studies, non-sectarianism, perfectibility of individuals, and lifelong learning."[18] As Tom Olbricht has demonstrated, non-sectarian instruction in the Bible is the hallmark of Campbell's vision of universal education suited to the capacity of the learner and emphasizing moral education.[19] Olbricht points out that for Campbell moral education addresses five subjects: "the origin, the nature, the relations, the obligations and the destiny of man."[20] Campbell prefers modern philosophers to ancient ones, but insists on the preeminent value of the Bible as the resource for moral development, especially since the Bible can be academically taught as history in a non-sectarian way.[21] Olbricht finds that Campbell's approach to this use of the Bible was unique to American colleges in his day.[22]

Segar reports Campbell's emphasis on the Bible as the core of the college curriculum:

> Mr. Campbell took upon himself, not only the duties of president, but also the daily labor of lecturing on the Bible. Indeed, he made the daily and thorough study of the Bible the peculiar characteristic of Bethany College. As he regarded the Bible, and the Bible alone, as the only authority to the church, in all matters of faith and practice, and the only infallible source of a perfect morality, so he conceived it should form the basis of all Christian education, and he made it the leading text-book of educational instruction. This great thought he ever cherished, as the ruling principle of his college labors. And to raise up men who would sympathize with him in his sublime aim of magnifying the value

18. D. Duane Cummins, *The Disciples Colleges: A History* (St. Louis: CBP Press, 1987): 35.

19. Thomas H. Olbricht, "Alexander Campbell as an Educator," in *Lectures in Honor of the Alexander Campbell Bicentennial, 1788–1988* (Nashville: Disciples of Christ Historical Society, 1988): 81. This essay places Campbell's educational ideas in the context of European and American education.

20. Ibid., 91, citing Alexander Campbell's 1840 address to the Charlottesville Lyceum, "Is Moral Philosophy an Inductive Science?" published in Campbell's *Popular Lectures and Addresses*, 99. Note the resemblance to Campbell's opening statement recorded by Pangburn on October 2, above, n. 8.

21. Olbricht, "Alexander Campbell as an Educator," 91–92, 94. Olbricht notes that Campbell in the 1860 *Millennial Harbinger* (510ff.) prefers the "five books of Moses" and the "five historical books of the New Testament" for this purpose.

22. Olbricht, "Alexander Campbell as an Educator," 95.

of the Book of Books, and enforce its claims to authority over the hearts and consciences of men—was the great motive which prompted him to superadd to his already oppressive labors, the additional responsibility of Bethany College.[23]

Robert Richardson recalls the formative intent of Campbell's morning lectures:

He addressed himself to the work of moulding the minds of the youths present in conformity with the great principles developed in the Bible. The sacred volume was at once made the text-book for the whole college, and he proceeded to develop every morning to the entire class, as he alone could do it, the great facts which it presented. His wonderful power of presenting these facts in their most extended relations, his simple yet comprehensive generalizations, opening up new fields of thought and enlarging the horizon of knowledge, enchained the attention of even the youngest members of the class, and Sacred History became at once the favorite study.[24]

Campbell's Rhetorical Method in the Lectures

Campbell's method in the lectures is neither critical-exegetical treatment nor Sunday-School Bible drill, but what he would have called "developing" the truths of Christianity from "Sacred History." This activity is the main function of the teacher: "Where the preacher "proclaims *facts* and proves them by *witnesses*; a *teacher* ascertains and developes [*sic*] *truth*, and supports it by *arguments*; an *exhorter* selects *duties*, and recommends and enforces them by *motives*"[25] (emphasis his). In today's vocabulary we might call these forms of discourse apologetics, theological reflection, and ethical application. The remark from Richardson just quoted describes how Campbell "develops" the facts by showing their relationship to general principles. When they "develop" truth, teachers explain the meaning and behavioral impact of the gospel narrative: "The apostolic epistles . . . are expressive of the meaning of the gospel facts. They taught the new converts the legitimate bearing and results of the facts believed."[26] Teachers broaden their students' views:

23. "Life of Alexander Campbell," in *Familiar Lectures*, 36.

24. Richardson, *Memoirs of Alexander Campbell*, vol. 2 (Philadelphia: Lippincott, 1870): 485.

25. *Millennial Harbinger* 1835: 487.

26. Alexander Campbell, *Debate on the Evidences of Christianity . . . Held in the City*

The *preacher* singly aims at the conversion of his hearers, while the *teacher* intends the development of a passage, a doctrine, a theory; or in vindicating the tenets he has espoused, and wishes to commend to the understanding and acceptance of his people. The preacher reclaims the heart; the teacher cultivates the understanding and enlarges the conceptions of his pupil. The preacher aims at producing *faith* in his auditory; the teacher at imparting *knowledge* to his disciple; the exhorter excites his auditory to action.[27]

The questions he asked of his students—for example, "Why is so large a part of the scriptures historical?" or "How many positive ordinances [are there] in Christianity?" or "What are the classes of supernatural evidences concerning the Savior?"[28]—reveal that Campbell is concerned that the students develop cognitive scaffolds for their intellectual and spiritual growth. Simultaneously, he clearly intends to motivate them to appreciate their opportunities and to pursue them diligently. For example, he says,

I have only to hope, that a true appreciation of the advantages which must accrue to you, from the thorough and comprehensive course of instruction in our college, will prompt you to acquit yourselves honorably before God and men; and thereby secure to yourselves, all the advantages, which a kind and beneficent Providence has placed within your reach.[29]

So his discourse has both teaching and motivational elements, appealing both to the intellect and to the feelings.

According to Campbell's "natural" rhetoric rooted in Scottish faculty psychology, although knowledge precedes imagination, emotion, and will in producing human action, imagination and the emotions are necessary to move people from knowledge to action.[30] Campbell focuses on the narrative biblical books because he believes that before people can choose well, they must understand the facts: what God has done and what it means in God's grand scheme of things. But while Campbell's morn-

---

of Cincinnati, Ohio, from the 13th to the 21st of April, 1829 (Bethany, VA: A. Campbell, 1829): 374.

27. *Millennial Harbinger* 1853: 546.

28. Pangburn journal, entries for June 13 and June 18, 1856.

29. *Familiar Lectures*, 67.

30. For a detailed treatment of Campbell's natural rhetoric, see Carisse Mickey Berryhill, "Alexander Campbell's Natural Rhetoric of Evangelism," *Restoration Quarterly* 30.2-3 (1988): 111–24.

ing lectures certainly inform the students and call their attention to the historical narrative, his lessons do not appeal solely to their powers of understanding. He uses vivid language to engage their imaginations in order to arouse proper emotion that will in turn motivate wholesome choices. He frequently employs imaginative illustrations and affecting language to promote their desire to conduct themselves as Christian gentlemen.

Campbell's Extemporaneous Eloquence

This series of speeches recorded by the best means of the day stands with the Campbell-Owen debate of 1829, also transcribed by a stenographer, as a vibrant witness to the extemporaneous speech of Campbell. The ease, warmth, imaginativeness, and lofty emotional power of these discourses may surprise readers who think of Campbell as a cold rationalist whose reliance on Enlightenment empiricism produced a flat dogmatism in his spiritual heirs. Admittedly, the lectures are occasionally repetitive or sometimes incomplete when interrupted by the campus bell (any professor will sympathize), and have a distinctly nineteenth century cadence. But here is a living voice, full of color, rhythm, and glimpses of sublimity—elevated, expressive, exclamatory, and affecting.

Campbell presented himself to his student audience in a paternal role. His biographer Richardson noted that his "urbanity and kindness and his genial manner gave him great personal influence with the students."[31] Although he was lionized as a champion debater, Campbell was also admired as a master of extemporaneous speaking, especially of the type where he could generalize from particular examples to create grand panoramas.[32] The biographical sketch compiled by Segar comments that his discourses were "so clear in statement, cogent in argument, rich in diction, and forcible in illustration, as to hold his auditors in rapt attention to the close."[33] It was this voice that he brought to the

---

31. Richardson, *Memoirs*, 2:485.

32. Ibid.; See also Richardson, *Memoirs*, 1:12, where Richardson observes that Campbell's "imagination displayed itself, not in poetic creations, but in the far-reaching grasp by which, as an *orator*, he seized upon principles, facts, illustrations and analogies, and so modified and combined them as to render them all tributary to his main design. It was in the choice of arguments, in unexpected applications of familiar facts, in comprehensive generalizations, widening the horizon of human thought and revealing new and striking relations, that this faculty manifested itself; subservient always, however, to the proof of some logical proposition or to the development of some important truth."

33. *Familiar Lectures*, 46.

morning classroom to attract and sustain his student's attention to the import of the work of God in history.

The Language of Imagination and Emotion in the Lectures

In addition to his abilities in meta-narrative construction, Campbell's repertoire of eloquence included powerful imagery and compelling narrative vignettes. Examples of these are abundant in the lectures. Let us consider some of them. Here is how Campbell imagines the moment when Adam and Eve realize they are naked:

> You have a beautiful lamp burning before you. It must have a wick and pure oil, in order to produce a brilliant light. This brilliancy continues while it burns, but it goes out and nothing is left but smoke and blackness, which can only be seen by the light of another lamp. There was a halo of glory about the persons of Adam and Eve, as about the blaze of the beautiful lamp. The beauty and glory of their persons, in their primeval state, was doubtless superior to the beauty and glory of the sun; but the moment they ate of the forbidden fruit, the lamp of their glory went out, the brilliant halo vanished, and they stood in the presence of God, and of one another, naked and ashamed.[34]

The concrete image of an oil-burning lamp is something his young men can recall and picture in their minds, along with its sudden extinction: "The lamp of their glory went out."

Here is his depiction of the rejection of Cain's sacrifice:

> We see, by the eye of faith, the fire descend from heaven, like the lightning's flash, and kindle a flame beneath the offering of Abel. The smoke and flame ascend up to heaven; but we see Cain standing, cold and stern, by his lifeless and bloodless offering, under which no fire is kindled, and from which no flame nor smoke curls upward toward the heavens . . . Cain becomes incensed; he frowns, his heart burns with pride and envy; and, forgetful of the natural relation between them, as men, as brothers, his resentment kindles against Abel . . .[35]

Here Campbell retells the laconic Genesis 4:4, "And the LORD had respect unto Abel and to his offering; but unto Cain and to his offering he had not respect," by imagining that God sends fire to consume the acceptable

34. Ibid., 81.
35. Ibid., 112.

offering. Fire descends from heaven, and ascends from Abel's offering, but no smoke curls up from Cain's. Campbell's young auditors know about kindling fires, about waiting for the curl of smoke that indicates fire. This passage uses "kindle" three times, and the third time, it is Cain's resentment that kindles. Cain "becomes incensed" and "his heart burns." Campbell presents his listeners with images not only familiar but emotionally powerful for them. Moreover, the images are arranged in striking and memorable patterns.

Moses's life is vividly imagined. For example, baby Moses "was exposed to death, under a law of Egypt. He was put into an ark, and placed upon the river Nile, in the midst of crocodiles."[36] Babies may not be of that much interest to young males, but crocodiles are exceedingly interesting, even if they don't appear in the biblical account. Another example: when Moses receives the stone tablets of the law at Mount Sinai, "A grand ladder, composed of shining angels, reaching from one to another, extended from Heaven to Mount Sinai; and upon this splendid monumental ladder, the stones were carried, from Moses to the Lord, who engraved upon them, with his own hand, the whole category of the relations between God and man, and between man and man; and then returned them to Moses."[37] This angelic ladder is not present in the Exodus account at all, but, inspired perhaps by the "message spoken by angels" in Hebrews 2:2, it echoes Jacob's ladder.

Campbell focuses the fourteen lectures from Exodus, Leviticus, and Hebrews on the symbolic significance of the tabernacle and its sacrifices as physical portrayals of the principles of redemption, the "remedial scheme." To accompany this cognitive exposition, he makes full use of the aesthetic power of imagining the beauty and ornamentation of the tabernacle, its furnishings, and the vestments of the High Priest. A striking passage in which we find Campbell's imaginative immersion in one of the tabernacle texts appears in Lecture 32, where he meditates on the spiritual comfort in the fact that the high priest wears golden bells on the hem of his robe:

> When the high priest went into the innermost department, he wore a holy robe, upon which were many tinkling bells. When enveloped in darkness—shrouded from the view of those for whom he was interceding, these bells gave evidence of the life of

36. Ibid., 190.
37. Ibid., 207.

the high priest—hence, so long as they heard the bells, they were assured of his safety, and could pray with confidence. Had the high priest gone presumptuously, and without due preparation, into the holiest of all, he would undoubtedly have been made the object of divine wrath; but while he conducted himself with propriety, and wore the holy robe with the names of the twelve tribes upon the shoulders and heart, he was safe; and the bells continued to give a comforting assurance, that he was interceding for the worshiping assembly without. . . . Our High Priest has entered into the literal heavens, with the names of his followers engraven upon his heart.[38]

Campbell seems determined to capture his students with the mystery of the interior of the tabernacle, for he frequently mentions its darkness: "There were no rays of the sun, no glimmering of the pale moon, and no twinkling light of the stars in the holy room."[39] Similarly, "In the tabernacle, after the high priest had gone into the holiest of all, he stood in silence and total darkness, having the twelve tribes represented in his person . . . ;"[40] and "In the holy place was perfect darkness, not a ray of light from sun or moon or star penetrated that sanctified and hallowed spot. An artificial light indicated that singular interposition—that mystery of mysteries—God's enlightenment of the world by the incarnation of his beloved son, and by giving to him, without measure, the spirit and light of life . . . ."[41] In the twenty-first century, when Earth has so much ambient electric light that astronomers have difficulty finding territory dark enough to set up a telescope, we might overlook the impact of a lamp, a kindled fire, a candle—but Campbell's students knew well enough how it felt to have a gust blow out the light. His pictures touched their experience to engage their imaginations, motivating them to appreciate the spiritual truths he wished to teach.

The Moral Force of Biblical Narrative

In almost the last entry in his journal, Pangburn telegraphically notes, "Matters of fact be such that man can be sensible by the eye and ear / These facts were publicly exhibited / Public monuments are kept up /

38. Ibid., 248–49.
39. Ibid., 211.
40. Ibid., 229.
41. Ibid., 247.

also outward acts be performed / Such monuments commence from the time the fact transpired."[42] As much at the end of the session as at the beginning, the students hear Campbell asserting evidences of the historicity of biblical narrative. But what is the import of these facts once they are established? They function as moral monuments, telling the story of God's work down through the ages. They have meaning that is intended to form the lives of humans. This is Campbell's task in the lectures to draw out the moral force of the narrative in terms suitable to character development in his young hearers.

Campbell's last lecture in the published volume reiterates that the purpose of the biblical narrative is "to indicate intelligently to man his relations to God, to himself, and his destiny; and thus enable him to know himself, a matter of vast importance to every man."[43] Thus people understand their spiritual poverty and the grace of a God who would answer prayer: "Can man conceive of any thing which should so inspire him with gratitude, with veneration and love, as that, upon the throne of his glory, God should hear the prayers of the frail denizens of earth—should listen to their supplications?"[44] "What an exhortation to man," Campbell exclaims, "to bend his heart and soul in thanksgiving and adoration, to the bountiful Fountain of his being."[45]

42. Pangburn journal, entry for June 17, 1856.

43. *Familiar Lectures*, 260.

44. Ibid., 264.

45. Ibid.

3

J. W. McGarvey's *Authorship of Deuteronomy* and the Rhetoric of Scholarship[1]

MARK W. HAMILTON

The last decade of the nineteenth century saw significant changes in the structures, knowledge bases, and practices of theological higher education in the United States. At the new University of Chicago, William Rainey Harper, himself a leading scholar of Hebrew and the Old Testament, built the historical-critical orientation to biblical studies into the structure of the university itself, with the Divinity School handling the New Testament and the Oriental Institute the Hebrew Bible. In New York, the 1892 trial of Charles Briggs on charges of heresy spread the very theories of higher criticism that his opponents sought to repress.[2] More broadly, the spread of Darwinism (social or biological) and the widening gaps between urban and rural members of the same denominations, signaled also in the popularity of political Populism in the South and West, portended the divisions and realignments that would shape twentieth-century Protestantism in its resurgence and decline. We are still dealing with the problems raised by the intellectual shifts of that era.

1. By paying attention to both argumentation and historical setting, Mike Casey greatly expanded our understanding of the rhetorical dimensions of the Stone-Campbell Movement, illuminating features that have made that group of churches so richly creative for the past two centuries. It is thus an honor to dedicate this study to his memory. One wishes it had appeared in a Festschrift he could read at his leisure in a long and productive retirement. That it appears in a memorial volume, instead, indicates the extent of both my esteem for him and my sadness at his much too early death.

2. See Charles Augustus Briggs, *The Defence of Professor Briggs before the Presbytery of New York* (New York: Scribners, 1892).

The person from this period who most influenced the biblical scholarship of Churches of Christ and Christian Churches/Churches of Christ,
the two more conservative branches of the Stone-Campbell Movement,
was John William McGarvey (1829–1911). A prolific preacher, editor,
and author of commentaries, works of apologetics, and a beautifully illustrated and, for its time, insightful historical geography of the "lands of
the Bible," McGarvey considered himself, and was widely considered by
others, to be a major representative of conservative biblical scholarship.[3]

His last and most ambitious major work was *The Authorship of
the Book of Deuteronomy: With Its Bearing on the Higher Criticism of
the Pentateuch*,[4] which sought to refute "destructive" higher criticism,
especially arguments in favor of a multisource view of the origins of
the Pentateuch. McGarvey correctly noted that an understanding of
Deuteronomy held the key to criticism of the Pentateuch in general.

McGarvey's *Authorship* offers contemporary historians an interesting
window onto several aspects of the major intellectual debates of American
theology at the turn of the twentieth century. Although biblical scholarship has long since reframed many of the issues exercising both McGarvey
and his opponents, some elements of both his and their proposals remain
in play. Deuteronomy does indeed offer an important key to understanding the development of the Bible and of Israelite faith. But the aim here
is not to place a century-old book in the mix of biblical studies today,
nor is it to attempt a refutation of McGarvey's case.[5] The aim, rather, is to
understand his arguments by sorting out his rhetorical strategies. Placing
his rhetoric within the intellectual climate of his time and place should

---

3. McGarvey's major works include *Acts of the Apostles* (Lexington: Transylvania, 1863);
Matthew and Mark (Cincinnati: Chase and Hall, 1876); *Lands of the Bible: A Geographical
and Topographical Description of Palestine, with Letters of travel in Egypt, Syria, Asia Minor,
and Greece* (Louisville: Guide, 1880); *Evidences of Christianity* (Cincinnati: Standard,
1886); *New Commentary on the Acts of the Apostles* (Cincinnati: Standard, 1892); and,
with P. Y. Pendleton, *The Fourfold Gospel* (Cincinnati: Standard, 1914). In addition, he
published numerous articles in several journals, as well as collections of sermons and of
Sunday school lessons.

4. J. W. McGarvey, *The Authorship of the Book of Deuteronomy: With Its Bearing on the
Higher Criticism of the Pentateuch* (Cincinnati: Standard, 1902).

5. On the state of current scholarship, see, e.g., Eckart Otto, *Das Deuteronomium im
Pentateuch und Hexateuch: Studien zur Literaturgeschichte von Pentateuch und Hexateuch
im Lichte des Deuteronomiumrahmens*, Forschungen zum Alten Testament 30 (Tübingen:
Mohr/Siebeck, 2000); Gary Knoppers and Bernard Levinson, eds., *The Pentateuch as
Torah: New Models for Understanding Its Promulgation and Acceptance* (Winona Lake, IN:
Eisenbrauns, 2007).

allow greater understanding of, and appreciation for, his work, even if one must ultimately reject his conclusions.[6] Like all his contemporaries, he made arguments that he thought would appeal to an audience open to his case, and thus, like all his interlocutors, his work is susceptible to rhetorical analysis.[7] By trying to identify the implied audience of the book and tracing out the arguments by which McGarvey seeks persuade it can we place him and his work in its proper historical setting.

The Implied Audience and Author

McGarvey published his volume while writing a long series of articles on higher criticism published in the *Christian Standard*, whose owner, Standard Publishing, published *Authorship*.[8] While neither McGarvey's own correspondence nor the sales records for the work are available to me (and apparently are lost), it is possible to reconstruct the book's implied audience from the work itself. As Perelman and Olbrechts-Tyteca note in their classic study of the rhetorical dimensions of persuasion, a speaker who would be persuasive must know his or her audience and shape arguments to fit their assumptions of the world.[9] Ideally, one shapes these arguments to address all of the several groups one expects to find one's case at least potentially credible, while excluding those groups that do not.

From this rather obvious point, one can argue as follows. If a work has a claim to rhetorical success, that is, if it seems to persuade audiences over some period of time, then the structure of the work itself should reveal the assumptions of the implied audience, at least as the author understands them. Now, McGarvey's work remained in print for

6. There has been one dissertation studying McGarvey's rhetoric, but it focuses on four sermons, not his books. See John Clifton Trimble, "The Rhetorical Theory and Practice of J. W. McGarvey" (PhD. dissertation, Northwestern University, 1966). An MA thesis studied McGarvey's understanding of reason and paid some attention to *Authorship*. See C. Myer Phillips, "The Role of Reason in the Thought of John William McGarvey" (MA thesis, East Texas State University, 1969) 113–18.

7. It would be similar instructive to examine the sophisticated rhetoric of Charles Briggs, himself also a highly engaging polemicist. On the historical background preliminary to such a study, see Mark S. Massa, "'Mediating Modernism': Charles Briggs, Catholic Modernism, and an Ecumenical 'Plot,'" *Harvard Theological Review* 81 (1988) 413–30.

8. John William McGarvey, *Short Essays in Biblical Criticism: Reprinted from the Christian Standard 1893–1904* (Cincinnati: Standard, 1910).

9. C. Perelman and L. Olbrechts-Tyteca, *The New Rhetoric: A Treatise on Argumentation* (Notre Dame, IN: Notre Dame University Press, 1969) 20.

some time and received significant reviews in both Restoration circles and beyond.[10] It apparently persuaded some of its value, while leaving others unconvinced.

Who, then, are the members of McGarvey's ideal audience? One clue appears in an introductory passage stating the book's rationale in terms of the opposition between "conservative" and "destructive" critics:

> By what title these two parties should be distinguished, is as yet an unsettled question. As we have stated above, the party who favor the analysis have usually styled themselves critics, and their opponents traditionalists; but this is manifestly unjust to the latter; for while there are traditionalists on both sides – that is, men who accept what has been taught by their predecessors without investigation on their own part – yet it can not be denied that the leaders of this party have been as independent and as scholarly in their investigations as their opponents . . .[11]

Several features of the audience emerge here. First, McGarvey distinguishes two groups of scholarly readers of the Bible, one "conservative" and critical and the other "destructive" and critical. He insists that both groups pay attention to rules of evidence and common sense, that both may contain members who accept claims on the basis of authority rather than evidence, and that both wish to take the Bible seriously. On occasion, he also acknowledges that subgroups exist within the two main ones.[12] But his first move in audience construction is to insist that he

10. For example see the anonymous review in *Expository Times* 13 (June 1902) 419 ("there is an honest endeavour to let all the probabilities have their weight on the one side or on the other"); and J. W. Shepherd's (?) review in *Gospel Advocate* 44/18 (May 1, 1902) 288 ("This evidence is presented in a clear, logical, and forceful way, and convicts 'higher critics' of accusing Jesus himself of ignorance and deception"). The book appears in the annual book list in *Zeitschrift für die alttestamentliche Wissenschaft* 23 (1903) 183, with the annotation "Der Verf[asser] ist Mose" ("the author is Moses").

11. John William McGarvey, *The Authorship of the Book of Deuteronomy: With Its Bearing on the Higher Criticism of the Pentateuch* (Cincinnati: Standard Publishing, 1902) vi.

12. McGarvey deals with exceptions to his two categories in various ways, including accusing the moderates of naivete. For example, he writes, "many scholars, especially in Great Britain and America, have accepted the analytical theory without accepting the sweeping denial of all miracles . . . But this makes the evil tendency inherent in the theory itself all the more dangerous from the common habit among men of accepting injurious teaching from apparent friends of the truth much more readily than from avowed enemies" (xix). Or, again: "The radicals see the difficulty very clear, and they answer, with all candor, that Jesus was mistaken. The Evangelicals, as Professor Briggs calls them, have seen the difficulty; it would be disparaging to them to hint that they have not; but, so far

has, in effect, only two possible audiences, adherents of Christianity and infidels. This strict bifurcation allows him to associate arguments of one member of a group with all those within it, as becomes clear on almost every page of his work.

Second, McGarvey is at pains to dissociate himself and, by implication, the conservative-critical members of his audience from charges of obscurantism or traditionalism, conceived as mindless adherence to outworn ideas. In this, he certainly stands in the broad stream of nineteenth-century theology, and in particular in the Campbellian tradition.[13] Hence his insistence on "the laws of evidence, the maxims of common sense, and the principles of a sound exegesis"[14] and his care to cite the authors he seeks to refute. On the last point, he sums up the arguments in his "Introduction" by noting

> In representing the positions and arguments which I controvert,
> I have not usually stated them in my own words, lest I might be
> suspected of misrepresenting them, and lest I should in some in-
> stances unwittingly do so; but I have quoted freely from represen-
> tative authors. In pursuing this course, I have taken pains to follow
> on every leading issue the line of argumentation pursued by that
> scholar on the other side who seemed to present the case with the
> greatest force; and where it appeared important I have appended
> foot-notes referring for confirmation to other authors.[15]

as my reading has extended, they have not grappled with it" (281). *Authorship* is full of similar texts, illustrating the pains that McGarvey took at audience construction, by means of which he forestalled objections to his case on the grounds that some scholars found no inherent contradiction between orthodox Christianity and critical scholarship. Appeals to the structure of reality ("common habit among men") and one's own competence and diminution of an opponent's ("as far as my reading has extended" but "have not grappled with it") bolster his basic approach.

13. See, for example, the comments on science and relgion in Alexander Campbell, *The Christian System* (1835; 2nd ed. 1839; reprint ed., Nashville: McQuiddy, 1912) 14–15. For the context of *Authorship* in contemporary Stone-Campbell movement scholarship, see Anthony L. Ash, "Old Testament Studies in the Restoration Movement—No. IV," *Restoration Quarterly* 10 (1967) 149–60; M. Eugene Boring, *Disciples and the Bible: A History of Disciples Biblical Interpretation in North America* (St. Louis: Chalice, 1997) 221–53. For a more wide-ranging discussion of "tradition" as a problem in modern political and social philosophy, see Edward Shils, *The Virtue of Civility: Selected Essays on Liberalism, Tradition, and Civil Society*, ed. Steven Grosby (Indianapolis: Liberty Fund, 1997) 103–22.

14. McGarvey, *Authorship*, vi.

15. Ibid., xxi.

Such a strategy would pose significant problems for many scholars because it assumes what must be proven, i.e., that a group of authors actually share a unitary idea that each exposits more or less effectively. Yet, for McGarvey and his implied audience, this style of argumentation apparently made sense and demonstrated a basic sense of fairness. In this rhetorical move, McGarvey is attempting to deconstruct appeals to his opponents' authority (note his earlier dismissal of "assured results")[16] by substituting his own authority for that of other scholars. He has systematically undermined these authorities as "unbelieving," a point to which I will return momentarily. He establishes his own ethos by claiming a high level of fairness and intellectual integrity, on the assumption that such a self-portrayal would make his case more persuasive.

As Perelman and Olbrechts-Tyteca have again pointed out, an appeal to authority is an example of an appeal to the structure of reality and is, therefore, closely related to arguments that play on the relationship of an act and a person.[17] While it is common to see such arguments as fallacies, they in fact constitute a major method of persuasion because they allow for the place of discrete ideas in a web of belief, the patterns of credence in which all persons are enmeshed. McGarvey assumes that many of his audience will find convincing his appeal to christological claims as a way of trumping historical or philological arguments because they distrust the theologies, and perhaps even the personal integrity, of his opponents.[18]

Third, McGarvey's construction of himself and his implied audience demands the severance of his audience from other experts, namely the "destructive" critics. A common strategy for achieving this effect is the demonization of an opponent, so that otherwise commendable achievements (in this case, disciplined study, detailed knowledge, ability to communicate complex ideas to others) become negative.[19] McGarvey adopts

16. Ibid., v.

17. Perelman and Olbrechts-Tyteca, *New Rhetoric*, 305–10. As they put it, "As soon as there is a conflict between authorities, the problem of the basis of the authority is raised. The basis should help to determine what credit each of the respective authorities deserves" (309).

18. A review like that in the *Gospel Advocate* would confirm an author like McGarvey in such an assumption for it portrays the critical struggle as one about basic personal integrity. One must choose, according to this way of seeing things, between the integrity of Jesus and that of the critics. The core of Christianity is thus at stake for these readers.

19. See the discussion in Perelman and Olbrechts-Tyteca, *New Rhetoric*, 310–16.

such a strategy in *Authorship's* introduction. In describing the "analytical theory" of higher criticism, he writes, "Those who have wrought it out were unbelievers, and were moved in their labors by hostility to the Bible and the Christian religion. Especially is this true of the two scholars to whom, above all others, the present form of the theory owes its completion and defense, A. Kuenen, now deceased, and Julius Wellhausen, who is still living."[20] This appeal to the audience's assumptions about counter-authorities sets up an implied syllogism: ideas from unbelievers are bad; the documentary hypothesis is from unbelievers; therefore, the documentary hypothesis is bad.

The first term is obviously the most problematic, as McGarvey himself apparently realizes. If the documentary hypothesis could be shown to be compatible with Christian orthodoxy, as many nineteenth- and early twentieth-century scholars tried to show, then McGarvey's case would be damaged.[21] To solidify it, he employs the risky strategy of quoting a counter-authority, Charles Briggs: "Whatever may have been the motives and influences that led to these investigations, the questions we have to determine are: (1) What are the facts in the case, and (2) do the theories account for the facts?"[22] Given his earlier statements about the sanctity of evidence, it would seem that Briggs's arguments would be persuasive, but not so. McGarvey peremptorily waves off Briggs's attempt at dissociating agent from argument with, "But it is vain to attempt to allay suspicion by such remarks as these."[23] For McGarvey's implied audience, acceptance of the documentary hypothesis is tantamount to rejection of Christianity. Halfway positions cannot defensibly exist.

20. McGarvey, *Authorship*, xv.

21. See, for example, the discussion in Charles Augustus Briggs, *Biblical Study: Its Principles, Methods, and History* (New York: Scribners, 1887) 75–104; T. K. Cheyne, *Bible Problems and the New Material for their Solution* (New York: Putnam, 1904) 49.

22. McGarvey, *Authorship*, xvi; the quotation is from Charles Augustus Briggs, *Biblical Study*, 212. Briggs's prior paragraph, however, frames the issue differently than McGarvey's quotation of him would imply. For Briggs, three sorts of scholars exist: scholastic critics, rationalistic critics, and evangelical critics. He puts himself in the last category; McGarvey would fit the first, and Wellhausen and Kuenen the second. Briggs understands the principled opposition to criticism per se as "unreasonable, unhistorical, and unprotestant," and seeks to "take our stand with the evangelical critics of Europe against the rationalistic critics, and conquer the latter by a more profound critical interpretation of the literature, the history, and the religion of the Bible." By eliding the second and third of Briggs' categories, McGarvey seriously misrepresents the scholarly landscape of his own time.

23. McGarvey, *Authorship*, xvi.

To summarize, then, like any author, McGarvey takes pains to construct his own ethos and the rules he hopes his audience to follow in interacting with him. In doing so, he must also undermine his opponents, much as a lawyer would his counterpart in court.

The Structure of the *Authorship of the Book of Deuteronomy*

The legal simile is not gratuitous, for unlike most scholarly analyses of texts such as Deuteronomy, which would offer a detailed analysis of biblical texts, McGarvey constructs his book as a series of pro and con arguments. The structure has the merit of clarity, leading the reviewer in *Expository Times* to say, "This is a book to be read by students,"[24] though *Authorship* inevitably sacrifices careful analysis of the biblical texts to the needs dictated by its structure.

The book's introduction (iii–xxiii) lays the groundwork for the pro and con argument by describing the state of the question, as McGarvey sees it, and by making a list of "authorities" "chiefly consulted in preparing this volume" (xxi–xxiii). The list includes thirty-five books and encyclopedia articles, all by prominent British and American scholars, or by European scholars in translation (Kuenen, Wellhausen, Edersheim, and Hommel). No works in a foreign language are cited, and McGarvey does not consider relevant major commentaries or studies of his time, such as those of Dillmann (1897), Ewald (1864), Hartmann (1893), Klostermann (1893), König (1893), Naumann (1897), Reuss (1893), Staerk (1894), Steuernagel (1894), Wellhausen (1894), or Zahn (1890).[25] In other words, McGarvey's knowledge of continental scholarship is second-hand, though he does engage more or less accurately the best English-language scholarship of his time.

The body of the book (1–297) divides into two major sections. The first (1–191) discusses nine categories of evidence for a late date for Deuteronomy. These include (1) the story of the discovery of a book by Hilkiah, (2) alleged conflicts with previous legislation, (3) absence of early evidence for a central sanctuary, (4) the absence of an Aaronic priesthood in narrative texts, (5) a series of sixteen intrabiblical contradictions, (6) internal evidence for a late date (phrases such as "until this

---

24. *Expository Times* 13 (June 1902) 419.

25. For a partial bibliography, see Duane L. Christensen, *Deuteronomy 1:1—21:9 (revised)*, Word Biblical Commentary 6A (Nashville: Nelson, 2001) xliii–xliv.

day"), (7) evidence for a late date from the historical books and (8) the early prophets, and (9) evidence from style.

The second part of the book (195–297) discusses evidence for an early (Mosaic) date for the book. The topics include (1) internal evidence, (2) allusions to entering Canaan in the future, (3) incidental evidence, (4) the problem of fraud, (5) evidence from the books of Joshua, (6) Judges, (7) Samuel, (8) Kings, and (9) early prophets, and (10) the testimony of Jesus. A book-length study might analyze in detail every feature of his argument, its antecedents, and its survival in subsequent polemical literature, some of which owes a debt to *Authorship*. Here, however, it will suffice to examine two aspects of McGarvey's argumentation, his use of a christological[26] trump card and his undermining of historical and literary evidence for a late date for Deuteronomy. Departing from the surface structure of his book will make it possible to ascertain aspects of the deeper structure of his presentation of his case.

Deuteronomy and the Language of Jesus

To begin, although McGarvey makes a cumulative case for his position, he saves the clinching argument for the end. As he puts it, the testimony of Jesus "if explicit and unambiguous, should settle this controversy finally and forever."[27] He also acknowledges that his case depends on Jesus' both

---

26. By "christological," I am not implying that McGarvey offers a full-blown doctrine of Christ, merely that he assumes one that serves as reference point for his argumentations. He assumes that (1) Jesus said Moses wrote the Pentateuch; (2) Jesus would not have said so if he knew otherwise; (3) he could not be ignorant of the subject since then his divinity would be in question; and (4) thus his statements about Mosaic authorship constitute a claim that cannot be refuted without compromising the entire Christian understanding of reality. That is, his assumptions about Jesus' use of language function as an argument from authority (or even as an argument from the structure of reality). Arguments from authority play a time-honored role in rhetoric especially "when agreement on the question involved is in danger of being debated" (Perelman and Olbrechts-Tyteca, *New Rhetoric*, 308), though they are precarious when an interlocutor can either undermine an authority (hence McGarvey's selection of Jesus) or it can be shown that the authority does not support one's arguments (hence his pains to overthrow the case of the "evangelical" critics). For an earlier version of McGarvey's understanding of Jesus' use of language, see J. W. McGarvey, "Grounds on Which We Receive the Bible as the Word of God, and the Only Rule of Faith and Practice," in *The Old Faith Restated, Being a Restatement, by Representative Men, of the Fundamental Truths and Essential Doctrines of Christianity as Held and Advocated by the Disciples of Christ, in Light of Experience and of Biblical Research*, ed. J. H. Garrison (St. Louis: Christian Publishing, 1891) 11–48.

27. McGarvey, *Authorship*, 264.

knowing and making an explicit statement on the facts of the authorship of Deuteronomy—an off-handed statement on Jesus' part would not suffice. He thus engages the theological problem of kenosis, arguing that, at his baptism in the Holy Spirit, Jesus received limitless knowledge, equipping him to speak on any subject. In this way, McGarvey allows for Jesus' maturation as a child and forestalls too easy critiques of his position.[28]

Authorship's case for Mosaic authorship of Deuteronomy depends on a set of assumptions about christology, namely that the earthly Jesus was omniscient in matters about which he spoke (and presumably avoided speaking about other matters), and that his words were propositions that refuted all possible counter-propositions, not merely those that his interlocutors would have offered. Admittedly, this definition of christology is idiosyncratic, and arguably even contrary to orthodox Christian views of Jesus' real humanity, but it is McGarvey's operative understanding of the person of Jesus Christ.

He continues the argument with an extended discussion on Jesus' use of language, arguing that either Jesus knew that Moses did not write the Pentateuch but dishonestly refused to disabuse his hearers of their erroneous ideas, or that Jesus correctly believed, as did they, that Moses had written the texts attributed to him (269–81). Without trying to trace all of the mixture of arguments, one might consider a representative sample. After quoting S. R. Driver's claim that no one asked Jesus who wrote Deuteronomy and thus Jesus' statements use conventional language and, therefore, do not constitute evidence for Mosaic authorship, McGarvey writes

> [I]t is equally true that no advocate of the Mosaic authorship of the Pentateuch has ever claimed that such a question was submitted to Jesus. But Professor Driver knows, as well as he knows his own name, that a man may say who wrote a certain book, or part of a book, without having been questioned on the subject. I wonder if, in lecturing before his classes in the university, he never names the authors of books which he quotes till some student calls for the names. What kind of teacher would Jesus have been had he never given his hearers a piece of information till they called for it? And what would have been thought of him if, in quoting books to his hearers, he had never given the names of the authors quoted till they were called for? How could this ingenious writer [S. R. Driver] have penned the sentence just quoted

---

28. McGarvey, *Authorship*, 267–68.

without being conscious that he was evading the question which he was professing to discuss? If this is throwing doubt on his perfect candor, respect for his good sense forces me to it.[29]

The seemingly simple paragraph actually weaves together a series of arguments, culminating in a *reductio ad absurdum* ("as well as he knows his own name"; "How could this ingenious writer . . . ?") and a backhanded compliment that undermines an opponent ("respect for his good sense forces me to it").[30] More significantly, however, it hints at a theory of language with which McGarvey is operating. ("Theory of language" need not imply that he has worked out a comprehensive viewpoint, merely that he makes assumptions about possibilities for the functioning of words upon an audience.) Part of his rhetorical brilliance lies in his willingness to link this theory of language to his high christology,[31] thus appealing to a central, and ultimately unassailable, assumption of his audience.

It would take a more extended treatment than this one to work out all the dimensions of McGarvey's understanding of language. Perhaps a few brief points will suffice. First, in arguing that either Jesus' statements are true responses to every reasonable interrogation or that they are frauds, he works with an understanding of the relationship of sign to referent that is both very narrow (sign/verbal expression has a one-to-one relationship to its referent) and very expansive (propositions embrace all possible referents). For McGarvey, if Jesus prefaces a quotation of the Pentateuch with "Moses says" then Moses must literally, not only have said the statement in question, but have written it. "Moses says" cannot be shorthand for "the Pentateuch says." Moreover, even if the question is "what does the Torah say," the answer "Moses says" introduces the unspoken question "who said X?" and answers it with a name. Such a view of language only makes sense if sentences are understood as propositions that simultaneously respond to all imagined questions to which they could be an answer.

In a fascinating passage, McGarvey argues that Jesus, as a responsible teacher, was bound to correct false views of the authorship of

29. McGarvey, *Authorship*, 275.

30. Compare Mark Antony's "But Brutus is an honorable man" in *Julius Caesar*, act 3, scene 2. Dismissing an opponent by appealing excessively to his virtues is a time-honored rhetorical strategy.

31. Or rather a more or less docetic christology, in which Jesus' humanity does not imply any limits of knowledge.

Deuteronomy, if his hearers had them. Since he did not correct their views, he must have accepted them. Moreover, McGarvey makes an argument from the rhetorical nature of Jesus' statements on Mosaic authorship:

> What did he mean by the demand, "Did not Moses give you the law?"? [*sic*] In this question he employs the rhetoric figure of *erotesis*, which is the most emphatic form of making an assertion. It assumes that neither with the speaker nor with his hearers is any other answer possible but the one implied . . . His demand, then, is the most emphatic assertion possible that neither with himself nor with his hearers could there be any doubt that Moses gave them the law. Affirmation of the Mosaic authorship of the law more emphatic or more explicit there could not be. But Jesus could not thus affirm that which he did not know to be true; and it follows as an irresistible conclusion that Jesus knew Moses to be the author of the law which the Jews connected with his name.[32]

The appeal to the nature of argumentation is telling, reflecting again the sophistication of McGarvey's work and, he assumes, his audience. On the other hand, his understanding of questions as arguments is fairly narrow; question-putting seeks to find points of agreement and disagreement, and they do not work like assertions. Ordinarily, they do not cover all possible assertions into which they can be turned, as McGarvey assumes.[33] His argument works for those who already accept his position, namely, his constructed audience. While Jesus undoubtedly shared the premodern view that Moses wrote the Pentateuch and saw no need to question that assumption, the claim that either Jesus must have been right in his critical assumptions or the fabric of Christian theology is shredded beyond repair rests on assumptions that were highly controversial in McGarvey's time, hence his taking pains to assign the opposite view to heretics and unbelievers. His careful work of audience construction is crucial here.

It would be desirable to place McGarvey's view of metaphor in the context of nineteenth-century theories, but perhaps it is sufficient here to cite his teacher, Alexander Campbell, who laid down in his work *The Christian System* two rules for understanding metaphorical language:

> Rule 5: *In all tropical language ascertain the point of resemblance and judge of the nature of the trope, and its kind, from the point of resemblance.*

---

32. McGarvey, *Authorship*, 278.

33. See Perelman and Olbrechts-Tyteca, *New Rhetoric*, 159–60, 492–93.

> Rule 6: In the interpretation of symbols, types, allegories and parables, this rule is supreme: *Ascertain the point to be illustrated; for comparison is never to be extended beyond that point—to all the attributes, qualities, or circumstances of the symbol, type, allegory, or parable.*[34]

Campbell's laudable concern for eliminating free-association from exegesis leads, unless supplemented with a much more robust understanding of metaphor, to a rigid understanding of language as rigorously propositional, a view that today's emphasis on performative and conventional aspects of language would certainly correct, and which was already under fire in McGarvey's time.[35]

Second, this rigid understanding of language fits well with a similarly rigid understanding of history. As his biographer Morro points out, "If one accepts the fluid, static philosophy of the ancient world, he will follow McGarvey. But if he adheres to the fluid, progressive philosophy which postulates change, growth, and development he will give his approval to the position of the critics."[36] McGarvey understood Christian doctrine as a historical artifact, one that existed in human history, but nevertheless as something static, to be lost or recovered, but not essentially altered, except as a form of corruption.[37]

Thus the view of the Bible and its language with which McGarvey works contrasts with that of his opponents precisely as a function of shifts in views of both in the nineteenth century. While McGarvey repeatedly insists that his view is "modern," in fact, it reflects the modernism of the late eighteenth century, which saw the past as providing timeless moral exempla (even amid the constant shift of events) versus the Romanticism of the nineteenth century, which saw history as radically other than the present and fundamentally alien.[38] Like many of his contemporaries,

34. Alexander Campbell, *Christian System*, 17 (emphasis original).

35. See, for his example, his contemporary, Ferdinand de Saussure, *Cours de linguistique generale*, ed. C. Bally and A. Sechehaye (Lausanne: Payot, 1916) (published posthumously for his lecture notes from prior decades); differently, Bertrand Russell, "On Denoting," *Mind* 14 (1905) 479–93.

36. W. C. Morro, *"Brother McGarvey": The Life of President J. W. McGarvey of the College of the Bible Lexington, Kentucky* (St. Louis: Bethany, 1940) 176.

37. See Boring, *Disciples and the Bible*, 243–44.

38. On the shift in nineteenth-century views of the Bible as history, see Stephen Prickett, *Origins of Narrative: The Romantic appropriation of the Bible* (Cambridge: Cambridge University Press, 1996) 152–79

McGarvey was seeking a mediating position (in this, he resembles Briggs and Driver), but his viewpoint must seem to a contemporary historian fundamentally ahistorical, or, rather, differently historical.

The fact that his undeveloped and unstated theory of language, resting on his notions of history, drives much of his argument can be seen at many points in *Authorship*, but here perhaps one example suffices. In the discussions of arguments against Mosaic authorship of Deuteronomy, he devotes two pages (190–91) to "evidence from style." Its position at the very end of the section treating arguments for a late date might lead a reader to assume that such arguments from literary style would constitute the most challenging ones for McGarvey to overcome. Indeed, he acknowledges that possibility by noting that "In the early stages of destructive criticism its advocates depended chiefly on peculiarities of style for determining the relative age of documents."[39] Yet he moves quickly to cancel out the argument by claiming that "glaring exposures of its unreliability" leading to a "decisive victory of conservatism" have marginalized the discussion of style. His evidence for such a claim derives from the fact that S. R. Driver in his *Introduction to the Literature of the Old Testament* devotes only four pages to stylistic issues.[40] In this case, however, McGarvey ignores several features of Driver's own rhetoric: (1) his book is a textbook and therefore brief; (2) it gives a comparatively extensive treatment of Deuteronomy's style; and (3) it assumes that a late date for the book has been proven and needs no extensive argumentation. Thus McGarvey's evidence simply does not back his case, or at least would not for someone who had read Driver's work. Again, McGarvey's implied audience comes into view.

In any case, McGarvey goes on to clinch his argument by citing Driver's praise of the rhetorical skill of the author of Deuteronomy and then by responding, "What orator among all that graced the history of Israel is more likely to have deserved this encomium than Moses?"[41] From a strictly logical viewpoint, McGarvey has simply begged the ques-

---

39. McGarvey, *Authorship*, 190.

40. S. R. Driver, *An Introduction to the Literature of the Old Testament* (1897; reprint ed. New York: Meridian, 1956) 98–103. As Driver puts it, "The literary style of Dt. is very marked and individual. In vocabulary, indeed, it presents comparatively few exceptional words; but particular words and phrases, consisting sometimes of entire clauses, recur with extraordinary frequency, giving a *distinctive colouring* to every part of the work" (98–99; emphasis original). He has hardly abandoned arguments from style, as McGarvey claims.

41. McGarvey, *Authorship*, 191.

tion. But before charging him with such, it is helpful to remember that in rhetoric, begging the question only seems to occur when the argument depends solely on the claim made (as is not the case here) and when the audience entertains doubts about the arguer's case.[42] McGarvey, again, has constructed a sympathetic audience in his book's introduction, and that imagined audience relates closely to the actual purchasers of his book. He has also defanged a critical argument of his opponents, not by meeting it with an elaborate discussion of Hebrew stylistics (which a scholarly treatment would ordinarily require, but which lay beyond McGarvey's knowledge),[43] but with an appeal to his audience's assumed viewpoint. The very brevity of his treatment of the arguments from style create a sort of anticlimactic ending to the section of arguments for the late origins of the book, thereby presenting the entire case against Mosaic authorship as, implicitly, a weak one. One must admire the brilliance of McGarvey's polemical skill (if not scholarly acumen) at this point.

In taking this excursion through various dimensions of McGarvey's understanding of language, one must ask how it connects to his christology, or rather his understanding of Jesus' use of language. Why do the words of Jesus play such an important role, or, to put matters differently, why does McGarvey take such pains to insist that both his critics and Jesus must use language in just the way he does? It is not hard to guess why an appeal to the authority of Jesus would be so attractive to any Christian writer, and indeed, it is easy to find in Briggs and others just such appeals.[44] Nor can it be difficult to understand the gravity of charging one's opponents with disagreeing with Jesus, not only in their

42. Perelman and Olbrechts-Tyteca, *New Rhetoric*, 113.

43. McGarvey undoubtedly knew some Hebrew (see Boring, *Disciples and the Bible*, 240), but little evidence of the use of it appears in *Authorship*.

44. For example, see the discussion of the discussion of the validity of Christianity for all human beings in Brooke Foss Westcott, *The Gospel of Life: Thoughts Introductory to the Study of Christian Doctrine* (London: MacMillan, 1892) 228–84. He writes that Jesus "gathered into a brief compass and without admixture of alloy the noblest rules for life: He placed them in a natural connexion with the fulfillment of the simplest offices of common duty . . . The claim which He made for Himself and the claim of the first preachers was . . . that they should believe in Him, that they should recognise in Him a new source of power and life, by which obedience becomes possible and love becomes energetic, and so throw themselves wholly upon [H]im and enjoy fellowship with the fullness of His glorified Being" (266–67). This is quite different from McGarvey's understanding of Jesus as the settler of all critical questions, but operates within the same universe of discourse in which late-nineteenth-century theologians wrestled with the relationship between the historical locatedness of Christianity and its claims to absolute validity.

conclusions, but in their way of making arguments. In charging his opponents with infidelity, duplicity, and sloppy reasoning, and by framing his charges in a christological context, McGarvey associates his own ethos as an authority on the Bible with the ultimate authority, Jesus, and thus seeks to preempt any arguments on theological grounds against his position. Such a strategy works because his implied audience does not consist primarily of biblical scholars or theologians, but of preachers and laypersons for whom an appeal to common sense makes sense.

DEUTERONOMY AND THE DECONSTRUCTION OF HISTORY

While listing a great many arguments for or against his position, McGarvey often coordinates the two major parts of his book, and by comparing them, one can get a sense of his rhetorical strategy. Among many possibilities, I shall consider one such coordination that can stand for the whole, his two discussions of the relationship between Amos and Deuteronomy (171–75, 253–56). The discussion of Amos is not critical to his argument—since the argument is cumulative, no single text could be decisive—but does illustrate his methods.

In the first treatment of Amos, part of the section describing arguments for a late date for Deuteronomy, McGarvey lists texts that the "destructive" critics have cited as evidence that the prophet did not know Deuteronomy and attempts to refute their arguments. Quoting Robert Smith's claim that Amos "never speaks of the golden calves as the sin of the northern sanctuaries," McGarvey goes on to acknowledge that "This statement is true, but as respects the question at issue it is evasive and misleading." He then offers a counter-exegesis of Amos 3:13–14, according to which Amos's mention of the "altar" is a metonymy for the idolatry at it. The same goes for the mock call to worship Amos 4:4–5, which presumes the prophet's hostility to worship at Bethel per se. McGarvey does not seem to consider the possibility that his texts do not precisely assume that all worship at the sites in question are idolatrous for Amos. That is, he misses the point of his opponents because he has not read the biblical texts carefully enough.

In any case, he then cements his case against the critics with *ad hominem* arguments[45] that signal their incompetence:

45. I am not using the phrase *ad hominem* pejoratively, since attempts to diminish the character and therefore ideas of opponents is an essential part of all argumentation. My own usage, therefore, is not intended to denigrate McGarvey, merely to describe his argumentation.

> It is here worthy of remark that Robertson Smith, while seeming
> to set forth the attitude of Amos to these sanctuaries, and making
> assertions in direct contradiction of these three passages, fails to
> quote a single word from them . . . We leave the reader to ac-
> count for this as best he can. No one can claim that the scientific,
> the inductive method, which takes into view all the facts before
> reaching a conclusion, is here observed.[46]

By declining to quote the passages that his opponents read differently,
McGarvey implicitly makes an argument for the opponent's incompetence. One may question how closely McGarvey himself has read Amos
or paid attention to the book's theological argument (though he is probably right to question the claim, so common in his era, that the prophets
opposed the cult outright). Yet the point here is not to ask whether his
interpretation of Amos is accurate, but how he constructs his arguments
against opponents. The *ad hominem* nature of those arguments should
be clear.

McGarvey ends the first treatment of Amos by claiming that his
opponents suppress part of the evidence to make their case, while leaving
unstated the obvious conclusion that the comprehensiveness of his own
treatment is more fitting the gravity of the topic, and thus more just.[47] He
then promises to return to the topic in the second part of his work. An
implicit appeal to the greater accuracy of his own exegesis—left implicit
so as to emphasize his own scholarly detachment as opposed to the bias
of his opponents—serves to reinforce his audience's confidence in the
reasonableness of their assumed position.

In the second treatment of Amos, McGarvey examines three texts
(Amos 1:2; 2:4; and 2:11–12). The treatment of the second text provides
the best example of his rhetorical skill. After citing Wellhausen's claim
that the *torah* to which Amos appealed bore no relationship to the Priestly
material in the Pentateuch (a view most scholars today would qualify),[48]
he dismisses Wellhausen's "reckless" assertion[49] with a syllogism: Amos

46. McGarvey, *Authorship*, 173.

47. McGarvey, *Authorship*, 175.

48. See Shalom Paul, *Amos*, Hermeneia (Minneapolis: Fortress, 1991) 75; but Jörg
Jeremias, *Amos*, Old Testament Library (Louisville: Westminster John Knox, 1998) 44.

49. McGarvey, *Authorship*, 254. The use of epithets in persuasion is time-honored,
but hazardous. As Perelman and Olbrechts-Tyteca (*New Rhetoric*, 126) note, "The role of
epithets in argumentation is most clearly seen when two symmetrical qualifications with
opposite values appear equally possible . . ." Speakers avoid hazard when, in their choice
of epithets, "the various aspects of a reality are situated on different planes, and a more

was the first writing prophet; any written text he cites must come before him; therefore, the written text he cites comes before him. The flaw in the argument is, of course, that the *torah* Amos cites need not have been a written text, but could have been an oral tradition. In McGarvey's defense, such an appeal to oral tradition would have been rare in 1902, since Gunkel and other early form critics were just beginning to make their influence felt. Like Wellhausen, McGarvey thought in terms of written texts. However, his statement, "The words of Amos imply of necessity that there was a law of Jehovah, statutes of Jehovah, which had preceded the prophets, and which had been disregarded by the people of Judah for generations past"[50] does not lead inexorably to his conclusion that the *torah* equals the entire Pentateuch or even large portions of it. Accordingly, his last *ad hominem* argument on this text must fall flat:

> How completely blinded by a preconception must Wellhausen have been not to have seen that he was using this passage to teach the opposite of what it implies! And how completely he has pulled the wool over the eyes of such men as Robertson Smith, Driver, Cheyne, and others, that they should not have seen the trap into which he has led them. But "critical views" have become traditional.[51]

The last line reveals, again, an important part of McGarvey's self-presentation: he and his fellow defenders of traditional understandings of Scripture are the truly modern ones, the opponents of groupthink and the practitioners of rational argumentation. Such a strategy of self-presentation serves McGarvey well in an environment in which his readers must have felt themselves marginalized by the apparent sophistication of their opponents.[52]

---

complete vision of reality can consist only of a progressive multiplication of aspects to which attention is drawn." *Authorship* is full of argumentation through the use of adjectives and adverbs, again pointing to the fact that McGarvey assumed that his audience basically agreed with his position and so would not find his choice of epithets controversial. They would not, for example, substitute "brilliant" or "persuasive" for his choice "reckless."

50. McGarvey, *Authorship*, 255.

51. Ibid.

52. One must be careful here not to reassert the old saw that fundamentalism (or McGarvey's proto-fundamentalism) was a rural reaction to urban sophistication. McGarvey was no Elmer Gantry. He was an educated man and a very skilled writer. Much of the conservative reaction to higher criticism in his time came from urban centers, and the early conservative leadership was also primarily urban. Yet it would be hard to dismiss altogether social considerations from an analysis of his work, and one hopes for future studies along these lines. For the overall socio-religious issues of the time and slightly later, see George M. Marsden, *Fundamentalism and American Culture: The Shaping of*

Conclusions

In offering this analysis of McGarvey's study of Deuteronomy, I am keenly aware of the limitations of my work. Much remains to be done on the rhetorical dimensions of the debates on biblical criticism from the 1880s on. Yet it does seem clear that *The Authorship of Deuteronomy*, while it has not made a significant contribution to scholarship properly speaking, does exhibit a high level of rhetorical skill, piety, and attention to texts (both biblical and scholarly). As such, it has exerted significant influence among Churches of Christ and Christian Churches/Churches of Christ until recently. By adroitly constructing an implied audience and confirming their commitments to central Christian doctrines and their distrusts of certain styles of reading the Bible, McGarvey wrote a book that, in its complex texture and enjoyable skewering of opponents, made for both an exciting read and a supporter of traditional views on the Bible.

It might be useful, then, to end by proposing lines of continuing research. First, further studies of the intellectual environment of the Stone-Campbell movement that gave rise to McGarvey and created for him an audience remains a high desideratum. Such research should consider the attitudes of readers of the key journals and books of the movement, as well as the processes by which ideas and attitudes were disseminated. Research in this area is still at a preliminary stage. Second, the reception history of works like *Authorship* deserves greater study. As an undergraduate student, I was exposed to McGarvey's earlier commentaries, just as previous generations of students in Church of Christ schools had been. But what social or religious end did such exposure serve? That question seems unanswered, though one may hazard guesses. Third, more exhaustive rhetorical and literary-critical studies of *Authorship* (and other such works) could lead toward a comprehensive understanding of the past and present uses of the Bible in the conservative branches of the Stone-Campbell movement, a research project of which only the beginnings currently exist. My hope is that this work marks a small contribution to these larger ends. The issues that McGarvey faced remain significant as readers of the Bible seek to understand its function in their own lives. His approach to scholarship, while arguably insufficiently supple to interpret adequately the biblical texts he obviously loved, deserves respect and engagement.

Twentieth-Century Evangelicalism 1870–1925 (Oxford: Oxford University Press, 1980) 199–205; see the essays in Martin Marty and R. Scott Appleby, eds., *Fundamentalisms and Society* (Chicago: University of Chicago Press, 1993).

4

The Struggle for the Soul of Churches of Christ (1897–1907)

Hoosiers, Volunteers, and Longhorns

JOHN MARK HICKS

When the division between Churches of Christ and the Christian Churches was recognized by the religious census of 1906, the theological perspectives among the Churches of Christ were fairly diverse. While there was an ecclesiological consensus to separate from the Christian Churches, the diversity between three major "traditions" among Churches of Christ threatened that unity.

The Traditions and the Papers

This diversity in the late nineteenth century has been previously identified as (1) the Tennessee Tradition (or Nashville Bible School tradition, represented by the *Gospel Advocate* [hereafter *GA*] published in Nashville, Tennessee), (2) the Texas Tradition (represented by the *Firm Foundation* [hereafter *FF*] published in Austin, Texas), and (3) the Sommer Tradition (represented by the *Octographic Review* [hereafter *OR*] published in Indianapolis, Indiana).[1] While the multiple "traditions hypothesis may be flawed and need correction," Michael Casey found it "compelling."[2] In

---

1. John Mark Hicks and Bobby Valentine, *Kingdom Come: Embracing the Spiritual Legacy of David Lipscomb and James Harding* (Abilene, TX: Leafwood, 2006) 19.

2. Michael Casey, Stone-Campbell History Archive List, October 1, 2007, under the subject line "'Baptist Baptism' and Soteriology."

Mike's honor, this essay explores this typology by surveying the decade when the Churches of Christ emerged as a "distinct and separate" body from the Christian Churches.

1897 is a *terminus ad quo*.[3] Lipscomb opened 1897 with this observation: "I am fast reaching the conclusion that there is a radical and fundamental difference between the disciples of Christ and the society folks."[4] Later that year Lipscomb questioned whether they were "disciples of Christ" because of Cave's inclusivism (saved without explicit faith in Christ), Garrison's unionism (uniting with churches that sprinkle infants), and Minton's denominationalism (building up societies and organizations that supplant the work of the church).[5]

1907 is a *terminus ad quem*. Lipscomb published his letter to S. N. D. North, the Director of the Bureau of Census in 1907 and made a clear distinction between the "Church of Christ" and the "Disciples of Christ" (or Christian Churches). "There is," he wrote, "a distinct people . . . calling their churches 'churches of Christ' or 'churches of God,' distinct and separate in name, work, and rule of faith from all other bodies of people."[6]

The Churches of Christ were led by several major papers. While smaller papers proliferated, the editors of at least three papers functioned as *de facto* "Editor-Bishops": *GA* (edited by David Lipscomb and E. G. Sewell), *FF* (edited by Austin McGary [1884–1902], George Savage [1902–1905], and N. L. Clark [1906–1907]), and *OR* (edited by Daniel Sommer and L. F. Bittle). *The Way* (edited by James A. Harding [1899–1903]) and the *Christian Leader* (edited by John F. Rowe [1886–1897] and James S. Bell [1898–1903], hereafter *CL*) were also significant. They merged as *The Christian Leader and the Way* [hereafter *CLW*] in 1904. This united northern and southern readers. The *GA*, *CL* and *The Way* shared a similar editorial policy.[7] *CLW* also absorbed the Texas *Gospel Review* in 1904. Through these mergers, as Casey has noted, *CLW* "became a national journal rivaling" the others.[8]

3. William Woodson, *Standing for Their Faith: A History of the Churches of Christ in Tennessee, 1900–1950* (Henderson, TN: J & W Publications, 1979), 56.

4. Lipscomb, "The Churches Across the Mountains," *GA* 39 (7 January 1897) 4.

5. Lipscomb, "The Vital Point," *GA* 39 (19 August 1897) 516.

6. Lipscomb, "The 'Church of Christ' and the 'Disciples of Christ,'" *GA* 49 (18 July 1907) 450.

7. Harding, "An Intricate Problem Solved," *CLW* 18 (5 January 1904) 8; "Shall We Stop Discussion?" *CLW* 21 (26 March 1907) 8.

8. Michael Casey, "*Christian Leader*," in *The Encyclopedia of the Stone-Campbell Movement*, ed. Douglas A. Foster, et. al. (Grand Rapids: Eerdmans, 2004) 193.

For my purposes the Texas Tradition is represented by the *FF* under its multiple editors and the Hoosier Tradition by the *OR*. The Tennessee Tradition, in this essay, is represented by the *GA* (1897–1898), *The Way* (1899–1903), and *CLW* (1904–1907) since Harding, the "epitome" of the Tennessee Tradition,[9] is the trajectory's most prolific editor and antagonist during the decade.

Two words of caution are necessary. First, the geographical designations neither limit the traditions to those regions nor was everyone in those regions an adherent. There was considerable cross-fertilization between the traditions. Second, these trajectories are not rigid but fluid. While there are clear loyalties, there is also variety within the traditions themselves. Consequently, while discerning the common thrusts of these traditions is legitimate, reductionism and oversimplification should be avoided.

A Common Tradition: Separation from the Christian Church

Whatever differences Hoosiers, Volunteers, and Longhorns had, they were united against a common foe. "The great enemy to the Church of Christ today is the sect called Christian Church," wrote Denton.[10] Across the spectrum there were incessant warnings about the failure of the Christian Churches to remain true to the "old paths" recorded in the New Testament. From 1897 to 1907 the Christian Church was increasingly regarded as another denomination. "[W]hat of the Christian Church?" Harding asked. "It is the youngest of the denominations," he answered.[11] "All denominations, including the Christian Church with its fast notions," Sommer wrote, "are a compromise."[12] In 1900 Sommer thought it was a "hopeful sign" that "now the churches of Christ are drawing the lines of demarcation more deeply and widely."[13] While there are obvious sociological and sectional causes of the division between the Churches of

9. Richard T. Hughes, *Reviving the Ancient Faith: The Story of Churches of Christ in America* (Grand Rapids: Eerdmans, 1996) 138.

10. J. W. Denton, "The Difference Between the Christian Church and Church of Christ," *FF* 19 (10 February 1903) 1.

11. Harding, "The Church of God *Versus* the Denominations," *The Way* 5 (17 September 1903) 866.

12. Sommer, "Epistles to Elders and Deacons. Number Twelve," *OR* 43 (20 March 1900) 1.

13. Sommer, "Epistles to Elders and Deacons. Number Thirty Seven," *OR* 43 (25 September 1900) 1.

Christ and the Christian Church,[14] there were also significant hermeneutical and theological grounds as well which our editors thought were the primary reasons for separation.

An Ecclesio-Hermeneutical Principle

Their common ground between the editors was hermeneutical. Many issues generated conflict between the two religious bodies. They ranged from instrumental music to choirs, from fund-raising festivals to funding missionary societies, from one-man pastor systems to female evangelists. Though diverse all these "sources of contention" were opposed on the basis of a legal hermeneutical "principle." Succinctly stated, it is a call to "an immediate return to New Testament faith and practice, in which nothing shall be taught that has not the apostolic sanction, and no expedient allowed that is not necessary to carry out the Lord's commands."[15] This is rooted the Reformed Regulative Principle,[16] assumed that positive law was the basis of obedience,[17] and obligations were discerned through command, example and necessary inference.

This "principle" is what divides Churches of Christ from Christian Churches, according to Harding. "The difference is one of principle. It is radical and the chasm" between the two bodies "must of necessity become wider and wider" since the difference will evidence itself in increasing ways. "It is not directly a question about organs, choirs, missionary societies, etc.," Harding notes, "but about abiding in the word of Jesus as expressed in the New Testament."[18]

·

14. David Edwin Harrell, *The Social Sources of Division in the Disciples of Christ, 1865–1900* (Atlanta: Publishing Systems, 1973) 2:323–50.

15. Bittle, "Concerning Division," *OR* 47 (21 June 1904) 4 (original stated in all caps).

16. John Mark Hicks, Johnny Melton, and Bobby Valentine, *A Gathered People: Revisioning the Assembly as Transforming Encounter* (Abilene: Leafwood Publishers, 2007) 96–102, 119–24.

17. Benjamin Franklin, "Positive Divine Law," in *Gospel Preacher: A Book of Twenty-One Sermons* (Cincinnati: G. W. Rice, 1877) 1:193–217.

18. James A. Harding, "Primitive Christians and Progressives—The One Difference Between Them," *The Way* 4 (24 July 1902) 130.

Biblical-Theological Ground

While some thought the above was sufficient for separation (e.g., Sommer, Harding, McGary), the rise of Higher Criticism and a new understanding of unity entailed a clear break for others (Lipscomb, Bell, Rowe).

Higher Criticism. When Sommer attended an Indianapolis convention in 1897, he found "that 'higher criticism'—otherwise the higher conceit which tampers with the integrity of the Sacred Text—was a subject of controversy."[19] This "unrest" within the Christian Church distanced them from the Churches of Christ.[20] Harding, for example, considered H. L. Willett "an unbeliever in and blasphemer of the Word of God . . . an infidel."[21] The "theological seminary," the Disciples Divinity House in Chicago, was the main source of these ideas among Disciples.[22] Such a seminary, of course, was anathema to all editors among the Churches of Christ.

Church Federation. When of the National Federation of Churches invited the Disciples of Christ to participate in their unity efforts in 1902, papers among Churches of Christ saw further evidence of a different spirit. Sommer's response was a kind of "I told you so" attitude. This is what one reaps when churches sow a worldly gospel driven by innovations.[23] Bell declared it a power grab similar to the "kingdoms of this world."[24] Savage called the development "disgusting and inexcusable."[25] When Garrison and anointed other religious bodies as "churches of Christ," a torrent of articles attacked this "new" agenda. Armstrong saw Garrison's position as affirming that "all denominations are churches of Christ, and taken together constitute the church of God," and "this is the foundation of all federation of churches."[26] The Christian Church became a charter member of the Federal Council of Churches in 1908.

---

19. Sommer, "Signs of the Times. First Article," *OR* 45 (10 June 1902) 1, 8.

20. Bittle, "Unrest," *OR* 44 (20 May 1901) 4.

21. Harding, "H. L. Willett and the Story of the Brazen Serpent," *CLW* 21 (3 Dec 1907) 8; cf. "Are They Christians or Infidels?" *CLW* 19 (16 May 1905) 8.

22. Sommer, "Signs of the Times. Sixth Article," *OR* 45 (22 July 1902) 8.

23. Sommer, "Poor Joseph! Always Wrong!" *OR* 46 (21 May 1903) 1.

24. James S. Bell, "Church Federation—What It Would Be," *CL* 17 (23 June 1903) 8.

25. George W. Savage, "Federation of Churches, Doctors, Doctored, and the Reason Why," *FF* 19 (6 February 10 1903) 4.

26. J. N. Armstrong, "Faris' Letter and Church Federation," *CLW* 20 (8 May 1906) 1.

This implied a different understanding of unity. While supporters of the Federation understood unity at a Christological level—faith in Jesus, Churches of Christ understood unity at an ecclesiological level. "We can not afford to go in and federate with them, and the Lord will not allow them to come in and federate with us," Kidwell wrote, "unless they will submit to being immersed."[27] Unity has prescribed ecclesiological boundaries: right baptism, right Supper, right worship, and right organization. It is better, thought Skagg, that the Christian Church be "absorbed by the other denominations and then the churches of Christ will not be deceived by the plea that 'we be brethren.'"[28]

Separation

Separation was the intention of Churches of Christ in the first decade of the twentieth century. Some divisions, McGary's co-editor Jackson wrote, "are right and necessary."[29] There was no longer any "neutral ground" and any kind of "neutrality is...treason against" God.[30] Though delighted that others had caught up with his initial attempts at separation in the 1889 "Address and Declaration,"[31] Sommer complained that it took "ten to twenty years . . . to convince [the] leading opponents that the spirit of innovationism was a deep-rooted heresy."[32]

Responding to "innovationism," Sommer noted, "apostolic disciples began to draw the lines between 'the church of Christ' and 'the Christian church.'"[33] In 1891 A. M. Morris, an *OR* writer, entitled a pamphlet *Difference Between the Church of Christ and the Christian Church*.[34] In 1903 James A. Harding lamented that "in the forty-three years that have passed," congregations have divided in "hundreds of places all over our land" with the result that in "the same city, town or village we find the

27. W. T. Kidwell, "Is the 'Federation' Spirit Any New Thing?" *FF* 22 (26 June 1906) 1.

28. W. P. Skaggs, "Digression Gone to Seed," *FF* 19 (4 January 1903) 1.

29. J. W. Jackson, "Divisions," *FF* 13 (9 March 1897) 4.

30. Bittle, "Our Ideal," 44 (29 October 1901) 4.

31. Sommer, "An Address," *OR* 32 (5 September 1889) 1, 5, 8; the "Declaration" also appeared in the *CL* 4 (10 September 1889) 2.

32. Sommer, "Signs of the Times. Eleventh Article," *OR* 45 (26 August 1902) 1.

33. Sommer, "Signs of the Times. Sixth Article," *OR* 45 (22 July 1902) 1.

34. A. M. Morris, *Difference Between the Church of Christ and the Christian Church* (Moberly, MO: Sentinel Printing, 1891).

'Church of Christ' and the 'Christian Church' the two having no Christian fellowship for each other."[35]

Divergent Traditions: The Struggle for Identity

Though the *FF*, *OR*, *CL*, *The Way*, *CLW*, and *GA* were heremeneutically and ecclesiologically united against the Christian Church, there was significant theological diversity among them. There was so much diversity and so much "strife over foolish and unlearned questions" that many feared that it would undermine the fight against innovations.[36] Bittle, for example, cautioned that "the friends of the ancient order of things should discard minor issues and personal interests, and unite in a vigorous campaign" for apostolic practices.[37] Yet, when George Savage, the new editor of the *FF* in 1902, sought to purge it "from evil speakings,"[38] he was accused of adopting the "digressive 'sweet-spirited' policy plan."[39] Given the intense heat of separation from the Christian Church and identity formation among Churches of Christ, suspicion and mistrust reigned.

Differences ranged from polity issues to conditional immorality, from mutual edification to located evangelists, from the corporate practice of the right hand of fellowship to the necessity of confession before baptism, from a prescribed order of worship to legitimate uses of the Sunday contribution, from women working outside the home to female participation in the assembly, from involvement in politics to institutionalism, from debating the relation of the kingdom to the church to whether the Sermon on the Mount applies to Christians, from war-peace questions to social involvement in temperance movements, from the nature of special providence to the reality of contemporary miracles, and from biblical names for the church to eschatology (millennialism, renewed earth theology).

This section will focus on four prominent issues where Hoosiers, Longhorns and Volunteers collided: (1) Faith and Baptism, (2) Indwelling of the Holy Spirit, (3) Institutionalism, and (4) Sunday Schools. While Texas and Indiana both took different positions from Tennessee on the

35. Harding, "Our Practice," *The Way* 5 (13 August 1903) 786.

36. Lottie Johnson, "From Sister Johnson," *FF* 14 (5 July 1898) 213.

37. Bittle, "Flattering Words," *OR* 40 (19 October 1897) 4.

38. Savage "The Policy of the Firm Foundation Will Be to Manifest the Spirit of Christ," *FF* 18 (23 September 1902) 4.

39. Savage, "An Unjust Charge—We Think It Is Not True," *FF* 20 (29 March 1904) 4.

latter two, Indiana and Tennessee occupied the same general ground on the first two. These are but a few of the many windows through which these traditions might be compared. Others are worthy of attention, particularly providence, eschatology and kingdom theology where Tennessee differed from both Texas and Indiana, but the limitations of space prohibit a thorough comparison.

In general, though not exclusively, Tennessee embraced dynamic divine action in the world as the in-breaking kingdom of God, Indiana stressed the non-institutional and anti-worldly character of that kingdom, and Texas rejected any semblance of dynamic divine action other than a cognitive understanding of the Bible. The Tennessee Tradition stressed divine dynamics rather than human mechanics. The Texas Tradition embraced human cognition and ability as the critical factor in humanity's relationship with God. Though the Indiana Tradition shared some formal characteristics with Tennessee, it stressed non-institutional ecclesiology and opposition to worldly wisdom, wealth and power as the centerpiece of its agenda. Essentially, the Tennessee Tradition transcended an ecclesiological focus on form and function with an eschatologically-driven kingdom vision.

Faith and Baptism

Over two hundred articles were exchanged on the subject of reimmersion between 1897–1907. Harding debated the question with both McGary and Tant; Burnett debated McGary. Lipscomb and McGary exchanged numerous articles. It threatened to split the church. McGary believed that the *GA* acted on the same principle as those who "justify instrumental music" and the "missionary society" since they "violate [Scripture's] silence here by teaching other ways that sinners may be forgiven and enter the kingdom of Christ." McGary thus regarded this as another step toward a "divided brotherhood."[40] Tant, however, expected that within "fifteen years" that people "coming into the fellowship of the church of Christ on their sectarian baptism [would] be a thing of the past" because "the *gospel* is having its leavening influence in Tennessee."[41]

---

40. McGary, "The Firm Foundation—Its Aims and Principles," *FF* 16 (8 January 1901) 8. Cf. McGary, "Some Splendid Words," *FF* 16 (9 January 1900) 24; and "Editors Must be Criticized," *FF* 18 (29 April 1902) 4.

41. J. D. Tant, "Too Many Papers," *FF* 15 (10 January 1899) 23 (emphasis mine).

For Texas it was a "*gospel*" issue because the *GA* received as Christians those who were not authentically Christian. Tennesseans, by "shaking in the Baptists," embraced a broader vision of the kingdom than was comfortable for Texans.[42] By so doing Tennesseans were acknowledging Christians among the sects. The *FF*, Savage declared, "has never 'fallen' so far as to teach this conglomeration of faithless 'union' and communion."[43]

The Texas charge was accurate. "I suppose," Harding wrote, "there are people among all the so-called 'Christian denominations' who have believed in Christ with their whole hearts" and been immersed. Whether these believers ever came out of denominationalism or not, baptismal and sanctifying grace entailed that God is gracious with their failings. "Wherever an [immersed believer] is," according to Harding, "if he is daily, diligently seeking the truth, if he is promptly walking in it as he finds it, we may expect him to be saved."[44] This gracious attitude toward those who walk sincerely among the denominations enlarged the kingdom beyond the borders of the *FF*'s vision of the church.

For Tennesseans faith is the issue rather than baptism. "The Firm Foundation," Burnett wrote, "says that faith in Christ is not the faith that qualifies for baptism, but faith that baptism is for the remission of sins."[45] What one "must believe," according to Harding, "is that Jesus is the Christ, the Son of God. This is the faith that saves" as "devotion to Christ, resolution to follow Christ."[46] Jesus saves through faith that is a matter of discipleship rather than intellectual assent. It is faith in the work of God rather than faith in the human understanding of baptismal design.

Opponents of rebaptism accused the Texans of sectarianism. "The rebaptism extreme . . . is an intensely sectarian idea," according to Sommer.[47] Rebaptists "adopt the sectarian plan of sitting in judgment on the fitness of persons for baptism."[48] In 1891 Sommer published a tract defending his views because the *FF* was intent on "working division in the brotherhood" and consequently he permitted "no discussion of the rebaptism question" in *OR*.[49]

42. J. W. Denton, "Burnett's Reply to Pearson," *FF* 22 (17 March 1906) 3.

43. Savage, "Brother Burnett's Charges," *FF* 21 (28 November 1905) 4.

44. Harding, "Questions and Answers," *The Way* 4 (17 July 1902) 122.

45. Burnett, "Burnett's Budget," *GA* 39 (26 August 1897) 533.

46. Harding, "The Faith That Prepares for Baptism," *CLW* 18 (1 November 1904) 8, 9.

47. As quoted by N. L. Clark, "On the Firing Line," *FF* 22 (6 November 1906) 4.

48. Sommer, "A Letter with Comments," *OR* 47 (2 Feb 1904) 3.

49. Sommer, "Let Patience Have Her Perfect Work," *OR* 40 (29 June 1897) 1, 8.

Indwelling of the Holy Spirit

Other than rebaptism the indwelling Spirit was the most controversial topic from 1897 to 1907. More than fifty articles were exchanged among the papers in 1897–1898 and over one hundred in 1904–1906. These involved some heated interactions, e.g., the explosive discussion between J. C. Holloway and Harding in the 1905 *CLW*.[50] When *The Way* and *CL* merged in 1904, Harding's belief in the enabling Spirit was opposed by some elements of the *CL*.[51] The Holloway-Harding exchanges were anticipated in 1897–1898 when Denton (*FF*) and Burnett (*GA*)—and in 1905 as well[52]—discussed the question.

Generally, the *OR* ignored these discussions because they assumed the personal indwelling of the Spirit was a settled question. Bittle answered questions as if there were no dispute—it is "as most Christians allow."[53] "In dwelling personally with and in the saints," according to Bittle, "the Holy Spirit acts as the representative of Christ and God."[54] Sommer dismissed attempts to reduce the presence of the Spirit to information. God gives "obedient believers" the Spirit "personally, entering their hearts and dwelling in them."[55] The *OR* had no patience for "word-alone" theorists, but neither did it emphasize the reality, power and function of the indwelling Spirit in any significant way.

The *FF* argued that the Spirit indwelt through the word alone by faith.[56] It opposed the personal, enabling power of the Spirit as a form of "mysticism," an "absurd idea" that is "purely sectarian in origin."[57] It rendered the word insufficient because the Spirit operates directly. If "the Spirit comes from God to the Christian, then" this is "direct operation" and if the "Spirit (as a person) dwells in the church today, then the days of miracles are not past and the Mormons are right."[58] Instead, the word is sufficient as God "leads, guides, controls men by his Word" and he does

50. Hicks and Valentine, *Kingdom Come*, 60–66.

51. B. F. Bixler, "Another Voice," *CLW* 30 (18 July 1905) 2.

52. Denton, "The Spirit and Word," *FF* 21 (4 July 1905) 1 plus five more articles.

53. Bittle, "The Invocation of the Spirit," *OR* 40 (11 May 1897) 4.

54. Bittle, "The Gift of the Holy Ghost," *OR* 44 (26 November 1901) 4.

55. Sommer, "Concerning What the Holy Spirit Says to Sinner and Saints," *OR* 46 (14 July 1903), 1.

56. G. A. Trott, "The Indwelling Spirit," *FF* 22 (13 March 1906) 4.

57. G. T. Walker, "The Indwelling of the Spirit," *FF* 15 (20 June 1899) 385.

58. Denton, "Reflections on the Spirit," *FF* 20 (9 February 1904) 1.

not "have to be here personally to do it."[59] That was only for the apostles and those gifted in the apostolic age. The general contention was that the Spirit dwells in the heart through the word of God in the same way that Christ and the Father dwell in the hearts of believers.[60]

According to Denton, God comforts by the words of his Holy Spirit because "you can not comfort anything that has no ideas, and you can not have ideas without words."[61] The "Spirit does not have to be here in person to teach, rule and guide by His word any more than Blackstone must be here to rule, guide or settle a point of law." [62] The Spirit helps our infirmities or comforts our souls through epistemology alone since we live by the word of God alone rather than "comforting us in some unknown and unspeakable way."[63] The work of the Spirit is thus reduced to an empirical epistemology of language.

Many in the Tennessee tradition were horrified by such statements though some were rather ambiguous, e.g., Lipscomb.[64] Burnett called it the "word alone doctrine" or "Spirit-in-the-word theory." "They have the idea," he wrote, "that the thought or idea in the word is the Holy Spirit."[65] In contrast to past Stone-Campbell luminaries (e.g., Campbell, Franklin, Lard, Brents), the *FF* "is so shy of the sectarian theory of the Spirit alone that [it] has switched off on the other side of the track to the word-alone doctrine." Burnett contended for a "Spirit-and-word theory" where the Spirit "dwells in the temple or church of God on earth today" and wields the word as a sword.[66]

The denial of the indwelling Spirit who enables transformed living was "semi-infidel[ity]."[67] Such a denial is a "withering, deadly curse to those that believe it."[68] "Does the Holy Spirit do anything now except what the Word does?" Harding asks. "Do we get help, any kind or in any

---

59. Denton, "Bro. Burnett's Muddle Again," *FF* 14 (6 September 1898) 282.

60. Savage, "Brother Burnett's Charges," *FF* 21 (28 November 1905) 4.

61. Denton, "Bro. Burnett's Muddle Again," *FF* 14 (6 September 1898) 282.

62. Denton, "Question and Answer," *FF* 21 (29 August 1905) 1.

63. Savage, "The Spirit in Christians," *FF* 20 (1 November 1904) 4.

64. Lipscomb, "The Spirit Before Pentecost," *GA* 40 (10 November 1898) 716

65. Burnett, "Owen to the Rescue," *GA* 40 (21 April 1898) 251.

66. Burnett, "On the Holy Spirit," *FF* 20 (10 May 1904) 3.

67. Harding, "Another Effort to Get Dr. Holloway Out of the Fog," *CLW* 19 (24 October 1905) 8.

68. Harding, "Saving Souls, Special Providence, Dr. Holloway," *CLW* 21 (29 January 1904) 8.

way, from God except what we get by studying the Bible?"[69] The specific point was whether there was any power available to the Christian that was not simply a matter of ideas or cognition. Rather than the mind passively receiving ideas, the Tennessee tradition embraced—in the words of R. H. Boll—that "there is an influx of power" through the personal presence of the Spirit.[70] The Spirit is the believer's divine enabler and transformer.

The Texas Tradition distanced themselves from these "sectarian" ideas. In fact, Chisholm, among others, linked the rebaptism and Spirit controversies. It is "no wonder" that those who ask "questions about spiritual influence" are also the same ones who "have said that men need not know just when God forgives their sins."[71] Both derived from denominational theology and demonstrated the impurity of the Tennessee heresy.

Institutionalism

In 1902 Sommer named two extremes, "innovationism" and "hobbyism." Both introduce "dissentions and divisions" as the innovators advocate "human devices" and the hobbyists strain "Scripture against sectarians." Generally, Sommer means the Christian Church by innovators and the *FF*, *GA*, and others by hobbyists. "[C]hurches in several southern states," particularly the *GA* and *The Way*, have "thrust upon" the apostolic churches "a new and modified phase of innovationism," that is, the Sunday School, its literature and the Bible College.[72] These are embarkations "on the 'high seas' of human institutionism."[73] Due to southern agitation Sommer began a campaign against both the colleges and the Sunday Schools in first few years of the 20th century.[74] Several exchanges in the papers ensued, including debates with J. N. Armstrong and B. F. Rhodes.

Sommer objected to "Bible Colleges" at several levels. Alexander Campbell set a precedent which "implied that the church" was "not a sufficient pillar and basis of truth, but needs *a college* to supply its defi-

---

69. Harding, "Questions and Answers," *The Way* 4 (17 July 1902) 123.

70. R. H. Boll, "The Spirit's Indwelling," *CLW* 19 (16 May 1905) 1.

71. L. C. Chisholm, "Spiritual Influence," *FF* 21 (14 November 1905) 2.

72. Sommer, "Signs of the Times. Eleventh Article," *OR* 46 (26 August 1902) 1, 8.

73. Sommer, "Signs of the Times. Tenth Article," *OR* 46 (19 August 1902) 1.

74. Sommer, "Sunday-Schools and Sunday-School Literature," *OR* 44 (26 February 1901) 1.

ciency," such as the training of preachers.[75] The college was, in effect, a "religio-secular educational society" analogous to missionary societies.[76] Moreover, this worldly connection prompted disciples "to make a show of greatness" and thereby manifest a "lack of gospel humility." Colleges, like Bethany, were human institutions designed to do the work of the church, sustained by the Lord's money, and promoted worldly values.[77]

Sommer regarded it as the "most unpleasant task of [his] editorial life" when he began opposing the Nashville Bible School (founded 1891) and Potter Bible College (founded 1901). "[C]ertain southern editors and preachers, supposed to be apostolic," he wrote, "have been prominent in planning, founding and managing religio-secular institutions with the Lord's money which they have called 'Bible School' and 'Bible College.'" Not only was "Campbell's institutionalism" not a "sufficient forewarning for [the] southern brethren," they have added to the "heresy" by sacrilegiously using "Bible" in the name.[78] When southerners responded that Sommer was against education, he clarified that "all" that he had "written on the subject has been under these two headings, namely, *the mistake of thus using the Lord's money,* and the *mistake of thus naming such institutions.*"[79] The "southern brethren" were following the same trajectory as Campbell. "*Human institutions have been the curse of the disciple brotherhood.*" When Campbell adopted them, they became "the rock upon which the ship of Zion [was] split." The South is now following his example, and the "Sunday school, with its extra officers and special literature" was the "first human institution which they adopted in connection with the church." Now their adoption of religio-secular colleges is another step away from the simplicity of Christ.[80] "We judge the future," Sommer observed, "by the past."[81]

---

75. Sommer, "Signs of the Times. Ninth Article," *OR* 45 (12 August 1902) 1.

76. Sommer, "A Serious Letter," *OR* 29 (18 July 1905) 3.

77. Sommer, "Signs of the Times. Ninth Article," *OR* 45 (12 August 1902) 1.

78. Sommer, "Signs of the Times. Ninth Article," *OR* 45 (12 August 1902) 1, 8.

79. Sommer, "A Plain Statement and Challenge," *OR* 46 (4 August 1903) 1. See Daniel Sommer, "Concerning the Unscripturalness of Establishing Religio-Secular Schools with the Lord's Money," *OR* 46 (8 September 1903) 1, 8, followed by eight more articles.

80. Sommer, "Signs of the Times. Ninth Article," *OR* 45 (12 August 1902) 1, 8.

81. Sommer, "Signs of the Times. Tenth Article," *OR* 46 (19 August 1902) 1, 8.

Sommer judged himself unique as only the *OR* was opposed "to all *sectarianism*, to all *innovationism*, and to all *hobbyism*."[82] Sommer was, in effect, the last refuge of apostolicity within the Stone-Campbell Movement. In his own view, his opposition to Bible Colleges in the first decade of the 20th century effectively "save[d] the churches of Christ north of the Ohio River from being deceived by the 'college craze,' which was common in the Southland."[83] Though Sommer's non-institutionalism was eventually shared by some within the *FF* orbit such as Tant,[84] it would be another forty years before many would take up Sommer's aggressive stance toward institutionalism among Churches of Christ.

Sunday School

While Sommer opposed the Sunday School as a form of institutionalism that subverts parental obligations and the work of the church,[85] some Texans opposed it primarily on hermeneutical grounds. The distinction is important because while Sommer opposed the human institution (as did Lipscomb), others opposed separate classes and female teachers in children's classes. N. L. Clark and G. A. Trott, two of the *FF*'s four editors (1906–1907), opposed Sunday schools. While opposition to the Sunday school and its literature in the *FF* predated Clark, none of the prior editors opposed the division of the church into classes on Sunday morning for the purpose of teaching. All editors among Churches of Christ, however, opposed any Sunday School organization independent of the church.

Clark's rationale is hermeneutical. "I have opposed the Sunday School because it is not in the Book"[86] and "unknown to the New Testament."[87] He opposed it on the same ground he opposed other innovations, that is, the unqualified adherence to the motto of the Restoration Movement—to speak where the Bible speaks and be silent where the Bible is silent. For

---

82. Sommer, "'Let Patience Have Her Perfect Work.' Third Article," *OR* 40 (20 July 1897) 1.

83. Sommer, "A Record of My Life," *Apostolic Review* 86 (15 July 1941) 9, as quoted by James Stephen Wolfgang, "A Life of Humble Fear: The Biography of Daniel Sommer, 1850–1940" (M.A. Thesis, Butler University, 1975) 114.

84. Tant, "Information Wanted," *FF* 27 (21 March 1911) 6.

85. Sommer, "The Sunday School Question Considered. Chapter I," *OR* 44 (3 November 1903) 8, followed by two more articles.

86. Clark, "What Shall We Do About It?" *FF* 23 (12 March 1907) 4.

87. Clark, "An Explanation," *FF* 23 (24 September 1907) 4.

Clark the rejection of the Sunday school is a matter of biblical authority just like his opposition to rebaptism, instrumental music, and the societies. He opposed limiting public teaching to a single preacher and argued that the maturing and education of the church belonged in the hands of the elders. Advocating mutual edification, he believed the Sunday school gave more power to the preacher by dividing the church. Since "everybody will agree" that it is Scriptural for the church to "meet regularly" under the leadership of elders for teaching, why divide the church by introducing a Sunday school about which Scripture is silent.[88]

The Sunday school was also the means by which innovations were introduced. Societies were first organized through Sunday schools, instruments were first introduced in them, and there women were first given "prominence." Consequently, the "Sunday school is the first move to set aside the word of God" and the "first innovation the church ever accepted came through this" seemingly "harmless institution."[89] Opponents saw the Sunday school as a threat. In the suspicious climate of 1897–1907, the Sunday school posed a danger to the purity of the church.

In 1896 there were few congregations using Sunday schools in Texas but within twenty years there were "good Bible Schools in all the congregations."[90] The opposition to Clark by Robert L. Whiteside[91] and others encouraged the growth of Sunday classes in Texas churches. This growth alarmed opponents and the "harmless institution" became heretical. "I regard the Sunday School as an innovation," Clark wrote. "I can't see it in any other light."[92]

The Tennessee Tradition promoted Sunday schools under the oversight of elders and the *GA* published class literature. Lipscomb, for example, suggested that the Leiper's Fork church near Nashville suspend their institutional Sunday School work and incorporate that work into the life of the local congregation. "Brethren," he pleaded, "can't we come together here, or anywhere else as the church, and do the work that the Sunday School is doing?"[93] If so, then the question is: "May Christians

---

88. Clark, "What Shall We Do About It?" *FF* 23 (12 March 1907) 4.

89. Chisholm, "Reminiscences of the Past," *FF* 19 (3 November 1903) 1.

90. Lee P. Mansfield, "Then and Now," *FF* 22 (14 March 1916) 3.

91. Robert L. Whiteside and N. L. Clark, "The Sunday School Question," *FF* 22 (4 September 1906) 4 followed by other exchanges.

92. Clark, "Editorial Notes," *FF* 23 (29 January 1907) 4.

93. Lipscomb, "Sunday Schools," 39 (28 January 1897) 52.

meet together at other than the chief meeting, and teach one another and others the word of God in classes arranged according to advancement and knowledge?" The answer was obvious to Lipscomb.[94] Sunday schools, as part of the work of the local church, were an expedient means for Christians to teach Scripture.

Conclusion

From 1897–1907 the Tennessee Tradition was the most substantial influence among Churches of Christ. The tradition encouraged irenic discussion among Churches of Christ without division. W. J. Brown of Cloverdale, Indiana, for example, noted that the "tone and spirit" of the *GA* and *The Way* were different from other papers whose "lordly editors" subverted the unity of the brotherhood.[95] Free discussion among those who disagree lies behind the title of Armstrong's article "United, Yet Divided."[96]

The eschatological, dynamic and countercultural kingdom vision of the Tennessee Tradition, however, was displaced in the mid-twentieth century. The Texas Tradition gained ascendancy in the 1930s–1940s. Foy E. Wallace, Jr. and John T. Hinds, writers for the *FF*, were appointed as *GA* editors in the 1930s and the *CL* morphed into a gentler mirror of the *FF* in the mid-1930s. Rebaptism was no longer a live issue and the personal indwelling of the Holy Spirit was a minority position. Other dimensions of the Tennessee Tradition had also faded, including millennial eschatology, special providence, and a broader kingdom vision. By the late 1950s there was little theological difference between the *FF* and *GA*.

Though the *OR*'s subscription list numbered 10,000 in 1924 [then the *Apostolic Review*], the *FF* was double that number.[97] The *OR* was marginalized by its Northern and Midwestern constituency. As a minority voice in the Stone-Campbell Movement in the Midwest, it had little influence on southern churches in Texas and Tennessee. The Sommer Tradition was ultimately lost in the expanse of the Stone-Campbell Movement and overwhelmed by the sheer numbers of southern Churches of Christ. At the same time, however, the noninstitutional

94. Lipscomb, "The Sunday School," 39 (26 August 1897) 534.

95. W. J. Brown, "Let This Mind Be In You," *The Way* 3 (13 June 1901) 88.

96. Armstrong, "United, Yet Divided," *The Way* 4 (14 August 1902) 156.

97. Wolfgang, "Sommer," 119, n. 2; and Lane T. Cubstead, "The Firm Foundation, 1884–1957: The History of a Pioneer Religious Journal and Its Editors" (MA thesis, University of Texas, 1957) 117 n. 17.

emphases of the Indiana Tradition were embraced by southern noninstitutional churches in the 1950s.

But just as Churches of Christ achieved a measure of uniformity in the 1940s under the Texas Tradition they began to implode with disputes over the precise legal application of the received hermeneutic. As non-institutional Churches of Christ emerged in the late 1940s and 1950s, they renewed an anti-worldly stance that was overshadowed by technical hermeneutical debates. A socially alienated non-institutional Church of Christ in the Texas Tradition lacked the dynamism of the Tennessee Tradition and the deep-rooted counterculturalism of the Sommer Tradition. Generally, 1950s non-institutionalism among southern Churches of Christ was a Texas "Sommerism" without the nonsectarian (e.g., rebaptism) and dynamic (e.g., indwelling of the Spirit) nature of the Tennessee Tradition or even the Indiana Tradition. At the same time, institutional Churches of Christ also lacked the nonsectarian and dynamic nature of the Tennessee Tradition. In essence, the 1950s division devolved into a fight over how best to apply the hermeneutic of the fathers that was reminiscent of the Sunday School discussion in the first decade of the century. The institutional division was, largely, a squabble within the Texas Tradition.

The critical turn in the story is the loss of a dynamic sanctifying presence of God in the hearts of believers through the personal indwelling of the Spirit which symbolized the broader loss of divine dynamics within Churches of Christ as a whole. At an earlier point in history, the forefathers of Churches of Christ had chosen Fanning's Baconian rationalism over Robert Richardson's openness to the work of the Spirit.[98] The first decades of the twentieth century were a similar fork in the road. The Texas Tradition ultimately won the day on the Spirit among Churches of Christ. The loss of dynamic divine power in sanctification and the reduction of the Spirit's work to an empirical epistemology fostered debates over patterns and mechanics rather than an emphasis on a transformed life enabled by the Spirit.

But this Spiritual theology was not wholly lost. Though K. C. Moser "was brought up at the feet of teachers who denied the indwelling of the Spirit," in the late 1920s he discovered for himself "that no doctrine is

---

98. C. Leonard Allen, *Things Unseen: Churches of Christ in (After) the Modern Age* (Siloam Springs, AR: Leafwood, 2004) 71–98.

more plainly taught than the doctrine of the indwelling Spirit."[99] Moser understood this as the hinge of grace and legalism since to "deny the indwelling of the Holy Spirit [is to] leave grace for law." "Legalism," he wrote, "is the father of the denial of the personal indwelling of the Spirit."[100] Moser's emphasis was a renewal of the Tennessee Tradition as represented by Harding, Boll, Armstrong, and others. Predictably, Moser was ostracized by the *FF*.[101]

While Foy E. Wallace could commend Moser as "sound to the core" in 1923, J. N. Armstrong could subsequently commend Moser as "sound to the core" in 1934.[102] Moser's shift from Texas to Tennessee is remarkable and bucks the general trend in Churches of Christ. Wallace and Armstrong were representatives of two different traditions and neither was well-disposed toward the other. As the Texas tribe increased, the Tennessee tribe decreased but not without hope that it would again rise to prominence. That subsequent rise is due, in part, to the Moser-prompted "Man or the Plan" controversy and a renewed emphasis on the personal indwelling of the Spirit in the late 1950s and early 1960s.[103]

---

99. K. C. Moser, "Brother Colley Seeks Information," *FF* 47 (11 March 1930) 3. See Bobby Valentine, "In with Wallace, Out with Brewer: K. C. Moser and the *Herald of Truth* in the 1920s," Christian Scholar's Conference paper, Rochester College, 2007.

100. Moser, "Reply to Brother Colley," *FF* 47 (6 May 1930) 3. See K. C. Moser, *The Way of Salvation* (Nashville: Gospel Advocate, 1932), 137.

101. G. H. P. Showalter, See "The 'Faith Alone' Idea," *FF* 51 (3 April 1934) 4.

102. Foy E. Wallace, Jr., "A Summary and A Tribute" *Herald of Truth* 3 (October 25/ November 1 1923) 11; J. N. Armstrong, "Extemporaneous Meeting" *GA* 76 (29 March 1934) 317. I am indebted to Valentine's "In with Wallace, Out with Brewer" presentation for demonstrating this shift and illuminating these commendations.

103. Hicks, "The Man or the Plan? K. C. Moser and the Theology of Grace Among Mid-Twentieth Century Churches of Christ," Presentation for the 18th Annual W. B. West Lectures for the Advancement of Christian Scholarship, October 5, 1993, available at http://www.mun.ca/rels/restmov/texts/moser/jmhindex.html.

5

Recovery of Coventantal Narratival Biblical Theology in the Restoration Movement

THOMAS H. OLBRICHT

The movement of which the Churches of Christ are a part began with a narrative about God's salvific work in which the church founded by Jesus Christ played a major role. The primordial church, so the first preachers declared, though concealed through the Middle Ages, was recovered in part by the magisterial reformers. Our forefathers especially Alexander Campbell and Walter Scott believed that in their efforts to restore the ancient order and ancient gospel that the glorious church of the New Testament was on the verge of breaking upon the horizon in splendor. God envisioned the redemptive work of Jesus, the Son, before the creation of the worlds. He declared it openly to humankind through his covenant promises especially to Abraham. The heralds of God's salvation should therefore highlight the narrative of God's word and work from the beginning, bring it into present, and proclaim its culmination in the distant future. The contours of this narrative are especially evident in the writings of Walter Scott and Robert Milligan, but may also be discovered in the works of Alexander Campbell. This redemptive narrative in Scott and Milligan was, in effect, their theology of the Bible.

My long seated conviction has been that narratival Biblical Theology is the indispensable foundation for restoration theology. Unfortunately many churches by and large have lost the urgency of that narrative. Somewhere early in the twentieth century our leaders turned from Biblical theology and soteriology to ecclesiology. Some of our foremost authors have abandoned the salvific narrative for systematic reflection upon the church and declared that ecclesiology is the overarching fountainhead for our theology. I believe it is urgent to recover the earlier covenantal narratival Biblical theology. By recover, I don't mean that front running thinkers need to internalize the narratival aspects of the writings of Scott and Milligan. I, however, am convinced that this unfolding of the promises of God is fundamental to a restoration theology that is Biblically based. We are in a much better position than were our nineteenth century fathers to pursue Biblical redemptive history so as to focus upon the great salvation of our God.

In this essay I intend to examine briefly the roots of this covenantal theology among the reformers, and then ascertain the manner in which Campbell, Scott and Milligan flesh out this redemptive history. I will conclude with ways in which, informed by Biblical theology, we highlight such a narrative for believers in our time.

The Roots of the Redemptive Narrative

Scripture itself couched the recovery of the ancient faith in a narratival framework. When Moses gave instructions for offering sacrifices after Israel came into the land he told them that first they needed to recount how God had preceded them into Egypt, and there they became slaves. But God powerfully delivered them from the hand of the Egyptians and gave them a land flowing with milk and honey (Deut 26:5–10). After the temple was rebuilt some years following the destruction by the armies of Nebuchaddnezer, Ezra recounted the narrative of God's mighty acts beginning with creation, running through the exodus, and of Yahweh's irrevocable promises to Abraham, Moses and David. At that point he declared that Israel recovered a land, a temple and a faith (Nehemiah 9). Stephen recounted the same basic narrative to the Jerusalem crowds the day he was martyred. He spoke of God's dealings with his people from the days of Abraham, continuing through Joseph, then the law given through Moses, and David and Solomon's building of the temple. He concluded by pointing out to those present that their ancestors had opposed God throughout their history and that now they had killed the Righteous one, Jesus Christ, who as he spoke was standing on the right hand of God (Acts 7).

Nearer the time of our forefathers, the Swiss reformer Heinrich Bullinger (1504–1575) especially affirmed the covenantal approach to

God's redemptive commitment in unfolding history. Bullinger in turn influenced the Scottish and English reformers. Bullinger held that God's relationship with humankind was through a conditional covenant that permeated the whole of the Scriptures. This one covenant began with Adam. The promise of God to all of humankind was made to Abraham and continued through the prophets and with Jesus Christ and his Apostles. The requisite conditions were the moral law and it was incumbent upon both the officials of the church and the government to enforce these laws. The covenant ceremonies of the Old Testament were typological foreshadowings of the liturgies in the church. According to McCoy and Baker in their book on Bullinger and the covenant,

> When Christ fulfilled the promise of the covenant it had been necessary to change the sacraments of the covenant. The old sacraments—circumcision and the Passover—had been fulfilled by Christ. They were replaced, therefore, by Baptism and the Eucharist. Just as infants before Christ had been initiated into the covenant and the church of God by circumcision, so they were, after Christ, enrolled among the people of God by baptism. Bullinger concluded his treatise on the "Federalism" with a section in which he argued that Christianity had begun with Adam when the covenant had first been made with humans.[1]

For Bullinger the church is that body of persons elected by the God of Scriptures though his covenant promises.

At least one other person needs to be considered when exploring the covenant backgrounds for the thought of the Campbell, Scott and Milligan. Johannes Cocceius (1603–1669)[2] was born into a reformed family in Bremen and probably read Bullinger as a young man. Cocceius studied at Franeker in the Netherlands and ended his long teaching career at Leiden. The writings of the faculty from these Dutch universities were widely read by the English and American Puritans. Cocceius was well trained in Biblical languages, philology and exegesis. His best

---

1. Charles S. McCoy and J. Wayne Baker, *Fountainhead of Federalism: Heinrich Bullinger and the Covenantal Tradition* (Philadelphia: Louisville: Westminster John Knox, 1991) 20.

2. W. J. van Asselt, *The Federal Theology of Johannes Cocceius (1603–1669)*, trans. Raymond A. Blacketer (Leiden: Brill, 2001).

known work on federal or covenantal theology was published in 1648.[3] Campbell's dispensational theology clearly reflects that of Cocceius.[4]

> His [Cocceius'] favorite method of setting forth theology was the *historical*, as the unfolding of the successive stages of the covenant entered into before all worlds by the Father and the Son . . . Of these there are three dispensations—that of the Promise during the time of the patriarchs, that of the Law given from Sinai, and that of the Gospel; although the two former are also classed as one, as preceding the advent of the Redeemer. The fall of man was self caused, and not necessitated by any act of God . . . but all his posterity were involved with Adam in the guilt and curse of his sin. This required a Mediator who could not be of the number needing redemption, and yet must be a partaker of their nature; a problem that was solved by the Son of God being made man. He, standing as the sponsor of the eternal covenant, gave unto the Father the obedience that was due from men, and also endured the penalty of death, the curse for sin, thereby making a true expiation and atonement.[5]

Campbell embraced these threefold covenants or dispensations even though he disagreed with Cocceius' hermeneutical rule that the meaning of words are derived from the whole of Scripture rather than from the specific documents.[6]

Alexander Campbell

We turn now to the restoration fathers and the manner in which they launched their theology by employing the covenant narratives. When he discussed the kingdom of heaven Alexander Campbell essentially held to the three dispensations proposed by Cocceius, the patriarchal, the Mosaic or Jewish, and the Christian, though he at times reduced them to

---

3. Johannes Coccejus, *Summa Doctrinae De Foedere Et Testamento Dei. Explicata A Johanne Coccejo Edito quinta variè Emendata, &, cùm ceatera, tum imprimus novo Indice locorum Scripturea tum citatorem tum explicatorum aucta* (Amsterdam: Joannis à Someren, 1683).

4. It is clear that Campbell read Cocceius, (*Millennial Harbinger* 32 [1831] Extra, 25) but I have not located a quote from Cocceius' *Summa Doctrinae De Foedere*.

5. John McClintock, and James Strong, *Cyclopedia of Biblical, Theological, and Ecclesiastical Literature* (New York: Harper, 1885, 1887) 2:41.

6. Alexander Campbell, *The Christian System* (reprint ed.; Nashville: Gospel Advocate, 1956) 113–31.

two, the Jewish and the Christian.[7] Each of these two involved a divine covenant. The Jewish dispensation was established upon the first promise made to Abraham. The Jews had the kingdom of God, but they did not have the "Kingdom of *Heaven*" as proclaimed by Matthew [21:43]. God envisioned the kingdom of heaven from eternity. "We must trace the constitution of this kingdom into eternity—before time began."[8] God authored the constitution of the kingdom.

> The Lord Jesus Christ is the constitutional monarch of the Kingdom of Heaven . . .[9] Neither are the statutes and laws of the Christian kingdom to be sought for in the Jewish scriptures, nor antecedent to the day of Pentecost; except so far as our Lord himself, during his life time, propounded the doctrine of his reign.[10]

The kingdom of Heaven is to reach throughout the earth, "but the new heavens and earth are to be its *inheritance*.[11] The kingdom of Heaven or the church began on the day of Pentecost in Jerusalem.[12] The kingdom of Heaven for Campbell therefore differed from the kingdom of God the latter being the eternal reign of God.

As Campbell set out his systematic theology in the first hundred pages of the *Christian System* he developed the narrative of God's salvific work, especially beginning with a chapter on "The Purpose of God Concerning Man." He first depicted how humans were created by God and provided whatever was needed for their happiness. But Adam and Eve brought death and the propensity to sin. God, however, promised Eve, Adam, Abraham, Isaac, Jacob, and David that he would redeem humankind through his son.[13] All these promises came to fruition in Jesus Christ.

> Two things are evident as demonstration itself:—The first,—that all the *purposes* and *promises* of God are in Christ—in reference to him, and consummated in and by him; and, in the second place, they were all contemplated, covenanted, and systematized in him and through him *before the foundation of the world*. These two propositions are so intimately connected, that they are gen-

7. Ibid., 143.
8. Ibid., 158.
9. Ibid., 159.
10. Ibid., 163.
11. Ibid., 164.
12. Ibid., 182–84.
13. Ibid., 30.

erally asserted in the same portions of Scripture. For example: "He hath saved us and called us with a holy calling, not according to our works, but according to his own purpose and grace which was given us *in* Christ Jesus before the world began; but is *now* made manifest by the appearing of our Saviour Jesus Christ." (2 Tim 1:9, 10)[14]

Through him human redemption is secured for those who are obedient. Campbell depicted the narrative beginning with Christ in this summary statement.

> III. Therefore, in "the fulness of time"—"in *due* time, God sent forth his Son, made of a woman"—for "the WORD became flesh, and dwelt among us; and we beheld his glory, the glory as of an only begotten of the Father, full of grace and truth." "He showed us the Father." He died as a sin-offering—was buried, rose again the third day—ascended to heaven—presented his offering in the true Holy Place—made expiation for our sins—"forever sat down on the right hand of the Supreme Majesty in the heavens"—sent down his Holy Spirit—inspired his Apostles, who "preached with the Holy Spirit sent down from heaven"—persuaded many Jews and Gentiles that he was made "the author of an eternal salvation to all who obeyed him." He commanded faith, repentance, and baptism to be preached in his name for remission of sins to every nation and people under heaven.[15]

Alexander Campbell presented more than a skeletal outline of the five steps of salvation or of the characteristics of the New Testament church. He set these in the overarching framework of the covenantal narrative.

Walter Scott

In the concluding section of *The Gospel Restored* (1836), Walter Scott developed a chapter for each of his six steps of "The Ancient Gospel": faith, repentance, baptism, remission of sins, the Holy Spirit, and the resurrection.[16] The chapter on faith, however, doesn't commence until page 225. The pages prior to that consisted of a detailed description of

14. Ibid., 33–34.

15. Ibid., 73.

16. Walter Scott, *The Gospel Restored, A Discourse of The True Gospel of Jesus Christ in which the Facts, Principles, Duties, and Privileges of Christianity are Arranged, Defined, and Discussed, and the Gospel in Its Various Parts Shewn to Be Adapted to the Nature and Necessiteis of Man in His Present Condition* (Cincinnati: Donogh, 1836; reprinted, Kansas City: Old Paths Book Club, 1949). This is a facsimile reproduction.

the fall and redemption of humankind. In the earlier pages as a succinct introduction to the Biblical story line Scott depicted the redemptive account as a divine drama.

> The fall of man, and his recovery by Jesus Christ our Lord form a great drama, of which God is the author. The chief personage is the Messiah, and his mighty and subtle antagonist is an archangel in arms. The parties are demons and angels, the theatre is the universe, the stage the world, and its government the subject in debate. The plot lies in bringing good out of evil, happiness out of misery, almighty power from feminine weakness, light out of darkness, glory from the grave. The catastrophe consists of the seizure and perdition of the traitor angel with all his powers, and of the final triumph of the son of man with all his saints.[17]

In the concretion that followed Scott set out the details into which the redemptive narrative is ensconced. The narrative commences with Adam and Eve in the garden and depicted first their happiness, but then their sin and condemnation. Their punishment and Satan's, and their being barred from the garden came in for considerable attention. Scott discussed many details of this narrative and essentially moved from the problems created by the human eviction from the garden to the appearance of the solution, that is, the advent of the Lord Jesus Christ and the many ways in which he was announced.[18] He covered little of the Old Testament between Exodus and Malachi. In his last book *Messiahship or Great Demonstration* (1859), Scott gave greater attention to the details between Adam and Christ. He was especially interested in the manner in which other persons and events served as types for Christ. He discussed the flood, the Assyrian Empire, Melchizedek, the Persian Empire, Moses, the Greek Empire, Aaron, the Roman Empire, and God's kingdom.[19]

Scott believed the key to understanding the meaning of history came about through discerning God's activity within history. Based upon his understanding that God worked within history to achieve divine purposes, Scott divided history into sacred ages which for the biblical period, are as follows:

17. Ibid., 9.

18. Ibid., 129.

19. Walter Scott, *The Messiahship or Great Demonstration, Written for the Union of Christians, on Christian Principles, as Plead for in the Current Reformation* (Cincinnati: Bosworth, 1859) 34–119.

> The Adamic or Antediluvian Age
>
> The Noahitic or Patriarchal Age
>
> The Mosaic Age, or Age of Organized Religion
>
> John's or the Baptistic Age
>
> The Christian Age[20]

Scott's breakdown was essentially that of Cocceius' dispensations thereby embracing earlier convenantal theology, but with additional specifics. The Adamic and Noahitic age are a fine tuning of Cocceius' patriarchal age, and Cocceius included John the Baptist in the Mosaic age.

Like most Protestants of his time, Scott divided post-biblical Christianity into eras. He wrote: "The history of christianity, from Christ to the Millennium, may be divided into three parts, *Primitive Christianity*, the *Apostasy* and the *Reformation*."[21] He located the beginnings of the Reformation in the fourteenth century with Wycliffe and Hus. From the magisterial reformation Scott mentioned Luther, Calvin, Knox, and Wesley. It was not until Scott's own time, so he believed, that the Reformation had moved in the direction of complete restoration. He was therefore not reticent in asserting that God, since the biblical period, has continued to work in stages of history in order finalize his purposes. All of history was leading into the great contemporary movement, led by the Campbells and by Scott. And Scott believed the successes heralded by the beginning of this "restoration" warranted the conclusion that the millennium would soon break into history.[22]

Robert Milligan

Milligan, much like Walter Scott, subsumed ecclesiology (the church) under soteriology, that is, *The Scheme of Redemption*.[23] The Scheme of redemption was in the mind of God from the beginning and culminated in the salvific action of Jesus Christ. The first book of comprising about a sixth of the whole contained remarks on God, creation, man's primi-

20. Ibid., 142. On the background of Scott's theology see my essay, Thomas H. Olbricht, "Walter Scott as Biblical Interpreter," in *Walter Scott: A Nineteenth-Century Evangelical*, ed. Mark G. Toulouse (St. Louis: Chalice, 1999) 79–107.

21. Scott, *The Evangelist* (2 January 1832) 19.

22. Ibid., (1 April 1833) 88–93.

23. Robert Milligan, *An Exposition and Defense of the The Scheme of Redemption as It Is Revealed and Taught in the Holy Scriptures* (St. Louis: Christian Board of Publication, 1885), reprint 11th edition (St. Louis: Christian Board of Publication, 1894).

tive state and man's fall. The second book or about a third covered from Adam through Christ. The third book, about a half of the total, centered on the church in its various aspects. Milligan's focus was upon how God struggled with humans so as to bring them into a relationship with himself that ultimately culminated in the advent of Jesus Christ. At the heart of his comments was soteriology, that is as he depicted it—redemption. His remarks upon the words and works of Christ were minimal. Milligan wrote that the primary object of the Bible is to "develop one great and glorious System of Divine wisdom, justice, goodness, mercy, and love through Jesus Christ, for the redemption of fallen man."[24] In terms of dispensations or covenants Milligan set forth the typical three, that is the patriarchal, the Mosaic and the Christian.

Milligan clearly took up the promise highlighted by Paul, that is the Abrahamic covenant. He did not mention the charge to Adam and Eve in the garden, so important to the Calvinist covenant (Gen 2:15) covenant of works, nor the promise to Noah and all existing creatures that he would never again destroy the earth by water. Milligan argued that there were two sides to the Abrahamic covenant, the spiritual side and the carnal side. It was the spiritual side that he perceived as being fulfilled in Christ.[25] Though Milligan mentioned that through Abraham and his seed the nations of the earth would be blessed he did not elaborate upon this promise. He commented at length on the Mosaic law, but did not focus on the promise or covenant aspect. He argued that the ten commandments are suitable laws for all times and thus remain in force by being repeated in various ways in the New Testament. Milligan mentioned neither the promise to David that one of his seed would reign continuously, nor the implications that might have for the significance of Jesus Christ. So though we may wish to quarrel with the focus of Milligan's narrative, nevertheless it is important that he sets the work of Christ and the church in such a narrative. The end of the scheme of redemption for Milligan was the gathering up of the church into the everlasting kingdom of God.

The Recovery of Covenantal Narratival Biblical Theology

We may question the specific fleshing out of earlier covenantal Swiss and Restorationist theologies, nevertheless this trajectory laid the right foundation. The narratival account of God's covenants with the forefathers,

24. Ibid., xii.

25. Ibid., 79.

Israel and the church provided the groundwork upon which the whole theology of the Scriptures is fleshed out. N. T. Wright has recently given recognition to the redemptive narrative that lies behind the biblical faith in his book *Simply Christian*.[26] He earlier noted this account in his commentary on Romans in which he insisted that in order to understand Paul's perspectives on justification and righteousness it is important to keep in mind Paul's narrative of God's salvific actions in human history. "But in this letter at least . . . these vital and highly important topics are held within a larger discussion. Paul's aim, it seems, is to explain to the Roman church what God has been up to and where they might belong on the map of these purposes."[27]

Certain recent restorationist theologians have given renewed attention to the covenantal narrative nevertheless much dedicated effort is needed. In my judgment it is most critical that our scholars indefatigably work back and forth from Biblical narrative to contemporary thinking in order to present a viable restorationist theology for our churches. In the last section of this essay I will set forth the unfolding story-line as I have perceived it in the Scriptures. I have elaborated upon the narrative in much more detail in two books, the first on the Old Testament, *He Loves Forever*,[28] and the second on the New Testament, *His Love Compels*.[29]

The Biblical Narrative in Schematic Presentation

1. God created the heavens and the earth and all its creatures, including humans. God ascertained that everything he created was good inasmuch as it was in harmony and mutually beneficial (Gen 1:29–30). Humans were created in God's image and charged with being managers and caretakers (Gen 1:28; 2:15).

2. Humans soon defiled the goodness of creation through willfully disobeying God. They presumed his prerogatives in deciding for themselves what was right and wrong (Gen 3:22). As the result evil pervaded human life. Cain murdered Abel. God concluded "that every inclination of the thoughts of their hearts was only evil continu-

---

26. N. T. Wright, *Simply Christian: Why Christianity Makes Sense* (San Francisco: HarperSanFrancisco, 2006).

27. N. T. Wright, "Commentary on Romans," in *The New Interpreters' Bible*, ed. Leander Keck (Nashville: Abingdon, 2002) 404–5.

28. Thomas H. Olbricht, *He Loves Forever* (Joplin, MO: College Press 2000).

29. Thomas H. Olbricht, *His Love Compels* (Joplin, MO: College Press, 2000).

ally" (Gen 6:5) and he determined to destroy humankind through a great flood.

3. God, however, relented and covenanted to save animate creation. He promised that never again would he destroy the earth through flood. This proclamation, God's first covenant, encompassed all creatures. "Then God said to Noah and to his sons with him, 'As for me, I am establishing my covenant with you and your descendants after you, and with every living creature that is with you, the birds, the domestic animals, and every animal of the earth with you, as many as came out of the ark'" (Gen 9:8–10). The Noachic covenant was an everlasting covenant (Gen 9:16). Succeeding covenants did not cancel nor render the Noachic null and void. A problem in traditional covenant theology was that covenants were connected with dispensations in such a way that succeeding covenants were viewed as canceling prior covenants. Later covenants according to the Biblical vision incorporated and built upon former covenants.[30]

4. God pledged anew to bless the earth despite human sin by advancing a second promise or covenant, that is, the one with Abraham and through him to all humankind. The world does not fully manifest its God intended goodness because of human perversity, but despite that, because of Abraham and his seed, some semblance of justice and integrity persists. God promised to bless the nations through Abraham and his descendents. "I will bless those who bless you, and the one who curses you I will curse; and in you all the families of the earth shall be blessed" (Gen 12:1–3). Those who are the seed of Abraham are to be a servants to the world, a light to the nations (Isa 49:6)

5. God promised Abraham that his seed will form a great nation (Gen 18:18; 46:3). "I will bring you into the land that I swore to give to Abraham, Isaac, and Jacob; I will give it to you for a possession. I am the Lord'" (Exod 6:8). This nation Israel will be a servant to the nations. In order that Israel be a righteous people God entered into a new covenant with them through Moses. The Mosaic covenant did not cancel or replace the Noachic or the Abrahamic covenants. It built upon them. Through Moses God conferred a covenant with stipulations to carry out (Exodus 20; Deuteronomy 5). The Mosaic covenant

30. These promises and covenants are often mentioned in creedal-like statements in the Old Testament in Joshua 24; Nehemiah 9; Psalms 78; 105; 106; 136.

could not be revoked as the result of human sinfulness because it was God given. Only God can withdraw the covenant. But God will remove humans from the covenant blessings who violate its statutes and laws. "They have turned back to the iniquities of their ancestors of old, who refused to heed my words; they have gone after other gods to serve them; the house of Israel and the house of Judah have broken the covenant that I made with their ancestors" (Jer 11:10). God gave Israel the covenant presented through Moses so that Israel would benefit from the goodness of God's creation. By keeping the statutes of the covenant the Israelites would live long in the land and it would go well, "...and so that you may multiply greatly in a land flowing with milk and honey" (Deut 6:1–3).

6. God selected Israel in order to bless them and through them to bless the nations. God desired that the other nations know his teachings and enjoy his beneficence.

> In days to come
>   the mountain of the Lord's house
> shall be established as the highest of the mountains,
>   and shall be raised above the hills;
> all the nations shall stream to it.
>   Many peoples shall come and say,
> "Come, let us go up to the mountain of the Lord,
>   to the house of the God of Jacob;
> that he may teach us his ways
>   and that we may walk in his paths."
> For out of Zion shall go forth instruction,
>   and the word of the Lord from Jerusalem (Isa 2:2–3).

7. God also covenanted with Israel to guarantee a forever line of kings from the lineage of David. This new covenant with David by no means nullified the covenants with Noah, Abraham or Moses. In fact, the Davidic covenant remembered the promise to Abraham and incorporated the Mosaic covenant. The commandments by which the Davidic kings were to be judged are those found in the Mosaic covenant.

> Thus says the Lord: If any of you could break my covenant with the day and my covenant with the night, so that day and night would not come at their appointed time, only then could my covenant with my servant David be broken, so that he would not have a son to reign on his throne . . . Thus says the Lord: Only if I had not established my covenant with day and night and the

ordinances of heaven and earth, would I reject the offspring of Jacob and of my servant David and not choose any of his descendants as rulers over the offspring of Abraham, Isaac, and Jacob. For I will restore their fortunes, and will have mercy upon them (Jer 33:20–26).

I will establish his line forever,
  and his throne as long as the heavens endure.
If his children forsake my law
  and do not walk according to my ordinances,
if they violate my statutes
  and do not keep my commandments,
then I will punish their transgression with the rod
  and their iniquity with scourges;
but I will not remove from him my steadfast love,
  or be false to my faithfulness.
I will not violate my covenant,
  or alter the word that went forth from my lips (Ps 89:29–34).

8. God promised that in the later days a new descendant of David would reign in justice and righteousness.

For a child has been born for us,
  a son given to us;
authority rests upon his shoulders;
  and he is named
Wonderful Counselor, Mighty God,
  His authority shall grow continually,
and there shall be endless peace
  for the throne of David and his kingdom.
He will establish and uphold it
  with justice and with righteousness
from this time onward and forevermore.
  The zeal of the Lord of hosts will do this (Isa 9:6–7).

9. At that time God also will bequeath a new covenant. This new covenant will transcend the old nevertheless it will retain certain of the laws of the Mosaic covenant. The problem with the Mosaic covenant was that the people did not incorporate it into their hearts, nor did it provide permanent forgiveness of sin.

The days are surely coming, says the Lord, when I will make a new covenant with the house of Israel and the house of Judah. It will not be like the covenant that I made with their ancestors when I took them by the hand to bring them out of the land of

Egypt—a covenant that they broke, though I was their husband, says the Lord. But this is the covenant that I will make with the house of Israel after those days, says the Lord: I will put my law within them, and I will write it on their hearts; and I will be their God, and they shall be my people. No longer shall they teach one another, or say to each other, "Know the Lord," for they shall all know me, from the least of them to the greatest, says the Lord; for I will forgive their iniquity, and remember their sin no more (Jer 31:31–34).

10. The writers of the New Testament believed that Jesus of Nazareth, born of woman and conceived by the Holy Spirit (Matthew 1:18), was the one who in a new and unique way blessed people of all nations and formed a new Israel made up of both Jews and Gentiles. By the sending of his only begotten Son God was faithful in his promises, that is, his covenants with Abraham, Moses and David. Jesus was declared to be both the son David and the Son of Abraham (Matt 1:1). In him the promises of God to bless the nations were fulfilled in momentous ways. He was both the anointed Davidic king (the Messiah) and savior. "He has raised up a mighty savior for us in the house of his servant David" (Luke 1:69). He is to save people from their sins (Matt 1:21) once for all (Heb 9:26) as contrasted with the repetitive sacrifice of animals.[31]

11. Jesus was anointed by the Holy Spirit after his baptism so that he could carry out his ministry of teaching and healing (Matt 3:16; 23). He was anointed (*meshiach* Hebrew; *christos* Greek) king by the Holy Spirit. This anointment was set forth in respect to a future scion of David.

> The spirit of the Lord God is upon me,
>   because the Lord has anointed me;
> to bind up the brokenhearted,
>   to proclaim liberty to the captives,
> and release to the prisoners (Isa 61:1)

---

31. The reiteration of God's covenant promises are found in sermons to Jewish audiences in the New Testament especially in Stephen's speech at his martyrdom (Acts 7) and Paul's address in the synagogue at Antioch of Pisidia (Acts 13:16–47). The work of God in Christ is also found in creedal-like formats in the sermons in Acts, for example, Peter and the house of Cornelius (Acts 10:34–43) and in more explicit statements in Paul for example (1 Cor 15:1–9).

12. Central to the claim about the mission of Jesus as Messiah, Son of God, was that he was "handed over to death for our trespasses and was raised for our justification" (Rom 4:25). It was by his death that Jesus fulfilled God's promise to Abraham that all nations will be blessed through his seed. John argued that it was time for Jesus' death on the cross when the Greeks sought him (John 12:20–26). At the end of Matthew Jesus sent the twelve to "make disciples of all nations, baptizing them in the name of the Father and of the Son and of the Holy Spirit" (Matthew 28:19). Paul especially utilized the promise to Abraham to argue for God's drawing both the Jews and the gentiles to himself through Jesus Christ. Paul also made it clear that the Mosaic covenant did not cancel the Abrahamic one.

> Now the promises were made to Abraham and to his offspring; it does not say, "And to offsprings," as of many; but it says, "And to your offspring," that is, to one person, who is Christ. My point is this: the law, which came four hundred thirty years later, does not annul a covenant previously ratified by God, so as to nullify the promise. For if the inheritance comes from the law, it no longer comes from the promise; but God granted it to Abraham through the promise (Gal 3:16–18).

13. Paul proclaimed that all of humankind who accepted Jesus as Lord and Savior comprised the people of God. "There is no longer Jew or Greek, there is no longer slave or free, there is no longer male and female; for all of you are one in Christ Jesus" (Gal 3:28). Earlier prophets had envisioned such a new day and Paul declared that it had come to fruition in Jesus Christ.

> On that day there will be a highway from Egypt to Assyria, and the Assyrian will come into Egypt, and the Egyptian into Assyria, and the Egyptians will worship with the Assyrians. On that day Israel will be the third with Egypt and Assyria, a blessing in the midst of the earth. (Isa 19:23–24)

All those in the church of Jesus Christ will be united in him. God in Christ is creating a new humanity.

> He has abolished the law with its commandments and ordinances, that he might create in himself one new humanity in place of the two, thus making peace, and might reconcile both groups to God in one body through the cross, thus putting to death that hostility through it. (Eph 2:15–16)

14. God will bring human history to a close through the coming again of his Son Jesus Christ (1 Thess 4:15—5:11). The heavens and earth as now constituted will be destroyed by a consuming fire (2 Pet 3:11–13). Those who are in Christ Jesus will dwell with God in the new Jerusalem.

> And I saw the holy city, the new Jerusalem, coming down out of heaven from God, prepared as a bride adorned for her husband. And I heard a loud voice from the throne saying,
> "See, the home of God is among mortals.
> He will dwell with them;
> they will be his peoples,
> and God himself will be with them." (Rev 21:2–3)

Conclusion

At this juncture in our history we are in a much better position to present and flesh out the salvific narrative through the two Testaments as the result of the many additional insights that scholars of Old and New Testament theology have brought to bear since the nineteenth century. I am especially impressed with the writings of N. T. Wright.[32] Additional works on the Old Testament include Wright,[33] Kaiser,[34] Goldingay,[35] and on the New Testament Dodd,[36] Ladd,[37] Goppelt,[38] and Marshall.[39]

---

32. N. T. Wright, *The New Testament and the People of God* (Minneapolis: Fortress, 1991); and *Jesus and the Victory of God* (Minneapolis: Fortress, 1996).

33. G. Ernest Wright, *God Who Acts: Biblical Theology as Recital*, Studies in Biblical Theology 1/8 (Naperville: Allenson, 1952); and *The Old Testament and Theology* (San Francisco: Harper, 1969).

34. Walter C. Kaiser, *Toward an Old Testament Theology* (Grand Rapids: Zondervan, 1978).

35. John Goldingay, *Old Testament Theology* (Downers Grove, IL: InterVarsity, 2003) vol. 1.

36. C. H. Dodd, *Apostolic Preaching* (London: Hodder, 1936, 1963).

37. George Eldon Ladd, *A Theology of the New Testament* (Grand Rapids: Eerdmans, 1974, 1993).

38. Leonhard Goppelt, *Theology of the New Testament* (Eerdmans, 1981, 1982) 2 vols.

39. I. Howard Marshall, *New Testament Theology: Many Witnesses, One Gospel* (Downers Grove, IL: InterVarsity, 2004).

Now on the cusp of the twenty-first century we are in a very favorable position for constructing a salvific narrative that dialogs with contemporary commitments and thought patterns. The outcome of such dialogue will hopefully be a viable and vibrant restorationist theology.

6

Clement Nance (1757–1828)

Stoneite Pioneer in Southern Indiana

HANS ROLLMANN

While Clement Nance has been acknowledged as being the earliest preacher of the Stone-Campbell movement in Indiana, no historical study has ever been published focusing on his life and contribution to the Restoration Movement.[1] The reason for this neglect may be the paucity of sources and the fact that the most pertinent biographical information about him was published in the New York and New England journals of the Christian movement engendered by Elias Smith and Abner Jones. This paper attempts to sketch Nance's religious development and theological profile as well as his ecclesiastical activities during the first three decades of the nineteenth century. One of the issues emerging among the western churches during Nance's ministry was the need for more effective communication. Such communication included the establishment of a journal for news and theological discussion among the Stoneite churches in Kentucky, Tennessee, Ohio, Indiana, Illinois, Missouri, and

---

1. Henry K. Shaw, *Hoosier Disciples: A Comprehensive History of the Christian Churches (Disciples of Christ) in Indiana* (St. Louis: Bethany, 1966) 32; L. C. Rudolph, *Hoosier Faiths: A History of Indian Churches and Religious Groups* (Bloomington: Indiana University Press, 1995) 64. To my knowledge, no study has ever been published that focused specifically on this Indiana Restoration Movement pioneer. There was a respectable unpublished student paper on Nance prepared for J. W. Roberts at Abilene Christian College, which, however, remains largely biographical. See Richard M. Adey, "A Historical Study of the Life of the Elder Clement Nance" (Abilene Christian University, Center for Restoration Studies, 1968).

Alabama. Michael Casey has singled out the print medium as an important factor shaping the culture of the Stone-Campbell Movement. This study is dedicated to Michael Casey, whose scholarship will remain a benchmark for all students interested in the Restoration Movement. His personal support and encouragement has greatly stimulated and kept alive my own academic interest in this exciting area of nineteenth- and twentieth-century Believers' Church history.[2]

From Virginia to Kentucky

Clement Nance was born in 1757 in the southern part of Virginia near the Dan River. Shortly after his marriage to Mary Jones in 1775, the 19-year-old became "convinced" of his "lost state by sin." Upon joining the local Methodist Society in 1776 and "after considerable exercise," he "found the Lord precious to [his] soul." In 1783 he "began to call sinners to repentance, being convinced that it was the will of God."[3] As a local Methodist preacher in Pittsylvania County, Virginia, he never appeared in the Minutes of the larger conferences of Methodism, but his ministerial status is attested to in several marriage bonds during the 1790s.[4]

P. J. Kernodle in his *Lives of Christian Ministers* (1909) and W. E. MacClenny in his *Life of Reverend James O'Kelly* have suggested and in so doing misled subsequent historians in assuming that Clement Nance left the Methodist Church shortly after O'Kelly's departure in 1792/3.[5] But Nance's own recollections date his joining the O'Kelly Christians considerably later, in 1800. He traces his break with Methodism in an autobiographical letter to Elias Smith in 1812 as a process of several years when he writes:

2. One of the latest contributions of Mike Casey to Restoration Studies was devoted to the importance of the printed media. See Michael Casey, "Mastered by the Word: Print Culture, Modernization, and the Priesthood of all Readers in the Churches of Christ," in *Restoring the First-century Church in the Twenty-first Century: Essays on the Stone-Campbell Movement (in Honor of Don Haymes)*, edited by Warren Lewis and Hans Rollmann (Eugene, Oregon: Wipf & Stock, 2005) 311–22.

3. "Religious Intelligence (Letter of Clement Nance of 18 August 1812 to the Editor of the Christian Herald)," *Herald of Gospel Liberty* 5.2 (18 Sept 1812) 423.

4. Some Select Marrriage Bonds Pittsylvania County, Virginia: http://www.rootsweb .ancestry.com/~vapittsy/marriage.htm.

5. P. J. Kernodle, *Lives of Christian Ministers* (Richmond, Virginia: The Central Publishing Company, 1909) 55; W. E. MacClenny, *Life of Reverend James O'Kelly* (1910; facsimile reprint: Ann Arbor, Michigan: Cushing-Malloy, 1950) 131.

After several years had elapsed, I began to see, from reading the Scriptures, that the Episcopacy I lived under was both unscriptural and oppressive; —other Local Preachers and myself for several years strove with my travelling brethren, for some alteration, and in particular that Local Preachers should have the privileges the Lord Jesus had assigned them; the matter was debated by General Conference both in 1796, and 1800; and put to vote and both of it went against us. Feeling the importance of the work of God to which he had called us, and being satisfied that it was needless to make any further applications, we (several Local Preachers and some members) declared ourselves no longer under the power of the Conference, and joined with Brother O'Kelley [sic] and the church in connection with him, who had previously renounced all human creeds, confessions, and party names, and after the example of the primitive Christians, had taken the Holy Scriptures for their only rule for faith and practice, and the Christian name as the only name of distinction - I was then living in Pittsylvania County, Virginia, August 1800.[6]

Several preachers, Rice Haggard included, withdrew with O'Kelly from the Methodist Episcopal Church once they had lost at the 1792 General Conference in Baltimore their struggle for greater rights of preachers, notably the right to appeal appointments to the General Conference.[7] There was also a biblically motivated opposition to the emerging hierarchical administration as well as a strong suspicion of committed "republicans" against the "aristocratic" structures enacted by Thomas Coke and Bishop Francis Asbury, the latter having been as well a British sympathizer during the American Revolution. There continued a nearly decade-long seepage of ministers dissatisfied with Asbury's and Coke's

---

6. *Herald of Gospel Liberty* 5.2 (18 Sept 1812) 423.

7. The best primary sources for the so-called "O'Kelly schism," reflecting the views of the dissidents, are James O'Kelly, *The Author's Apology for Protesting Against the Methodist Episcopal Government* (Richmond Virginia: John Dixon, 1798); James O'Kelly, *A Vindication of the Author's Apology: With Reflections on the Reply, and a Few Remarks on Bishop Asbury's Annotations on His Book of Discipline* (Raleigh, NC: Gales, 1801); William Guirey, *The History of Episcopacy in Four Parts, from its Rise to the Present Day* (n.p.: n.p. [1801]). Secondary literature since MacClenny's biography of James O'Kelly, specifically devoted to O'Kelly, includes Charles Franklin Kilgore, *The James O'Kelly Schism in the Methodist Episcopal Church* (Mexico City: Casa Unida de Publicaciones, 1963) and the more recent unpublished dissertation by J. Timothy Allen, "A Man of some Means: Ambitious Values, Evangelical Theology, and the Reverend James O'Kelly" (Greensboro: University of North Carolina at Greensboro, 2004).

leadership. Some of these ministers and lay people joined the Christian Movement under O'Kelly's leadership.[8]

Jesse Lee, a contemporary of Nance and O'Kelly who remained in the Methodist Episcopal Church, writes about the continuing tensions that Coke's and Asbury's leadership created well beyond O'Kelly's departure in 1792. One major point of dissatisfaction surfacing in the 1796 and 1800 General Conferences singled out by Nance centred on the status and clout of local preachers and lay members within the church. Lee writes: "Some of them contended that the local preachers ought to have a seat and a vote in all our conferences; and others said, there ought to be a delegation of lay members."[9]

By 1800, when Nance joined the Christians around O'Kelly, the Republican Methodists had abandoned their original self-designation and, under the influence of Rice Haggard, adopted the name "Christians." They retained an annual conference structure by which their churches maintained ministerial contact and ecclesiastical cohesion. If the institutional development of Methodism and the question of local and lay representation in the church were the initial reasons for the departure of Nance and his fellow ministers, we observe in Nance's recollections two points that defined early on his religious and institutional identity, restoration and union. These two foci became also two identity markers of the future Stone-Campbell Movement.

Nance notes that the O'Kelly "Christians" whom he joined had "renounced all human creeds, confessions, and party names" and adopted "after the example of the primitive Christians" Scripture as "their only rule of faith and practice" as well as "the Christian name as the only name of distinction."[10] Nance's early restitutionist agenda sought to reject also all human traditions and creeds and promote instead "Christian love and Christian union." He expressed his thoughts on Christian unity first in a hymn that was printed in early Stoneite and Jones/Smith hymnals and later became a common possession of Stone-Campbell hymnody: "Come my Christian friends and brethren, Bound for Canaan's happy land."

8. Some biographical profiles of these ministers are detailed in chapter 10 of W. E. MacClenny, *Life of Reverend James O'Kelly*, 125–38.

9. Jesse Lee, *A Short History of the Methodists in the United States of America . . .* (Baltimore: Magill & Clime, 1810) 213. On the general unrest in 1796, see Dee E. Andrews, *The Methodists and Revolutionary America, 1760–1800* (Princeton, New Jersey: Princeton University Press, 2000) 203–4.

10. *Herald of Gospel Liberty* 5.2 (18 Sept 1812) 423.

The hymn is a plea for a unified Christianity and articulates in verse a creedless, word-oriented and spirit-driven loving fellowship of believers in Christ.[11] Similar to Thomas Campbell's irenic and peaceful Zion imagined in the 1809 *Declaration and Address*, Nance's postmillennial optimism anticipated a *kairos* and reign in which God's righteous kingdom would be realized.[12] Evangelization was a crucial human co-labor with God in ushering in this Zion so that, in the words of the hymn, "Thousands, millions be converted, / Round the earth his praises ring; / Blessed day! O joyful hour!"

Sometime during 1803 Nance left Southern Virginia for Kentucky. According to Barton W. Stone he appeared in the company of James Read and Rice Haggard at Cane Ridge in October 1804, only a few months after the *Last Will and Testament of the Springfield Presbytery* had been signed by the dissident Presbyterians,[13] and joined Stone's New Light Christians.[14] Rice Haggard's views persuaded Stone and his associates to adopt the Christian name as a sufficient and biblically approved self-designation, just as Haggard had earlier likely influenced O'Kelly's Republican Methodists to abandon their name in favour of being simply called "Christians."[15]

11. See, e.g., Stith Mead, *A General Selection of the Newest and Most Admired Hymns and Spiritual Songs Now in Use* (Richmond, 1807); *Christian Hymn-Book*, compiled by B. W. Stone and Thomas Adams (Georgetown, KY: Miami Christian Conference, 1829).

12. On Thomas Campbell's eschatological action plan of ushering in Zion, see Hans Rollmann, "The Eschatology of the Declaration and Address," in *The Quest for Christian Unity, Peace, and Purity in Thomas Campbell's Declaration and Address: Texts and Studies*, edited by Thomas H. Olbricht and Hans Rollmann, American Theological Library Association Monograph Series 46 (Lanham, MD: Scarecrow, 2000) 341–63.

13. This signal document was signed in June 1804. On the chronology of the Presbyterian secession, see R. Marshall & J. Thompson, *A Brief Historical Account of Sundry Things in the Doctrines and State of the Christian, or as it is Commonly Called, The Newlight Church* (Cincinnati: Carpenter, 1811) reprinted in Levi Purviance, ed., *The Biography of Elder David Purviance . . .* (1848; 3rd ed., Kimberlin Heights, TN: Johnson Bible College, 1940) 272.

14. Barton W. Stone, "History of the Christian Church in the West, No. VIII," *The Christian Messenger* 1.11 (25 September 1827) 243.

15. On Rice Haggard, see his pamphlet *An Address to the Different Religious Societies, on the Sacred Import of the Christian Name* (Lexington: Joseph Charless, 1804), facsimile reprint with introduction by John W. Neth, in the series "Footnotes to Disciple History," No. 4 (Nashville: The Disciples of Christ Historical Society, 1954); R. L. Roberts, "Rice Haggard (1769–1819) 'A Name Rever'd,'" *Discipliana* 54.3 (1994) 67–81; Colby D. Hall, *Rice Haggard: The American Frontier Evangelist who Revived the Name Christian* (Forth Worth: Stafford-Lowdon, 1957). On the development of the Stone Movement, see J. W. and R. L. Roberts, Jr, "Like Fire in Dry Stubble—The Stone Movement 1804–1832," *Restoration Quarterly* 7.3 (1963) 148–58 (Part 1); and 8.1 (1965) 26–40 (Part 2).

Stone wrote in his autobiography: "With the man-made creeds we threw it overboard, and took the name *Christian*--the name given to the disciples by divine appointment first at Antioch. We published a pamphlet on this name, written by Elder Rice Haggard, who had lately united with us."[16]

Nance was no stranger to Stone since the two men had known each other already in Virginia. Stone wrote in his obituary of Nance in 1828 that he was "intimately acquainted with him at least 40 years, being his neighbor in Virginia."[17] Nance, after joining Stone's fellowship of Christians, did not stay long in Kentucky but moved in 1805 to Indiana Territory.

Pioneer Preacher in Indiana

The Nance family travelled via a flatboat down the Ohio and arrived on 5 March 1805 near today's New Albany Holiday Inn. Here, at the Falls of the Ohio, adjacent to Louisville, Kentucky, Clement built a cabin, while waiting for his livestock to arrive overland. The family's stay was only temporary, however, since they soon moved into the nearby Knobs. A challenger, Joseph Oatman, jumped the claim and registered in Vincennes the land the Nances were squatting on. Oatman's action was allegedly in revenge over Nance's refusal to give him his daughter in marriage.[18]

In Franklin township, Nance established a prosperous 500-acre farm with a horse-run grist mill. But even before relocating, Nance had preached in the area where he first settled, thus being the earliest Stoneite preacher on Indiana Territory. It is likely that church services were conducted in an eight-cornered log school house, which the New Light, Baptist and Methodist ministers shared.[19] In his autobiographical sketch of 1812, Nance speaks about the initially sparsely populated area but also about his eventual preaching success, in which he was soon supported by an unnamed "Christian brother." The two men assembled the converted "into a Christian Church upon the true foundation Stone, the

---

16. *The Biography of Eld. Barton Warren Stone, Written by Himself: with Additions and Reflections by Elder John Rogers* (Cincinnati: J. A. & U. P. James, 1847; facsimile reprint, 1972) 50.

17. Barton W. Stone, "Obituary," *The Christian Messenger* 2.10 (August 1828) 239.

18. Geo W. Nance, *The Nance Memorial* (Bloomington, IL: Burke, 1904) 11–12; see also Marti Bergstrom, "Nance Home Could be Oldest in Floyd County," *The Tribune Scope*, Wednesday, 3 October 1980.

19. *History of the Ohio Falls Cities and their Counties* (Cleveland, OH: Williams, 1882) 250–52.

Lord Jesus Christ; his Word the only rule for faith, practice, doctrine, and discipline."[20] In all likelihood, the unidentified brother, who had been raised as a Presbyterian, was the Scottish Stoneite pioneer John McClung, who arrived in the area shortly after Nance but preached and established churches in the Madison area, somewhat further east.[21]

Nance indicates that most of the converted "were baptized upon confession of their faith, after the example of our Lord, by going down into the water and being buried with him in baptism." Coming from the O'Kelly wing of the Christian movement, the mode of baptism was still very much a matter of discussion. O'Kelly opposed adult immersion, but the Jones/Smith people and increasingly Stone's Christian Churches opted for believer's baptism by immersion. Nance and McClung show this process of moving from infant baptism to believer's baptism during the first decade of the 19th century. The two preachers were "fully convinced of the impropriety of Infant Sprinkling" but had not yet been immersed themselves.

> We being in this remote section of the Union, and having none of the true gospel order to apply to, convenient to us, and believing that our mission to preach and baptize fully authorized us to baptize, we appointed a day, when in the presence of a numerous congregation, after we had each of us preached to the people, descended into a certain water with singing and prayer, where we baptized each other after the primitive mode of *immersion*, which was in June 1808.[22]

Nance remarks that their own baptism occurred at "about the same time" when the brethren "in Kentucky gave up their Infant Sprinkling, and were also baptized in the primitive mode." During 1807 and 1808 there was an intense discussion among Kentucky Stoneite preachers about the issue of infant baptism. In a large meeting at Lexington in October of 1808, all of the assembled 47 preachers acknowledged believer's immersion as a "gospel ordinance," although they left its administration up to the discretion of the individual minister.[23]

20. *Herald of Gospel Liberty* 5.2 (18 Sept 1812) 423.

21. Love H. Jameson dates McClung's arrival one year after that of Clement Nance. See Love H. Jameson, "Origin and Progress of the Reformation in Indiana," *The Christian-Evangelist* (12 November 1891) 724.

22. *Herald of Gospel Liberty* 5.2 (18 Sept 1812) 424.

23. D. Newell William, *Barton Stone: A Spiritual Biography* (St. Louis: Chalice, 2000) 129–32.

Among the events that stimulated the growth of the Christian Movement in Southern Indiana was a spectacular series of earthquakes that had their epicenter near New Madrid, Missouri. The earthquakes in December 1811 were so powerful that they made church bells ring in Boston and had also a strong impact in Southern Indiana, notably in the Louisville and Jeffersonville area.[24] Abraham Snethen, a Kentucky New Light preacher, records vividly in his autobiography the religious effect of the earthquake in Kentucky. The violent shakes and rumblings of the earth frightened people so much "that they gathered in groups and huddling together, they silently awaited the coming of the end of all things." Apocalyptic texts of the Bible and their predictions of earthquakes as signs of the end enhanced the impact and led to a visible moral change among the people.[25] Nance mentions that "the tremendous shaking of the earth last winter alarmed numbers" so that "a glorious revival took place," in which he baptized twenty people and interested many more.[26]

The autobiographical narrative in which Nance reflects for Elias Smith on his life and ministry in Southern Indiana was occasioned by the reading of some copies of the *Herald of Gospel Liberty*. Nance had seen these issues along with Smith's hymnal at the home of a fellow Virginian who had been baptized by Frederick Plummer, a well-known New England preacher. Nance writes that reading what fellow Christians in the east were accomplishing "created in me an anxiety to get farther acquainted with you, and our Northern brethren." The news from the east compelled him to initiate a fraternal communication. His rhetoric is imbued with millennial fervor and apocalyptic biblical imagery derived from the book of Daniel. Similar to the note struck in his earlier hymn, Nance was convinced of the eventual global success of evangelization. "I give you this abstract," he wrote to Smith, "to inform the brethren in the *North* and *East* of the spread of the gospel of peace in these parts, and I believe the Lord in the end will cause this little stone of truth so effectually to smite the image of error as to beat it to dust, and become a great mountain and fill the whole earth."[27]

---

24. Samuel L. Mitchill, "A detailed narrative of the earthquakes which occurred on the 16th day of December, 1811 . . . ," *Transactions of the Literary and Philosophical Society of NY*, 1:281–307; http://pasadena.wr.usgs.gov/office/hough/mitchill.html.

25. *Autobiography of Abraham Snethen, the Barefoot Preacher* (Dayton, OH: Christian Publishing Association, 1909) 59–62.

26. *Herald of Gospel Liberty* 5.2 (18 Sept 1812) 424.

27. Ibid.

Civic Activities

And, yet, Clement Nance was by no means an otherworldly visionary but stood with both feet in society and contributed his own share of civic involvement even before Indiana had achieved statehood. Nance was a judge in the Court of Common Pleas of Harrison County from 1809 on. The documented court actions he presided over included two cases of indentured servitude by which the bondage of southern slaves who had moved with their masters to Indiana continued in Indiana Territory. The territorial legislature had rejected arguments of the aristocratic faction in territorial politics of introducing slavery to encourage resettlement of southern planters in the territory. But it adopted in 1805 an act that allowed slaveholders who had moved to the territory to keep slaves over the age of 15 for an indefinite period in servitude. Males and females under 15 had to be released at ages 35 and 32 respectively. One case that Clement Nance dealt with under the provisions of the new law involved a slave from North Carolina by the name of Jacob Ferrel, who still owed his master thirteen years of indentured servitude after which he would be set free. For such service the slave would receive from John Smith "on demand one gray mare four years old, named 'Til,' and a red cow with a white face."[28] The other case related to a four-year indenture of a slave who had been owned by Clement Nance's son-in-law, Patrick Shields, a farmer and Christian Church preacher, who had brought 35-year-old Samuel Wilson from Virginia to Indiana. Shield and Nance promised that they would take care of Wilson once he received his freedom before the age of forty.[29] Although Indiana law changed in 1810 so that no new slaves could be brought into the territory, *de facto* slavery of African Americans who had been enslaved before coming to Indiana survived even after the granting of statehood in 1816, so that the census of 1820 still listed 190 slaves as serving in long-term indentured relationships in Indiana.[30] In 1809, Clement Nance also confirmed before a fellow judge

28. Indiana Court of Common Pleas (Harrison County) Deeds, 1809, Folder 1, Manuscript and Visual Collections Department, William Henry Smith Memorial Library, Indiana Historical Society, Indianapolis; http://www.indianahistory.org/library/manuscripts/collection_guides/SC2695.html.

See also W. H. Perrin, *Biographical and Historical Souvenir, Harrison County, Indiana* (Chicago: Gresham, 1889) 121–22.

29. Ibid.

30. On the important issue of slavery in the early history of Indiana, see Ralph Gray, *The Hoosier State: Readings in Indiana History*: Vol. 1: *Indiana Prehistory to the Civil War* (Bloomington: Indiana University Press, 1989) 95–108.

his emancipation of a slave named "Will" in 1799 in Pittsylvania County, Virginia, after having received a compensation of $200 from the slave.[31] Family tradition also mentions another female slave, "Old Marge," previously owned by Clement Nance and set free in Virginia as well as other slaves whom Nance is said to have freed and sent to Liberia.[32]

Nance continued his judicial activities after the formation of Floyd County and from 1819 until 1825 served as one of its associate judges. One of his cases is remembered in the annals of the county's history, the capital murder case of John Dahman, who was accused of having murdered Frederick Notte. On 18 May 1821, the jury found Dahman guilty, and he was sentenced to hang on 6 July 1821. Unlike his fellow New Light Abraham Snethen, who was an avowed opponent of the death penalty, Clement Nance had no hesitation in sentencing John Dahman to death.[33] Allegedly, when Nance pronounced the verdict that Dahman was "to be hanged by the neck til he be dead-dead-dead," Dahman is reported to have said: "and damned." To that Nance replied: "And may God have mercy on your soul," which Dahman countered with: "and the devil too."[34]

Upon moving from the Falls of the Ohio into the Knobs west of New Albany, Nance became the postmaster of Nanceville, a postal station named after him, where later he also served as one of the local agents for the *Christian Messenger*. Today, Nance's presence in the area is still remembered by the geographical location of Nance's Corner, the many Nance family members in a local cemetery, and a nearby residential dwelling that contains the structure of the pioneer's original log house.[35]

Soteriological and Christological Theological Concerns

The published correspondence of Nance in the *Herald of Gospel Liberty*, *Gospel Luminary*, and *Christian Messenger* gives us some indication of the theological preoccupations of contemporary Christian Church preachers. Live theological issues concerned soteriology, notably the atonement, Christology, and ecclesiology. An unnamed contributor to the *Herald of*

31. W. H. Perrin, *Biographical and Historical Souvenir, Harrison County*, Indiana, 121–22.

32. Nance, *The Nance Memorial*, 13.

33. *Autobiography of Abraham Snethen, the Barefoot Preacher*, 55–56.

34. Nance, *The Nance Memorial*, 19.

35. Marti Bergstrom, "Nance Home Could be Oldest in Floyd County," *The Tribune Scope*, Wednesday, 3 October 1980.

Gospel Liberty from New England, staying in January 1815 at the home of Clement Nance, recounted some of their conversations. These conversations open a window on what engaged Nance and religious folk in the west theologically. According to the visitor, "the doctrine of Christ" was "recovering its ancient ground in the hearts and understandings of believers." By "ancient ground" the visitor meant that people rejected the "error of their opponents, the imputation of the first Adam's sin, and that of the righteousness of the second." Instead, in salvation "the grace of God arrests as it were the operations of his Justice." Justice thus "forbids the suffering of imputed guilt," in fact "imputation of sin" is for our visitor at the Nance residence "the most monstrous absurdity in all ethics" since God himself is the source of all justice and mercy." "In short," the Christians in Indiana and Kentucky "preach that Jesus was made an offering for sin, and that by grace in the fullest extent of its meaning, the believer receives his acquittal from the curse of broken law." If the visitor represents correctly the *sensus communis* on soteriology in the west, Nance and his fellow believers shared Stone's moral view of the atonement.[36] Victor McCracken has drawn attention to the fact that theories of the atonement concerned not only Stone but also his contemporaries very much. Stone's opposition to substitutionary atonement, while drawing on a trajectory developed in American Unitarianism, challenged his contemporaries with an alternative to penal substitution that did not lead to universalism because each individual retained "the capability of either accepting or rejecting the divine call."[37] It appears that Stone's views were also held and discussed among preachers like Nance in Indiana. Next to the general background of British and American Unitarianism suggested by McCracken, one might thus fruitfully widen the context for Stone's soteriology to include also the Christians of the Jones/Smith movement, where the western Christological discussion found an open ear.[38] Other

36. "Imprimatur (Anonymous letter from Franklin Township, Harrison County, Indiana, of 11 January 1815 to the Editor)," *Herald of Gospel Liberty* 7/11 (Friday, 3 March 1815) 663.

37. Victor McCracken, "The Unitarian and Orthodox Backgrounds of the Stone-Campbell Atonement Debate," *Discipliana* 58.4 (1998) 113.

38. On Stone's views of the atonement, see also D. Newell Williams, "The Power of Christ's Sacrifice: Barton W. Stone's Doctrine of Atonement," *Discipliana* 54.1 (1994) 20–31; On the afterlife of atonement theology in the Stone-Campbell movement, see John Mark Hicks, "Atonement Theology in the late Nineteenth Century: The Pattern of Discussion," *Discipliana* 56.4 (1996) 116–27.

topics covered in passing by Nance's visitor are a polemic against the "*Thritheistick notion*" of Trinitarians and the Calvinism of Baptists.

But the pathos and the distinctiveness in the appeal of the Christian Movement in the west lay primarily in its rejection of ecclesiastical traditions and the promotion of a non-sectarian and gospel-oriented Christianity. The visitor hoped that the communication of the successful evangelization in the "western country" would also "refresh" the New England brethren and provide them with "great encouragement to go forward in the glorious cause."[39]

In April of the same year, Elias Smith extracted a letter of Nance, in which both men take issue with a preacher in Indiana who held what amounts to modalist Monarchian views about Christ, who as eternal God died for sinners. Nance raised the classical objections against such a view when he wrote: "I thought while he was speaking, if the eternal God died, what situation could the world be in when God was dead; and if Jesus Christ was the eternal God, into whose hands did he commit his spirit when he died."[40] Christological differences continued in Indiana well into the 1820s, as the minutes from 1827 attest, when Elder Adam Payne left the New Light connexion "because he could not be reconciled to the Church's view of the Son of God."[41]

Links with Christian Churches in the East and Questions of Organization and Communication

In 1817, a year after Indiana achieved statehood, it also constituted its first Christian Conference of Stoneite churches. Most of the early preachers serving in Indiana came from Kentucky and were New Lights like Nance and his early associate John McClung.[42] In 1818, the Conference of Illinois or Wabash separated from the Indiana Conference.[43] In December of 1825, William Kinkade, who like Joseph Thomas, the White Pilgrim, was a bridging figure between the western and eastern Christian Churches,

---

39. *Herald of Gospel Liberty* 7.11 (Friday, 3 March 1815) 663.

40. Extract of an undated letter of Clement Nance to the Editor, in *Herald of Gospel Liberty* 7.15 (28 April 1815) 679–80.

41. "Minutes," in *The Christian Messenger* 2.1 (November 1827) 15.

42. Love H. Jameson, "Origin and Progress of the Reformation in Indiana," *The Christian-Evangelist* (12 November 1891) 724; (19 November 1891) 740, and the Minutes mentioned below.

43. "Elder Kinkade's Letter (11 December 1825)," *Gospel Luminary* 2 (1826) 79–80.

wrote optimistically from Ohio about the growth of the Christian movement in the west. "If we compare the present age, with the ages that are past," the evangelist wrote, "we cannot fail to see that the light is shining brighter, and that divine power in the church is increasing."[44]

In the same month, Elder Joseph Badger, a leading preacher from New York, visited Stone and the churches in Kentucky and Ohio and sought a closer linkage between Christians in the north and east and the Christian Church movement in the west.[45] At Georgetown, Kentucky, he brought to preachers greetings from Christians in New England and New York. His greetings were reciprocated with an address of solidarity signed by Thomas Smith, the moderator of the assembly, and Barton W. Stone, its Clerk. Eastern Christians, according to Smith and Stone, were "as one family with us—governed by the same rule, directed by the same spirit, animated by the same hope, and engaged in the same cause."[46] Badger then went on to Ohio, where he also met with the Ohio Conference of Christian Churches. Later, the 1825 statistics for all western churches as well as the Proceedings of the two meetings Badger had attended were published in one of the major eastern periodicals, David Millard's New York based *Gospel Luminary*.[47]

The available statistics show the strength of western churches in 1825, which numbered nearly 13,000 members and were ministered to by 225 preachers. They were distributed over three conferences in Kentucky (3,350), and one each in Tennessee (1,800) and Alabama (600). The largest membership, however, could be found in the six conferences of Ohio (4,390), and smaller numbers in Indiana (1,200), Illinois (600), and Missouri (1,000). Altogether the statistics also list 64 church buildings as being owned by these churches.[48]

The strength of Christian Churches raised questions about the need for better communication and the viability of an annual conference comprising all western churches, beyond the regional quarterly and annual

---

44. Ibid., 80–81.

45. On Badger, see E. G. Holland, *Memoir of Rev. Joseph Badger* (New York: Francis, 1854); and Thomas H. Olbricht, "Christian Connexion and Unitarian Relations 1800–1844," *Restoration Quarterly* 9.3 (1966) 160–86.

46. "Proceedings of a Conference in Kentucky, and Address to Elder Badger, &c.," *Gospel Luminary* 2 (1826) 86.

47. Ibid., 82–93.

48. Ibid., 90–93.

district conferences existing at the time. After successive failures to arrange "a general Conference in the west," the Ohio Conference attempted once again to arrange a meeting of representatives of all regions in the west, this time for October 1826. The visiting Badger, while acknowledging some local resistance to such a General Conference, saw the benefits far outweighing its costs and dangers. In fact he envisioned in the future three General Conferences, which would link the east with the south and the west. The geographical center for western churches was in Badger's opinion "the great emporium of the west," Cincinnati.[49]

Beyond the conference structure, more effective means of communication were sought for preachers, members, and churches. This need was addressed by the Ohio Conference when it sought to establish a journal and an associated book room serving the western churches. Again, Badger felt that all three conferences would need a medium of communication, where now only New York had such a journal in the *Gospel Luminary*. The Conference of Ohio thus established a committee to arrange an annual conference, whose object it was "to form a correspondence throughout the Churches, in the western States, and acquire a correct knowledge of the churches in general—and also to consult about establishing a periodical work, to be edited in the western country."[50] Badger assumed that Barton W. Stone's "distinguished gift of writing" would make him the likely choice of being the editor, which in fact he became when the *Christian Messenger* was started in 1826. It is important to note, however, that the ensuing journal, *The Christian Messenger*, was by no means the single initiative of Barton W. Stone. Rather, it had been the resolution of churches in the west to have such a periodical voice and medium of communication.

When the Indiana Christian Conference met in Harrison County in September of 1826 under Elisha Gunn as their leader and Clement Nance as clerk, the Hoosier preachers suggested organizational procedures and policies for more effective ministerial work among the churches. This included regular attendance and representation of churches at quarterly meetings, the registration and printed roster of accredited ministers, better record keeping among local churches, and the subdivision of Indiana and Kentucky churches into separate regional districts.[51]

---

49. Ibid., 87–88.

50. Ibid., 89.

51. *Christian Herald* 2.11 (Jan 1827) 165–67.

All throughout this period, Nance kept his lines of communication open to the east and sought light on biblical issues from brethren nationwide. In December of 1826, he rejoiced over news about the work of the brethren in the east, which he had read in the *Herald of Gospel Liberty*. He was especially happy that his "old friend and brother Elias Smith had renounced his universal system, and was lovingly invited once more to resume his stand in fellowship with his former brethren." As before, Nance sought out opportunities, "to hold a Christian correspondence with the eastern brethren, by conveying intelligence from each other from time to time, of the state of Religion—the state of the churches, and number of Gospel ministers approved in each section of the country." And in his postmillennial fervor, he had no doubt that "in the space of a few years the BIBLE will be the only RULE for faith and practice for a large portion of our dear American Christians; creeds and confessions of faith (merely human) are fast falling, and the numerous isms, badges of sectarianism, are by many now publickly opposed as an evident mark of the beast."[52]

The last two religious issues that Nance raised in the periodicals dealt with church and ministry. In the *Gospel Luminary* he expressed, together with Sherman Babcock, a fellow minister from Indiana, the conviction that since the office of bishop and elder was the same, each church needed a "plurality of elders" according to the "ancient order of things" and that without such plurality "no Church of Christ is properly organized." His discussion ended with the prayerful invocation "Oh, that the ancient Apostolic order of things may be speedily restored."[53] In the same month, Nance also posed some queries for discussion in the *Christian Messenger*, seeking clarification on the work and office of an evangelist.[54]

Representatives of the newly separated Indiana and Kentucky districts met in September of 1827 at Rood's Creek, Hardin County, Kentucky, for a union meeting. Nance served once more as their conference clerk. The conference resolved that the Minutes of their meeting be printed in the *Christian Messenger*, the new medium of communication for the western churches. Among the usual business, such as the

52. Ibid.

53. *Gospel Luminary* 3.10 (October 1827) 245–47.

54. "Queries Proposed for Investigation by Elder C. Nance," *The Christian Messenger* 1 (25 August 1827) 232. See also Barton W. Stone, "Elder Nance's Queries," *The Christian Messenger* 1 (25 October 1827) 273.

listing of *bona fide* ministers and the appointment of messengers and correspondence with other Conferences, the Indiana district supported Ohio's effort in organizing a General Conference of all Christian districts and conferences in the west. Nance concluded these minutes with an air of optimism in light of recent conversions. "I expect," he wrote, "that the state of Indiana will, in a short time, be filled with Churches or Congregations, who will own no other Lord but Jesus, and submit to [no] other creed but the Bible.[55]

This annual union meeting would be the last one that Clement Nance attended, for he died on 21 July 1828, on his farm in the Knobs near New Albany. He was remembered by Barton W. Stone as "a useful and laborious preacher" who "left a good testimony of his unwavering faith in Christ, and is now gone to receive the reward of his labours," sentiments also echoed in an obituary notice by Nance's son, published in Elias Smith's New England journal, *The Morning Star and City Watchman*.[56]

Conclusion

Clement Nance's life and labor demonstrate the ease with which a Virginia Christian in fellowship with James O'Kelly became a preacher among the Christians around Stone in Kentucky and subsequently a pioneer on the expanding western frontier in Indian Territory. His own life also illustrates the transition among western churches from the practice of infant baptism to that of believer's immersion. Nance's theological profile resonates with some of the Christological and soteriological issues proposed by Stone and discussed among preachers in the west, notably a moral understanding of the atonement as alternative to the evangelical substitutionary model.

Since his departure from the Methodists, Nance's ecclesiastical views were strongly focused on the two poles that also became identity markers for the subsequent Stone-Campbell Movement: restoration and union. Nance's restorationist pathos employs a language anticipating Alexander Campbell's "Ancient Order of Things." Also the optimism over massive conversions and the erection of a creedless, Word-oriented Zion in America speak the postmillennial language of Thomas Campbell's *Declaration and Address*.

55. "Minutes," *The Christian Messenger* 2.1 (1827) 16.

56. "Obituary," *The Christian Messenger* 2.10 (1828) 239; "Death of Elder Nance," *The Morning Star and City Watchman* 2.1 (1828) 47.

Nance remained confident that a Christian could be actively involved in government, as his judicial activities and those as postmaster attest. Unlike in the Lipscomb and Harding pacifist and separatist tradition, quite a few O'Kelly Christians had actively championed the Revolution and fought in it. Clement Nance did not hesitate to be a judge, and among the early prominent New Lights one finds progressive politicians like David Purviance, who was a Kentucky and Ohio state legislator, and William Kinkade, who was a member of the Illinois state convention. Both men brought their Christian convictions to bear in the political process, Purviance in opposing slavery and the fugitive laws.

Nance kept his lines of communication open to fellow Christians in the north and east and actively pursued the sharing of religious intelligence in the eastern Christian papers. His desire to clarify theological issues and communicate and document ecclesial strengths and evangelistic activities nationwide was shared by fellow Christians in the west, who sought to establish more effective means of communication via a common journal, which became a reality with the *Christian Messenger* still during Nance's lifetime.

The other institutional issue commanding attention among the western churches in the 1820s was the ultimately futile attempt to organize the Stoneite churches into a General Conference. This institutional structure, some hoped, would enhance greater communication and collaboration. As favorably as such a General Conference was viewed by Joseph Badger and the eastern Christians, strong internal opposition to such a superstructure with dubious biblical precedent prevented its establishment. Elijah Goodwin, for example, who supported annual meetings for consultation, became a fierce opponent of "a standing body, separate from churches." In fact, the relatively tenuous and regional Indiana Conference established in 1817 collapsed a few years later in 1830. The impending encounter and merger with the reform movement of Alexander Campbell heightened the suspicions towards larger structures and also closed the lines of communication to the Christian Churches among the Jones and Smith people in the east, connections that Clement Nance had nurtured and maintained throughout his lifetime.[57]

57. James M. Mathes, *Life of Elijah Goodwin, the Pioneer Preacher* (St. Louis: Burns, 1880) 119.

7

Washington Territory's Klickitat County (1861–1893)
Christian Beginnings in an Isolated Corner

JERRY RUSHFORD

The American Restoration Movement (Churches of Christ/Christian Churches) had its origins in West Virginia, Kentucky and Tennessee in the early years of the nineteenth century. It grew rapidly in the Midwestern states of Ohio, Indiana, Illinois, Missouri, and Iowa, and following the Civil War many members of the movement migrated to the northwest corner of the country. This essay focuses on Christian beginnings in isolated and sparsely-populated Klickitat County in Washington Territory.

The members of the Restoration Movement who migrated to Washington Territory in the nineteenth century insisted on calling themselves "Christians." However, they did not imply by this preference that they were the only Christians. On the contrary, they were motivated by an intense desire to unify all professing believers into one church family. It was their aversion to all denominational distinctions that drove them to insist on a pure speech in Biblical matters. With an obvious depth of passion, Thomas Campbell admonished members of the movement to never relinquish the precious right of wearing the name "Christian" for the very reason that it was consistent with what they had been about from the beginning, namely "the restoration of pure, primitive, apostolic Christianity in letter and spirit, in principle, and practice."[1]

The Restoration Movement arrived in Klickitat County in Washington Territory in March of 1861 when Meriel S. Short and his wife, Louise, settled south of Goldendale near the Columbia River. They had been living in Marion County, Oregon following their marriage in 1859. They were most likely members of the Bethany Church of Christ in that area. The Shorts filed on a Klickitat County homestead where the wagon road from Columbus started to climb over the Columbia hills.[2]

The Shorts were devout members of the Church of Christ. M. S. Short had been baptized into Christ in Indiana in 1845, and one his brothers, Washington Short, was a preacher in the Church of Christ for more than fifty years.[3] Mr. Short owned a blacksmith shop on the Columbus Road for 5 years and he also served as the first mail carrier ("Pony Express" on a saddle horse) for Klickitat County. One account says: "He was a short, stockily built man . . . because of this the pioneers christened him with the nickname of Pony."[4]

In 1866 Short moved his family to Chamberlin Flat on the Columbia River and engaged in cattle raising. One source notes: "In 1875 he organized a church on Chamberlin Flat. This church was later moved to Goldendale."[5] Another account confirms that "in 1875 he organized his first church with ten members."[6] This 1875 congregation on Chamberlin Flat may not have continued to meet, or it may have only met sporadically. Three years later, when Short organized a church at Spring Creek schoolhouse near Goldendale, he called it "the first Christian Church east of the Cascade Mountains and north of the Columbia River."[7]

T. D. Adams observed:

> Meriel (Pony) Short wished to become a minister in the Campbellite faith, but the church never licensed him to preach in my knowledge. However, some of the young people urged him to preach. I have heard my brother, Elder J. E. Adams, say that he knew Pony Short was called to preach for he helped call him. After he moved to Chamberlin Flat on the Columbia River he continued to preach at Pleasant Valley and other places.[8]

Actually, Short was ordained to the Christian ministry in October 1881.[9] This ceremony may only have consisted of the leaders of the Goldendale Church laying hands on Short and praying for God's blessings on his ministerial efforts, but he always remembered their confidence in him and he was always faithful to his ministerial responsibilities. He became one of the most respected church leaders in Klickitat County. One history recorded that he was "a minister of the Church of Christ, engaged in farming and stock raising" and that he was "one of Klickitat's earliest and most honored pioneer citizens."[10]

The Methodists were ahead of the Christians in establishing a presence in Klickitat County. They organized their first congregation at a camp meeting in the fall of 1871, and they erected a meetinghouse in Goldendale in 1872. The Christians built their church house in Goldendale in 1879.[11]

When the Edmund B. Robertson family moved from Oregon to Klickitat County in the 1870s, M. S. Short welcomed a co-laborer in the gospel. He and Robertson rode together on a circuit around Goldendale preaching in meetings and encouraging the Christians to organize churches. In February 1878 they held a meeting at Spring Creek schoolhouse northwest of Goldendale and were successful in organizing a congregation of ten members.

Nearly four years later, Short reflected back on this historic meeting in a letter to the editor of the *American Christian Review* in Cincinnati, Ohio. He wrote:

> The rise and progress of the Christian cause in this country dates from the 22nd of February next, four years ago. At that time Bro. Robertson and myself with eight others met at Spring Creek and organized the first Christian Church east of the Cascade Mountains and north of the Columbia River in Washington Territory. Our number was ten, all told.[12]

For the next two years, Short and Robertson worked to enlarge the Klickitat County congregation. Sometimes the church met at Spring Creek and sometimes at Goldendale, but it was the same congregation. Progress was slow, but Short and Robertson got an unexpected break in the summer of 1879 when a veteran preacher from Missouri, Robert Milne, arrived in the county.

In a July 22, 1879 letter to the *American Christian Review*, Short wrote:

> We have had two meetings in this month, two days each—one at Goldendale, the other at Spring Creek—but the same congregation, or nearly so, we having but one organized body in this country. We had a good, large audience; the people behaved very well indeed. Since our last report, we have received in all, eighteen by letter and recommendation, some not having letters; two by faith, confession and baptism—making a total of twenty new additions; and more came forward and confessed the Lord, that we expect will be baptized the first Lord's day in next month,

according to their request. Some of the new additions were from the Baptist and some from the M. E. Church. The brother that did the preaching is lately from Missouri. His name is R. Milne . . . He is able to use the sword of the Spirit, which is the word of God, to the best advantage . . . We shall do all we can to help him along in doing good. This is to let you know that we are trying to do something for the cause away over here in Klickitat, W. T. The *A. C. Review* is doing good.[13]

Less than two weeks later, and writing again from Spring Creek, Short provided the *American Christian Review* with another progress report:

We closed a meeting at Goldendale, in this county, August 2 with good results, having received ten additions: one who had been a member of the Christian Church; two who had been baptized, we did not learn by whom; five by faith, confession and baptism. The same brother, Milne, is laboring for us. The church thinks of keeping him for a year. We have now about fifty-five members, with good prospects for more. We have got a subscription for a church-house, and have almost enough to put it up. So you may see that we have but started here in the good work. When we get our house up we shall try to have a Sunday-school started.[14]

In a January 27, 1882 letter to the *American Christian Review*, Short looked back on the progress of four years and wrote:

Our number was ten, all told. Bro. Robertson and myself labored for about eighteen months and had collected about thirty members. I tried to preach the first sermon ever made by the Christian order in the old school house in the town of Goldendale, about two years ago, to a few faithful ones. About this time Bro. Milne came to this country and preached once a month at Goldendale. We built a house at this place and the organization was located here, accumulating about seventy-five names, principally of emigrants locating in this country.[15]

Several sources confirm that the Christians erected a meetinghouse in Goldendale in 1879 on the southwest corner of Third and Court streets.[16] Although there have been a number of renovations over the past 130 years, some of the original building remains in the current facility used by the Church of Christ. It is the oldest church building still in use in Goldendale.

A new town named Centerville, located about eight miles south-west of Goldendale, was platted in 1877. In that same year a small group of Christians settled in Centerville and began to meet for prayer and Bible study in the local school house. Prominent among this group were Frederick and Emily Eshelman and their children who had migrated from Missouri. These Christians would meet in the Centerville school house and in private homes for nearly seven years before organizing themselves as a church in January of 1884.[17]

With the Centerville Christians meeting regularly in the Centerville school house and the Spring Creek/Goldendale congregation meeting regularly in either the Spring Creek school house or its own new church house in Goldendale, Short and Robertson began to set their sites on establishing a congregation in Pleasant Valley about eleven miles to the east of Goldendale. In a February 2, 1880 letter to the *American Christian Review*, Short wrote:

> It has been some time since you had any news from us, as I had nothing good to send. I think we have good news now. Bro. Robertson and myself held a protracted meeting in Pleasant Valley commencing the fourth Lord's day in January and ending Wednesday night, with fourteen additions—nine by confession, four by immersion and one from the Baptists. Four had belonged, and were reclaimed. There is not any church organization in Pleasant Valley of any kind yet. The Methodists have been hold-ing prayer-meetings in the neighborhood, and met with us and assisted in carrying on the meeting. There was a good degree of love manifested among the people during our stay with them. We have got our church house in Goldendale, so we can hold meet-ings in it. We have preaching in it once a month by Bro. Milne; reading and prayer-meeting once a week. Bro. Milne preaches at Spring Creek once a month.[18]

In the January 27, 1882 letter in the *American Christian Review*, Short described his actions after building the meetinghouse in Goldendale and the strengthening of the Spring Creek/Goldendale congregation. He reported:

> Bro. Robertson and I held the first Christian meeting in Pleasant Valley, resulting in the confession of forty persons, who were baptized. Brethren Milne and Hunt also did some preaching there, adding about twenty-two more to the membership. Bro. Robertson and I, within the past 5 months, have added thirteen

new members—eight by confession and baptism and five from
the other denominations, principally from the M. E. Church.
Our total membership in the county now is about one hundred
and twenty. We have four ordained preachers, six elders, two
churches—one house built by the church at Goldendale. The
church at Pleasant Valley have one ordained preacher—Meriel S.
Short—who was ordained October last. The church there is in a
flourishing condition at present. We hold prayer-meetings twice
each week, preaching two times a month, and the brothers and
sisters manifest much of the spirit of Christ.[19]

Plans were made to conduct a camp-meeting near Goldendale in
the summer of 1880. A correspondent named J. W. Fulton sent a report
of this meeting to the editor of the *Pacific Christian Messenger* in Monmouth, Oregon. He wrote:

During the past week the brethren of Goldendale have been
holding a camp-meeting a few miles from the town. It com-
menced on Saturday, June 26th, and closed on Sunday, July 4th.
Quite a number were present and intense interest was manifested
throughout the meeting. All seemed to be in unison and harmony, and united prayer went up to the God of heaven. Love
seemed to flow freely from heart to heart, while sweet Gospel
songs of praise rang through the woodland with an echo—"God
is love."

Satan and his emissaries were driven back to their hiding places and the Gospel of Christ triumphed, not only in the conversion
of sinners, but also in building up those already in the faith.

The brethren of this place should be commended for their
zeal and piety, and the warm brotherly feeling they have for one
another.

During the meeting there were two added to the church by
immersion and one by relation. The preaching brethren present were Bros. Robert Milne, J. W. Elder, D. P. Hewitt and D. F.
Gilstrap; also two others, Jacob Eshelman and F. N. Roberts, who
have just started into the ministry by preaching their first sermon. An uncommon occurrence which took place at the meeting is that a brother sixty years old (J. W. Burnett) preached his
first public discourse, and a person over sixty-five years of age
obeyed the Gospel.

A protracted meeting conducted by R. H. Moss, of Oregon,
will commence at Goldendale on Friday evening before the third
Sunday in August.[20]

Just prior to the beginning of the Goldendale camp-meeting, some stirring news reached the Christians who were living in Washington Territory. The news bulletin came out of the Republican National Convention meeting in Chicago, Illinois, on Tuesday, June 8, 1880. It was reported that a former Christian preacher and Christian college president, Representative James A. Garfield from Ohio, had been nominated as the Republican candidate for President of the United States. There were numerous articles in the nation's press inquiring about Garfield's religious affiliation, and the Christians began to acquire a level of recognition they had not enjoyed before.

No letters were sent to the church papers giving the results of the summer meeting with Rufus H. Moss, but in the spring of 1881 the Goldendale church decided to host another gospel meeting. In the meantime, James A. Garfield was elected 20th President of the United States on November 2, 1880, and the Christian movement received unprecedented publicity. Joseph Warren Downer, an Oregon Christian who had only recently settled in the Goldendale area, attended the Goldendale meeting and sent a report to the *Pacific Christian* Messenger back home in Monmouth, Oregon. He wrote:

> The Goldendale protracted meeting, held by Elder J. P. McCorkle, commencing March 5th and ending the 21st with the following result: 11 by confession and 13 by fellowship, total 24.
>
> Bro. McCorkle has done much good, having stirred up the people to thinking and removing prejudice from the minds of many. The plea as set forth by the disciples lost none of its power as set forth by that powerful advocate of the truth, Bro. McCorkle.
>
> He seemed to hold his congregation spellbound, from first to last. It was sad parting on the eve of his last sermon, when the brethren were asked to give Bro. And Sister McCorkle the parting hand; three-fourths, yes near four-fifths of the congregation went forward; many unbelievers gave the parting hand. He has endeared himself greatly to the brethren, and had the best wishes from outsiders.
>
> We are trying to induce him to remain with us this summer, with fair prospects. The doctors have advised him to go to California for his health. He will no doubt go this fall.[21]

Originally from Missouri, John Provines McCorkle had been living and preaching in Northern California for nearly 30 years. He had baptized thousands of converts during his illustrious ministry, and he was often the Sunday morning preacher when the Christians assembled for their large annual meetings in northern California. The presence in Goldendale of such a veteran preacher gave a tremendous boost to the Christian cause. Although he went home to California that fall, he returned to Goldendale in 1885–86.

One of the sons of Frederick and Emily Eshelman, Jacob Thomas, had shown considerable promise as a young preacher in the late 1870s. Following his marriage in 1880, J. T. Eshelman began preaching more often for both the Centerville and Spring Creek/Goldendale groups. At some point following his 29th birthday, Eshelman accepted a call to preach regularly for both congregations, and he continued this dual ministry for six years.

In his January 27, 1882 letter, M. S. Short had estimated the number of Christians in the county at 120 divided between two congregations. He clearly was talking about Spring Creek/Goldendale and Pleasant Valley and he must not have included the Christians in Centerville in his numbers. This was probably because the Centerville group had not formally organized themselves as a church at that time. In round figures, it appears from Short's letter that there were about 70 members in the Spring Creek/Goldendale congregation and about 50 members in the Pleasant Valley congregation.

Meanwhile, the group of Christians meeting in Centerville was thinking of organizing themselves into a church. They had probably been meeting regularly for worship in the school house as far back as 1877, but they did not organize themselves into a church until January, 1884. In that same year, the Church of Christ at Centerville constructed a frame church building with a prominent spire. Today, 125 years later, it remains standing at its original location and is still used by the Church of Christ.

The annual summer camp-meetings continued to be hosted by the Goldendale Christian Church in the 1880s. In June 1886 a Christian preacher from Columbia County, Thomas McBride Morgan, was invited to preach. Morgan had preached in Oregon from 1874 to 1882 before moving to eastern Washington. In his report submitted to the *American Christian Review*, Morgan observed:

> The audiences in the main were good, and the brethren seem to be in peace and harmony, and a nobler band of brethren I never met with. The meeting closed on Lord's day night, May 30, with good interest. There was not a big ingathering, but certainly much

good was done . . . I find among these brethren quite a number of subscribers to and warm friends of the "Old Reliable."[22]

When Morgan used the phrase "Old Reliable," he was referring to the *American Christian Review* which was often called that by its friends and supporters who appreciated its consistently conservative and middle-of-the-road position in the church.

Two months after the Goldendale camp-meeting, Short sent a brief note to the *Christian Standard* in Cincinnati, Ohio on July 23, 1886. He wrote: "We had a good meeting the second Lord's day in this month. Two sermons by Elder J. T. Eshelman and fourteen came forward and made the good confession. Ten of them were immersed on the same day."[23]

Several church papers circulated among the Christians in Klickitat County in the mid 1880s. In addition to the *American Christian Review, Christian Standard,* and *Christian Leader*, all of which were published in Cincinnati, Ohio, the *Christian Oracle* from Des Moines, Iowa, the *Christian-Evangelist* from St. Louis, Missouri, and the *Christian Herald* from Monmouth, Oregon were well-represented in the county.

In a letter to the *Christian Leader*, dated September 4, 1887, Joseph E. Beeks from the Pleasant Valley Church wrote: "We now have a Bible class here, and intend to conduct it on the Lord's plan, without the aid of human ordinances."[24] One of the controversial "innovations" at that time was the use of Bible School quarterlies and other "lesson leaves" to aid teachers and students in their Sunday school classes. Joseph Beeks, and others like him, were skeptical of "human" commentaries on the Bible, and preferred the combination of open Bibles, animated discussions and common sense.

After six years of fruitful ministry with Centerville and Goldendale, as well as occasional visits to Pleasant Valley, J. T. Eshelman left the county in November, 1887, and began a new ministry with the Christian Church in North Yakima. In a note to the *Christian Standard* he wrote: "Our six years' labor in and for the churches at Goldendale and Centerville closed the second Lord's day in November, at which meeting we report 4 confessions and baptisms."[25]

The town of Bickleton was founded in April, 1879, and the town of Cleveland, four and a half miles to the west, was founded in 1880. Several families of Christians settled in these areas, but a church was not organized until the early 1890s.

By the decade of the 1880s the American Christian Missionary Society, often referred to as the General Christian Missionary Convention, was exercising tremendous influence in the Christian movement. This was happening not only through the actions of the national board, but in a more pervasive way through the various state conventions and state boards. It was inevitable that the national board would eventually turn its eyes toward the growing population in the Northwest, and this happened in 1887. In that year the ACMS began its operations in the Northwest by providing and supporting preachers for Seattle and Tacoma and several smaller communities.

The Christian movement in Washington Territory underwent a dramatic change with the arrival of Freeman Walden in 1888 and William Franklin Cowden in 1889. Both men were talented preachers and gifted organizers, and in a very short time their shaping influence was being felt throughout the territory. Freeman Walden had served on the state board of the missionary society in Iowa for sixteen years, and from the moment he set foot in the territory in January, 1888 he began calling for the creation of a missionary society in Washington. His efforts were largely successful, and the eager delegates met in Ellensburg on October 4, 1888 and organized the Washington Christian Missionary Convention with Freeman Walden as the first president.

With demands of statehood for Washington increasing on all fronts, the national board of the ACMS did not want to be left behind. In 1889, moving quickly to secure its own presence in the Northwest, the American Christian Missionary Society appointed W. F. Cowden to be "General Superintendent of Missions for the Pacific Northwest" with his salary guaranteed by the Honorable T. W. Phillips of New Castle, Pennsylvania.

On November 11, 1889, Washington territory became Washington state. With Walden and Cowden working in tandem, a significant number of preachers were recruited for service in the newest state in the union. When they arrived in Washington they were indebted to either the American Christian Missionary Society or the Washington Christian Missionary Convention for their new positions. But it wasn't just the preachers who were interested in the newest state. Large numbers of Christians began migrating to the Northwest. By the early 1890s, Walden and Cowden were trumpeting the news that the Christians were the second largest Protestant group (after the Methodists) in Washington.

Walden and Cowden were aided tremendously in their considerable efforts to showcase Washington by a weekly periodical called the *Christian Oracle*. Begun in 1884 and published in Des Moines, Iowa, the *Christian Oracle* was thoroughly supportive of the ACMS and all state missionary conventions. Walden had a regular column in the *Christian Oracle* entitled "Notes of Travel" and later "Washington Notes" in which he described the weather, geography, agricultural crops, and church life in his new home. He often mentioned the names of Christians he met in his travels through the state. His lively column, read by hundreds and perhaps thousands, was certainly a motivating factor in persuading many Christians to leave Iowa and other Midwestern states in favor of carving out a new home and a new life in the Northwest.

Following the creation of the Washington Christian Missionary Convention in 1888, there were not many churches that chose to retain an independent position relative to the state missionary board. The first Territorial evangelist chosen by Walden and the board was C. F. Goode from Wakefield, Nebraska. He accepted their offer and moved to Washington immediately, beginning his labors in November 1888. For his first evangelistic foray into Washington Territory, Goode chose Klickitat County. J. T. Eshelman had been gone for a year, and his former churches at Centerville and Goldendale had not replaced him. C. F. Goode spent a month working with the Church of Christ at Centerville, or as Walden described it in his weekly article: "Bro. Goode, our Territorial evangelist, is in that county working it up, with a view to locating a preacher."[26]

Walden was certainly pleased that both the Washington Christian Missionary Convention and the Territorial evangelist were now a reality, and he wrote with obvious pride in his weekly column:

> Bro. Goode is doing excellent work as Territorial evangelist. I am in receipt of a letter from one of the leading members at Centerville, where Bro. Goode spent a month, and in this way I learn that his work is very satisfactory. There were but three additions, all by confession and baptism, but the church was aroused to greater activity, and their spiritual strength was revived. If Bro. Goode succeeds in raising the tone of spirituality among our churches where he goes he will do a good work.[27]

Two weeks later, Walden offered more information on Klickitat. "Bro. Goode has just returned from Klickitat County where he has spent six weeks arranging so as to locate a preacher there," he wrote. "The field is all ready, and we are now looking for a suitable man. The brethren will not only support a man, but will help him to secure a home. Here is a fine opening for some good preacher. The brethren want a man of some experience and one who will go there to stay."[28]

One week later, C. F. Goode submitted his own report to the *Christian Oracle*. Under the heading of "Washington Territory" he wrote:

> I have just returned from Klickitat County. We have in that county not less than 175 disciples. At Centerville and Goldendale (county seat), and at Pleasant Valley they are organized. Centerville and Goldendale are ready for a preacher. They want and deserve a good able man, and will give him a reasonable salary.
>
> There are fine opportunities in that county for the right man— I mean a talented, energetic, godly man—one who has no time nor disposition to growl at Sunday-schools, missionary societies, organs etc. . . .[29]

In retrospect, this is a significant letter. As Goode knew only too well, there was a level of uncomfortableness in the church over all three of these issues. Sunday schools had been introduced into Washington churches in the mid to late 1870s. For the most part they were accepted as a positive tool for educating both children and adults about the contents of the Bible. However, there was some discontent among older members about the use of man-made study guides.

Organs to aid the singing in the public worship of the church were another recent addition. Not all Christians thought they were an improvement. The state missionary society was less than four months old, and the jury was still out on whether Washington Christians would unanimously accept the authority of this parachurch organization and its state board. Most Christians were naturally disposed to favor the autonomy of each local church. Given all of that, Goode's decision to throw down the gauntlet and challenge anyone who disagreed with him seems both brazen and unwise.

In his work as Territorial evangelist, Goode left Klickitat County and began traveling and preaching through eastern Washington. However, when his wife and small children arrived from Nebraska it was difficult to be away from them. After less than four months of service as Territorial evangelist, Goode made a decision to work full-time with the Christians in Klickitat County. Walden wrote: "Bro. Goode, our Territorial evangelist, has resigned and settled in Klickitat County. He could not well be away from his family. We have not yet filled his place."[30]

Walden traveled to Goldendale at the end of May to support Goode in the annual camp-meeting, where there were "about a dozen additions." On Decoration Day Walden was invited to deliver the featured address and "spoke to the largest audience I have yet addressed in Washington Territory. The number present in the armory was estimated at from 1,000 to 1,500."

However, Walden's visit was marred by his encounter with one of the preachers who had helped to establish the Church of Christ at Centerville. David F. Gilstrap was distributing copies of the *Christian Leader* during the camp-meeting and speaking out against missionary societies and the use of organs in Christian worship. Walden wrote: "The *Leader* has some adherents in these parts and they are antis of the out and out school . . . I had a long talk with this brother and warned him of the sin he is committing, but I presume that it will all amount to nothing so long as the *Leader* advocates such foolish and sinful things."[31]

There was no more mention of Klickitat County in the church papers for the next 6 months, but in his column of January 16, 1890 Walden informed his readers that someone had seen J. T. Eshelman on the train returning from Goldendale where he had gone to settle a dispute. Walden wrote the *Christian Oracle*: "There had been some confusion and strife in the Goldendale Church, but harmony was restored. Bro. Eshelman will do good wherever he goes."[32]

C. F. Goode responded with some embarrassment: "Bro. Walden is wrongly informed. There is not, nor has not been any strife nor confusion in the Goldendale Church since I have been here. The brethren in Centerville, eight miles away from here, had some difficulty last year, but we settled the matter ourselves and I think wisely, too. Am sorry such an explanation is necessary."[33]

In 1891 William Worth Stone, a Christian preacher living in Ellensburg, began editing a monthly periodical called the *Gospel Preacher*. Stone was a conservative and he launched his journal primarily to counteract Freeman Walden and the growing influence of the Washington Christian Missionary Convention. As expected, he found considerable support among conservative Christians in Klickitat County. In fact, David F. Gilstrap agreed to serve as a co-editor of the *Gospel Preacher*, thereby insuring its wide distribution in the county.

Among the first subscribers to the new paper was Wesley Short, a resident of Goldendale and a brother to M. S. Short. In 1893, W. W.

Stone ceased publication of the *Gospel Preacher* and gave his mailing list to the *Primitive Christian* in Wellington, Kansas. In exchange, the editors of that weekly journal asked Stone to contribute a regular page entitled "The Gospel Preacher" which he agreed to do. Stone's page contained news from Churches of Christ in the Northwest. In one issue he included a note from Wesley Short that read: "Brother Stone, I will say, although I have never met you in the flesh, still I hold you as one of God's noble defenders of the pure faith; and I invoke the aid of divine blessings of our heavenly Father upon your efforts to maintain the pure gospel."[34]

In 1891, the majority of Christians in the Centerville and Goldendale churches approved of the work of the Washington Christian Missionary Convention and favored the use of organs and pianos in the public worship assemblies of the church. There were conservatives in both congregations who, although disapproving of these "innovations," nevertheless continued to attend and support the church.

However, in three other districts of Klickitat County there were small congregations of Christians where the conservatives had more representation. These congregations were located at: Bickleton-Cleveland in the northeastern section of the county; at Pleasant Valley, eleven miles east of Goldendale; and at Sand Springs south of the Goodnoe Hills.

In April-May of 1891 the Pleasant Valley and Sand Springs congregations invited a 71-year-old veteran preacher from Missouri and Illinois, Craven Peyton Hollis, to preach in a one-week gospel meeting at each location. Hollis was living at Dayton in Columbia County at the time. Following the meetings, David F. Gilstrap submitted a report to the *Christian Leader*:

> On the fourth Lord's day in April, Bro. C. P. Hollis of Dayton, Wash. Began a meeting with the little band of brethren worshiping at Sand Springs, Klickitat Co., Wash., continued one week and went to Pleasant Valley and continued one week. The visible results in each case was the strengthening of the faithful brethren and the stirring up of the opposers until, I hope, their investigations will lead them to the truth. This county is sparsely settled and pretty much occupied by innovationists and other sects, so that the hearing for the truth was not as good as was hoped for. Bro. H. is an earnest, fearless, able proclaimer of the gospel as delivered by the apostles of the Son of God. He has a wonderful memory for one so old (he is seventy-two years old this summer), and his exegesis is as good as the best. His style and delivery are

with life and force, but his face is set as steel against innovation and all opposition to the truth, for which cause the opposers have tried to starve him out here in Washington.[35]

On April 30, 1893, David F. Gilstrap sent another letter for publication to the editor of the *Christian Leader*. Writing from Sand Springs, Washington, Gilstrap reported:

> Today at our regular Lord's day meeting, after preaching I took the confession of and baptized two noble souls (Bro. and Sister Mobly), which brings our little congregation up to eight in number. Although we are few in number and live in a sparsely settled country where there is but little material to work on to make Christians of, still we are determined by a godly walk, apostolic worship and sound teaching to save ourselves and all honest-hearted people who will listen.[36]

The General Missionary Convention began publishing annual "Year Books" at some point in the 1880s. These volumes contained a wealth of statistical information on Churches of Christ/Christian Churches in every state in the union. Washington may not have been included until after it achieved statehood. The first "Year Book" I have seen that includes Washington is the one dated 1892. In that volume, Washington is credited with 86 churches and 4,812 members (only baptized believers would be included in this figure as the Christians did not baptize infants nor count them in membership totals).

Of the 86 congregations listed, four were located in Klickitat County. Those churches and their membership totals were: Goldendale (60); Centerville (50); Bickleton (40); and Luna (35). Luna was an early name for Pleasant Valley. According to this data, there were 185 Christians distributed in four congregations in the county. The congregation at Sand Springs was not listed, but as Gilstrap pointed out, there were only eight Christians in that group.

A young Kansas preacher, M. J. Walters, came west in the summer of 1893 and preached in several gospel meetings along the way. He was "field editor" for the weekly *Primitive Christian*, and he was zealous in his attempt to secure subscribers in the Western states. In July he traveled through Klickitat County and stopped in the Cleveland area to preach for a week. According to the "Year Book" there was a 40-member congregation meeting in Bickleton, but there was no congregation meeting in Cleveland four miles away.

Writing from this temporary base in Klickitat County, M. J. Walters informed the readers of the *Primitive Christian* that:

> We are now in an interesting meeting at Cleveland, Wash. What the end will be, no one can tell. But we hope to do much good in sowing the seed of the kingdom, if we do not get to reap any of the ripened grain.
>
> We have no organization here at this place, but if some good evangelist could come in and locate at some point where he could reach this much neglected spot, there could be a permanent one, as we have a few members scattered about over the country. We will do all we can in holding forth the words of life, to give our hearers something to think about.[37]

After preaching for a week, Walters wrote again on July 25 to report: "Four were added to the church of Christ in a week's meeting at this place—two immersions, one from the Baptists and one reclaimed."[38]

Walters was an effective spokesman for the *Primitive Christian*, and copies were soon circulating among Christians in the county. One church leader who welcomed the new paper was William Dudley Smith, one of the elders of the Centerville Church of Christ. Although Centerville used an organ in worship and supported the missionary society, Smith appreciated the conservative thrust of the *Primitive Christian*. Corresponding with its editor, Smith wrote:

> I like the *Primitive Christian* very much and wish I were able to give it financial aid. I hope it may survive these hard times, and surmount all difficulties, and long live to do battle against sin and rebellion, and to be a mighty factor in restoring the ancient order of things. May the blessings of God, our Father, through our Lord, Jesus Christ, rest upon the editor and contributors.[39]

From Pony Short's rejoicing in "the rise and progress of the Christian cause" in Klickitat County in the 1870s to William Dudley Smith's passion for "restoring the ancient order of things" in the 1890s, many of the Christians in isolated and sparsely-populated Klickitat County were faithful to their vision of the kingdom of God.

NOTES

1. *Millennial Harbinger* (January 1840) 19. Unearthing quotations from long-forgotten nineteenth-century periodicals may not seem very exciting to modern day descendents of the Restoration Movement, but this is exactly the kind of data

that enthralled Mike Casey. On countless occasions, I was the beneficiary of Mike's encyclopedia knowledge of Christian periodicals. For two decades we worked together to build up the collection of Restoration periodicals in Payson Library at Pepperdine University. Our late night phone calls were never brief. We routinely talked too long because the data was always so enchanting. He was a beloved colleague, and I miss him.

2. Robert Ballou, *Early Klickitat Valley Days* (Goldendale: Klickitat County Historical Society, 1997) 287–88.

3. *An Illustrated History of Klickitat, Yakima and Kittitas Counties* (Chicago: Inter-State Publishing, 1904) 433.

4. Ballou, *Early Klickitat Valley Days*, 287.

5. Ibid., 288.

6. *An Illustrated History*, 433.

7. *American Christian Review* (March 2, 1882) 78.

8. Ballou, *Early Klickitat Valley Days*, 396.

9. See Short's letter of January 27, 1882, published in the *American Christian Review* (March 2, 1882) 78.

10. *An Illustrated History*, 432.

11. Pete May, ed., *History of Klickitat County, Washington* (Goldendale: Klickitat County Historical Society, 1982), 81.

12. Written January 27, 1882, and published in the *American Christian Review* (March 2, 1882).

13. Written July 22, 1879, and published in the *American Christian Review* (August 19, 1879).

14. Written August 4, 1879, and published in the *American Christian Review* (September 9, 1879).

15. Written January 27, 1882, and published in the *American Christian Review* (March 2, 1882).

16. Pete May, 100 *Golden Years: A 1972 Look at the History of Goldendale, Washington, at the End of Its First Century* (Goldendale: The Goldendale Sentinel, 1972) 74, 76.

17. Letter from Wayne Eshelman to Jerry Rushford, January 15, 2000.

18. Written February 3, 1880, and published in the *American Christian Review*, (March 9, 1880).

19. Written January 27, 1882, and published in the *American Christian Review* (March 2, 1882).

20. Written July 5, 1880, and published in the *Pacific Christian Messenger* (July 16, 1880). J. W. Elder was a young preacher who had just graduated from Christian College in Santa Rosa, California. Dr. D. P. Hewitt lived in Pleasant Valley. David F. Gilstrap was a young preacher who had just settled in Klickitat County. He would remain there for two decades. Jacob Thomas Eshelman had been in the county for about three years. He would begin a six-year ministry with the Goldendale and Centerville congregations in the summer or fall of 1881. Rufus H. Moss was the son of a well-known gospel preacher, Jesse Jasper Moss. Rufus had fought in the Civil War and returned nearly blind. He preached in Oregon throughout the 1870s but was moving into Washington Territory about the time of this gospel meeting in Goldendale.

21. Written on March 26, 1881 and published in the *Pacific Christian Messenger* (April 1, 1881).

22. Written in June 1886 and published in the *American Christian Review* (July 1, 1886).

23. Written July 23, 1886 and published in the *Christian Standard* (August 14, 1886).

24. Written September 4, 1887 and published in the *Christian Standard* (September 20, 1887).

25. Written November 21, 1887 and published in the *Christian Standard* (December 13, 1887).

26. *Christian Oracle* (January 3, 1889) 14.

27. Ibid.

28. *Christian Oracle* (January 17, 1889) 7.

29. *Christian Oracle* (January 24, 1889 14.

30. *Christian Oracle* (March 21, 1889) 7.

31. *Christian Oracle* (June 13, 1889) 14.

32. *Christian Oracle* (January 16, 1890) 14.

33. *Christian Oracle* (February 13, 1890) 7.

34. *Primitive Christian* (February 15, 1894) 6.

35. *Christian Leader* (June 23, 1891).

36. *Christian Leader* (May 16, 1893) 3.

37. *Primitive Christian* (August 3, 1893) 5.

38. Ibid., 4.

39. *Primitive Christian* (August 9, 1894) 5. The "hard times" Smith referred to was the two-year depression of 1893–94 that gripped the entire nation and led to many bank closings.

8

Lipscomb of Texas vs. Lipscomb of Nashville

R. L. Whiteside's Rejection of David Lipscomb's Pacifism[1]

BOBBY VALENTINE

The Emergence of a Texas "Lipscomb"

Robertson Lafayette Whiteside was born in Hickman County, Tennessee on December 27, 1869, not far from Salem on Swan Creek. Having lost both of his parents by the time he was twelve, Whiteside was raised by his sister Martha Jane and her husband Jack Sisco. Education was difficult to come by in war torn and impoverished Tennessee but Robertson grew into a sought after Bible scholar and a theological architect of the "Texas Tradition."[2]

Hickman County was not only devastated by the Civil War but was victim to constant religious fratricide as well. Whiteside reminisced "I was born into a fight,"[3] and in his early years did not align with any particular denomination. In October 1888, however, at the encouragement of H. W. Sisco, Whiteside responded to the preaching of Brown Goodwin

---

1. It is an honor to offer this essay in memory of Michael W. Casey. Mike always exhibited the marks of peace that evidenced his walk with the Spirit.

2. For more on the "Texas Tradition" and the "Nashville Bible School Tradition," see John Mark Hicks and Bobby Valentine, *Kingdom Come: Embracing the Spiritual Legacy of Lipscomb and James Harding* (Abilene: Leafwood, 2006); and Bobby Valentine, "Robertson Lafayette Whiteside: Systematic Theologian for the Churches of Christ" (Unpublished Guided Research Paper, Harding University Graduate School of Religion, 2001).

3. Whiteside, *Doctrinal Discourses*, ed. Inys Whiteside (Denton, TX: Inys Whiteside, 1955) 4–5.

and later recalled, "At the age of 18 I made a resolution to serve the Lord to the best of my ability, and that is still my resolution."[4] Specifically his new resolution in his baptism was to engage in systematic Bible study, cease his bad habits and war with the sects. He explained, "If he loves the Lord, he will find no satisfaction in indulging in that which is questionable. When I first grew up, I made a 'good hand' at the old square dances, and liked it immensely; but after I became a Christian toward the close of my eighteenth year, I never saw another dance . . . they did not fit into my program of life."[5]

If Whiteside's program did not include dancing it did education. He entered into West Tennessee Christian College in 1890[6] but remained in Henderson for six months because "little Bible was taught."[7] When Whiteside heard that David Lipscomb and James A. Harding would be starting a new school in Nashville, he enrolled in the first class on October 5, 1891. J. N. Armstrong remembered that Whiteside was one of a group of students who sat on the steps waiting for Harding to open the doors.[8] Due to finances Whiteside's education was broken up with sojourns into Alabama and Texas and he did not finish Nashville Bible School until 1898.

In Corsicana, Texas, Whiteside put into practice his resolution to engage in combat with any and all error, as he understood it. He became embroiled in the "order of worship hobby" espoused by W. J. Rice in his *Gospel Missionary*.[9] The contest with Rice concerned a fringe element but Whiteside's engagement with two consecutive editors of the *Firm Foundation* was not. George W. Savage advanced the notion that only a traveling man could be an evangelist but one who located his ministry within a particular congregation became a pastor. Whiteside noted, "Within the last few decades an idea has grown up that an evangelist is one who goes from place to place and holds protracted meetings of a few

4. R. L. Whiteside, "It is New Year," *Gospel Advocate* 83 (16 January 1941) 66.

5. Whiteside, *Doctrinal Discourses*, 4–5.

6. Earl West dates this to the fall of 1889, *Search for the Ancient Order*, 3: 251. Whiteside himself stated that he was only a student for six months before leaving for the Nashville Bible School to join its first class in 1891, cf. Whiteside, "Brewer's Benedict Arnold," *Firm Foundation* 67 (5 September 1950) 2.

7. Ibid.

8. Armstrong, "Martin, Janes, Whiteside," *Firm Foundation* 45 (12 June 1928) 5. See also Lipscomb, "Nashville Bible School," *Gospel Advocate* 36 (7 June 1894) 362.

9. Whiteside, "Texas Notes," *Gospel Advocate* 51 (17 June 1909) 761.

days duration at each place. But if this same man lives in one community and preaches with any degree of regularity at one place, these custom-bound, traditionalized brethren call him a 'pastor.'"[10] Whiteside inquired "how often must one preach in order to be an evangelist."[11] Savage was so thoroughly demoralized through this exchange he resigned from his editor's chair.[12]

No sooner had the smoke cleared when one of "the most volatile"[13] controversies to face the brotherhood arose, the issue of Sunday Schools. This issue had been simmering for years but with the ascension of N. L. Clark as editor of the *Firm Foundation* it became contentious. Clark declared, "I regard the Sunday School as an innovation. I can't see it in any other light."[14]

At the urging of others, Whiteside engaged Clark in the first written debate on the Sunday School issue.[15] Whiteside insisted that churches need "to teach the children" and countered the anticipated objection, "One says, 'It is the parents duty to teach their children.' Don't get excited my brother . . . if a child were to ask you a question, you would not tell him to run along and ask his parents . . . I know it is my duty to teach my children and I do teach them, but I want all the help I can get. Get the children to come to your Sunday meeting."[16] According to Whiteside it was a false distinction between a written and oral explanation of a biblical text.[17] Nor could he understand why Clark would object to the term "Sunday School" simply because the phrase did not occur in the Bible. Whiteside pointed out that terms like "conversion," "church," "prayer

10. Whiteside, "Evangelists," *Gospel Advocate* 50 (5 March 1908) 147.

11. Whiteside, "Preachers and Preaching," *Firm Foundation* 21 (24 October 1905) 3. See also "Preachers and Preaching," *Firm Foundation* 22 (30 January 1906) 2; and "Preachers and Preaching," *Firm Foundation* 22 (13 February 1906) 4–5.

12. Whiteside would debate this same issue again ten years later with G. A. Trott in the pages of *Burnett's Budget* running from May 1915 and May 1916. Whiteside published a sermon on hermeneutics which addressed this issue, "The Essentials and Incidentals: or, the Law and Circumstances," in *Live Sermons by Live Men*, vol. 1, eds. C. R. Nichol and R. L. Whiteside (Clifton, TX: Mrs. C. R. Nichol Publisher, n.d) 47–64. This work was published in 1916.

13. Earl West, *Search for the Ancient Order*, 2:74.

14. N. L. Clark, "Editorial Notes," *Firm Foundation* 23 (29 January 1907) 4.

15. Kent Ellett, "Non-Sunday School Churches of Christ: Their Origins and Transformation," *Discpliana* 60 (Summer 2000) 52.

16. Whiteside, "Methods of Teaching," *Christian Monitor* 1 (18 August 1906) 1.

17. Whiteside, "The Sunday School Question," *Firm Foundation* 22 (23 October 1906) 4.

meeting," though not in the Bible were used and accepted by Clark.[18] As their exchange developed, Clark, like Savage before him, stepped away from the helm of the *Firm Foundation*.[19]

Whiteside took on the "digressive" churches with equal fervor. When unity became the "buzzword of the day" he noted that churches should not "waste time chasing this Christian union will o' wisp . . . he who fails to follow Christ, to be perfectly united with him severs himself . . . and is himself responsible for all division."[20] Whiteside lent his considerable reputation to the religious census of 1906 by promoting the census among Texas Churches of Christ and working as the Census Bureau's collecting agent. Through the *Firm Foundation* he urged churches to send the address of a responsible member in order to collect the necessary information. He urged churches to file again because some had mistakenly sent data to G. A. Hoffman who represented "digressive" churches.[21]

In the wake of his religious controversies, Whiteside became a man of considerable influence. Large crowds assembled to hear him preach.[22] But it was the caliber of his pen that earned Whiteside accolades from his constituency. George Savage, a former adversary, publicly appealed for Whiteside's contributions to his new journal, the *Christian Monitor*. "Whiteside is doing some splendid writing," Savage exclaimed. The editor stated he was setting aside a page for "Brother Whiteside to fill . . . we want our paper to be, not good, but very good."[23] Not long after Whiteside joined Savage to become the journal's editor and in August 1907 Savage called on Whiteside to take the helm of the journal.[24] Whiteside invited

18. Whiteside, "The Sunday School Question," *Firm Foundation* 23 (19 February 1907) 4.

19. This controversy would rage for years to come however and sadly ended up with a recognizable division by the 1920s.

20. Whiteside, "Unity," *Gospel Guide* 1 (1 April 1905) 28. See also "Union Meeting in Corsicana, Texas," *Gospel Advocate* 50 (16 April 1908) 242–43.

21. Whiteside, "How Many Churches of Christ?" *Firm Foundation* 23 (24 September 1907) 8. See also "How Many Churches," *Firm Foundation* 23 (26 November 1907) 7; and J. W. Shepherd, "United States Church Statistics," *Gospel Advocate* 50 (23 February 1908) 53.

22. "Last Nights Services," *Christian Monitor* 2 (6 July 1907) 2. See also D.S. Ligon's glowing appraisal of Whiteside's earlier ministry, "Meetings in Texas," *Gospel Advocate* 41 (21 September 1899) 607.

23. George W. Savage, "About Bro. Whiteside," *Christian Monitor* 1 (9 March 1907) 9.

24. Savage, "Editorial," *Christian Monitor* 2 (10 August 1907) 4. See also Whiteside, "Golden Nuggets," *Gospel Guide* 3 (October 1907) 26.

Foy E. Wallace, Sr. to join him on the staff but the venture would soon die from the economic woes of the day.[25]

In 1908 the College Church in Abilene invited Whiteside to preach for them and teach in the new college. For the next six years he would serve as teacher, president and vice president of Abilene Christian College. M. Norvel Young noted that Whiteside "brought to the school greater recognition and support from the membership of the Churches of Christ."[26]

J. C. McQuiddy claimed that under Whiteside's influence Abilene Christian College became neither "sectarian nor denominational" but a "thriving Christian" college in the center of Texas.[27] Whiteside's special "Bible Reading and Training Courses" would become the ancestor of the annual lectureship at ACU. He announced that in January and February, 1909, Abilene Christian would offer a special session for preachers. "Many preachers and active church workers realize their need of just such a course as we are now offering. Their opportunities for gaining an education have been limited, and they now feel that they cannot spare the time to attend an entire nine months session. . . . We expect this to be a permanent feature in the school."[28]

When Whiteside stepped aside from his official relationship with Abilene Christian College he worked with Sabinal Christian College. He was asked to take over leadership but declined.[29] He became associated with Harding and Armstrong in editing *The Gospel Herald* in October 1912. Over the next several years Whiteside would be a regular at Cordell Christian College[30] and collaborated with C. R. Nichol on what could

---

25. Whiteside and Foy E. Wallace, "To the Christian Monitor Readers," *Gospel Advocate* 50 (6 February 1908) 89. For more on the fate of the Christian Monitor see Valentine, *Robertson Lafayette Whiteside*, 20–22.

26. M. Norvel Young, *A History of Colleges Established and Controlled by Members of the Churches of Christ* (Kansas City: Old Paths Book Club, 1949) 176.

27. J. C. McQuiddy, "Abilene Christian College," *Gospel Advocate* 51 (9 December 1909) 1544.

28. Whiteside, "Abilene Bible Reading and Training Course," *Firm Foundation* 24 (24 November 1908) 7. See also Jesse P. Sewell, "Abilene Christian College Special Courses for January and February," *Gospel Advocate* 55 (25 December 1913) 1293.

29. Whiteside, "Views and Reviews," Firm Foundation 28 (2 April 1912) 1; See Isaac E. Tackett, "Sabinal Notes," Firm Foundation 26 (25 April 1911) 8.

30. Whiteside, "My Cordell Visit," *Gospel Herald* 2 (18 December 1913) 5; "Program for Thanksgiving Week, Cordell, Okla.," *Gospel Herald* 3 (11 November 1915) 3. See also "Thanksgiving at Harper College," *Christian Worker* 7 (17 November 1921) 7.

pass for a Church of Christ systematic theology, the four-volume *Sound Doctrine*. These books were highly influential being used in hundreds of churches and colleges to train preachers and church leaders. A testament to these books is that George S. Benson used *Sound Doctrine* in his mission work in China[31] and years later Cled Wallace confessed "without shame" that he "soaked up like a sponge" *Sound Doctrine* which were "in my grip along with my Bible" during gospel meetings.[32] Whiteside was recognized among his peers for his expressive thought and confidence to promote his positions in the premillennial fight and the flowering of the Texas Tradition.

Within the first decade of the twentieth century Whiteside had become well established as a leader among Texas Churches of Christ. This is evident from Nichol's short biographical sketch in *Gospel Preachers Who Blazed the Trail* (1911) where he labeled Whiteside the "Lipscomb of Texas." When Armstrong introduced Whiteside as the editor of the *Gospel Herald* he also referred to him as the "Lipscomb of Texas."[33] Knowing the stature of Lipscomb helps us appreciate the loftiness of this appellation bestowed upon Whiteside. But it was not because of his theology that Whiteside became known as the Lipscomb of Texas. Indeed, Whiteside eventually disagreed with all the "unique" features of the Nashville Bible School Tradition helping pave the way for a "Texas Consensus" that permeated the Churches of Christ through the mid-20th century. Foy E. Wallace Jr., who regarded Whiteside as his "mentor"[34] complimented him this way,

> He is known to the reading members of the church as one of the ablest writers in the brotherhood. He is in every sense a Bible scholar, and his writings have a depth of thought carried in a simplicity of style peculiar to R. L. Whiteside. In this respect he

31. George S. Benson, "Sound Doctrine for the Chinese," *Gospel Advocate* 71 (24 January 1929) 77. See also C. R. Nichol, "A Letter from China," *Gospel Advocate* 71 (21 March 1929) 271.

32. Cled Wallace, "Dealing in Personalities," *Gospel Guardian* 2 (15 February 1951) 1, 13.

33. Armstrong, "Editorial," *Gospel Herald* 1 (31 October 1912) 4. Whiteside was also dubbed the "Lipscomb of Texas" in *The Whiteside-Clark Discussion*, 5.

34. Foy E. Wallace, Jr. *The Christian and the Government* (Nashville: Foy E. Wallace, Jr. Publications, 1968) 46.

has been compared by thoughtful and discriminating brethren to the term "Lipscomb."[35]

Lipscomb's Pacifistic Apocalyptic Worldview

David Lipscomb's little classic *Civil Government*,[36] birthed in the aftermath of the Civil War, formed the heartbeat of the worldview of the Nashville Bible School Tradition. This work envisioned a radical apocalyptic interpretation of life in the present, conceived as being lived in the shadow of God's all consuming in-breaking kingdom. The same radical apocalyptic orientation under girded Harding's theological worldview.[37]

According to the scheme embraced by the founders of the Nashville Bible School, God created humanity out of his gracious love to enlarge his royal family. Adam and Eve, as proto-typical humans, were to be trained in the art of ruling in order to share regency with God. Yet humanity rejected God's gracious reign and sought to establish a rival government apart from that of God's. Thus, humanity turned God's creation over to Satan. As a result of this tragic turn of events the earth knew evil and suffering while envy, hate and war became humanity's lot.

Yet, the Lord sought to "deliver the earth from Satan, and destroy his hosts."[38] God had been progressively reclaiming his creation, first through Israel and supremely in the work of Christ culminating in the destruction of rival human kingdoms.

> The object of God's dealing with man, and especially the mission of Christ to the earth, was to rescue the world from the rule and dominion of the evil one, from the ruin into which it had fallen through sin, and to rehabilitate it with the dignity and the glory it had when it came from the hand of God.[39]

35. Foy E. Wallace, Jr., "Editorial," *Gospel Advocate* 73 (19 November 1931) 1444.

36. Lipscomb, *Civil Government: Its Origin, Mission, and Destiny, and the Christian's Relation to It* (Nashville: McQuiddy Printing, 1913).

37. See especially Harding, "The Kingdom of Christ vs. The Kingdoms of Satan," *The Way* 5 (15 October 1903) 929–31. Harding endorsed Lipscomb's *Civil Government* without reservation, "Civil Government is the best book on the subject of the Christian's duty to civil government in the world, so far as I know." "Books," *The Way* 2 (May 1900) 71.

38. Ibid., 930.

39. Lipscomb, *Salvation from Sin* (Nashville: McQuiddy, 1913) 114. See also Lipscomb, *Civil Government*, 12–13.

Or again,

> The Holy Spirit came to earth to . . . guide that kingdom to its future growth, to its final and perfect development, when the kingdoms of the earth shall become the kingdom of God and his Christ, when the will of God shall be done on earth as it is in heaven, and when earth itself shall become heaven and God shall dwell with his people and be their God and they shall be his people.[40]

It might be helpful to graph this Harding-Lipscomb perspective on salvation history in the following manner:

Creation (Eden)   Renewed Earth (God's Reign)

Israel   Sabbath Rest/Millennium

Incarnation/Age of the Spirit

This structure is not just an "end time" scenario for the Nashville duo but rather fills and provides coherence to Lipscomb's entire theological perspective. God's kingdom and rival human kingdoms exist like "matter" and "anti-matter" in a science fiction novel. The kingdom of God will come, and is coming, not to simply break apart but to totally "*consume them, the last vestige of them.*"[41] Human kingdoms are satanic in origin and doomed to destruction. Lipscomb explained, "Every act of affiliation, partnership, friendship or treaty with them was regarded and punished as treason against God. The spirit of complete antagonism, and the wide separation between the two, were marked, emphasized and fostered by Almighty God."[42]

As a result of their theology Lipscomb and Harding were not simply pacifists but apocalyptic pacifists. Their theology of God's kingdom led them to "avoid adulterous alliance[s]" with the fallen governments around them.[43] They made concrete application of their theological tenant to the Monroe Doctrine approximately the same time R. L. Whiteside was finishing his education at Nashville Bible School.

From 1895 to 1896, the United States used the Monroe Doctrine to interfere in a dispute between Britain and Venezuela. Lipscomb thought it ironic that Americans of all persuasions, Republicans and Democrats,

40. Lipscomb, "The Kingdom of God," *Gospel Advocate* 45 (21 May 1903) 328.

41. Lipscomb, *Civil Government*, 27. See also pp. 28 and 83.

42. Ibid., 89.

43. Lipscomb, "An Explanation," *Gospel Advocate* 8 (3 July 1866) 427.

had joined the war wagon in support of America's foreign policy. Since the English posed no legitimate threat to American security, only mindless "Christian patriotism" moved people to embrace the Monroe Doctrine. Lipscomb expressed a radically different perspective,

> When the leading lights among politicians begin to advocate war in defense of the Monroe doctrine it is high time for the chief luminaries in the church of God to commence preaching peace on earth and good will among men in defense of the doctrine of the Sermon on the Mount. And if the government of the United States decides to go to war to uphold the Monroe doctrine, the disciples of Christ should determine with equal firmness to take no part in the bloody business in order to maintain the principles and spirit of the doctrine of Christ.[44]

With rhetorical irony Lipscomb asked, "Should the Christian patriots of America kill the Christians of England because they are patriots too?"[45]

The crises passed and war with England never materialized. However, such was not the case with Spain in 1898. Though many humanitarian reasons were put forth to justify conflict with Spain, Lipscomb believed the real reason for the war was the same as all wars. Since politicians use war to further personal agendas and the rich use war to make money and the poor will kill and be killed, "Christians have no part nor lot in such affairs."[46]

According to Lipscomb the United States had charted a course that was antithetical to Jesus. When a person embraces the Messiah, Lipscomb wrote, the values of Jesus are also embraced. "This is what being a Christian means," he declared.[47] Since every Christian is "pledged" to do what Jesus would do if he were present, Lipscomb asked his readers, "Would Jesus join the army of the United States to fight Spain, or join the army of Spain to fight the United States? Would he kill and destroy men?"[48]

According to his own testimony, during his student days Whiteside embraced the pacifistic theology of Lipscomb and Harding. He was "as dogmatic as any in opposition to voting and holding office."[49] But, during

44. Lipscomb, "From the Papers," *Gospel Advocate* 38 (9 January 1896) 17.

45. Lipscomb, "The Monroe Doctrine," *Gospel Advocate* 38 (16 January 1896) 37.

46. Ibid.

47. Lipscomb, "War-Is Spirit," *Gospel Advocate* 40 (28 April 1898) 269.

48. Ibid.

49. Whiteside, "The War Question Again," *Gospel Advocate* 78 (23 July 1936) 702; "Concerning War," *Bible Banner* 5 (June 1943) 1.

Whiteside's 1895 break in his education he met the man who overturned his pacifism, G. G. Taylor. Indeed when Whiteside returned to finish his education at the Nashville Bible School, Harding made it known he was looking for a man to expose the students to a different view point but did not know anyone. Whiteside quoted Harding, "We would like to have some able man who believes it right for Christians to take part in the affairs of civil government to give some lectures on that side, but we don't know who to get."[50] Thus at Whiteside's suggestion, Harding secured Taylor who became a regular in offering a dissenting voice in Nashville. Whiteside remembered "Brother Lipscomb heard all that Brother Taylor had to say, and so did Brother Harding, and no man ever received a more courteous hearing."[51]

Whiteside always held his teachers in Nashville in the highest personal regard although he came to disagree strongly on virtually every point of the Nashville Bible School Tradition.[52]

R. L. Whiteside's New Theology of Government

During the opening decades of the twentieth century there was a deep struggle for the identity of the Churches of Christ. They had been slowly separating from the "digressive" Disciples but what kind of people would they be? Streams flowed from Nashville, Texas and north of the Ohio. The apocalyptic tradition nurtured by Lipscomb and Harding came under frontal assault first through Harding's Holy Spirit debates with J. C. Holloway (1905),[53] Harding's debate with L. S. White over special providence (1910)[54] and finally the war on Boll.[55] Already under attack, pacifism was just one more feature of the Nashville Bible School Tradition to retreat in the early years of the twentieth century.[56] In many

---

50. Whiteside, "The Memory of Three Great Men," *Bible Banner* 6 (May 1944) 6.

51. Ibid.

52. See Whiteside's respectful reflection on Lipscomb and E. G. Sewell after a visit to Nashville in 1905, "The Work in Tennessee," *Firm Foundation* 21 (24 October 1905) 6.

53. See John Mark Hicks and Bobby Valentine, *Kingdom Come*, 59–74. Cf. Bobby Valentine, "Harding's Theology of the Indwelling Holy Spirit: Highlighted by His Discussion with Dr. J. C. Holloway," Christian Scholar's Conference Papers, 1999.

54. Ibid, 43–57. Cf. Richard T. Hughes, *Reviving the Ancient Faith: The Story of Churches of Christ in America* (Grand Rapids: Eerdmans, 1996) 139–40.

55. Ibid, 163–77; Cf. Hughes, *Reviving the Ancient Faith*, 141ff.

56. Professor Mike Casey has greatly expanded our understanding of the demise of pacifism among Churches of Christ. See his "From Pacifism to Patriotism: The Emergence

ways Whiteside's transition to vocal opposition to Lipscomb's pacifism is a microcosm of the journey of the Churches of Christ.

As the United States entered into World War I immense social pressure was put on Americans to line up and conform. The conflict in Europe was cast as a struggle between light and darkness, virtue against sin, God against the Devil. Michael Casey noted that by the time the US entered the war there was a "xenophobic hatred of anything German."[57]

Yet those who with an apocalyptic heartbeat remembered well the lessons of Lipscomb and Harding. A mere three weeks after the declaration of war, Samuel P. Pittman stood before an audience in Murfreesboro, Tennessee and delivered a classic discourse on "My Kingdom Not Of This World."[58] Pittman declared "the kingdoms of this world—they must *fall*."[59] Countering the claim that horrible times demand horrible actions he declared, "If there ever was a time when man was justifiable in taking the sword, it would have been when the apostle took his sword from its sheath in the garden of Gethsemane."[60] But, Jesus rebuked Peter rather than justified him.

The tenacity of apocalyptic pacifism in the face of severe adversity is the witness of Armstrong and the demise of Cordell Christian College.[61] Trouble brewed when faculty member S. A. Bell published an article perceived as seditious in *The Gospel Herald*. On July 23, 1918 the school was informed that it would be "[R]eorganized and will unreservedly conform to all military policies and requirements of the government in the present war. All 'doctrines or teaching' in the school must 'comply strictly and

---

of Civil Religion in Churches of Christ During World War I," *Mennonite Quarterly Review* 66 (July 1992) 376–90; "From Religious Outsiders to Insiders: The Rise and Fall of Pacifism in Churches of Christ," *Journal of Church and State* 44 (2002) 455–75; "The Closing of Cordell Christian College: A Microcosm of American Intolerance during World War I," *Chronicles of Oklahoma* 76 (Spring 1998) 20–37; and with Michael A. Jordan, "Free Speech in a Time of War: Government Surveillance of Churches of Christ in World War I," *Free Speech Yearbook* 34 (1996) 102–11.

57. Casey and Jordan, "Free Speech in a Time of War," 103.

58. *Murfreesboro Addresses: Delivered at Murfreesboro, Tenn. Covering a Period of Eight Days from April 26 to May 6, 1917* (Cincinnati: Rowe, 1917) 87–99.

59. Ibid., 96. Pittman's emphasis.

60. Ibid., 97.

61. See Hicks and Valentine, *Kingdom Come*, 145–61; Cf. Michael W. Casey, "The Closing of Cordell Christian College." Armstrong also published an essay on "Noncombatant Service," *Apostolic Way* (June 1918) 424.

to the fullest extent with the military policy of the government."[62] The faculty and board of Cordell became a martyr to conviction however and the school closed its doors rather than cave into a human government. Austin McGary viewed the pacifist tradition coming out of Nashville with disdain. "Nashville, Tennessee is the headquarters of that character of slackery. These sanctimonious fanatics claim that their 'citizenship is in heaven' in such an exclusive sense as will not admit of their being citizens of any nation."[63]

With many traditional venues for expressing countercultural points of view closed, Churches of Christ did not address the issue openly until after World War I. Indeed, Whiteside apparently liked the "silence" government imposed upon the pacifists. He wrote that a few were assuming the role of "prosecuting attorney" in trying to "convict some one on his war record."[64] Compelled to defend those who fought in the war, Whiteside challenged the pacifist preachers, "Have an honest interview with yourself. Perhaps you will then feel more like repenting in humility than assuming your war record is so superior that you can now ... attack someone else's."[65]

Whiteside defended war veterans because he had come to view the government in a different light than Lipscomb and Harding. God not only ordained government God used government as his "minister."[66] Contrary to Lipscomb's position in *Civil Government*, he argued that Romans 13 demonstrates that God's government and human government are not antagonistic.[67] As such Christians were the "most law-abiding" citizen in the community.[68] Whiteside labeled pacifists "anarchists" and any one who willingly disobeyed a law were rebelling against God. "It is a Christian's duty to obey the laws of his government."[69] The rebellious spirit of con-

62. Casey, "Closing of Cordell Christian College," 29.

63. Cited in Flavil Hall, "Field Notes and Helpful Thoughts," *Christian Leader* (6 November 1917) 6.

64. Whiteside, "What About Your War Record," *Gospel Advocate* 62 (28 October 1920) 1048.

65. Ibid.

66. Whiteside, *Annual Lesson Commentary on Bible School Lessons,* 1944 (Nashville: Gospel Advocate, 1943) 264.

67. Whiteside, *A New Commentary on Paul's Letter to the Saints at Rome* (Denton, TX: Inys Whiteside Publisher, 1945) 257–59.

68. Ibid., 263.

69. Whiteside, "Christianity and Democracy," *Gospel Advocate* 86 (9 November 1944) 732.

scientious objection was "the essence of anarchy" and no Christian can "afford to be guilty of dishonorable conduct toward anyone, especially toward the rulers of his country."[70] For Whiteside "obedience to civil authorities is a fundamental requirement of the gospel."[71]

While Whiteside defended the veterans, R. F. Duckworth remembered the young men who sat in prison rather than serve in the military. He believed churches should secure official government recognition as a "peace church." When Whiteside was asked "should not a Church of Christ come out openly against war?" he claimed that if a congregation published articles in opposition to war it had created a creed.[72] Harvey Riggs disagreed, "Is it creed making to ask to be excused from violating one's conscience?" He added,

> Military service is the one thing men may be forced to do legally, while believing it to be wrong. Think it over: the law forces no one to drink, gamble, prize fight, or even to 'follow the multitude' to such affairs, while many citizens and church members exercise their personal liberty to do all. No one has professional or political activity forced upon him, and a man is even excused from jury service as a 'conscientious objector.'[73]

For Whiteside, thinkers like Lipscomb, Harding, Riggs and others were not discriminating enough. A failure to make a distinction between "wars of aggression" and "wars of defense" was the root of the argument.[74] If it was wrong to defend the constitution of the United States, ratcheting up the rhetoric, Whiteside opined, then one must also stand "idly by while a fiend raped and murdered his wife or daughter."[75]

With the rumblings of war in 1930s Europe the "c.o." issue became one of the "most controversial and explosive" issues among Churches of Christ.[76] For many, pacifism was linked with premillennialism. O. C.

70. Whiteside, *Annual Lesson Commentary on the Bible*, 1944, 269–70.

71. Whiteside, *A New Commentary*, 258.

72. Whiteside, "War," *Gospel Advocate* 76 (7 June 1934) 549.

73. Harvey W. Riggs, "Faith, Conscience, and War," *Gospel Advocate* 78 (16 July 1936) 681.

74. Whiteside, "The Christians Duty as to War," *Gospel Advocate* 78 (18 June 1936) 585; "The War Question Again," *Gospel Advocate* 78 (23 July 1936) 702.

75. Whiteside, "Christians Duty as to War," 585.

76. Michael W. Casey, "The Courage of Conscience: The Conscientious Objectors of World War II and the Churches of Christ," Christian Scholars Conference, Lipscomb University, 1991, p. 6.

Lambert, who claimed to have sat at the feet of Lipscomb, published a blistering attack upon him.[77] Lambert, as did others, believed he found "Russellism" throughout *Civil Government*. So disturbing was Lipscomb's small book to Lambert that he suggested "we call all of them in and burn them."[78] Foy E. Wallace, Jr. was not "only amazed but ashamed that any recognized leader in churches of Christ, past or present, should espouse and promote such a doctrine."[79] Pacifism had become an embarrassment for many leaders among Churches of Christ.

Whiteside found his own distaste for pacifism intensified by pacifists themselves. H. Leo Boles was asked in the pages of the *Gospel Advocate* if it was biblical to pray for victory over the enemy. Boles responded negatively, citing the example of Jesus in the Garden of Gethsemane as the proper attitude for the Christian by praying that "God's will be done."

Whiteside was incredulous! Speaking to pacifists in general, he said "I do not see how they can think that any conclusion arrived at by force of arms can not be a just conclusion." Not only did Whiteside gladly affirm that he desired victory over the Germans and Japanese but that he prayed for it. He exhorted Boles to "free himself from any such unsavory position."[80]

In a revealing essay written in 1934, and published several times by Whiteside, he bitterly attacked pacifism as a hiding place for false doctrine and even described it as a cult. "The design of this treatise is to show that the doctrine of pacifism is a hiding place of false doctrine, and to answer with logic and scripture the claims and the creed of this nondescript religio-politico cult, showing the views to be unethical and unbiblical and in all respects untrue."[81] Whiteside further described conscientious objectors as "a generation of rebels against the government,

---

77. John T. Lewis disputes this claim. He reproduces a letter from H. Leo Boles that shows Lambert entered into the Nashville Bible School in September 1917 while Lipscomb died on November 11, 1917. See *The Christian and Government or A Review of the Bible Banner's Position on Christians Going to War* (Birmingham, AL: John T. Lewis, 1945) 9.

78. O. C. Lambert, "The Lipscomb Theory of Civil Government," *Bible Banner* 6 (October 1943) 3.

79. Foy E. Wallace Jr. "Lipscomb Theory of Civil Government," *Bible Banner* 6 (October 1943) 5.

80. R. L. Whiteside, "Prayer During War," *Bible Banner* 7 (September 1944) 1, 5.

81. R. L. Whiteside as quoted in Foy E. Wallace Jr., *The Christian and the Government* (Nashville: Foy E. Wallace, Jr. Publications, 1968) 67. This article appeared as "Logic—The Argumentum Ad Hominem," *Gospel Advocate* 75 (7 December 1933) 1164–65; and "Logic—Argumentum Ad Hominem," *Bible Banner* 6 (May 1944) 7.

a generation of anarchists." Being a pacifist in the face of national crises did not make one a paragon of faith to Whiteside. Rather "mortal fear and lack of trust in the cause of right make cowards of men, and this is mistaken for conscientious objection"[82]

Lipscomb vs. R. L. Whiteside: Conclusions

Lipscomb had embraced a radical countercultural stance largely because of his apocalyptic worldview. The kingdom of God was central to his understanding of the mission of God in creation and redemption. His apocalyptic radicalism led him to embrace the Sermon on the Mount as central to the life of the church. It was the Spirit of Christ that pervaded the Sermon. If we reject the values of Christ's sermon, Lipscomb declared, "we are not and cannot be children of our Father which is in heaven."[83] When the Sermon is lost on the church "the spirit of Christ is driven out of the church and the spirit of the world takes its abode in it."[84]

H. Leo Boles had written that the true spirit of Christianity was "altruistic." "The altruistic spirit is a spirit of Christianity . . . . Vicarious suffering must be endured in order to live the Christian life."[85] Whiteside took a very different point of view. We are not called to altruism, but "self-preservation." "The law of self-preservation is embedded in our nature; God made us that way for our own good. We may never feel the need of resisting evil men further than to lock our doors; . . . . Self-preservation is a law of our own being—it is a God-given law. I cannot believe that God is the author of two conflicting laws."[86] Whereas Lipscomb pointed to the essential nature of the Sermon on the Mount, Whiteside down played the words of Jesus. In commenting on how one is to love his neighbor Whiteside stated tersely "It is impossible for him to have the same feel-

---

82. Ibid., 68. Whiteside believed that pacifists were dangerous to Christianity and America. He criticized James D. Bales for defending the rights of Jehovah Witnesses as conscientious objectors during World War II, see "This Government and Jehovah Witnesses," *Gospel Advocate* 84 (30 April 1942) 416, 428.

83. Lipscomb, *Civil Government*, 133–34.

84. Ibid., 135.

85. H. Leo Boles, "Christian Nonresistance," *Gospel Advocate* 78 (18 June 1936) 602.

86. R. L. Whiteside, "Concerning War," *Bible Banner* 5 (June 1943) 1. See John T. Lewis' response to Whiteside in *The Christian and The Government*, 163–70. Whiteside played a significant role in Lewis' work.

ings toward a neighbor, or an enemy, that he has toward the members of his own family, and God does not require him to have such . . . ."[87]

Texans needed their own David Lipscomb and found him in R. L. Whiteside. Like his Nashville counterpart he spoke the language of the average man and woman in the pew. He became a leader and trainer of preachers among whom Cled Wallace and Foy E. Wallace Jr. are two of his most famous protégés. Through writing hundreds of articles he was able to shape opinions on everything from hermeneutics to the indwelling of the Holy Spirit to pacifism. In the eyes of his comrades in arms he was a giant of spiritual wisdom. When he passed into his reward, Foy E. Wallace Jr. spoke these words, "[T]he inimitable R. L. Whiteside, who was more than any other teacher my mentor and model to me, and who was more responsible than any other for changes that were made from earlier years to the later years in my own thought and study."[88] No doubt many felt the same.

---

87. Whiteside, "Christianity and Democracy," 732.
88. Foy E. Wallace, Jr., *The Christian and the Government*, 46.

PART II

Studies in Rhetoric and Homiletics

9

Conversation as a Resource for Character Formation in Proverbs

DAVE BLAND

Mike Casey and I first met while we were in graduate school at Abilene Christian University in the late 1970s. At the time we were both teaching introduction to speech classes as teaching assistants. Over the subsequent years, Mike established a reputation as a gifted scholar, one who was committed to excellence. As a rhetorician Mike believed that a good person speaking and writing well could influence the lives of others for better. Influencing others for good was what drove Mike to the careful and thoughtful research he undertook. As a researcher he made sure he understood and represented others' ideas with integrity. Mike embodied integrity in all his work and relationships.

Mike enjoyed good conversation. He wanted to learn from others' insights. He challenged the perspectives of others and in return was willing for others to challenge his ideas. What follows is a treatment of the essential role dialogue plays in the shaping of moral character as described by the sages in Proverbs. Even though the field of biblical wisdom was not Mike's area of study, he did know and appreciated the value of conversation. Mike always made a good conversation partner.

Introduction

Biblical scholarship and theology have made worthwhile contributions in identifying the value of wisdom for character development.[1] Still there

1. For example, see William P. Brown, *Character in Crisis: A Fresh Approach to the*

remains a tendency for some contemporary scholars to ignore the book of Proverbs as a viable resource in this regard. James Crenshaw makes the pronouncement that the "vast majority of proverbial sayings tends toward the banal, hardly commending themselves as worthy of careful study by serious students."[2] Theologian William Willimon announces, "Generally, I dislike the book of Proverbs with its lack of theological content, its long lists of platitudinous advice, its 'do this' and 'don't do that.' Pick up your socks. Be nice to salesclerks. It doesn't hurt to be nice. Proverbs is something like being trapped on a long road trip with your mother, or at least with William Bennett."[3]

As scholars, educators, and even political leaders continue their quest to identify those genres that provide vital resources for shaping character, Proverbs is all too often presumed beyond moral resuscitation. However, I believe that the autopsy report is highly premature.

Character and Proverbs

I would like to argue that the book of Proverbs contributes a healthy understanding to the subject of character and the process of character development. It is a welcome sight to see scholarship beginning to explore more in depth the dimension of character formation as developed in Proverbs and wisdom material.[4] According to Michael V. Fox, this quality of character is the thicker, richer meaning of wisdom.[5] He observes, "Proverbs consistently applies the word *hokmah* to wisdom as manifest in the skill and knowledge of right living" in the ethical and pragmatic senses.[6] By its definition wisdom is the ability to develop expertise in living responsibly.[7] Near the end of his work, Fox states wisdom's objec-

---

Wisdom Literature of the Old Testament (Grand Rapids: Eerdmans, 1996). See also Alyce M. Mckenzie, *Hear and Be Wise: Becoming a Teacher and Preacher of Wisdom* (Nashville: Abingdon, 2004).

2. James L. Crenshaw, *Education in Ancient Israel: Across the Deadening Silence*, Anchor Bible Reference Library (New York: Doubleday, 1998) 232.

3. William H. Willimon, *Pastor: The Theology and Practice of Ordained Ministry* (Nashville: Abingdon, 2002) 255–56.

4. Brown, *Character in Crisis*, viii. Crenshaw affirms the same goal: "The goal of all wisdom was the formation of character"; *Old Testament Wisdom: An Introduction*, rev. ed. (Louisville: Westminster John Knox, 1998) 3.

5. Michael V. Fox, *Proverbs 1–9*, Anchor Bible 18A (New York: Doubleday, 2000) 29.

6. Ibid., 33.

7. Fox, *Proverbs 1–9*, 32.

tive succinctly, "And fostering moral character, it is no overstatement to say, is at all times the greatest goal of education."[8] Proverbs' interest in character is pragmatic. It directs character to its implementation in life and gives character rigor, keeping it from becoming just another "bog of blessed assurance."[9] Proverbs is Scripture's effort to put character in working clothes.[10] Its goal is to develop people of mature moral character. The process is not easy or simple but the end product is worth more than the finest silver.

There are many resources the sages used to help foster character formation. In this essay I want to explore the role conversation plays in achieving this goal. However before I address the use of conversation, I must briefly place it in the context of two broader perspectives. First, we must understand the conversation in which the sages engage is a part of a larger theological context. Second, their conversation is a part of the bigger process of character formation.

The Theological Context of Conversation

Wisdom is relational. The process of character formation takes place in the context of relationships. In coming into relationship with God and becoming involved in the lives of others, character takes shape.

The process is first and foremost grounded in the sage's relationship with God, that is, in the fear of the Lord. The introductory poem in Proverbs (1:1–7) announces this foundational quality by quoting one of the most repeated lines in the book: "The fear of the Lord is the beginning of knowledge" (v. 7a; "knowledge" and "wisdom" in Proverbs are often used synonymously; cf. v. 7b). That the fear of the Lord is the *beginning* of wisdom means that without this relationship one will never acquire true wisdom or character. This "beginning" is not in the *horizontal* sense of missing the first tire in an obstacle course and just skipping to the next. Rather it is in the *vertical* sense of a ladder. If a person misses the first step of the ladder then progress cannot be made to the next step.[11] What the

8. Ibid., 348.

9. This is a phrase used by Fred B. Craddock in, "The New Homiletic for Latecomers: Suggestions for Preaching from Mark," eds. David Fleer and Dave Bland, *Preaching Mark's Unsettling Messiah* (St. Louis: Chalice, 2006) 28.

10. Derek Kidner, *The Proverbs: An Introduction and Commentary*, Tyndale Old Testament Commentaries (Downers Grove, IL: Tyndale, 1964) 35.

11. Bruce K. Waltke, *The Book of Proverbs: Chapters 1–15*, New International Commentary on the Old Testament (Grand Rapids: Eerdmans, 2004) 181.

letters of the alphabet are to reading and notes to music, the fear of the Lord is to wisdom.[12] In wisdom's world the fear of the Lord means that one lives life focused not on self but on seeking God (Prov 3:5–7).[13]

The sages' use of conversation is more clearly understood in this theological context. Out of a relationship with Yahweh, one learns to live responsibly with others. Therefore the conversation in which the sages engage does not create an ethical lifestyle out of nothing. Rather out of their relationship with Yahweh, conversation enables the sages to develop a deeper understanding of the kind of lifestyle Yahweh calls them to live and to more faithfully embody that lifestyle. Conversation is a resource out of which the sages discover God's will.

The Process of Character Formation In Proverbs

The book of Proverbs begins with the image of a gang, which embodies the vices of greed and violence (1:8–19). They steal, abuse, and mistreat others in order to selfishly gain wealth for themselves (vv. 10–14). They are the fools, the antitype of character. Ultimately, their selfish lifestyle results in their own downfall; they "kill themselves" (v. 18, NRSV). The sage concludes with this observation, "Such is the end of all who are greedy for gain; it takes away the life of its possessors" (v. 19). Proverbs thus begins with a full-blown image of a group that is void of moral character.

From this opening scenario, the book works its way through a plethora of instructions, sayings, and admonitions building to the final image in chapter 31:10-31, the woman of noble character. This woman of noble character is wisdom incarnated. Her life is the culmination of a life focused on *becoming*. She serves, she shows compassion, instructs, and leads. She demonstrates kindness. Her diligent pursuit of wisdom shapes her into God's woman. Yet at the same time the wisdom she acquires is ultimately a gift from God (Prov 2:6-8; 1 Kgs 3:9; James 1:5). She is the model for all (men and women) who, by God's grace, desire to become what God wants them to be. It is the journey of life.

In Proverbs the journey from the gang to the woman of noble character is arduous. The sages do not orchestrate the journey in a nice step-by-step process. Rather these chapters are a storehouse of rich rhetorical

---

12. Ibid.

13. Diogenes Allen, "Wisdom of the World and God's," *Princeton Seminary Bulletin* 23 (2002) 197.

forms and a variety of images and themes that often times stand in tension and even blatantly contradict one another. Proverbs is not a "how to" manual; it is a "how to be" book. That is, the focus is on character and not on lists or rules and regulations. For faith communities, such a perspective implies that the most important question they must ask is not, "What are we doing?" but "Who are we becoming?" The pedagogy of Proverbs is complex and demanding but so is the process of building character. Such a goal remains at the center of concern for the sages. Even though, as I have said, the sages use many different tools to accomplish the goal of character formation in the life of a student, I want to focus on their use of vigorous verbal conversation. It is to this focus that I now turn.

Talk as a Tool for Character Development

In order to challenge students to grow, the sages engage in the process of verbal conversation between individuals. Such conversation assumes the involvement of the faith community whose investment in the process is essential for growth. One of the most popular views today, however, is that one attains wisdom through a lifetime of quiet meditation. The book of Proverbs would not deny the important place of time spent in personal reflection. But that is not the center of focus for attaining wisdom. Notice where Woman Wisdom resides when first introduced in the book. She dwells in the street, at the marketplace, and in the city gate (Prov. 1:20–33). Wisdom finds herself in a city teeming and bustling with the traffic of human life. According to Proverbs, wisdom is acquired at the hub of human activity. This implies that wisdom is not primarily cerebral; it is first and foremost relational. Through entering into relationship with Yahweh (1:7), with parents (1:8; 13:1), with one's spouse (5:18; 18:22; 31:10-31), and with the wise (20:18; 27:17), the student gains wisdom and thus the resources necessary for moral development.

That is why Proverbs places such a heavy emphasis on the value of dialogue. The fool, in contrast, is the one who is "wise in his own eyes" (3:7; 26:5). Fools rely exclusively on self-evaluation and as a result remain morally inept. The wise, however, do not depend solely on their own perceptions but rely heavily on the counsel of others. The book of Proverbs makes this clear: "Without counsel, plans go wrong, but with many advisers they succeed" (15:22). Wisdom teachers do not give pat answers to perplexing issues of life. Rather students engage in conversation with the community and out of that dialogue make decisions, carry out actions, and create moral order. Students are not shaped in a cookie-cutter fashion.

Wisdom believes that two heads are better than one. Because of a high regard for human ingenuity, the wise seek out the insights of others, whether from other cultures or from the wise in their own communities. Sometimes in these encounters talk goes awry; relationships turn dysfunctional. However, when individuals and communities seek out the best in others, wisdom is acquired, new insights are gained, and character takes shape. Character is shaped and refined in the rigor of exchange between two interlocutors.

Conversation and Conflict

In studying sapiential instruction, one discovers that conversation and conflict are close cousins. Character development flourishes only in a community where healthy confrontation exists. Without the rigors of such an environment, individual character becomes undisciplined, anemic, and even destructive to community life. The sages believe strongly in the principle that "iron sharpens iron" when it comes to human conversation (27:17). Relationships thrive on a healthy dose of constructive conflict.

The proverbs clustered in chapter 27 speak to this phenomenon. Many describe the dialogue between two individuals; many of them also refer to the "friend" or "neighbor" (vv. 5, 6, 9,[14] 10, 14, 17, and 19). As a specific example, I want to explore verses 14-19. The proverbs in this text portray both constructive and destructive verbal exchange between two individuals:

> v. 14   Whoever blesses a neighbor[15] with a loud voice,
>   rising early in the morning,
>   will be counted as cursing.

> v. 15   A continual dripping on a rainy day
>   and a contentious wife are alike;

14. Verse 9b is problematic, as comparing various translations will indicate. The text literally reads "sweetness of his friend from the counsel of soul." The LXX does not believe the line stands in good antithetic relationship to 9a so it emends the text to read, "but the inner being is torn down by trouble," which the NRSV adopts as its reading. But the NIV offers a good interpretation in trying to make sense of the text as it stands: "and the pleasantness of one's friend springs from his earnest counsel." The verse is an analogy. The enjoyment received from the sweet aroma of perfume is compared to the pleasant counsel received from a friend.

15. The word can be translated either "neighbor" or "friend."

v. 16 to restrain her is to restrain the wind
or to grasp oil in the right hand.

v. 17 Iron sharpens iron,
and one person[16] sharpens the wits of another.

v. 19 Just as water reflects the face,
so one human heart reflects another.[17]

This cluster of proverbs brims with tension and vignettes of spirited talk. There are times when dialogue with others results in harm. Such is the case with the one who blesses a neighbor with a loud voice early in the morning. The blessing ends up being a curse. For one reason, the person blesses in a loud voice. That is, perhaps the person does it for show. For another, the blessing is offered early in the morning, an inappropriate time. What the friend expresses is positive. The friend extends greetings to the neighbor, offering "encouragement." The problem is, the timing is off! For the sage, timing determines the appropriateness of a word or deed. Because of the friend's poor timing, his or her words become irritating, perhaps abusive; the blessing turns to a curse. The exhilarating songs and words of the early riser translate into nothing more than clanging cymbals to the late sleeper. The friend disguises insults with a lighthearted demeanor. Beneath the image of the early-morning riser lies a larger issue. It is the churlish attitude of tactlessness toward others. Such insensitivity creates dysfunctional discourse.

Not only are such destructive patterns of communication developed among friends, they also spring up in the home. Husbands and wives can develop communication patterns that eventually lead to incessant quarreling. Verses 15 and 16 compose one proverb that presents a picture of dysfunctional dialogue in the family. It is the infamous image of the contentious spouse. The image is not, however, of a leaky faucet but of a more serious nature, a leaky roof.[18] Thus such contentiousness is not simply a nuisance; it can potentially destroy a whole house. These two images, the image of the insensitive friend and that of the contentious spouse, depict conversation gone awry. This kind of communication becomes an obstacle in the process of character formation.

16. The same word is used here that is translated "neighbor" in v. 14.

17. Literally this verse translates: "As water, the face unto the face, so the heart of man to man."

18. Compare this with the image in 19:13. See also Ecclesiastes 10:18.

In contrast, healthy conversation creates a more morally responsible community. Such dialogue is depicted in the following images in verses 17 and 19:

> v. 17   Iron sharpens iron,
> and one person[19] sharpens the wits of another.

> v. 19   Just as water reflects the face,
> so one human heart reflects another.

The first line of verse 17 contains an old saw: "Iron sharpens iron." The figure portrays someone using metal to sharpen a knife or sword or a farming implement. The metaphor of steel rubbing against steel in the first line is applied in the second line to the abrasion or friction necessary for personal and moral growth.

As iron sharpens iron, so one friend sharpens another. The principle is at work, for example, in the relationship between spouses in the home or colleagues at work or students in a class. Each challenges the other to grow and stretch their mental capacities. The process requires individuals to exercise the mind in the disciplined work of dialoguing, listening, thinking, reflecting, and sharing. When one engages the intellect in interacting with others over issues that matter, mental faculties sharpen.

The principle of iron sharpening iron is a necessary part of physical, mental, and moral development. But the image of iron sharpening iron is not an isolated image in this text. The proverb in verse 19 compliments it: "Just as water reflects the face, so one human heart reflects another." This proverb, like many, is intentionally ambiguous, though more cryptic than most.[20] Two possible interpretations exist. Some understand the second line to refer to one person reflecting on her own thoughts.[21] Through thoughtful introspection, an individual comes to a better understanding of the self. Others understand the second line to refer to two people engaged in reflecting on each other's thoughts.[22] Through engaging con-

---

19. The Hebrew word is actually "neighbor" or "friend."

20 Because of the figurative and metaphorical language used, proverbs are by nature relatively indeterminate.

21 William McKane, *Proverbs: A New Approach*, Old Testament Library (Philadelphia: Westminster, 1970). The second line, McKane says, "has to do only with one man whose self is mirrored in his *lev* [heart], and the meaning . . . is that it is through introspection . . . that a man acquires self-knowledge" (616).

22 Robert Alter's analysis of the imagery is especially apropos: "The terseness makes you work to decipher the first verset. Once it dawns on you that what is referred to is the

versation, a person comes to a better understanding of the self. So how should the verse be interpreted, as introspection or conversation?

One possibility for determining the proverb's meaning lies in examining the surrounding context. Granted, not all proverbs have a context. Many are randomly collected or quite loosely connected with their surroundings.[23] This proverb, however, has a thematic connection with the proverbs that precede it. The focus of verses 14–19 is not the individual in isolation but the self in relation to friends, family, and community. In addition, two proverbs located earlier in chapter 27 reinforce the idea of spirited conversation:

> v. 5 Better is open rebuke
> than hidden love.
>
> v. 6 Well meant are the wounds a friend inflicts,
> but profuse are the kisses of an enemy.

Within the context of chapter 27, with its heavy emphasis on conversation between individuals, it is more fitting to interpret the reflection of verse 19 not as self-reflection but as inter-reflection.[24] Individuals come to know themselves not primarily through introspection but through talk.

Verse 19 is also thematically connected with another proverb in the cluster. Verse 21 reads: "The crucible is for silver, and the furnace is for gold, so a person is tested by being praised." That is, the kind of reputation

---

reflected image of a face in water, further complications ensue: Does each man discover the otherwise invisible image of his own heart by seeing what others are like, or, on the contrary, is it by introspection (as we say, "reflection"), in scrutinizing the features of his own heart, that a person comes to understand what the heart of others must be? And is the choice of water in the simile merely an indication of the property of reflection, or does water, as against a mirror, suggest a potentially unstable image, or one with shadowy depths below the reflecting surface?" See Alter, *The Art of Biblical Poetry* (New York: Basic Books, 1985) 178.

23. Tremper Longman maintains that the sentence literature is more or less random with a few isolated collections here and there. There is, in his opinion, no overarching systematic structure to the book. He observes, "a systematic collection of proverbs may give the wrong impression . . . that life is systematic and that Proverbs was a 'how-to' fix-it book" (40). The lack of structure is intentional and "reflects the messiness of life" (ibid.). He believes the trend to see structure and clusters is imposed rather than discovered. See Tremper Longman III, *Proverbs*, Baker Commentary on the Old Testament Wisdom and Psalms (Grand Rapids: Baker Academic, 2006).

24 Van Leeuwen writes: "The idea is of water as a mirror: man comes to self-knowledge through confrontation with the other." Raymond C. Van Leeuwen, in *Context and Meaning in Proverbs 25–27*, SBL Dissertation Series 96 (Atlanta: Scholars, 1988), 125.

that a person develops has much to say about that person. Reputation receives its shape from the furnace of struggle within the community. The community has ways of testing the character of an individual that are just as rigorous as the means used to separate the dross in silver and gold. In exposing our vulnerability to the community, we refine and strengthen character. Thus the image of verse 19 is surrounded by proverbs that depict spirited conversation between two or more individuals. The portrayal of engaging rhetoric pervades this chapter and represents the essence of verses 14–19.

Verse 19 conveys a potent image: "Just as water reflects the face, so one human heart reflects another." When one engages in rigorous conversation with another who reflects with her, offers counter ideas, expresses alternatives, or just listens, she discovers new insights. Until individuals can verbalize their ideas to another, the thought process remains incomplete. That is to say, unless individuals can express their thoughts to others, they do not understand them as well as they might think. When thoughts and ideas are clarified to others, we better understand them ourselves.

The proverb in verse 19 revolves around the image of water, incorporating two dynamic qualities of human nature. Unlike the predictable reflection in a mirror, reflection on the surface of water is ever changing, a quality also characteristic of people. And unlike the mirror, the reflection in water implies depth.[25] More is there than meets the eye. A parallel proverb makes a similar observation: "The purposes in the human mind are like deep water, but the intelligent will draw them out" (20:5). The image is of a deep well. It takes a person with a bucket and long rope to draw out the water. In the same way, it takes time, patience, and one who is indeed a friend to plumb the depths of another's thoughts.

The images of iron sharpening iron and one person reflecting the mind of another serve to compliment each other. They describe the constructive conflict necessary for growth to occur. Character is sharpened when individuals put defensiveness aside and engage in open discussion about life issues that will lead to stronger faithfulness. Sometimes when iron sharpens iron, sparks fly. But when two friends in conflict have the best interest of the other in mind, such conflict results in good. Character does not develop in a vacuum but only in community with others. It is a collaborative process.

25 See Alter's remarks on this verse in n. 19 above.

The Use of Reproof

Whereas the proverbs in chapter 27 appear to describe the rhetoric between two friends of equal authority, there is another type of conversation that takes shape between individuals of unequal authority. This kind takes place more often between a parent and a child or a teacher and a student. In this relationship the communication is somewhat less interactive. The authority figure shares experiences and reflects on life with the youth or the student. The sage often refers to this type of communication as "rebuke" or "reproof."

The sages used the rhetorical tool of reproof to help shape the character of the student.[26] The noun "reproof" appears in Proverbs more often than in any other book in the Hebrew Scriptures.[27] Reproof in Proverbs has to do with training in moral instruction (see Prov 19:25 and 21:11). Reproof does not involve verbal abuse or persistent nagging. Neither the quarrelsome man (26:17–28) nor the quarrelsome woman (27:15–16) demonstrates the appropriate way to reprove. Nor does the reproof talked about by the sages necessarily come in the context of an angry moment. In the context of wisdom and experience, reproof becomes a constructive instrument. The sages describe it as a work of art (25:12). The sages describe reproof as "wholesome admonition":

> The ear that heeds wholesome admonition[28]
>   will lodge among the wise.
> Those who ignore instruction despise themselves,
>   but those who heed admonition gain understanding.
> The fear of the LORD is instruction in wisdom,
>   and humility goes before honor. (15:31–33)

This text envisions the instruction the sage gives to youthful minds. It uses the familiar sapiential language of "admonition" or "reproof" (vv.

---

26 The term "reproof" (תוכחת) is often paired with the word "discipline" (מוסר) in Proverbs (see 3:11; 5:12; 6:23; 10:17; 12:1; 13:18; 15:5, 10, 32). The Hebrew word for "reproof" is also the word for reasoned argument such as would be put forward by a lawyer in the courtroom (cf. Job 13:6; 23:4; Ps 38:14).

27 It occurs twenty-four times in the Old Testament, sixteen of those are in Proverbs. The verb יכח occurs fifty-nine times in the Old Testament. Its most frequent occurrence is found in Job (seventeen times) and Proverbs (ten times).

28 The phrase for "wholesome admonition" is תוכחת חיים, literally "admonition of life."

31, 32). This is not just any kind of reproof; this is wholesome, life-giving instruction.

Reproof has as its goal instruction in the ways of prudence, righteousness, justice, and equity (1:3). In its broadest sense, the whole of Proverbs is a collection of advice that could be classified as reproof. In the opening paragraph of 1:8–19, a wise father offers reproof to the listening ear of the son warning the young adult about the dangers of living by the rules of a gang-type lifestyle. The sage in 7:6–27 describes in graphic details the enticing and destructive ways of the temptress. This is wise reproof to the attentive ear. King Lemuel recalls with appreciation the reproof his mother gave him (31:1–9). She warns him about the baleful temptations of the seductress and the ruinous effects of wine and strong drink. His mother admonishes him as king to practice justice and righteousness toward the poor and afflicted (31:5, 8–9).

In Proverbs offering reproof is a way of holding up experiences of life before young minds in order for them to receive concrete images of how to live responsibly. Through listening to the insights of the experienced, students receive moral training. Though rebuke can turn into nagging and even verbal abuse (26:17–28), its constructive function is to develop character. In fact, reproof that is forthright but wise is more productive than a superficial demonstration of love.[29] Reproof profits even the advanced student: "The wise when rebuked will love you" (9:8). Reproof finds its theological moorings in the way in which Yahweh instructs his children:

> My child, do not despise the Lord's discipline
>   or be weary of his reproof,
> for the Lord reproves the one he loves,
>   as a father the son in whom he delights. (3:11–12)

In this text a close relationship exists between the discipline of the Lord and the discipline of a parent. The discipline of a loving parent reflects the discipline of God. The reproof given is not easy to accept; it is a wearisome and painful process. That is the reason for the exhortation. The sage gives encouragement to the youth to accept the reproof because it is offered out of love.

---

29 Compare the following proverbs: "Better is open reproof than hidden love" (27:5); and "Whoever reproves a person will afterward find more favor than one who flatters with the tongue" (28:23). See also Ecclesiastes 7:5: "It is better for a man to hear the rebuke of the wise, than to hear the song of fools."

Such an exhortation suggests the need for students to respond appropriately to the reproof. It is a matter of life and death. Because the way one responds to reproof is critical, further investigation into this dimension is necessary.

The Response to Reproof: A Listening Ear

In Proverbs, the one who is a fool is the one who does not listen to reproof. However, those who are wise are those receptive to the instructions of the parent and the teacher. They develop a listening ear. Solomon asked God for a "listening heart" which pleased the Lord (1 Kgs 3:9). Such a heart is open to the words of God and others. This is the quality necessary for receiving instruction in Proverbs. The following proverbs describe the appropriate kind of conversation necessary:

> A word fitly spoken
>> is like apples of gold in a setting of silver.
> Like a gold ring or an ornament of gold
>> is a wise rebuke to a listening ear. (25:11, 12)

Both proverbs use the image of precious metal as an analogy for proper speaking and listening. Both describe the crafting of gold into an aesthetically pleasing piece of artwork. In one case (v. 11), the beautiful golden artwork is inlaid on a silver frame. Such a masterpiece of human art is compared to the artistic use of words. When used aptly, words can generate a response similar to that of experiencing a beautiful work of art.

The proverb in verse 11 does not detail the kind of word spoken, whether it was an affirming word or a confrontational word. However, it really does not matter because the word spoken was right and necessary for the occasion; it was a wise word. The proverb in verse 12 may indicate that it was a word of reproof or rebuke. Such communication covers a variety of speech forms including warning, correcting, instructing, and exhorting (cf. Prov 1:9–19). The proverb describes a collaborative effort between teacher and student. Successful instruction requires a teacher who delivers a "wise rebuke" and a student who develops a "listening ear." When the two come together, they are compared to a precious piece of jewelry. The process of molding and shaping the character of another individual open to change is truly a work of art. Learning the language of wisdom involves a team effort. On the one hand, it takes wisdom to know how to exhort or offer rebuke (25:12). On the other hand, it takes a "listening ear," that is, an open mind, to receive the instruction properly (25:12).

Fools are held up as the antitype to the receptivity of a rebuke. Because they do not accept reproof, they do not learn from their mistakes or the mistakes of others. To develop a listening ear means that one is open to hearing about one's own blunders and missteps.[30] The fool is the one who is defensive and refuses to admit mistakes. The truly wise person desires to know when he or she has made a mistake and takes steps toward correcting behavior. Thus the sage observes, "Whoever heeds instruction is on the path to life, but one who rejects a rebuke goes astray" (10:17). The wise appreciate insightful criticism because it enables them to live life better and experience more satisfaction.[31]

Scoffers do not like rebuke; they will not go to the wise (15:10, 12). "Scoffer" (לֵיץ) (XEl)[32] is another term the sages use to describe a fool.[33] The scoffer is the one who is "wise in his own eyes" and therefore not open to correction or rebuke. He or she manifests arrogance (cf. 21:24). The wise person develops the humility necessary to be open to correction and criticism from others. The wise are in constant dialogue with others not only instructing and leading but also learning and following. Wise are good listeners (15:5)! Longman expresses the situation succinctly, "If one cannot bear to hear about one's mistakes and take steps to correct them, then one is doomed to be perpetually wrong."[34] Hearing criticism and changing wrong behavior is integral to wisdom (3:1–11).

The give and take of dialogue is only a medium in the process of character formation. It works in tandem with one's mental faculties. For moral transformation to take place, it is assumed that the student must be able to nurture the ability to think. Attitudes, emotions, and behaviors are changed when the mind is actively involved. Otherwise a student will only imitate and react mechanically to the behavior of others. It is this final dimension that I now want briefly to address.

---

30. As Longman puts it, "Only the wise are willing to admit mistakes . . ."; Longman, *Proverbs*, 323.

31 Ibid., 316.

32. לֵיץ is used eighteen times in Proverbs. The NIV usually translates this word "mocker" (Prov 9:7, 8, 12; 13:1; 14:6; 15:12; 19:25; 20:1; 21:11, 24; 22:10; 24:9).

33. See Dave Bland, *Proverbs, Ecclesiastes, Song of Solomon* (Joplin, MO: College Press NIV Commentary, 2002) 16.

34. Longman, *Proverbs*, 313–14.

Conversation as a Way of Engaging the Mind

That sages encouraged students to interact with one another demonstrates the concern they had for teaching students the art of discernment. They were not content with students regurgitating ideas simply learned through rote memory. Rather the sages demonstrate an interest in equipping students to process ideas through spirited dialogue with others. Students must learn to think. They had to interact with others. Those who accepted the challenge came to realize that understanding is a process that comes through the exchange of ideas between individuals.

The sages want students to internalize moral values and learn the art of discernment (1:2, 6). The discerning student is the one who develops a "listening ear" and the ability to think critically.[35] The very quality of wisdom itself invites the reforming and rethinking of ideas. The sages give no pat answers. For instance, while the proverbs in chapters 10–15 generally emphasize the simple, conventional theology of wisdom (wise people prosper, foolish people suffer), those in chapters 16–22 quickly dispel any mechanical or mindless approach to that theology. For example, Proverbs 16:1–9 throws a wrench in the conventional cogs of wisdom, claiming that humans may make their plans but Yahweh has the final say. This cluster of proverbs in verses 1–9 describes the complexity of a world that lives with the tension between human freedom and divine sovereignty. No simple answers exist.

It appears, however, that some students looked for the easiest route to acquire wisdom, as the sage sarcastically observes, "Why should fools have a price in hand to buy wisdom, when they have no mind to learn?" (17:16). Some students believed they could gain understanding apart from using the mind. If they paid the tuition cost, wisdom was theirs for the taking. They viewed wisdom as a commodity, a matter of learning some techniques, accepting certain beliefs, and memorizing a few proverbs. But it was not so in the eyes of the sage. For the sage, the acquisition of wisdom is an arduous process. But the demanding process is worth the outcome as character is shaped and life enriched. One could not, however, acquire wisdom and its byproducts without developing the

---

35 See John Eaton, "Memory and Encounter: An Educational Ideal," in *Of Prophets' Visions and the Wisdom of Sages: Essays in Honour of R. Norman Whybray on His Seventieth Birthday*, eds. Heather A. McKay and David J. A. Clines, JSOT Supplement Series 162 (Sheffield: Sheffield Academic, 1993) 179–91.

art of critical thinking. And that art was best nurtured in conversation with others.

Conclusion

When humans understand the rhetorical potency of conversation, they can no longer approach talk with another lightly. As a faith community, when we talk about conversation we are not simply talking about sharing information and ideas, we are dealing with the shaping of a worldview based on the moral universe created by Yahweh.

Christian character does not develop in a vacuum but only in dialogue with others. Dynamic and continual conversation is a part of any community wanting to grow morally and spiritually and dissonance remains endemic to that process. Being open to different opinions on various issues and experiences is a sign of a healthy family, a healthy friendship, and a healthy community. Engaging constructively in dialogue indicates that we take each other seriously. When individuals engage in a healthy exchange of ideas and perspectives, individuals grow and the faith community is able to create an environment governed by righteousness, justice, and equity (Prov 1:3).

Rhetoric is embedded in the very fabric of wisdom and wisdom is fundamentally relational. Thus we come to understand who we are through conversation with others. We engage others in sparring, conflict, and discussion and out of that dialogue grows new understanding and insight. We are able to see things from a different perspective. Hans-Georg Gadamer refers to this phenomenon of conversation as "play." As one engages in "play," that person participates in a kind of dialectical movement. As one participates in the dialectic, the player becomes absorbed and loses himself or herself in the activity. In the context of being totally absorbed in the "play," new meaning arises from the experience. In the play of conversation humans do not simply reproduce information or regurgitate ideas, but collaboratively produce new understanding.[36] John Stewart puts it this way, "By engaging both proactively and responsively in the play of language events, humans participate" in creating their world.[37] They cannot create any world they want because they are

36. Hans-Georg Gadamer, *Truth and Method*, 2nd rev. ed., trans. Joel Weinscheimer and Donald G. Marshall (New York: Crossroad, 1991) 102–3.

37. John Stewart, *Language as Articulate Contact: Toward a Post-Semiotic Philosophy of Communication* (New York: SUNY Press, 1995) 119.

constrained by the limits of wisdom as well as by the sovereignty of God. But within these constraints, humans can create an order that manifests the virtues of wisdom.

The wise embark on a fascinating and often unpredictable adventure. Intrigue, disappointment, joy, suffering, conflict, dialogue, and satisfaction fill the journey. It is a journey initiated within the context of the family and perpetuated by the faith community. Wisdom offers no guarantees along the way regarding rewards or financial security or physical well-being. But the journey with wisdom does guarantee the kind of character that enables individuals to live responsibly in community and that reflects the very nature of the God they serve.

10

Christology and Logology

Rethinking Burkean Frames for Interpersonal Consubstantiality and Guilt Purification through the Lens of Christian Theology

ROBERT C. CHANDLER and JEFFREY DALE HOBBS

"[T]he relation between theology and logology should not be conceived simply as proceeding in one direction."
—KENNETH BURKE[1]

Introduction

The center point of the Johanine prologue is that the Word (*the Logos*) was before the beginning, intertwined with God, and was God and that through the Word came all things subsequent. The center point of Kenneth Burke's prologue in *The Rhetoric of Religion* (1961) is that, if theology is "words about God," then *logology* means "words about words" and that the creation came forth from the power of naming. Juxtaposing these two opening premises gives us an opportunity for exploratory ponderings in the space between theology and logology.

Too frequently scholars and believers have posed a false dichotomy between *Christological* and *Logological* approaches. Despite St. Augustine's (and many subsequent) efforts at reconciliation of pagan rhetoric with Christian faith, far too often the assumption is that it is an either/or

1. Burke, *The Rhetoric of Religion* (Berkeley: University of California Press, 1970) 36.

approach. In this essay, we seek a path in this conversation that transverses both sacred and scholarly ground. Burke, we would argue, leads us to be suspicious about dichotomies that imply either/or polarized extremes that force us into mutually exclusive alternatives. Furthermore, we think that, in the Burkean frame of rejecting the divisive "or" and inserting the conjunctive "and," Kenneth Burke would be in favor of a conversation in the expanse that lies between the theological and the logological. So we ask, how each might inform the other in helpful ways? Specifically, are there approaches to human relationships and communication that are *both* Christological *and* Logological?

Much has been written in both spheres concerning the interpersonal relationship principles implied in Christian doctrine as well as the power of words. While we make no claims in this essay as to offering a "last word" (so to speak) on some of the questions raised, we do seek to offer a word or two in the conversation that we hope will be forthcoming and on-going. As "believing scholars," we seek to engage in a dialogue with two communities that have largely remained disconnected—although each might be beneficially informed by a conversation with the other. We are indebted to Kenneth Burke for suggesting a fruitful conversation at the intersection where Christology and Logology might illuminate one another.

First, this essay examines the framework that a logological posture provides for our questions. Second, a correspondence of identification and the association (consubstantial identification) function is considered. Third, we address the nature of words and how rhetorical scholarship might inform practical faith. Fourth, we address Christians and consubstantial relationships. Fifth, we address Christians and forgiveness and how faith might inform scholarship. Finally, this essay reconsiders Kenneth Burke's purification ritual (cult of the kill) in light of corresponding Christian thought. This necessitates a look at the form of language (logology) itself in order to offer a new page for understanding the rhetorical moves of scapegoating, mortification, and transcendence from a Christian theological frame—extending the traditional Burkean typology along a trajectory that is consistent with Burke, himself, but with a greater logological inference.

Logos

In ancient Hellenistic common usage, *logos* appear to have had two identifiable but overlapping meanings. One meaning appears to have referred to speaking, talk, oration, and spoken words. The other meaning usually referred to "mere words" or "mere talking" and seems to involve the juxtaposition of words with tangible action or activity (much as a contemporary speaker might use the derogative description of "mere rhetoric" compared with actually doing something tangible). According to H. G. Liddell, R. Scott, H. S. Jones, and R. McKenzie's (1925) *A Greek-English Lexicon* (entry: *logos, lexis*); the term for a "word" in a semantic or linguistic sense was *lexis*, so perhaps the conventional English translation of the prologue in John's Gospel (as *logos*, or "Word") is, at first glance, somewhat problematic for our purposes (although both *logos* and *lexis* derive from the same root verb).

In ancient Hebraic common usage, many words were considered sacred. Utterances were assumed to invite the participation (positively or negative) of the divine. The idea of words as mystical, magical, sacred, pious, and supernaturally powerful is scattered across the Biblical text. Perhaps, given the dominant secular influence (even on believers), some of these presumed qualities of language and words may be overlooked by contemporary readers of the ancient text.

Logos and Christology

While it is not the purpose of this essay to explore all of the theological and doctrinal implications of this well-discussed and long debated Biblical passage that is in the prologue of John's gospel, this passage clearly undergirds central assumptions of mainstream and traditional Christian faith and doctrine including fundamental confessions of faith as related to the claims of the inherent and eternal nature of Jesus Christ.

The Word and the Name in Hebrew and Christian Scripture

It is useful for our purposes to recall that (as Burke and others have as well), in the creation account given in the opening line of the Torah, the act of "creation" was via the means of words: i.e. "God said, 'let there be *light*' and there was '*light*'" (emphasis added), and at least, in the first creation account, God spoke humanity into existence, calling Adam "human" (Hebrew: אדם). God brought all of creation before "human" to see "what he would *name* (emphasis added) them." The word/term/name was there before the beginning, was intertwined with the act of creation, and, according to Hebrew theology, through the word came all things subsequent. Certainly there is an implicit assumption of the "power" of words in the opening narrative of scripture. However, there is more in Torah to call our attention to the reverence for words.

The name of God in the Hebrew Bible (embodied in the tetragrammaton, traditionally written as YHVH [יהוה], and customarily assumed as "Yahweh") offers an interesting consideration from a logological perspective. Traditional Jews generally would have never spoken the name (except once a year by the High Priest during Yom Kippur in the Holy of Holies within the Jerusalem Temple). Therefore, we have only conjecture to support the choice of vowels and syllable emphasis. The name YHVH (יהוה) was only written on paper or stone that would never be discarded or destroyed. In prayer, an observant Jew might use the name Adonai. But, in most other settings, the euphuism used to refer to God would most probably be a variation of *HaShem* ("The Name") or *Shem HaMeforash* ("The Ineffable Name"). Contemporary Orthodox Jews continue this tradition and one might hear references to God that include "the ineffable name," "the unutterable name," or the "distinctive name." Exodus 3:15 documents the declaration that "This is my Name forever; and this is my memorial to all generations."

God as embodied in the Name (word) is seen throughout scripture as expressing attributes, presenting authority, and connected with supernatural actions. Perhaps, most significantly, the prophets who call upon the Name of God—and the congregants when they concur—find themselves delivered, protected, and triumphant.

The term *logos* also appears to reflect the term "Word of God" as used variously in the Hebrew Bible. For messianic Jewish readers of John's narrative, the linkage with the utterances of God creating all things and His sovereignty were embodied in this linkage. For Hellenistic Pagan and Jewish readers of John's narrative, the linkage with the eternal logos as a pattern for all creation would have resonated with this imagery. The New Testament writers certainly carry forward the sacred notion of the Name of God. Believers are instructed in scripture that "salvation is found in no one else, for there is no other name under heaven by which we must be saved" (Acts 4:12); "everyone who calls upon the name of the LORD will be saved" (Romans 10:13); "God gave him the name that is above every name" (Phil 2:9); "do it all in the name of the LORD Jesus" (Col 3:17); and "the name that he [Christ] has inherited is superior to [the angels]" (Hebrews 1:4).

In Christian church tradition, the "Name of God" (*Holy Name*) takes on a spiritual (occasionally mystical) quality in the life of the church and believers. Invoking the Holy Name is a powerful embodiment of the divine presence and is involved in requests for both divine action and intervention. Christian church rituals are empowered by the Name with an invocation of the holy Name—for example; baptism done *in the name* of Jesus or *in the name* of the Holy Father, Holy Son, and Holy Spirit brings consubstantial identification and spiritual power to the ritual. Thereby, an action done in this Name provides a sacred "incantation" that transforms a mundane action (immersion in water) into a sacred act—spiritually and symbolically powerful. Doctrinal disputes have arisen over the sanctification efficacy of baptism rituals performed with differing arrangement and formula of "words" spoken during the ritual. In fact, schisms in fellowship have resulted from differences in the words used before, during, or after the rite of baptism.

Returning to the texts of both the Genesis and Johannine prologues, we can call attention to the interplay between the word and the Name. Perhaps considering that "the Name said, 'let there be [a name] *light*' and there was [the name] '*light*,'" and thereby light was created into existence. The Name created "all things" in the beginning by naming them into existence—as there was no existence before the words called things (into being). In the beginning was the Name/Word; and the Word/Name was with God; and the Name/Word was God. The Word/Name was with God in the beginning. Through the Name/Word all things were created; without the Name/Word nothing was made that has been made.

This is our opportunity, as scholars of words and as believers, to explore the constructs of a theologically Christian view of a God who is the Word and the Word that is God. Further, the interconnection between God and words—and, more specifically, the functions, purposes, and meanings of words—is a fertile field to plow in thinking about the interconnection between the role of the *theological* and the *logological*. Martin Buber may have been onto something close to this topic when he concluded that we need to search for the role of God in human communication as a precursor to understanding human communication. In our opinion, Christian theological treatment has far too often run parallel to, but uninformed by, rhetorical critics seeking to understand the nature of language and words. Likewise, the well of theological thought has been left untapped by secular rhetoricians trying to grasp the persuasive power of words. Could it be that elements of the divine are at the heart of all true human communication?

Logos and Logology

Logos is a foundational concept in classical rhetorical thought. Aristotle created a category system for argument that defined *logos* (arguing from reason) as one of the three primary forms of argument along side of *pathos* and *ethos*. However, other ancient Greek rhetoricians argued that *logos* was the active reason for the universe which gave it functionality (e.g., *logos spermatikos*). Among some classical schools (including the Stoics), this notion was extended to identify *logos* with the gods, or a divine power. Platonists tended to argue that *logos* was the necessary "inter-mediator" between the imperfect (material world) and the perfect (idea). The Platonist-Jewish philosopher Philo of Alexandria argued that "logos" was the divine wisdom or a discernable pattern of the image of God (but not God). It was this image that Philo suggested the human mind was patterned after in the creation.

Rhetorically, there is a comparable move for logos—the word/the name that we recognize in the Christian theological tradition. For our purposes, we are interested in the contributions that Kenneth Burke's Dramatism has made to the discussion of *logos*. Creation, or naming according to Burke, implies the authority of the designer/author of the term in a "terministic interrelationship" between the namer and the named. This "verbal principle" or terministic ontology is a central aspect of Dramatism and the examination of the relationship between words and the things they name. We believe that we are on an appropriate footpath with our exploration, as Kenneth Burke calls our attention to John's logological prologue as well as the ancient Hebrew description of the verbal act (symbolic action) of creation in his essay "On Words and The Word." Kenneth Burke also sees this "verbal principle" very much at the core of other approaches to this topic—including Martin Buber's "I-Thou relation"—since it involves, on both surface and core levels, "a grammatical distinction to do with the personality implicit in certain forms of address [of the other]."[2]

Kenneth Burke writes: "All of these considerations should indicate why, in a kind of "linguistic fundamentalism," we should keep ourselves

2. Ibid., 12.

reminded of this strongly verbal connotation in the word *Logos*, quite as the translation of the Bible does (in translating it as "Word"), even while commentators often stress the more philosophic meaning."[3]

With Logology, Burke starts with the systematic study of theological terms to see what he can learn from their use about the function of language as a creative "instrument" by which humans are separated from their natural condition. By Christology, we intend an (albeit loosely defined) exploration of the nature of Christ as a meaningful center point for learning how believers should functionally pattern themselves as distinctive from their "natural condition."

As professors of Communication, we see a connection between the function of words in human society and the role of Jesus in the life of a Christian. George Marsden, in *The Outrageous Idea of Christian Scholarship*, writes: "Scholars who have religious faith should be reflecting on the intellectual implications of that faith and bringing those reflections into the mainstream of intellectual life."[4] Nicholas Wolterstorff adds, "the religious beliefs of the Christian scholar ought to function as control beliefs within his [or her] devising and weighing of theories."[5] At the same time, Wolterstorff notes that there are instances where the results of academic study should cause one to revise his or her Christian beliefs.[6]

This relationship between Christian faith and academic scholarship is keenly salient in the act of looking at Jesus as the Word. One such look occurs in the writings of Kenneth Burke and his concept of logology. He writes:

> If we defined "theology" as "words about God," then by "logology" we would mean "words about words." Whereupon, thoughts on the necessarily verbal nature of religious doctrines suggest a further possibility: that there might be fruitful analogies between the two realms. Thus statements that great theologians have made about the nature of "God" might be adapted *mutatis mutandis* for use as purely secular observations on the nature of *words*."[7]

3. Ibid., 13.

4. Marsden, *The Outrageous Idea of Christian Scholarship* (New York: Oxford University Press, 1997) 3–4.

5. Wolterstorff, *Reason within the Bounds of Religion*, 2nd ed. (Grand Rapids: Eerdmans, 1984) 70.

6. Ibid., 92–97.

7. Burke, *The Rhetoric of Religion*, 1.

In this essay, we would like to take another look at Burke's logology —however, not as "purely secular observations." We hope to illustrate what happens when Christian communication scholars examine Christ as the Word and allow their scholarship to inform their faith and their faith to inform their scholarship.

Ontology of a Name

A student of realism, referential, or semantic meaning might remind us that, in an absolutist sense, the term is not the actual thing. However, a Burkean lens allows us to "see" the term or label for the thing, when taken as the thing, used as if it were the thing, or when its role is defining the thing. Dramatism reminds us that "terms," as hortatory (sermonic) expressions, direct or misdirect our attention by reflecting, selecting, and deflecting "reality." This is not dissimilar to the mystical power that a Christological view of the Name/Word provides.

William Barclay, in *Jesus As They Saw Him*, wrote, "It can very often happen that a name given to a [person] can be a one-word summary of what he [or she] has done and of what he [or she] is."[8] He continued: "All this is especially true of Jesus. All through the New Testament we find [people] giving Jesus titles which are at one and the same time affirmations and confessions of their faith in him and summaries of what they believed him to be."[9]

Following these words are the explanations of forty-two of these names, such as the Messiah, the Good Shepherd, the Lamb, and the Bread of Life. One of the most meaningful names to a scholar of Communication is the Word. "In the beginning was the Word, and the Word was with God, and the Word was God" (John 1:1).[10] A few verses later, the passage states, "The Word became flesh and lived for a while among us" (John 1:14).

Identification and Association in Dramatism

Perhaps it is also useful to draw upon Burke's extension of identification (beyond its persuasive functions) to the power of association—the power of identification as the associative degree of sharing a common substance and a mutual combined identification of A with B. Burke borrows from

8. Barclay, *Jesus As They Saw Him* (Grand Rapids: Eerdmans, 1962) 9.

9. Ibid.

10. All Scripture quotations from the NIV.

the theological realm (transubstantiation and consubstantiation) with his notion of so shared an identity of two things that they become one in common and in communion with each other. In the context of our present conversation, the notion that one becomes so closely identified (consubstantial) with another that he or she is transformed into sharing a common substance might well inform our theological understanding of the dramatistic function of a "Christian" who "becomes the (body of) Christ." In fact, in Christian theology, the corpus of believers is terministi- cally labeled (and rhetorically recreated) as "the body of Christ." Perhaps, it is more than simply a surface metaphor to think of the transformation (rebirth) of an individual who becomes part of the (transubstantiated) Christ as Christ (likewise by this rhetorical function) becomes one with the believers. Believers are the Christ and Christ is the believers. Such would be the projected transformation of associative identify.

The Nature of Words—Scholarship Informing Faith

One theory of language argues that words perform various functions in human society. This view of language has been influenced greatly by the works of Kenneth Burke. As Em Griffin noted, "Kenneth Burke is perhaps the foremost rhetorician of the twentieth century. Burke writes about rhetoric; other rhetoricians write about Burke."[11] Three of the func- tions that language performs, according to this theory, are that words transfer meanings and feelings, words influence our view of reality, and words influence our actions.

First, words transfer meanings and feelings. That is, words have both denotative and connotative meanings. A word's denotative meaning is its "dictionary" meaning, while a word's connotative meaning is a personal- ized emotional response to a word that is derived from an individual's experience. This is the most basic function of language that we are all familiar with. We use words to communicate—to share our thoughts and ideas with other people. One must choose his or her words carefully to be understood. According to Mark Twain, "the difference between the right word and the 'almost' right word is like the difference between lightning and the lightning bug."[12]

---

11. Griffin, *A First Look at Communication Theory*, 5th ed. (New York: McGraw-Hill, 2003) 320.

12. Twain, quoted in Ronald J. Matlon, *Communication in the Legal Process* (New York: Holt, Rinehart & Winston, 1988) 187.

Second, words influence our view of reality. This function is known as the epistemological function of language. Epistemology is the study of knowledge, how we come to know what we know. Words influence what we know and how we come to know it. We use words to explain our reality and then we begin to see what our words say exist. When one of us was a little child (too young to remember this story other than from his father's repeated telling of this tale), he told his dad that, "There's a bull outside." He described with his words a most ferocious bull. When it came time to leave the house, he was afraid to venture outside because of this "bull." His words had created a reality—at least something real enough to cause this little child to cry. Grown-ups can create realities as well.

Kenneth Burke says that language reflects, selects, and deflects reality.[13] Language reflects reality in that it only gives us a picture of reality. Our words are not reality, just as our reflection in a mirror is not us. Language selects reality by telling us what is important to pay attention to. Humans are limited "information processors," we cannot pay attention to everything at once. We have to decide what to pay attention to and language helps us decide what is important. Language deflects reality in the sense that what is not selected is not seen. For example, college students learn complicated technical languages in their majors. The languages of the chosen major tell them what is important—what needs to be paid attention to. Thus, if a person comes to a group of different students saying he or she has a problem, a Bible major wonders what sin this person has in his or her life, a Communication major wonders what kinds of communication difficulties this person is experiencing, and a Pre-Med major wonders what type of chemical imbalance this person is facing. We see what our language tells us to see. People with different words live in different worlds.

Third, words influence our actions. We are persuaded by the words of others, and we are persuaded by our own words. As we write this essay, perhaps we are convincing ourselves of these ideas more than we are convincing our readers of them. Kenneth Burke, in *Language as Symbolic Action*, wrote: "Do we simply use words, or do they use us? An 'ideology' is like a god coming down to earth, where it will inhabit a place pervaded by its presence. An 'ideology' is like a spirit taking up its abode in a body: it makes that body hop around in certain ways; and that same

13. Burke, *Language as Symbolic Action* (Berkeley: University of California Press, 1966) 45.

body would have hopped around in different ways had a different ideology happened to inhabit it."[14]

The Bible makes a similar observation about the power of words to motivate us and control our actions. James wrote, "If anyone is never at fault in what he [or she] says, he [or she] is a perfect [person] able to keep [the] whole body in check" (3:2). He continued: "take ships as an example. Although they are so large and driven by strong winds, they are steered by a very small rudder wherever the pilot wants to go. Likewise the tongue is a small part of the body, but it makes great boasts" (3:4–5).

The Name of Christ

With this theory of language in mind, it is time to make the analogy between the function of words in human society and the role of Jesus in a Christian's life. The term Christian literally means "little-Christ" or "little-Christer." This originally derogatory term serves for believers as an organizing hub of the central idea of becoming "Christ-like" or "taking on the form of Christ." It is this aspect of "becoming Christ" or "imitating" (modeling, following, mimicking, enacting, repeating, or joining) Christ from which all of the other spokes of action, faith, practice, and meaning extend.

The nature of symbolic action of "taking on the name of Christ," from a Burkean perspective, is that such acts are not just a reflection or memoriam of the person whom the name symbolizes. The name and the adoption of the name by a believer is a symbolic act—a participation in and a shared common substance with the person to which it corresponds. Burke borrowed, from Roman-Christian theological concepts, the notion of transubstantiation (wherein the Eucharist host transforms into the literal body of Jesus Christ which becomes a real, immediate, and literal part of those who partake) of the body of Jesus Christ. For Burke, this opens up the possibility of consubstantiation—where through symbolic action people may be united into common substance. Traditionally, we consider the identification of one with a cause or a larger body through rhetoric as a primary enactment of consubstantiation. In this case, Burke's concept of consubstantiation may be borrowed (it only seems equitable to return the conceptualized loan) by those of us struggling with theological issues of the meaningfulness of "Christian" as united with Christ or as a "little-

14. Ibid., 6.

Christ," as symbolic action should suggest, making the individual one with (of common substance) Jesus Christ. This is not religious imagery only, but it is a move that is predicted by Burke's notion of the rhetorical symbolic act of becoming consubstantial with the Christ. It is not persuasion, but rather identification that is involved in the rhetorical principle at work in making the one who shares the name of Christ as being one with the ontological Christ. With this turn, our logology informs our theology. The term "Christian" is a consubstantial identification of the believer with the greater symbolic substance of Christ (and concurrently with all of those who share that common substance—the community of believers) all becoming rhetorically the "body" of the Christ—a transubstantiation of form via the mechanism of identification. In this sense, it is the name of Christ that compels Christians in their entelechical quest.

As the Word, Jesus Christ transfers the meanings and feelings of God, influences a Christian's view of reality, and influences a Christian's actions. In short, Christ is the Word, or language, of those who claim to follow Him.

First, Christ transfers the meanings and feelings of God. Christ is God's word to us. He is God's communication to us. "No one has ever seen God, but God the only Son, who is at the Father's side, has made him known" (John 1:18). William Barclay argues that: "John went out to Jews and Greeks to tell them that in Jesus Christ this creating, illuminating, controlling, sustaining mind of God had come to earth. He came to tell them that [people] need no longer guess and grope; all that they had to do was look at Jesus and see the mind of God."[15]

Second, Christ influences a Christian's view of reality. Christ becomes the "glasses" by which Christians view the world. Christians live in a different world because they have a different language—Christ as the Word. The apostle Paul wrote: "Those who live according to the sinful nature have their minds set on what that nature desires; but those who live in accordance with the Spirit have their minds set on what the Spirit desires. The mind of sinful [humans] is death, but the mind controlled by the Spirit is life and peace . . ." (Rom 8:5–6).

What do Christians see that others do not see? They see joy in suffering: "we also rejoice in our sufferings, because we know that suffering produces perseverance, perseverance, character; and character hope" (Rom 5:3–4). They see blessedness in poverty of spirit, mourning, meek-

---

15. Barclay, *Gospel of John*, rev. ed. (Philadelphia: Westminster, 1975) 1:36–37.

ness, righteousness, mercy, purity, peacemaking and persecution (Matt 5:3–10). They see people who need help rather than condemnation. Jesus said of those who do not share this vision, "The Son of Man came eating and drinking, and they say, 'Here is a glutton and a drunkard, a friend of tax collectors and sinners'" (Matt 11:19). Christians truly live in a different world because the reality they see is colored by their Word—Christ.

Third, Christ influences the actions of Christians. It does no good to see the world differently if one does not act differently. Christ is the motive for a Christian's actions and the Word that persuades. "And whatever you do, whether in word or deed, do it all in the name of the Lord Jesus" (Col 3:17). Paul exclaimed, "I have been crucified with Christ and I no longer live, but Christ lives in me" (Gal 2:20). It is Christ that makes Christians "hop around." Actions are qualitatively different when Christ is the motive. Jesus noted this distinction in motives in the religion of his time:

> Everything they do is done for [people] to see: They make their phylacteries wide and the tassels of their prayer shawls long, they love . . . the most important seats in the synagogues . . . [But] The greatest among you will be your servant. For whoever exalts [him or herself] will be humbled, and whoever humbles [him or herself] will be exalted. (Matt 23:5–12)

The oft cited questions of *What Would Jesus Do (WWJD)?* or *how would Jesus have seen that?* are perhaps unsatisfying to us in this logological Christology. We need to use the dramatistic frame to turn the discussion. This turn is telling. Christians would not merely therefore "see" the word around them "as Jesus saw (sees) the world." Rather, Christians would "see" the world *through* Jesus (the prism or lens). A believer's view of the world around her or him would be transformed, selected, deflected, and reflected by the prescription of Jesus as the (terministic) screen. The sense-making and relationship to others is bonded to the filters of interactions with those beyond (outside) the self—inherently tied to the identity and framing that Christ imposes when viewing the world through this prism.

From a logological Christian perspective, "What Would Jesus Do?" may be a misleading question for a believer to ask. Perhaps a more consubstantially relevant question (from a Christological theological perspective as well) is to not look externally at what Jesus (or the Christ) would do (have done) because the question itself appears to presume a partition or separation of the believer from the Christ. A believer who has been transformed into the body of Christ (consubstantial with the Christ) would now see the world transformed (distorted) by the prism of the Christ (see with "Kingdom eyes"). So identified, the question would be what would I (who has been transformed by the Christ—and share the Christ) do? Perhaps that is a bit long to abbreviate for a wrist bracelet (WWIWHBTBTCD?). Nonetheless, a logological Christology would suggest that the Name/Word of the Christ is transformative—making the believer the Name or the Word. In this sense, we are created anew—a new person—identified and consubstantial with the Christ. In our (new) beginning, we are the Word—we are with God—and we are the body of God. We participate in the body of Christ (logologically and theologically)—we participate in the life, death, and resurrection as a new person, a new body, a transformed (transcendent) eternal body. We connect with the beginning in our new beginning. It is in these terms that the Christian theology of "born again" is made apparent by the Dramatistic move of logology.

This logological move also opens other possibilities when we consider not just our relationship (identification) with Christ—but when we turn to our relationships with others.

Christians and Consubstantial Relationships

Just as words in human society function to transfer meanings and feelings, influence views of reality, and motivate actions; Christ as the Word transfers the meanings and feelings of God, influences a Christian's view of reality, and motivates a Christian's actions. Kenneth Burke, in *A Rhetoric of Motives*, wrote: "Whether there are gods or not, there is an objective difference in motivation between an act conceived in the name of God and an act conceived in the name of Godless nature."[16] We want to extend this thought by contending that there is an objective difference between an act conceived in the name of God and an act conceived with God. Buber is one scholar who kept God in his "theory" of communication.[17] (see *I and Thou*). Pfuetze wrote of this "triadic relationship" in communication for Buber: "For the relation to my neighbor is always a

16. Burke, *A Rhetoric of Motives* (Berkeley: University of California Press, 1969) 6.
17. See Buber, *I and Thou* (New York: Scribner, 1970).

part of my relation to God. God meets me in and through the neighbor. 'Every particular *Thou* is a glimpse through to the eternal *Thou*.'"[18]

Perhaps, like Buber, we need to search for the role of God in human communication. Perhaps we need to change our definition of communication to "a process through which persons *and* God create, maintain, and alter social order, relationships, and identities."[19] According to Jorgensen: "This is the crux of the Johannine prologue: the Word, the light became a human being. God is present; he encounters us in flesh and blood. And here we are at the heart of all true human communication: it always takes place in the person-to-person encounter. It is always communication between two, and not just communication of a message. The communication of is only realized in the communication between."[20] By way of example, this essay will briefly look at one of Christ's interpersonal encounters recorded in the Gospel of John—His encounter with the Samaritan woman (John 4:4–42). In this story, one can see that Christ behaved differently from the people around Him. The actions of the Samaritan woman and of the disciples illustrate the human tendencies in interpersonal communication to live up to other people's expectations (the Pygmalion effect), to limit our associations with people to those who are already consistent with the way we like to be (selectivity), and to enter into relationships on the basis of rewards (Social Exchange). Dodd and Lewis wrote: "In many respects these theories explain why interaction between people develops as it does. These principles also represent the basis for relationship formation, maintenance, and dissolution. By using these principles, you can better understand your own behaviors and the behaviors of others."[21] However, it is our contention that these principles are descriptive of human nature and not prescriptive in nature for Christians who are motivated by the Word. The actions of Jesus Christ gave us a new way of looking at people—a new set of directions for interpersonal relationships.

18. Paul E. Pfuetze, *Self, Society, Existence: Human Nature and Dialogue in the Thought of George Herbert Mead and Martin Buber* (New York: Harper & Brothers, 1954) 156.

19. Vernon E. Cronen, W. Barnett Pearce, and Linda M. Harris, "The Coordinated Management of Meaning," in *Human Communication Theory*, ed. Frank E. X. Dance (New York: Harper & Row, 1982) 85–86 [61–89].

20. Knud Jorgensen, "Models of Communication in the New Testament," *Missiology: An International Review* 4 (1976) 468 [465–84].

21. Carley Dodd and Michael Lewis, *Human Communication*, 2nd ed. (Dubuque: Kendall/Hunt, 1992) 61.

In the story, the Samaritan woman and the twelve disciples were living up to society's expectations that Jews and Samaritans did not associate with each other and, especially, that Jewish men did not associate with Samaritan women. The text even says in an aside, "For Jews do not associate with Samaritans." However, Jesus violated this expectation. He entered into a conversation with the woman, and this surprised both the woman and the disciples. The woman said, "You are a Jew and I am a Samaritan woman. How can you ask me for a drink?" And the disciples "were surprised to find him talking with a woman." Christ did not live up to the expectations of the people around Him; He surpassed them in unique and exciting ways. Jesus, by expecting the best of those around Him, helped others to change in positive directions.

The woman also illustrates the human tendency to enter into relationships for the benefits that relationship can bring. Jesus said, "whoever drinks the water I give him will never thirst." To which the woman replied, "Sir, give me this water so that I won't get thirsty and keep coming here to draw water." However, Jesus did not enter into the relationship with the woman for the benefits it would bring. Christ gave much more than He ever received. The Apostle Paul wrote "There is no difference, for all have sinned and fallen short of the glory of God, and are justified freely by His grace through the redemption that came by Jesus Christ. God presented Him as a sacrifice of atonement" (Rom 3:22–25). Christ's principle for interpersonal relationships was the Golden Rule, not Social Exchange—"In everything, do to others what you would have them do to you, for this sums up the Law and Prophets" (Matt 7:12). Earlier in the Sermon on the Mount, He cautioned, "You have heard that it was said, 'Eye for eye, and tooth for tooth.' But I tell you, . . . if someone strikes you on the right cheek, turn to him the other also" (Matt 5:38–39).

Re-Thinking Burkean Frames—Faith Informing Scholarship

This essay's second look at Burke's *logology*, along with demonstrating how scholarship can inform faith, illustrates how faith can inform scholarship. For Burke,[22] both conceptions of "the perfect" and "the negative" (commands) are creations of language—thus, the problem. Humans are not perfect and we break commands. We cannot live up to the words we create. This leads to guilt. In turn, guilt leads to the need for purifica-

---

22. Burke, *Language as Symbolic Action*, 16

tion through the three tradition paths of scapegoating, mortification, and transcendence.

Purification Cycle and Forgiveness

One way to achieve purification is through scapegoating. Victimage attempts to purge the guilt by blaming and punishing another. Burke cautioned that "inasmuch as substitution is a prime resource of symbol systems, the conditions are set for catharsis by scapegoat (including the 'natural' invitation to 'project' upon the enemy any troublesome traits of our own that we would negate)."[23] The quintessential form of victimage would be the genocide of the "perfect" enemy.[24] Burke wrote: "Men [and women] who can unite on nothing else can unite on the basis of a foe shared by all."[25] When scapegoating is not a workable option, mortification is contemplated "insofar as ritual transference of guilt feelings to the scapegoat is frustrated, motives of self-destruction must come to the fore."[26]

Mortification consists of the personal acceptance of guilt and it ranges from simply acknowledging blame to its ultimate form—suicide. Burke explained "the step from conscience-laden guiltiness to a regimen of mortification can be narratively translated into terms of the step from 'sin' to 'death.'"[27]

The third, and less used, path to purification is transcendence. Transcendence takes what is seen as "bad" and redefines it as "good." This strategy seeks society's granting of redemption to the degree that society can accept and see a new, transcendent order.

As Christian communication scholars, we would like to expand on these three strategies and argue for a fourth path of purification, forgiveness, as an extension of Burke's ideas.[28] Scapegoating and mortification

23. Ibid., 18.

24. Ibid.

25. Burke, *Philosophy of Literary Form* (Berkeley: University of California Press, 1973) 193.

26. Burke, *A Rhetoric of Motives*, 408.

27. Burke, *The Rhetoric of Religion*, 208.

28. Robert C. Chandler, Jeffrey Dale Hobbs, A. S. King, and Charles Walts, "Scapegoating,Transcendence, Mortification, and Forgiveness: Compensatory Arguments of Blame after Littleton," in *Argument at Century's End*, edited by Thomas A. Hollihan (Annandale, VA: National Communication Association, 2000) 528–36.

are tragic in nature. While transcendence approaches the closest to a comic path, the new social order may or may not be better than the existing one. We have faith that there is a fourth, and more consistently comic, path. This path is forgiveness and it is ultimately comic because it makes the guilt "disappear"—"But now he has appeared once for all at the end of the ages to do away with sin by the sacrifice of himself" (Heb 9:26). While Burke does not explicitly argue for forgiveness due to his "purely secular observations," we believe it is implicit in his writings for two major reasons.

First, extending Burke by introducing concepts from Christianity is consistent with his collected works. Burke's borrowing from the Judeo-Christian story is both obvious and substantial. Dramatism is logology: "If we defined 'theology' as 'words about God,' then by 'logology' we should mean 'words about words.'"[29] Since the Judeo-Christian story is borrowed by Burke to define the problem as the need for purification, we propose that it is necessary that we borrow from the Judeo-Christian story to define the solution as forgiveness. "'If you had known what these words mean, "I desire mercy, not sacrifice," you would not have condemned the innocent'" (Matt 12:7). Without the comic frame of forgiveness, it is impossible to become consubstantial with Christ.

Second, there is an analogy that can be made between the four master tropes of Burke and the four possible paths to purification. Burke identifies the four master tropes as metaphor (or perspective), metonymy (or reduction), synecdoche (or representation), and irony (or dialectic).[30] A subtle twist of each of the tropes invites their conjunction with corresponding purification moves.

Scapegoating is compatible with the concept of synecdoche as the scapegoat represents guilt. Mortification corresponds with metonymy as the mortified individual conveys intangible blame in terms of a tangible person. Transcendence is compatible with the concept of irony as "bad" is turned into "good" (its opposite). Finally, forgiveness corresponds with metaphor because, in forgiveness, we see humans as "divine." Paul wrote to forgive "each other, just as . . . God forgave you" (Eph 4:32). It is in forgiveness that we become like Christ.

It is important that Christian communication scholars offer the construct of forgiveness as a return contribution to Burke's insights, as it

---

29. Burke, *The Rhetoric of Religion*, 1.

30. Burke, *A Rhetoric of Motives*, 503–17.

allows people to avoid any tragic turns. Mortification and scapegoating privilege the cult of the kill, but forgiveness circumvents it. Christology teaches that one cannot be one with the body of Christ without forgiveness. Logology may yet discover forgiveness as the ultimate comic turn that allows society to avoid the "progressive" march towards perfection manifested in the cult of the kill. Thus, the rhetorical move of forgiveness provides the both/and comic alternative to the tragic means of guilt purification and ritual sacrifice—allowing Christology to repay the insights that logology offered theology. Adding forgiveness to the rhetorician's palate of illuminating constructs may be critical to our understanding of otherwise inexplictable rhetorical turns. As the central contribution of the critic, this understanding may offer us a way back to order over division and guilt—while avoiding the pains of mortification and the sacrifice of the scapegoat.

Conclusion

Christians, whose *language* is a vocabulary identified with the Word, are called to be different. Since a Christian's language is Christ, a Christian lives in a different world and is motivated by a force that is not of this world. Christ, as the Word, enters into a Christian's interpersonal relationships to create life-saving and life-transforming encounters as we forgive those around us.

To reach this conclusion, this essay explored the range that lies between the theological and the logological—seeking how each might inform the other in helpful ways. Specifically, this essay addressed the issue of interpersonal communication in terms of the power of words as well as the principles of relationships given in Christian doctrine. Secondly, this essay reconsidered Kenneth Burke's purification ritual (cult of the kill) and corresponding Christian thought, as well as language (logology) itself, in order to offer a new page for understanding the rhetorical moves of scapegoating, mortification, and transcendence from a Christian theological frame—extending the traditional Burkean typology along a trajectory that is consistent with a greater logological inference. In so doing, we have illustrated that it is appropriate, possible, and necessary for scholarship to inform faith and faith to inform scholarship.

11

Garrison Keillor's Chiasmus

A Study for Homiletic Form

DAVID FLEER

Keillor's Monogogues in the Literature

Garrison Keillor's Lake Wobegon has become such a staple of the American imagination that phrases and impressions from his monologue surface as metaphor or point of argument in a surprising variety of disciplines. Ralph's Pretty Good Grocery Store in Lake Wobegon, which operates under the sensible catchphrase, "If you can't get it at Ralph's, you can probably get along without it," is now a metaphor for democratic thinking.[1] Keillor's closing description of Lake Wobegon, "Where the men are good looking, where the women are strong and where all the children are above average," has been appropriated in education as the "Lake Wobegon Effect" to describe students who tend to overstate their academic accomplishments in student self-reported data.[2] The "effect" has been utilized for studies on work-related absenteeism,[3] and taken up by psychologists and theorists in the field of economic geography.[4]

Not only has Keillor's fictional work provided slogans and images for the academic world, it has also been a source of inquiry. Religious studies connect Keillor's essential themes with larger theological issues. Laura Smit claims, "Keillor's popularity is based on the accuracy with which he reflects his audience's own feelings about the home they left behind."[5] Similarly, Beldon Lane acknowledges that Keillor's "sensitivity for place"[6] is at the heart of his religious imagination. Like Lewis and

Tolkien before him, and Scripture writers before them, Keillor creates for his listeners a place in the imagination where "faith can be tried on for size . . . . [which] always involves a joining of geography and narrative."[7] Some commend Keillor's theology of "generic grace" because it speaks to those outside the Christian world,[8] while others note Keillor's strong appeal to those who live within the orbit of the church since he takes church so seriously.[9]

A Prairie Home Companion has even been cast as a type of church. Michael Nelson finds in the program all the earmarks of a Christian worship service: announcements that pertain to members of the audience, musicians on stage who take the place of a choir, Powdermilk Biscuits as the bread of communion and, especially, Keillor's monologue which usually runs the prescribed twenty minutes of a sermon.[10]

Analyses of Keillor's monologues typically focus on the program's themes and the orator's delivery. More than two decades ago Doug Thorpe noted that in Keillor's monologues, "details are kept to a minimum . . . the voice is personal, reflective; often it is strikingly moral . . . . Vulnerable himself, the narrator sees vulnerability everywhere."[11] Keillor eventually retired, moved out of the country, resurfaced in New York with a modified show and, a few years later, returned to St. Paul to resurrect the program.[12] Appreciation for Keillor's delivery, especially his voice, continues, "His mouth was so near the microphone that he did not need much volume. He seemed to be speaking directly in my ear, and he was so close that I could hear his breath whistling through his nose hairs."[13] One could not help but wonder at "all the things he was doing right."[14]

Keillor's work has received serious attention in rhetorical studies.[15] Sonja Foss and Karen Foss argue that Keillor's radio monologues rhetorically construct a feminine spectator by dismantling the male gaze, creating Lake Wobegon as a feminine setting, and employing a feminine speaking style.[16] Keith Michael Hearit uses Burkean analysis to label the rhetorical strategies that Keillor employs in creating identification with his audience. Hearit argues that in Keillor's characteristic work, "We are prepared less to demand a certain qualitative progression than to recognize its rightness after the event."[17]

The above work, notwithstanding, Keillor's oeuvre has not undergone serious examination for its arrangement. Hearit's observation that, "the elements of the [Keillor] story are anticipatory in nature and reach a logical conclusion" lacks precision.[18] Hearit's conclusion, "Within Keillor's narratives there is always that logical progression which comes to a climax,"[19] is generally true, but raises more questions than it answers. What is the progression of Keillor's narratives and where is the climax?

Foss and Foss elsewhere find in Keillor an example of a "stream of consciousness" speech, which they define as, "An unfocused organizational pattern that does not contain easily identifiable connections among main ideas. It is held together by a central idea, but this idea is not as explicitly stated as it is in other organizational patterns."[20] They do entertain the heuristic possibility that careful examination may reveal some system or idea that connects Keillor's "seemingly irrelevant fragments."[21]

Typical of the comments on Keillor's arrangement is that from James Wall, "The tales . . . still ramble on, starting at one point and finishing somewhere else . . . ."[22] Bob Frye notes that one monologue, which begins with a train derailment and ends with a man driving into a snow bank, is "artfully intertwined."[23] Like other observers, Frye fails to consider just how Keillor's narrative segments connect.

Are Keillor's monologues simply rambling streams of consciousness? If not, how does this artist "tie it all together?" In this essay I shall respond to Foss and Foss' heuristic suggestion that with closer analysis "some system or idea" holds together the fragmentary segments of the Keillor monologue. Based on these findings, I shall briefly explore some implications for the current discussion on sermonic form in the field of homiletics.

Approaching Keillor's Monogogues on Their Own Terms

Arrangement, defined by Cicero as the setting in order of the invented topics so that each might have a definite place in delivery, retains a supple life in rhetorical studies. Early in the first half of the twentieth century, neo-Aristotelianism dominated rhetorical criticism with *dispositio* playing a strong role. Today, the critic is more apt to frame a speech from what one finds in culture,[24] in the mind of the critic, or in the speech's own terms.[25] *Dispositio* has evolved from the observations of Aristotle, Cicero, and Quintilian, to the prescriptive ways in which later rhetoricians applied their views, and further to a careful examination of a text for its own sequential development. The creative potential of the expansive notion of *dispositio* is memorably summarized in Hugh Blair's suggestion that form steals itself upon the audience until they are surprised by its conclusion.[26]

Approaching a Keillor monologue on its own terms reveals a reoccurrence of images, themes, and terms. For example, in an early Spring broadcast Keillor opens his monologue by describing the signs of the new season, "Just a few dark shards of snow in the deep shadows back in the trees, a little tinge of green in the grass and a little faint haze of green, or is that our imagination, up in the branches of the trees?"[27] He then adds, "The other morning there was this beautiful fog, this thick fog, outlines of branches of trees back in the fog. You stood at your kitchen window and looked out at it and it made you think of the Yorkshire moors or Ireland or someplace where people live large, romantic, fictional lives."[28] The haze, fog, and shadows that stir the imagination in these opening comments appear again in the center of the monologue, this time as smoke from a cigar. Here, Keillor as narrator in the first person, recalls, "Little smell of cigar smoke drifted across the grass . . . Such an exotic smell. So foreign, so romantic. Cigar smoke . . . That smoke made me think of far away places."[29] When Keillor concludes the monologue he returns to a vaporous image. In an evocative scene he brings back to life family members in order to look out at him from a dated photograph, "I'm the man in the green checked suit with his head under the black cloth who drives the Chrysler and smokes a little black cheroot. They're looking at me now. And, they're thinking, 'How did you get there? What happened to you?'"[30] Images of smoke or fog that stimulate the creative memories of both narrator and audience, also work to connect content from different places within the monologue. The narrator who reports the week's weather, the narrator as young character, and finally the narrator as a reflective adult are all linked, anticipating or recalling specific narrative segments in the Family Portrait monologue.

Approaching Keillor's monologues on their own terms one finds that they are often filled with thematic and linguistic couplets. Usually, Keillor's pairing of words, themes, or characters progress a thought or develop a meaning. In the Family Portrait monologue Keillor's opening remarks set up the dichotomies: large/small, romantic/mundane, and fictional/real.[31]

Or, consider the arrangement of material within another monologue entitled "Vacation Bible School" (see figure 1). On the surface, the monologue's form appears to be little more than a string of events meandering along, connected only through a brief transition or a generic setting (early summer activities). There seems to be no tie between a fast driving senior citizen (segment I) and the local high school graduation (segment II). However, narrative segments throughout the monologue are linked by common words and themes.

FIGURE 1: KEILLOR'S JUXTAPOSITION OF THEMATIC MATERIAL IN THE "VACATION BIBLE SCHOOL" MONOLOGUE

Opening comments: Wood ticks in nice weather *comforts* complainers

Segment I   Senator Thorvaldson driving: a dis*comfort*ing thought

Segment II   *Children's* High School Graduation

                A   Pranks, *clowning* with Mr. Halverson

                        B   Graduates are off—but did we *cheat* them?

Segment III   VBS *Clown* (Pastor's Wife) and Church of the Brunch *cheat* their children

                        B′   Story which holds the source of true *comfort*: Job

                A′   Keillor as *clown*: but someone was paying attention

Segment II′   Return to the *Children*: what will become of them?

Segment I′   Return to Senator Thorvaldson driving: *comfort* from *Job*: "He won't take me out."[32]

Note how Keillor utilizes critical words to weave the material in the VBS monologue. For instance, *comfort* ends both segments I and I′. Keillor connects these segments with reference to Senator Thorvaldson, the source of his dis*comfort*. At the same time he casts an eye on the center of the monologue (III, B′), Job, the source of his *comfort*.

Again, Keillor concludes the graduation segment by wondering aloud if we have *cheated* our children by not telling them all they need to know. The same word connects with the next segment's theme, the Church of the Brunch, who *cheat* their children by not telling them about serious biblical stories. Even incidental words connect segments. For example, *rockets* tied to the spark plugs in the Superintendent's car later appear as an adjective (*rocket*ing) to describe Thorvaldson's driving speed.

Significant themes link segments, as well. Judy Ingqvist, the pastor's wife, is dressed as a *clown* (III, A) and Keillor describes his own *clownish* ways (III, A′). While the word is not used of the high school graduates,

Keillor does detail their *clownish* pranks on the principal (II, B). The difference between Keillor, the other clowns and the VBS, he explains, is that VBS has no one "paying attention" to the important stories (III, A'). That implied problem is resolved when listeners follow Keillor's cue and remember the previous segment and central focus, the story of Job (III, B').

Keillor's corresponding terms and themes link segments within the narrative. These connections function as more than chronological progression.[33] They manifest movement in another direction, from the narrative's extremities back to its center. Meaning foreshadowed in the opening remarks of the VBS monologue is articulated in the center section and is recalled in the conclusion.

I propose that Keillor's work, taken on its own terms, suggests a chiastic structure, a rhetorical form based on parallelism which creates a movement that is essentially concentric. Not denying a linear development that moves from the beginning to the end of a monologue, chiasm incorporates another sequence, from the exterior to the interior of the narrative. Chiasm works like a rhetorical spiral, with parallel lines converging on a center of meaning which is "the author's center of concern."[34] This convergence increases intensity and specifies Keillor's humor and social commentary. The pairings, thus, are for a particular rhetorical end. I shall additionally assert that the stability of the chiastic form is the grounding structure for Keillor's most effective work. It creates room for his distinctive delivery, evokes the imagination through inter-textual allusions, and deepens meaning through the pairing of words and themes.

Chiastic Frame: Creative Delivery and Imagination Educed

Keillor's chiastic form leaves its sequential trail, anticipating a certain direction that will link what has happened with what will transpire. This sure framework gives Keillor opportunity for creative expression. For example, Keillor will run on sentences,[35] or slow his delivery to complement an ominous phrase.[36] He can vocally imitate a word, like *snatch* or *crush* so that the sound of the word suggests its sense. He will pause after a comment for any number of reasons, an affect that creates time for his audience to consider his verbal images. Stability of form creates places where Keillor's s voice can represent the concerns of his favored characters. When Keillor maintains that tomatoes are an aphrodisiac, his crisp affirmation, "we know that," punctuated with a verbal pause, puts his claim in full sympathy with the true believers.[37] Nouns like *shoes* and *tires*, with no more than Keillor's hoarse and breathy voice, are given peculiar verbal emphasis. At times he picks up a Norwegian accent when a character needs it. Keillor's pauses signal transitions, emphasize a comic punch line, or point to an emotive scene.[38] Chiastic form gives Keillor the leisure to accent his perceptions and judgments and linger as long as rhetorically necessary.

We can draw further insight into the kind of work Keillor performs within a narrative segment by examining his use of sources, specifically employment of his published work. The structural stability of the monologue's chiastic arrangement allows Keillor to draw on previously published material, his stock scenes and characters, and re-position them in a new location, adapting previous characters and plots to meet a monologue's particular needs.

Consider, for example, one reference in Keillor's Family Portrait monologue. The scenic focus of this Lake Wobegon tale, the family photograph, appears previously in his novel, *Lake Wobegon Summer, 1956*. In the prior work, Keillor describes the experience of his extended family sitting for a group picture,

> Daddy is a man of the picture and he loves his Kodak box camera. At family picnics he loves to arrange family portraits in the backyard and place Al next to LeRoy and Uncle Sugar and Aunt Ruth and Mother in her new green dress and Aunt Flo, all in a row beside the hydrangeas, and cry 'Cheese!' and dash into the gap between Ruth and Mother and grin as the shutter goes *click!* Then get one of LeRoy mugging and get the earnest Al to hold out his hand for a trick picture in which he seems to be holding Flo's head in his palm. We have pictures of various dogs wearing hats and neckties.[39]

In a monologue delivered one year after the book's publication, Keillor uses the same event with significant alterations. During a Sunday gathering of the extended family, Aunt Eva announces, "It's time we had a good portrait of this family and not this sort of shadowy Kodak Brownie snapshot. I want a good picture of everybody."[40] Prior to the portrait, the grown ups sit on kitchen chairs arranged around the front of the house by the lilacs and hollyhocks and begonias.[41] Just before the shot is taken, "My Uncle Lee said, 'When you see [the photographer] squeeze the bulb it's a four second exposure. So, you two boys, you run as fast as you can around to the other side and stand over there and then you wait until you see the picture and you'll be in both places'. . . Right in front of him sat his dog, Buster Brown, an old mutt, a kind of terrier, black circle around one eye."[42] Moments later, "[M]y Uncle Lee has reached into his pocket and put on a fake nose and mustache and the hat is on the dog's head and it's tilted rakishly over one ear."[43]

Notice first the obvious places where Keillor follows the script: 1) attention to detail in positioning persons within the picture, 2) identified flowers as background, 3) dog wearing clothing, 4) practical jokes, and 5) running at the click (or, the squeeze of the bulb) to appear in two places in one photograph.

Consider, as well, the details where Keillor deviates from the earlier written script: 1) Eva, not Daddy, arranges the portrait, 2) the photographer is not Daddy, but first the unnamed man in a green checked suit, and then Keillor, himself, 3) placement of persons in the picture differs for both persons and place, 4) the dog wearing clothing is expanded with description, name, and reason for its name, 5) Kodak is not the camera that takes the picture but the inferior product that Eva wants to improve, and most important, 6) the *portrait setting has more than a silly purpose, it is opportunity for serious reflection.*

Other examples abound in monologues where Keillor mines his published works.[44] What is noteworthy in these connections between a particular monologue and a prior text is that Keillor uses a scene or a character like a commonplace, and in this re-use creatively adjusts or modifies the material to suit a monologue's particular need. Within this seemingly extemporaneous[45] structure Keillor relies on a larger narrative to evoke the imagination. Keillor seems to envision a locale or person as he describes it, aiding his listeners to do the same.

An example of the evocative echoes and allusions to previous material is seen in the references to Aunt Eva in the Family Portrait monologue. Eva has arranged the family portrait, kept her plans from Grandma, knowing she'd protest and abscond. When Grandma still tries to leave the scene "to fix her hair", Eva says, "You look just fine, Mother."[46]

Aunt Eva is given a fuller description in *Lake Wobegon Summer*, 1956, "I asked if I was going to hell and she said, 'Don't be ridiculous.' And then she did something that nobody in our family did, ever, she told me she loved me, and she threw her big arms around me, and I took a deep breath of her, and she squeezed and said, 'I wish you still lived with me, precious.'"[47] The novel discloses a certain mystery to Aunt Eva who is judged, by some, as crazy.[48] Yet, the familial image of innocence, of the preschool aged narrator snuggled during nap with one of Aunt Eva's dresses, her fragrance captured within its fabric, stays with the reader through out the novel. For Lake Wobegon connoisseurs, the monologue's quick reference to Eva arranging the family portrait brings up a full-bodied image of a warm and loving mother-like figure, supplying motive and fullness of character in the monologue.

This is how Keillor's stories work. Meaning is embedded in form. However, the essential question arises, "How does Keillor's sequential trail reveal meaning and character in his narrative?"

Chiastic Frame: Value Pairs and Deepening of Meaning

Functioning like "effective juxtaposition," Keillor's corresponding story segments, while spatially removed within the narrative, give rise to his narrative's motif. In the Family Portrait monologue, even the opening line suggests the importance of "imagination" and the relation of the real and romantic worlds.[49] The monologue's initial remarks foreshadow imagination's involvement in reconciling a dichotomous world and set out two contrasting pairs: spring/winter and romantic/real. The question thus arises, "Does Keillor maintain or reverse these dichotomies?" If the latter is true, "How does Keillor perform this reversal of values in relation to his chiastic form?"[50]

Consider again Keillor's linguistic pairings in the Family Portrait monologue. The entire narrative repeats a number of similar dichotomistic pairs related to the basic romantic/real. These include: present/past, faraway places/farm, and alive/dead. At the center of the monologue, Keillor develops yet another pair, laughter/serious. Keillor begins by reporting the comic details of a boat incident, with audience laughter greeting various moments in Keillor's delivery. The story is of a summer resident who tries out his new inboard boat,

> equipped with fish radar which is connected to a global positioning system that uses a satellite reading to lock in to the biggest fish in the lake . . . the onboard computer takes over the steering . . . so you're free to go up in the bow and drop the bait right down off that big Walleye's nose . . . for some reason the fish radar locked in on a merganser that was flying around, flying around, or maybe the shadow of the merganser, who knows, but suddenly the boat took off in these tight circles, going at top speed. The

man was hanging on for dear life. And then the duck came in and landed on the water and the boat tore towards him, the duck took off. People standing on shore watching.[51]

Once Keillor has his St. Paul audience laughing, characters within the narrative follow suit, "He could hear people on shore laughing. People hooting and cackling."[52] At this very moment in the monologue, Keillor begins to blur the laughter/serious pairing. In the subsequent narrative segment, laughter is reintroduced to describe Pastor Ingqvist's action during the citation of the creed.[53] The laughing pastor precedes a Keillor riff on wanting certain professionals (pilots, surgeons, and ministers) to not be "silly." The section concludes with a final reference to the Pastor Ingqvist incident, and ministers in general, "This is the guy who sends you off. You don't want people laughing when you go."[54] The initial clarity of the laughter/serious dichotomy reaches full ambiguity with Keillor's lengthy description of the staid practices of the Sanctified Brethren, who for amusement, "Would sit and plan their funerals . . . . They wept as naturally as you'd brush your hair."[55] The ambiguity pushes the monologue beyond simple comedy, beyond even the definition of satire, to shake the original value pairings.

This laughter/serious segment immediately precedes the lengthiest portion of the monologue where Keillor describes a point in time and then holds that moment for nearly the duration of the narrative. The "frozen frame" is the family posed for the photograph. Keillor maintains the instant by repeating one image with these seven phrases, "She got people lined up". . . "I stood there next to my uncle Lee" . . . "I stood next to my Uncle Lee" . . . "I stood next to him with my cousin" . . . "My Uncle Lee stood there" . . . "We stood and waited" . . . "and he started to squeeze the bulb." Following each of the seven lines Keillor makes comments that are either humorous, like describing Uncle Lee's brand of practical jokes, or images of the exotic possibilities of life, evoked by the photographer's cheroot smoke.[56] When the bulb is finally squeezed,[57] Keillor verbally examines the persons and details in the photograph. The entire monologue concludes when he has characters in the photograph look out at him. He, thus, becomes the photographer and embodies the imagination, "And they're all looking out at that picture at me, I'm the man in the green checked suit . . . ."[58] In a narrative that opens with Keillor looking out imaginatively at the fog, this is a stunningly evocative turn to self assessment, for narrator *and* listeners.

How has Keillor brought his audience to engage his fictive world? How are listeners moved to perform what he embodies in the narrative? Keillor, in the closing scene, reverses the two pairs, present/past and alive/dead. He accomplishes this by bringing the past into the present and making the dead (in the photograph) come alive.[59] Then, in the grand reversal, extended family members in the photograph look out at Keillor. At this closing moment, with Keillor's embedded chiastic cues, listeners longing to interpret the event, turn back to the middle section of the discourse, Keillor's comments on laughter. Now, Pastor Ingqvist's cackling during the creed is judged.[60] The original value pair, laughter/serious is reversed, with serious becoming the positive term. The serious creed itself assumes the valued position. All the valued pairs are flipped. The dead are now alive, the serious judge the silly, and the farm transforms to a place where Keillor could have "made something of himself."[61] The large and romantic have become reality. Opposite value pairs in proximity throughout the monologue are reversed, unearthing deep emotion and serious reflection. This process makes listeners both eyewitnesses and participants in the drama. Keillor's chiastically structured narratives are an example that meaning can be embedded in dispositional detail as Keillor performs what he beckons of his audience, to engage the photographic moment of our lives.

Keillor's Chiasm: Implications for Homiletics

Close analysis reveals a lively dispositional system that holds together the segments of a Keillor monologue. Reoccurring images, words, and themes are chiastically related and thus move, for clarity and meaning, to the monologue's center. The stable nature of this framing device allows Keillor to develop his signature style and delivery, even evoking the imagination through adaptation of a larger narrative. Within the monologue, Keillor's reversal of value pairs is accomplished, in part, through chiastic movement. Extended chiasm is an essential form of Keillor's monologues. But, how might *dispositio,* which "steals itself upon the audience" and creates a narrative world, inform homiletics?

This study poses serious implications for the discipline of homiletics, suggesting the *continuation* of the discussion of sermonic form. In Charles Campbell's substantial and intelligent critique of recent homiletic theology he rejects the New Homiletic's fixation on narrative form. Recalling, that "one of the marks of spiritually impoverished times is too great a concern for external form," [62] Campbell argues that plot *should be* dependant on character. He finds support for his claim in Scripture where the key is not narrative form, but the "One whose identity is rendered by the narratives in the Bible." Story does not save, Campbell reminds us, "Rather, it is God in Jesus Christ."[63] Thus, it is character and not plot that is primary. Campbell further clarifies, "It is the central character [Jesus of Nazareth] rendered by the gospel narratives, not narrative plot in general, that is at the heart of preaching shaped by the biblical story."[64] In other words, narrative serves Jesus' identity.

Campbell sternly rejects the simplistic move from narrative Scripture to narrative sermon, claiming that the narrative logic of the story of Jesus, and not general considerations of narrative structure, be the crucial connection between sermon form and content. "The relationship between narrative text and sermon is more complicated than many contemporary narrative homileticians have suggested."[65] Following Hans Frei, Campbell asserts that the general understanding of narrative (the movement of plot shaped by character and incident) is incomplete without the unity of Jesus who emerges in that narrative.

Ironically, however, attention to plot may help the preacher to "linger with the identity of Jesus before moving too quickly to his meaningfulness,"[66] the very quality Campbell urges and commends. Following Campbell's fundamental corrective to narrative preaching, I propose that we consider *more closely* how the text's form paints the details of character that summons listeners into the world depicted in Scripture and toward the character of Jesus.[67] As I have shown in Keillor's monologues, meaning and character can be embedded in chiastic form. Thus, should not preachers attend to the same matters in reading and preaching Jesus? To miss the form is to miss the depth of meaning and the allurement of the character who is central to the narrative.

In fact, the chiastic movement apparent in Keillor is similar to what one finds at places in Scripture.[68] For example, the tensions developed in the narrative segments within Keillor's monologues function in some ways like the tension of faith/fear in the collection of miracle pericopes in Luke 8:22–56. In the last of four stories in this cluster, fear and faith appear to be concepts of opposition, presented as a faith/fear pairing. After news of the death of Jairus' daughter, Jesus proposes, "Do not be afraid any longer, only believe" (Luke 8:50). Yet in the other neighboring miracle stories, fear is the *consequence* of Jesus' miracle. The disciples are afraid *after* the storm at sea is calmed (8:25), the townsfolk are "frightened" and "gripped with fear" *after* the legion of demons are cast out of the violent and possessed man (8:35, 37), and *after* her healing of the twelve year hemorrhage the woman responds with "trembling."[69] The tension is not easily resolved, especially when one observes that Jesus commends only the trembling woman. Luke pushes *fear*, initially the negative value in the faith/fear pairing, to an equivocal and imaginative status, thus embedding Jesus and his message in an intricate form.[70]

Campbell's emphasis on character is a vital corrective to the recent trend in homiletics. "Christians do not worship a particular genre, but rather the One whose identity is rendered through the story."[71] Campbell's critique is a necessary reminder that homiletic appropriation of form should never impede interpretation of content for which the form originally served. But, form and content are intertwined, as the complex tapestry of Keillor's monologues reveal. What *is* needed in the discipline, therefore, is attention to the form that crafts meaning and develops character.[72]

NOTES

1. So argues John Mueller, "Democracy and Ralph's Pretty Good Grocery: Elections, Equality and Minimal Human Being," *American Journal of Political Science* 36 (November, 1992) 983–1003.

2. Nan L. Maxwell and Jane S. Lopus, "The Lake Wobegon Effect in Student Self-Reported Data," *The American Economic Review* 84 (1994) 201. The "effect" is debated in J. J. Cannell, "The Lake Wobegon Effect Revisited," *Educational Measurement: Issues and Practices* 7 (1988) 12–15.

3. D. H. Harrison and M. A. Shaffer, "Comparative Examinations of Self-Reports and Perceived Absenteeism Norms: Wading Through Lake Wobegon," *Journal of Applied Psychology* 79 (1994) 240–51.

4. Risa Palm, "Catastrophic Insurance: Patterns of Adoption," *Economic Geography* 71 (April, 1995) 119–31.

5. Laura Smit, "The Image of Home," *Theology Today* 45 (1988) 305–14. William Lee Miller crowns Keillor "the nation's leading humorist-as-theologian"; Miller, "*Sola Gratia* in Lake Wobegon," *Christian Century* 104 (June 3–10, 1987) 526–28.

6. Beldon Lane, "Fantasy and Geography of Faith," *Theology Today* 50 (1993) 399–400.

7. Ibid., 398.

8. Miller, "*Sola Gratia*," 526–28.

9. David Heim, "Garrison Keillor and Culture Protestantism," *Christian Century* 104 (June 3–10, 1987) 518. "He finds the church humorous precisely because he grants that it is deadly serious." Miller, too, notes that "religion figures in Keillor's work not just as subject matter but also as point of view," 527.

10. Michael Nelson, "Church on Saturday Night: Garrison Keillor's A Prairie Home Companion," *Virginia Quarterly Review* 77 (Winter, 2001) 1–18. Similarly, "One could almost substitute these sketches for a sermon in a worship service (and in some instances that would no doubt be an improvement)," Miller, "*Sola Gratia*," 526–28.

11. Doug Thorpe, "Garrison Keillor's 'Prairie Home Companion': Gospel of the Airwaves," *Christian Century* 99 (July 21–28, 1982) 793–96. Thorpe claimed that the beauty of the program was set in the listeners' knowledge of its transience. With the publication of early broadcasts (*Leaving Home*), distribution of cassette recordings, and Internet access to past programs (www.prairiehome.org), Thorpe's theoretical position has vanished.

12. For a recent (2001) biographical sketch of Keillor's life, see Nelson, "Church on Saturday Night." The one book length biography, now quite dated, was unauthorized and opposed by Keillor: Michael Fedo, *The Man From Lake Wobegon* (New York: St. Martin's, 1987).

13. Barbara Brown Taylor, "A Manner of Speaking," *Christian Century* 117 (September 27–October 4, 2000) 968.

14. Ibid., 968.

15. For example, Keith Michael Hearit, "A Burkean Analysis of the Rhetoric of Garrison Keillor" (M.A. thesis, Central Michigan University, 1988); and Peter H. Schreffler, "Caught Between Two Worlds: The Spiritual Predicament and Rhetorical Ambivalence of Garrison Keillor" (Ph.D. dissertation, Bowling Green State University, 1990), in the fields of Communication and English, respectively.

16. Sonja K. Foss and Karen A. Foss, "The Construction of Feminine Spectatorship in Garrison Keillor's Radio Monologues," *Quarterly Journal of Speech* 80 (November, 1994) 410–26. On the latter trait, the authors claim, "The form and style of his narratives embody features that typically are associated with feminine patterns, including lack of closure, refusal to judge, and feminine speech forms," 421. Keillor's reiteration of words and phrases and his use of indirect adverbs and qualifiers ("kind of," "sort of," "I think") typify a feminine style.

17. Hearit, "A Burkean Analysis," 15.

18. Ibid., 53. Hearit's analysis tends to squeeze Keillor's material into Burkean forms without looking first to the trajectories suggested from Keillor's work.

19. Ibid., 52.

20. Sonja K. Foss and Karen A. Foss, *Inviting Transformation: Presentational Speaking for a Changing World* (Prospect Heights, IL: Waveland, 1994) 35.

21. Foss and Foss, *Inviting Transformation*, 35. A full transcript of one Keillor monologue appears on 137–40.

22. James Wall, "The Secret is Out About Lake Wobegon," *Christian Century* 102 (November 13, 1985) 1019.

23. Bob Frye, "Garrison Keillor's Serious Humor: Satire in Lake Wobegon Days," *Midwest Quarterly* 40 (Winter, 1999) 132.

24. As with the ethnographer, for instance, in Gerry Philipsen, "Mayor Daley's Council Speech: A Cultural Analysis," *Quarterly Journal of Speech* 72 (1986) 247–60.

25. As with a "close reading" of the text. See, for instance, Michael Leff, "Things Made by Words: Reflections on Textual Criticism," *Quarterly Journal of Speech* 78 (1992) 223–31. The approach was suggested in nascent form in Edwin Black, "A Note on Theory and Practice in Rhetorical Criticism," *Western Journal of Speech Communication* 44 (1980) 331–36.

26. I have made this application to *dispositio* from an overview provided by Barbara Warnick, "Leff in Context: What is the Critic's Role?" *Quarterly Journal of Speech* 78 (1992) 232–37.

27. Keillor, "News From Lake Wobegon," *A Prairie Home Companion*, broadcast 4/13/02 (page 1: lines 7–9). The notation for this and following references are from transcriptions made by the author and in his possession. For relative placement within a monologue, transcripts generally run four pages, single spaced.

28. Ibid. (1:19–22).

29. Ibid. (3:35–43).

30. Ibid. (4:44—5:3).

31. Here, and throughout this essay, I have placed the positive term in the top position.

32. Keillor, "News From Lake Wobegon," *A Prairie Home Companion*, broadcast 6/15/02.

33. In the VBS monologue, the progression is neatly framed with comments about Senator Thorvaldson's driving.

34. John Breck, *Scripture in Tradition: The Bible and its Interpretation in the Orthodox Church* (Crestwood, NY: St Vladimir's Seminary, 2001) 103.

35. "Mrs. Gunsel went down the line and she looked at them and she realized a terrible thing, that the man from Millett had the best tomato. This man who was stuffed into coveralls, who had three days growth of beard, old pony tail on the back, smelled like he'd been sleeping in a silo eating silage for a few weeks and he came from Millett. This is not a tomato-growing town, Millett. This is a town where a garden is full of weeds, a place where they throw their beer cans, it's a place where people pee after parties, it's a toxic waste site, a garden, these are not gardening people. They keep old appliances out there. And yet, here it was . . . ," Keillor, "News From Lake Wobegon," *A Prairie Home Companion*, broadcast 6/29/02 (3:23–30).

36. For example, the "tent caterpillar" in his tomato contest monologue, Keillor, "News" 6/29/02 (1:18).

37. Ibid. (2:15).

38. For example, Keillor's pauses while he "looks" at the family photograph create a stirring engagement. In the following quote, the asterisk (*) indicates a significant verbal pause of one to two seconds in duration. Audience laughter accompanying the pause is marked with double asterisk. "It's a great picture.** I look at it often.* I'm now older than everybody in that picture except Grandma herself and I'm catching up to her pretty fast.* Most of those big people in that picture are gone.* And yet, in this picture* they look utterly alive. They're so clear. You can see all the wrinkles. You can see strands of hair. You can see the scruff marks on the shoes* and you can see* two boys down at the left* and two boys over to the right.** I sometimes look at those twins of me* and I imagine that one boy stayed here and learned how to farm and made something of himself.* And, the other boy* went off somewhere and hasn't been heard of since.** Which one am I? I'm not sure.*" Keillor, "News" 4/13/02 (4:36–45).

39. Keillor, *Lake Wobegon Summer, 1956* (New York: Viking, 2001) 17.

40. Keillor, "News," 4/13/02 (3:23–24).

41. Ibid. (3:10–11).

42. Ibid. (4:10–14).

43. Ibid. (4:40–41).

44. The neighboring town of Millett, "a hotbed of robbery, rock and roll and matricide" (*Lake Wobegon Summer,* 1956, 32) is identified in the Tomato Competition monologue as the home of the man who threatens to win the Mist County contest. Millett is a place that "is not a tomato-growing town, Millett." Keillor, "News," 6/29/02.

45. Any number of examples could be used. One previously cited instance is Keillor's riff on the seriousness of the Sanctified Brethren, Keillor, "News," 4/13/02 (2:25—3:6).

46. Ibid. (4:18).

47. Keillor, *Lake Wobegon Summer*, 1956, 54–55.

48. Ibid., 198, 289. Aunt Eva has spells (170–71), hypnotizes chickens (254), has a morbid dread of strangers, and talks of poisoning herself (247–60).

49. So, too, in the VBS monologue, the opening words set forth the narrative's motif, "It's been just perfect, just perfectly beautiful, absolutely perfect, bright beautiful warm days and all the complainers in our midst had to search hard and long to find something to satisfy them. And then a mosquito came along and they were so happy. A wood tick came along, pleased them, satisfied them. The need to be bitten, I guess. Wood ticks are a blessing." The monologue's humorous initial remarks ironically foreshadow the serious theme of finding pain in times of delight. Keillor, "News," 6/15/02 (1:6–10).

50. I am following Chaim Perelman and Lucie Olbrechts-Tyteca's definition of reversal of value pairs, an effort to settle incompatibilities between appearance and reality through the modification of their very structure and ultimately the remodeling of the audience's perception of reality. With the reversal of value pairs, the audience is forced to reconstruct reality and assign value to what they had before perceived as negative. See, Chaim Perelman and Lucie Olbrechts-Tyteca, trans. John Wilkinson and Purcell Weaver, *The New Rhetoric: A Treatise on Argumentation* (London: University of Notre Dame Press) 411–59. What is new in my essay is connecting value pairs to chiastic arrangement.

51. Keillor, "News," 4/13/02 (1:43—2:6).

52. Ibid. (2:8).

53. He "laughed in church. A very strange, inappropriate laugh . . . He laughed, a kind of nervous, a kind of whinny, a kind of giggle." Ibid. (2:11–14).

54. Ibid. (2:23–24).

55. Ibid. (2:25—3:6).

56. Each comment lasts, in order, 59, 61, 43, 44, 29, 21, and 20 seconds. The shortest segment in the descending duration is the comedic activity that follows the squeeze of the bulb.

57. Keillor holds the moment for nearly five minutes, one quarter of the monologue.

58. Keillor, "News," 4/13/02 (4:44–45).

59. "They look utterly alive. . . . You can see all the wrinkles. You can see strands of hair. You can see the scruff marks on the shoes. . . . It's as if they were alive today all fifty of them. Children, people kneeling, people standing. Grandma trying to hide. You can see their faces, all of their hard work. And you can see their love of God and their fear of poverty and ruin . . . and the loyalty and such pride." Ibid. (4:36–45).

60. Judy Ingqvist will be similarly judged, in the VBS monologue, for playing the clown.

61. Keillor, "News," 4/13/02 (4:33).

62. Charles L. Campbell, *Preaching Jesus: New Directions for Homiletics in Hans Frei's Postliberal Theology* (Grand Rapids: Eerdmans, 1997) xiii.

63. Ibid., 172.

64. Ibid., 173.

65. Ibid., 211.

66. Ibid., 201.

67. I am attempting to circumvent the "grand assertions about unity of form and content . . . to support the turn to narrative . . . the cavalier moves to . . . narrative sermon structures"; ibid., 169–70.

68. See, for example, the suggestive arguments in Robert Stephen Reid, *Preaching Mark* (St. Louis: Chalice, 1999) 1–17; Ian H. Thomson, "Chiasmus in the Pauline Letters,"

Journal for the Study of the New Testament Supplements 111 (Sheffield: Sheffield Academic, 1995) 13–45; Roland Meynet, "Rhetorical Analysis: An Introduction to Biblical Rhetoric," *Journal for the Study of the New Testament Supplements* 256 (Sheffield: Sheffield Academic, 1998); and Breck, *Scripture in Tradition*, 89–158.

69. In Mark's parallel account, she responds to Jesus' post-miracle question, "in fear and trembling" (Mark 5:33). Luke drops the word "fear" allowing the accompanying action, "trembling," to work alone.

70. This is true for other Scripture writers, as well. For instance, note the similarity in character development in Keillor and Paul. As Campbell notes, "The allusiveness of Paul's language required a people trained to listen . . . they needed to know the story of Jesus," *Preaching Jesus*, 210. So, in Keillor, the fullness of characters like Aunt Eva and the Ingqvists is developed in careful relation to a larger narrative. As Campbell, following Richard Hays, claims, "[Paul's language] is rich with multiple meanings, inviting the participation and involvement of the hearers," ibid., 210.

71. Ibid., 202.

72. I conclude with this caveat, "It will *not* be good news when there are imitation Keillors all over the lot, peddling warm nostalgic memories of innumerable small towns" [even if developed in chiastic form! DF], Miller, *Sola Gratia*," 527.

12

Ronald Reagan, the Disciples of Christ, and Restoring America

JOHN M. JONES and MICHAEL W. CASEY

During his presidency, observers frequently discussed Ronald Reagan's appeal to the religious right, his use of religious language, and the influence of religious values on his presidency. Scholars also have provided a historical overview of Reagan's religious tradition in the Disciples of Christ.[1] Additionally, rhetorical critics have noted the tone of restorationism that pervades Reagan's discourse.[2]

To date, however, no analysis has directly linked Reagan's secular political rhetoric of restoration to his sacred religion of restoration, which he learned at an early age in the Disciples of Christ. In this essay, we endeavor to make that link. We argue that a sacred doctrine of restoration, advanced by the Disciples of Christ, served as a mythic template for a political doctrine of restoration for America, which saturates Reagan's political discourse over the many decades of his political career. We begin by discussing the "rhetoric of restoration," using Mircea Eliade's idea of the myth of the eternal return and tracing Reagan's religious roots in the Disciples of Christ. Next, we discuss how these teachings served as a pattern for his political rhetoric of restoration.

Reagan and the Disciples of Christ

Disciples of Christ theology, in Reagan's formative years, best could be described as a *rhetoric of restoration*. Eliade argues that the recovery of a lost golden age or ideal is a recurring theme in human history. This lost, but recoverable, ideal allows its possessors to rhetorically construct meaning for their lives and keep the "chaos" of meaningless or erroneous history at bay. Eliade says that the primitive person believed that primordial sacred time was real while profane time was unreal. By re-enacting periodic rituals and festivals revealed during the sacred primordial time of the gods, that sacred time was restored transforming profane time into the sacred cosmos. Time could be reversed and the chaos of profane reality remade into a perfect and whole world.[3]

For the Disciples, this restoration has five characteristics. First, such a discourse *assumes the original, primitive church as described in the New Testament is the ideal model.* To Disciples adherents, the early church was ordained by Christ and established and nurtured through the preaching of the Apostles, who themselves were inspired by God. The teachings of Christ and the Apostles, later assembled together in the New Testament, became a timeless pattern for the church. This pattern will bring about the pure primordial time. Second, a rhetoric of restoration *assumes emulation of that model should be the goal for all generations of Christians.* Because the New Testament is the church's blueprint, faithful adherence will produce the church that Christ intended to build throughout all generations. The primitive church is the only true church that God desires. Third, this unique rhetoric *emphasizes the danger and presence of apostasy.* To a pure restorationist, there is an ever-present possibility of drifting from the intent of Christ and the Apostles. Just as adherence would produce the church, deviation would produce a less-than-authentic version of the church. Such a departure would happen gradually, in tiny increments. Minuscule additions or subtractions from the original pattern would accumulate over time until eventually the modern church had abandoned its sacred doctrine and mission. Thus, the church must constantly stand guard against deviations from the New Testament church. These deviations would bring about the profane chaos that Eliade describes. Fourth, the rhetoric of restoration *assumes heresy or apostasy in any generation can be corrected by a return to first principles.* Thus the mission of the Disciples Movement was to call itself and other churches back to the New Testament pattern. This pattern is the means to restore the sacred cosmos or church in any age. The primitive church can and will transcend any chaos resulting from the corruptions of the church that occurred in human history. Fifth, Alexander Campbell, Barton Stone, and thousands of other Disciples believed *all Christians could be united on this primitivist basis*. By taking the Bible alone all Christians could discard the rubbish of the ages and enjoy perfect primordial bliss and be united together in one perfect church.[4] This plea for reform emanated from Disciples pulpits in the United States and throughout the world and was heard by thousands of adherents. Among them was Ronald Reagan.

Reagan's experience with the Disciples of Christ dates back to his childhood in Dixon, Illinois. Although his father, Jack, was Roman Catholic, his mother regularly attended the Sunday services of the Disciples of Christ, rarely missing a service. Baptized into the church in 1910, the year before Ronald Reagan was born, Nelle Reagan is described as "an admirably devout, indeed zealous, churchwoman." Early in her marriage, Nelle Reagan assumed responsibility for the spiritual training of her two boys and took them to her church. She gave her youngest son a book, *That Printer of Udell's*, a story of the child of an alcoholic who discovered that he had a gift for public speaking and became a traveling preacher. Young Ronald, whose own father was an alcoholic, was inspired by this story of a young boy who eventually carried his message of reform to Washington, DC.[5] Reagan decided to become a member of his mother's church and was baptized at the age of twelve.[6]

As a teen, Reagan "attended prayer meetings, taught Sunday School, acted in his mother's morality plays, and in 1926 led an Easter service."[7] During his high school years, Reagan met and fell in love with Margaret Cleaver, the daughter of his minister. Ben Cleaver, Margaret's father, served as a father figure for Reagan, and the teenager spent much time at the Cleaver's house.[8] Mentored by the religiously conservative Cleaver, Reagan was further grounded into Disciples' restorationist beliefs. Later he followed Margaret to Eureka College, a tiny Disciples of Christ school, where he graduated in 1932.[9]

After finishing his education at Eureka, Margaret Cleaver and Reagan parted company and he worked as a sports reporter in Iowa. He remained with the Disciples, however, and upon securing a movie contract with Warner Brothers, promptly joined the Hollywood-Beverly Christian Church. At a men's forum at Hollywood-Beverly he delivered a speech condemning neo-fascism. Shortly afterward, his minister urged him to adopt a similar stance against communism, which Reagan soon did.[10] On March 4, 1952, Ronald Reagan married Nancy Davis at the Little Brown Church in the Valley, a Disciples of Christ congregation.[11]

By the time he became governor of California, Reagan no longer attended the Disciples of Christ and "occasionally attended Bel Air Presbyterian Church."[12] Nevertheless, Reagan at times alluded to his heritage. For example, when asked whether he had been "born again," he explained the Disciples' interpretation of the phrase before answering, "yes, by being baptized."[13] After leaving Washington, the Reagan's returned to California and once again attended Bel Air Presbyterian Church.

While Ronald Reagan did not remain a lifetime member of the Disciples, he clearly was grounded in their fundamental teachings. In the next section, we discuss how closely his political rhetoric paralleled this restorationist pattern.

Reagan's Rhetoric of Restoration

Careful analysis of the speeches Reagan delivered over several decades reveals a pattern in his account of the American story. This narrative is characterized by four important phases—a God ordained beginning, a journey traveled by ordinary Americans who embraced this creed, (the perfect primordium) a gradual drifting away from the basic tenets of the creed (the start of the corruptions of profane time), and the pathway to restoration (the re-enacting of the sacred American primordium) led by Ronald Reagan and ordinary American citizens who supported his cause. Reagan's story remarkably resembles a restorationist's version of Christianity. As Disciples adherents traditionally believe the New Testament church was ordained by God, the discourse of Ronald Reagan reveals his conviction that America began in a miraculous fashion, guided by the hand of a Supreme Being, and was set apart for a special mission. The Constitution and Declaration of Independence became the New Testament for the nation, serving as the pattern which America should follow. These foundational documents contained essential, timeless doctrines such as freedom, individualism, faith, peace through strength, and limited government. By holding steadfastly to these virtues, Reagan's America had grown and prospered, often against the odds.

But, like the church, America always faced the possibility of drifting from these principles and eventually apostasizing. Preventing this (or reforming the nation once an apostasy had occurred) required a political rhetoric of restoration, which we describe in this essay. From at least the early 1950s, Reagan discussed America's origins and heroic journey. With the increased role of the Federal Government in the 1960s and a changing global scene, Reagan's rhetoric warned of a drifting away and called Americans back to the pattern established by the Founding Fathers. By 1980, what began as a gradual drifting had evolved into a full- blown apostasy and he became the central leader of a political restoration movement as he campaigned for and was elected president. When he left office in 1989, he triumphantly proclaimed that the mission was accomplished.

The Miraculous Inception

Reagan's story of America attributed the establishment and development of the nation to God. It portrayed the United States as a country with sacred principles and a sacred purpose, traced America's struggle against the odds, warned of the tendency to drift away from these "sacred" principles, and pointed the way back to the straight and narrow. Disciples restorationists believe the church began in Jerusalem in 33 AD when the twelve apostles began to preach salvation through Jesus Christ.[14] From there the message spread throughout the world.

America's Divine origin was one of the primary focuses of Reagan's speeches. In 1952, Reagan narrated America's story at home.[15] In a speech entitled "America the Beautiful," he told an audience at William Woods College that he "thought of America as a place in the divine scheme of things that was set apart as a promised land" (9). God, in "shedding his grace on this country," had always "kept his eye on our land and guided it as a promised land for these people" (10).

The Jerusalem of Ronald Reagan's America was the city of Philadelphia, where the Founding Fathers gathered in the Pennsylvania State House to frame the Declaration of Independence. In Reagan's account, the Founding Fathers were discussing the possible repercussions of signing the historic document that would sever the colonies' ties to Great Britain. They talked of being put on trial for treason and of possibly losing their lives. In the midst of it all, a man stood up and spoke to the assembly, imploring them to, "Sign that document, sign it if tomorrow your heads roll from the headsman's axe" (10). They promptly signed the Declaration of Independence and when they went to look for the man, they were unable to find him. He had departed from the hall even though the doors were locked and guarded. Five years later at the commencement of Eureka College, Reagan's alma mater, the actor repeated a slightly different version of the story and this time attributed the story to Thomas Jefferson. In this account, the voice from the balcony said:

> Sign that parchment. Sign it if the next moment the noose is around your neck. Sign it if the next minute this hall rings with the clash of falling axes! Sign by all your hopes in life or death, not only for yourselves, but for all ages, for that parchment will be the textbook of freedom—the bible of the rights of man forever. Were my soul trembling on the verge of eternity, my hand freezing in death, I would still implore you to remember this truth—God has given America to be free.[16]

Reagan's story serves two important purposes. First, it strongly implies that Divine force was at work in the foundation of the United States, which adds legitimacy to the nation itself. Second, the account strengthens what Reagan believed to be America's creed by linking it to the will of God.

Again, the parallel between Reagan's beginning of the nation and the restorationist's beginning of the New Testament church is striking. As the New Testament served as the pattern for the Disciples, the principle of freedom as outlined in the Declaration of Independence and the Constitution provided the blueprint for the United States. America's success lay in the fact that it had clung steadfastly to the blueprint and the foundational principle of freedom. As a result, America had grown into "last best hope of man upon the earth."[17]

THE DANGER OF DRIFTING AWAY

The late fifties and early sixties saw the escalation of the Cold War and the fear of Soviet domination increase in the United States. The sixties also were marked by a renewed call to expand the role of the Federal Government. Ronald Reagan was deeply concerned about both. As the biblical restorationist feared apostasy in the church, Reagan feared the gradually increasing role of the government. This was a sign of corruption that was moving America away from the ideals of the American primordium. He believed that slowly expanding the government would erode individual freedom, eventually stripping it completely away and making Soviet conquest inevitable—the ultimate "chaos." Reagan contended that the Soviets, having taken over much of the world, desired to do the same with the United States. This could happen if the role of the Federal Government were allowed to increase: "They are convinced that we will abandon our democratic institutions one by one under the stress of constant pressure. Nikita Khrushchev said, "we cannot expect the Americans to jump from capitalism to Communism. However, we can assist their leaders in giving Americans small doses of Socialism until they suddenly awake to find they have Communism."[18] Reagan called this acceptance of socialism in tiny increments "encroaching control" (4).

If this continued, "we will discover one day that we have given up so much of democracy, we have become so much like them—there is no longer any cause for conflict between our two peoples."[19] Americans could either stop encroaching control or find themselves "spending their sunset years telling our children what it was like when men were free." (14) Throughout the sixties, LBJ's Great Society became the target of Reagan's critiques, and he cited numerous instances of excessive government.[20] This demonstrated that the perfect American pattern or primordium was being abandoned for chaos.

As he always had done, Reagan proclaimed that freedom, the penultimate American primordial value, should be esteemed most highly. Upon taking office as governor of California, he warned, "freedom is a fragile thing and is never more than one generation away from extinction." He also cautioned, "it is not ours by inheritance; it must be fought for and defended constantly by each generation." And failure to guard against the enemies of freedom would lead to the demise of the nation since "those who have known freedom and then lost it have never known it again."[21]

During his years as Governor of California, Reagan made an initial attempt at restoration through the "Creative Society," a theme on which he had campaigned in 1966. Intended as an answer to LBJ's "Great Society," the Creative Society sought to "discover, enlist and mobilize the incredibly rich human resources of California, calling on the best in every field to review and revise our governmental structure and present plans for streamlining it and making it more effective."[22] Rather than depending on government bureaucracy, the Creative Society would tap into the expertise of talented men and women in the private sector to solve California's problems. When Reagan left office in 1975, he could point to a reduction of welfare recipients, lower taxes and peace on college campuses in California as evidence that some degree of restoration had taken place. However, he still believed in an overall American primordium that needed to be restored.

1980: CARTER'S APOSTASY AND REAGAN'S RESTORATION

In 1980, the timing could not have been better for Reagan's strategy of restoration discourse. Chaos seemed to loom everywhere and many Americans longed for a recovery or restoration of American pride and ideals in a time of confusion and discouragement. This set the stage for Reagan to campaign for president calling "for a restoration of national strength and pride."[23] After securing the Republican nomination, Reagan vigorously attacked incumbent Jimmy Carter and pledged to make America great again.

Reagan's view that a falling away from America's basic values and principles was occurring was never clearer than in his bid for the presidency in 1980. If the 1960s were characterized by a gradual drifting away, then what happened to America in the late 1970s amounted to virtual apostasy. What little of the pure ideals of America were left, Reagan believed had been completely engulfed by the chaos engendered by America's external and internal enemies. Reagan laid responsibility for America's ills at the feet of the Carter administration, condemning the president for failure to provide adequate leadership. He told his party's convention, "there may be a sailor at the helm of this ship of state, but the ship has no rudder."[24] and his campaign speeches were filled with a plethora of Carter's transgressions.

Reagan warned of "three grave threats to our very existence, any one of which could destroy us" (1). These threats were "a disintegrating economy, a weakened defense, and an energy policy based on the sharing of scarcity" (1). Reagan's speeches suggested that Carter not only directly caused these exigencies, but was powerless to correct them and appeared to be out of touch with the American people. Worst of all, Reagan suggested, the Democratic president had blamed them for their plight.

Reagan described the Carter record as "a litany of broken promises, of sacred trusts abandoned and forgotten."[25] Specifically, Reagan blamed the president for unemployment, inflation, tax increases, high interest rates, and growing budget deficits. Additionally, Carter's energy policies had resulted in "gas prices twice as high as when he took office . . . long gas lines and the ever-present threat of another oil cutoff" as well as "skyrocketing heating oil prices" (3). And Carter had mistakenly relied on the Federal government to correct the nation's economic problems.

And what was the result of the increased regulation? Reagan suggested that such policies had hindered research and development (4), led to lost world market share, stifled productivity (4) and cost many Americans their jobs (5). His policies, according to Reagan, had affected minorities, especially blacks, by casting many out of work.[26] They had hurt the nation's farmers, "forcing tens of thousands of farm families from the land"[27] And Carter had met these crises with vacillating policies. Reagan noted that Carter criticized Ford for a Misery Index of 12.5 percent. Four years later, the Index had reached 20.3 percent, thus "by the very standard Jimmy Carter used to define failure, he has failed. Of the economic slump, the GOP challenger said, "call this human tragedy whatever you want. Whatever it is, it is Jimmy Carter's. He caused it. He tolerates it. And he is going to answer to the American people for it" (1).

Reagan denounced Jimmy Carter for his handling of other issues as well. Besides creating the economic woes of the late 1970s, Carter also was personally responsible for a number of international crises and the decline of America's military preparedness. In his acceptance speech at the Republican convention, Reagan outlined the administration's foreign policy failings. Reagan pointed out that Carter had allowed the Soviets to surpass the United States in "all but 6 or 8 strategic military categories,"[28] perpetuated the doctrine of détente with Russia, and in the process, confused our allies (3). Furthermore, he pointed out that President Carter had allowed the military to weaken[29] and cut both the Veterans Administration and military pay increases,[30] making many enlisted personnel eligible for food stamps.[31] All of this pointed to a drifting from America's first principles.

The abandonment of the American primordium by Carter threatened America with ultimate chaos. But America's problems still could be overcome with the right leadership. In the next section we discuss Reagan's discourse of restoration as he outlined his vision for America's recovery in 1980.

Recovery by Restoration

Ronald Reagan frequently asked his listeners whether they were better off than they were four years ago. If they could answer in the affirmative, he suggested that they should vote for his opponent. If, however, they believed as he did that the condition of America had worsened between 1976 and 1980, they should join him for what he termed a "new beginning." His call to change the direction of the nation in 1980 was filled with the language of restoration. His speeches often contained such words as "restore," "restoring," "restoration," "reclaim," "renew," "new beginning," "rebirth," "revival," "rebuild" as well as a call to "make America great again." This new beginning was a restoration of the ideals of the miraculous American primordium. As he accepted the Republican nomination in Detroit on July 17, 1980, Ronald Reagan contended that, "We need a rebirth of the American tradition of leadership at *every* level of government and in private life as well" (220). He took his audience back to the origins of the nation and to another time in which a call for restoration had resounded before issuing a similar call: "Four score and seven years later, Abraham Lincoln called upon the people of all America to renew their dedication and their commitment to a government of, by and for the people. Isn't it once again time to renew our compact of freedom, to pledge to each other all that is best in our lives; all that gives meaning to them—for the sake of this, our beloved and blessed land?" (221).

The Republican theme in 1980 was "Together . . . A New Beginning." In his campaign addresses, Reagan specifically outlined what that beginning entailed. It required that the nation "pledge to restore to the federal government the capacity to do the people's work without dominating their lives" (222). It required that "we reindustrialize our cities" by creating "enterprise zones in depressed urban areas."[32] To solve the plight of America's urban areas, Reagan called the nation to "revitalize, not just redistribute tax resources from one part of the country to another" (2). And the candidate pledged to "recapture the momentum black enterprise experienced in the early 1970s (3).

Also, on the economic front, Reagan promised that:

> By contrast, a Reagan/Bush administration will be able to reverse the decline in American's standard of living, and we will begin working to do this our first day in office. Last month, I offered a comprehensive economic program geared at reducing the growth in Federal spending, in taxes, in regulation, in the money supply, and restoring predictability and stability to economic policy. These are steps this administration has utterly refused to take, but they will form the foundation of the Reagan/Bush economic plan. And when we carry out these steps, we will be able to gradually reduce inflation and unemployment at the same time. That way, we can restore the dream to Americans of a continually improving standard of living."[33]

He later proclaimed that "we must restore confidence by following a consistent national economic policy that does not change from month to month."[34]

Militarily speaking, Reagan was concerned that the nation had been weakened by the policies of the incumbent and he frequently spoke of "restoring the margin of safety...both in conventional arms and the deployment of troops."[35] This was necessary in order to "restore the confidence and cohesion of the alliance system on which our security ultimately rests" (2). It also was essential, he reasoned, that the Soviets know "that we are going about the business of restoring our margin of safety pending an agreement on both sides to limit various kinds of weapons" (2). This restoration, he suggested, gave the nation a greater chance for real peace "because we will never be faced with an ultimatum from anyone" (2). In other areas pertaining to military readiness, Reagan argued that a Republican Administration could, "restore our seapower, insure our access to vital raw materials and energy, and buttress America's foreign policy with a first-class modern Navy."[36]

Coupled with his pledge to restore America's armaments was his determination to restore pride in America's troops. In October 1980, he stated that: "Restoring a sense of pride in their careers for the men and women in our fighting forces is another important element of my program for peace. We must direct our attention to the urgent manpower needs of our services. In defense matters, we hear much about hardware, not enough about people. The most important part of our military strength is the people involved—their quality, their training, their welfare."[37] Accomplishing this aim meant that the United States "must do all in our power to make sure they are well trained and well-equipped" and making sure that "their economic sacrifice is not out of proportion to what we ask of them" (3).

In matters of intelligence, Reagan emphasized the importance of "restoring the ability of the C.I.A. and other intelligence agencies to keep us informed and forewarned about terrorist activities." Moreover, he resolved to "take the lead in forging an international consensus that firmness and refusal to concede or to pay ransom are ultimately the only effective deterrents to terrorism" (3). The military and foreign policy restoration of which Reagan spoke, however, could only occur if Democrats and Republicans united in their efforts. For this reason, the candidate pledged "to take every step necessary to restore the bipartisan tradition in American national security and foreign policy." This, he promised, would be at the center of his efforts at peacemaking.

But not all of America's decline had been in the areas of economics or foreign policy. Since part of the apostasy had been moral in nature, Reagan called upon his audience to return to faith: "I don't ask you to 'trust me' to do all that. I ask you to go back to an older vision of where trust should be placed. You see it written on a dollar bill. In fact, about the only thing about a dollar that's worth more today than it was four years ago are the words 'In God We Trust.'"[38] By returning to faith in God, Reagan predicted, "we *can* exert America's moral leadership in the world again" and affirmed that "in a struggle against totalitarian tyranny, traditional values based on religious morality are among our greatest strengths" (1). Furthermore, a renewed faith would assist the nation in its effort to "rescue young people from drugs, our elderly from crime, [fight] pornography and poverty" and a host of other objectives (2).

Although he stressed that time was of the essence, Reagan also predicted that "we still have time to use our renewed compact to overcome the injuries that have been done to America these past three and a half years."[39] Armed with faith, the possibilities for the nation would be limitless. He reminded his audiences that, "the eyes of mankind are upon us, pleading with us to keep our rendezvous with destiny" and assured them that "we have God's promise that if we turn to Him and ask His help, we shall have it."[40] And with the same Divine assistance that had set America in motion, America "can still become that shining city on a hill" (2). When that occurred, Reagan prophesied, "the world will once again look on in awe, astonished by the miracles of education and freedom, amazed by a rebirth of confidence and hope and progress."[41] And, of course, America's reply to the world would be, "Well, what did you expect? We are, after all, Americans" (7). Reagan saw himself as more than a political candidate that year, rather he viewed himself as leading a restoration movement or crusade and his campaign discourse was flooded with restorationist language. On November 4, 1980, Ronald Reagan was elected president in a landslide. In 1989, Reagan would boast of the success of his agenda.

Restoration Accomplished, for Now

On January 11, 1989, Ronald Reagan delivered his farewell address to the nation. More than simply a trip down memory lane, an expression of gratitude to the American people or the final words of wisdom from an outgoing president, the Reagan farewell was a proud boast of a successful restoration movement. It was essentially a shift from restoration to preservation and closely resembled the rhetoric of the religious restorationist who believes they have duplicated the primitive church and now must maintain what has been restored. In Eliadean terms Reagan believed that he had successfully recreated the American primordium and its ideals in his administration. Turning back would risk losing everything that had been gained and threaten America with ultimate chaos which would be the loss of our freedom, power and greatness as a nation. We would no longer be the Shining City on a Hill to civilization.

Reagan described the scene in the South China Sea in which sailors aboard the carrier *Midway* spotted a small, leaky boat full of refugees from Indochina who were bound for America: "The *Midway* sent a small launch to bring them to the ship and safety. As the refugees made their way through the choppy waters, one spied the sailor on deck, and stood up, and called out to him. He yelled, 'Hello American sailor. Hello, freedom man.' A small moment with a big meaning."[42]

The significance of this story, in Reagan's view, was that it symbolized "what it was to be an American in the 1980s," because in this decade, "we stood again for freedom" (19). After acknowledging that American always had stood for freedom, Reagan suggested that during his administration, "we ourselves rediscovered it" (19). He also cited what he considered his two greatest accomplishments. The first was economic recovery; the second was "the recovery of our morale" and the fact that "America is respected again in the world and looked to for leadership" (19).

Economically speaking, Reagan believed he had restored strength and prosperity. He had gone from being "the new kid in school" at economic summits to being the center of attention of all the world leaders, who beseeched him, "tell us about the American miracle" (19). Much had changed since his run for the presidency in 1980, when detractors predicted an economic collapse. Now he could proudly boast that the "opinion leaders were wrong" and that "what they called 'radical' was really 'right'" and "what they called 'dangerous' was really just 'desperately needed'" (20). And the recovery came because America once again had observed time-tested principles that it had known for years:

> And in all of that time I won a nickname, the "Great Communicator." But I never thought it was my style or the words I used that made a difference; it was the content. I wasn't a great

communicator, but I communicated great things, and they didn't spring full bloom from my brow, they came from the heart of a great nation—from our experience, our wisdom, and our belief in the principles that have guided us for two centuries. They called it the Reagan revolution. And I'll accept that, but for me it always seemed more like the great rediscovery, a rediscovery of our values and our common sense. (20)

Reagan then explained how the "great rediscovery" was implemented. In keeping with his principle of less government and a lowering of the tax burden, "we cut the people's taxes and the people produced more than ever before" (20). All of this, he contended, spawned the greatest peacetime expansion in American history, increased family income, made America competitive again on the world markets, and reduced the rate of poverty at home (20).

In matters of foreign policy, Reagan argued that he and the nation had rediscovered the common-sense doctrine of peace through strength. The nation had rebuilt its defenses, which had yielded a long-term result of fewer nuclear weapons, the Soviets beginning to leave Afghanistan, the Vietnamese preparing to leave Cambodia and Cuba starting the process of withdrawing from Angola (20).

Ultimately, Reagan was convinced that his revolution, or restoration, had succeeded because it was so closely aligned with the basic primordial principles of the Founding Fathers:

Ours was the first revolution in the history of mankind that truly reversed the course of government, and with three little words: "We the People." "We the People" tell the government what to do, it doesn't tell us. "We the People" are the driver, the government is the car. And we decide where it should go, and by what route, and how fast. Almost all the world's constitutions are documents in which governments tell people what their privileges are. Our constitution is a document in which "We the People" are free. This belief has been the underlying basis for everything I have tried to do these past eight years. (21)

Reagan then credited the American people with winning the victories of the restoration for him and beckoned them to support incoming president George Herbert Walker Bush. After warning of the danger of losing an informed patriotism, Reagan concluded his address on a congratulatory note:

> We've done our part. As I walk off into the city streets, a final
> word to the men and women of the Reagan revolution, the men
> and women across America who for eight years did the work that
> brought America back. My friends, we did it. We weren't just
> marking time. We made a difference. We made the city stronger.
> We made the city freer, and we left her in good hands. All in all,
> not bad, not bad at all. (24)

Reagan also drew a lesson from all of his reminiscing. He noted the in-
evitability of complex challenges, but assured listeners that, "As long as
we remember our first principles and believe in ourselves, the future will
always be ours" (20). Reagan also boasted that the principles upon which
America was founded had now extended beyond the nation's borders and
"countries across the globe are turning to free markets and free speech,
and turning away from ideologies of the past" (20).

The movement that Reagan and his supporters had begun had now
spread throughout the world and would continue as long as people adhered to the principles he had articulated for decades. There were now
two golden ages in American history: the era of the founding fathers
and the second one where Reagan had re-enacted the principles of the
founding fathers. Deviation from either meant apostasy and chaos for
Americans, but adherence promised a glorious sacred destiny.

As a child and young adult Reagan heard the restorationist mythic
call that God would gloriously bless a united and restored church based
on the perfect primordial pattern found in the New Testament. Now as
a retiring president he felt the same pride of uniting America through a
restoration of the American sacred destiny founded in the primordial
American Revolution. Reagan felt then as he did when he quoted Carl
Sandberg in his 1984 State of the Union address, "I see America in the
crimson light of a rising sun fresh from the burning creative hand of
God." Reagan's Disciples of Christ heritage left an indelible mark on his
political rhetoric.

NOTES

1. See for example Stephen Vaughan, "The Moral Inheritance of a President: Reagan
and the Dixon Disciples of Christ," *Presidential Studies Quarterly* 25 (1995) 109–27.

2. Kathleen Jamieson, *Eloquence in an Electronic Age* (New York: Oxford University
Press, 1988); Walter Fisher, "Romantic Democracy, Ronald Reagan, and Presidential

Heroes," *Western Journal of Speech Communication* 46 (1989): 299–310; William Lewis, "Telling America's Story: Narrative Form and the Reagan Presidency," *Quarterly Journal of Speech* 73 (1987) 280–302; Ernest Bormann, "Fantasy Theme Analysis of the Television Coverage of the Hostage Release and the Reagan Inaugural," *Quarterly Journal of Speech* 68 (1982) 133–45.

3. Mircea Eliade, *The Myth of the Eternal Return, or Cosmos and History* (Princeton: Princeton University Press) 151.

4. Michael Casey, "From British Ciceronianism to American Baconianism: Alexander Campbell as a Case Study of a Shift in Rhetorical Theory," *Southern Communication Journal* 66 (2001) 151–66.

5. Adriana Bosch, *Reagan: An American Story* (New York: TV Books, 1998) 31.

6. Ronald Reagan, *An American Life* (New York: Simon & Schuster, 1990) 32.

7. Bosch, *Reagan*, 33.

8. Garry Wills, *Reagan's America* (New York: Penguin, 1988) 22.

9. Reagan, *American Life*, 60.

10. Ibid., 106.

11. Ibid., 123.

12. Dinesh D'Souza, *Ronald Reagan: How an Ordinary Man Became an Extraordinary Leader* (New York: Free Press) 213.

13. Marjorie Hyer, "Reagan, Carter, Anderson: Three Born-Again Christians Who Differ on Meaning," *Washington Post*, July 25, 1980, A28.

14. It is important to recognize that the Disciples doctrine of which we speak was the Disciples doctrine of Reagan's generation. The Disciples of Christ Church has evolved significantly and is far less of a "restoration movement" today.

15. Reagan, *America the Beautiful Address at William Wood College*, May 3, 1952.

16. Reagan, *Your America to be Free Commencement Address at Eureka College*, June 7, 1957.

17. Reagan, *America the Beautiful*, 13.

18. Reagan, *Enchroaching Control Address at Evanston, IL*, May 8, 1961.

19. Reagan, *Address to Employees of Forest Lawn*, November 2, 1961, 3.

20. Reagan, *A Time for Choosing*, October 27, 1964.

21. Reagan, *Inaugural Address*, January 5, 1967.

22. Reagan, *The Creative Society*, April 19, 1966, 2.

23. Michael Schaller, *Reckoning with Reagan* (Oxford: Oxford University Press, 1992) 4.

24. Reagan, *Acceptance Address to the Republican National Convention*, July 17, 1980, 6. Note, all campaign speeches from 1980 can be accessed at *The Annenberg/Pew Archive of Presidential Campaign Discourse*.

25. Reagan, *Campaign Speech*, September 1, 1980, 1.

26. Reagan, *Campaign Speech*, August 5, 1980.

27. Reagan, *Campaign Speech*, September 30, 1980, 1.

28. Reagan, *Campaign Speech*, August 18, 1980, 2.

29. Reagan, *Campaign Speech*, August 20, 1980.

30. Reagan, *Campaign Speech*, August 18, 1980.

31. Reagan, *Acceptance Address*.

32. Reagan, *Campaign Speech*, August 5, 1980, 2.

33. Reagan, *Campaign Speech*, October 7, 1980, 3.

34. Reagan, *Campaign Speech*, October 24, 1980, 10.

35. Reagan, *Campaign Speech*, August 18, 1980, 2.

36. Reagan, *Campaign Speech*, August 20, 1980, 3.

37. Reagan, *Campaign Speech*, October 19, 1980, 3.

38. Reagan, *Campaign Speech*, August 22, 1980, 1.

39. Reagan, *Acceptance Speech*, July 17, 1980, 222.

40. Reagan, *Campaign Speech*, August 22, 1980, 2.

41. Reagan, *Campaign Speech*, October 8, 1980, 7.

42. Reagan, *Farewell Address to the Nation*, January 11, 1989, in D. Erik Felten, *A Shining City: The Legacy of Ronald Reagan* (New York: Simon & Schuster, 1998) 19.

13

Rhetorical Education and the Christian University

A Nationwide Survey of Major Catholic Institutions

MARTIN J. MEDHURST

"The fundamental proposition of the Catholic university is that
the religious and the academic are intrinsically related."
—MICHAEL BUCKLEY

"[W]hom they hire to teach . . . what they actually require students
to take . . . what they offer. These are the factors that determine
what a school will or will not be."
—RONALD HERZMAN

"The greatest contribution to pluralism in higher education
is to be a different kind of university."
—RICHARD JOHN NEUHAUS[1]

It has often been said that all scholarship is autobiographical in one way
or another, and this chapter is no exception. At its core, this chapter is
about me, and Michael Casey, and three things we both loved—rhetoric,

1. The opening quotations come from Michael Buckley, "The Catholic University and
Its Inherent Promise," *America*, May 29, 1993. Online at: <http://www.bc.edu/offices/
mission/exploring/cathuniv/buckley_inherent_promise/>; Ronald Herzman, "Catholic
Educations," *First Things* 106 (October 2000) 44; Richard John Neuhaus, "The Christian
University: Eleven Theses," *First Things* 59 (January 1996) 21.

Christianity, and the challenge of integrating faith and learning in our chosen vocations, professors of rhetoric. Mike and I had known each other in a casual way for about fifteen years, but it was not until the 2002–2003 academic year that our lives would become forever intertwined. In that year, Mike had taken a leave from Pepperdine University to serve as a visiting fellow at the Institute for Faith and Learning at Baylor University in Waco, Texas. I was beginning my fifteenth year of teaching at Texas A&M University, just 90 miles south of Waco. In January 2003, I received a call from Mike, asking if I might know of any Christian professors who would be interested in going to Baylor. I half-jokingly said that I might be interested. One thing led to another and by the fall of 2003, I was a Baylor faculty member.

That was the easy part. The hard part was trying to discern how a person who had spent the previous twenty-nine years teaching in secular, state-supported universities could make the transition to the world's largest Baptist university, where the notion of integrating faith and learning was central to the new vision.[2] It seemed intuitively obvious to me that Christian higher education had to be both philosophically and substantively different than secular education. But when I arrived at Baylor, it didn't seem to be so. In fact, it seemed as though the curriculum, the faculty, the goals, and the outcomes were pretty much the same as I had encountered at Texas A&M. To complicate matters further, I was an adult convert to Roman Catholicism. I had been raised as a Pentecostal, educated as a conservative evangelical Protestant at Wheaton College, and lived most of my adult life within the orbit of evangelical Protestantism of one sort or another. I had never been a Baptist, however. Maybe I was missing something. Maybe I just didn't understand.

Thus began a quest to try to discern what, if anything, should be different about Christian higher education. I had my undergraduate experience at Wheaton in the back of my mind, but that didn't seem to translate very well to the situation at Baylor. Neither did my experiences with other Christian colleges. So I attended some conferences, wrote a couple of essays,[3] talked to colleagues from around the country, and con-

---

2. For a history of Baylor University's Vision 2012 project see Barry G. Hankins and Donald D. Schmeltekopf, eds., *The Baylor Project: Taking Christian Higher Education to the Next Level* (South Bend, IN: St. Augustine's, 2007).

3. See Martin J. Medhurst, "Religious Belief and Scholarship: A Complex Relationship," *Journal of Communication and Religion* 27 (2004) 40–47; Martin J. Medhurst, "Between Athens and Jerusalem: On Putting the 'Christian' Back Into Christian Higher Education," *Cultural Encounters* 2 (2005) 7–17.

ducted the survey that is reported in this chapter. Although the survey focuses on Catholic institutions of higher education, I intend my findings to apply to all Christian higher education. As a practicing Catholic, I am deeply concerned with what is going on—or not going on—at Catholic schools across the country. As a Wheaton alumnus, I am concerned about higher education in the larger world of evangelical Protestantism. And as a Baylor faculty member, I am concerned with my own institution's experiences with the integration of faith and learning. Mike Casey was concerned with that integration at Pepperdine, as are a host of academics working in Christian higher education.

Rhetoric and Religion

Since I am by training and practice a rhetorician, I want to focus on the narrow question of how rhetorical studies and religious or theological issues might be usefully conceptualized and executed within the communication curriculum. As anyone who has ever studied the field of communication knows, it is notoriously heterogeneous. Even the names of departments differ from campus to campus. My own academic sojourn is illustrative. I started in a department of Rhetoric. It then changed its name to Rhetoric and Communication and, a few years after I left, to Communication. The job I left for was in a department of Speech Communication and I now teach in a department of Communication Studies. The combinations are almost endless: Communication Arts, Communication Sciences, Communication Arts and Sciences, Communication and Media, Communications, Journalism and Communication, Media Studies, Speech, Speech and Theatre, and the list goes on and on. Equally heterogeneous is what is taught in such departments. But my concern is not so much to discuss the nature of the field as to consider what a communication curriculum at a Christian college or university ought to look like, why it ought to look that way, and how that look will necessarily be different than what is found at secular universities.

My research question is straightforward: What would a university education that is both fully Christian and fully rhetorical look like? For my purposes, we can understand "Christian" to mean the classical, orthodox doctrines of the faith as articulated, for example, in the Nicene Creed and brought to life in the history and tradition of the Christian Church from the time of Jesus and the Apostles forward. We can understand "rhetoric" or the rhetorical as that art by which one seeks "to discover, in any given case, the available means of persuasion." That is, of course, Aristotle's definition of rhetoric.[4] Rhetoric is a mode of discovering things, a way of understanding, a systematic approach to human communication that involves real human beings in complex social, cultural, and political contexts. As such, rhetorical analysis can be applied to a wide range of human creations. Historically, rhetoric and Christianity have had a close, if at times contentious, relationship.[5]

In the pre-Christian world, rhetoric was most closely associated with Athens and Rome. It was used as a mode of invention, a theory of composition, a breviary of style, a sourcebook on the psychology of audiences—and much more. In the classical world rhetoric was both the predominant method and proximate end of education.[6] The goal of most rhetorical education was to produce leaders of indisputable character who were capable of creativity, critical thinking, analytical judgment, clear expression, persuasive argument, and informed decision making. Christianity was born into a Roman world where rhetorical education was normative, where the doctrines of Isocrates, Aristotle, Cicero, and later Quintilian ruled the classroom and where the practice of persuasion, whether philosophical or practical, ruled the day. Not all such teaching was compatible with Christianity.

St. Paul goes to some lengths to distinguish his teaching and preaching from the kind of discourses practiced by certain members of the profession at the dawn of what would come to be called the Second Sophistic.[7] "When I came to you, brothers, proclaiming the mystery of

4. See Aristotle, *On Rhetoric*, trans. and introduced by George A. Kennedy (New York: Oxford University Press, 1991). The definition is on 36–37.

5. For overviews of the intertwined relationships between rhetoric and Christianity see Werner Jaeger, *Early Christianity and Greek Paideia* (Cambridge: Harvard University Press, 1961); James L. Kinneavy, *Greek Rhetorical Origins of Christian Faith: An Inquiry* (New York: Oxford University Press, 1987); Wayne A. Meeks, *The Moral World of the First Christians* (Philadelphia: Westminster, 1986); Averil Cameron, *Christianity and the Rhetoric of Empire* (Berkeley: University of California Press, 1991); Peter Brown, *Power and Persuasion in Late Antiquity: Towards a Christian Empire* (Madison: University of Wisconsin Press, 1992); Robert M. Grant, *Greek Apologists of the Second Century* (Philadelphia: Westminster, 1988).

6. On rhetorical education in the Roman world, see Stanley F. Bonner, *Education in Ancient Rome* (Berkeley: University of California Press, 1977); Donald Lemen Clark, *Rhetoric in Greco-Roman Education* (Morningside Heights: Columbia University Press, 1957); Winifred Bryan Horner and Michael Leff, eds., *Rhetoric and Pedagogy: Its History, Philosophy and Practice* (Mahwah, NJ: Erlbaum, 1995).

7. On the Second Sophistic see Thomas M. Conley, *Rhetoric in the European Tradition*

God," Paul writes to the Church at Corinth, "I did not come with sublimity of words or of wisdom . . . my message and my proclamation were not with persuasive [words of] wisdom" (1 Cor 2:1–4).[8] Paul didn't want his audience to think that his teaching was a human creation, a mere tissue of words or a feat of oratorical genius. To him, both the Word and the Wisdom were Christ, and Him crucified. So right from the outset, it appears that rhetoric and Christianity were at loggerheads with one another. Yet later, in Acts 17:22–34, we find Paul speaking to learned pagans at the Areopagus in Athens. In that discourse, Paul is nothing if not the consummate rhetorician. He grounds his discourse by acknowledging the concerns of his audience ("I see that in every respect you are very religious"), he comments on his immediate surroundings ("For as I walked around, looking carefully at your shrines, I even discovered an altar inscribed, "To an Unknown God"), he sets forth his purpose ("What therefore you unknowingly worship, I proclaim to you"). And he proceeds to tell them about the God who made the world. In doing so, he quotes both a Greek philosopher and a pagan poet as a means of identifying with his audience. And what happens? Some scoff at his teaching. Some want to hear more. And some ultimately are converted. In this instance rhetoric becomes the handmaiden of Christian truth. It is used to make the Gospel, the good news of Jesus the Christ, available to people who have not heard the message and to do so in a way that will allow them to open their minds and hearts to the moving of the Holy Spirit.

This is the crucial distinction: It is not Paul's words that convert the listeners, for only the Spirit can lead people to Jesus. But it was the words that opened the minds of the audience to be able to hear the message. In rhetoric, we call that audience adaptation. Paul believed in that principle, too, for he writes in First Corinthians: "To the Jews I became like a Jew to win over Jews; . . . To those outside the law I became like one outside the law . . . to win over those outside the law; . . . To the weak, I became weak to win over the weak. I have become all things to all, to save at least some" (1 Cor 9:22). Paul adapted to the different audiences he faced. To do so successfully, he had to know who they were, what they believed, what they considered authoritative, what they valued, and what kinds of

---

(New York: Longman, 1990) 59–63; George A. Kennedy, *Classical Rhetoric and Its Christian and Secular Tradition from Ancient to Modern Times* (Chapel Hill: University of North Carolina Press, 1980) 37–40.

8. All quotations from Scripture come from the Revised Standard Version.

arguments, reasoning, and evidence would seem to them most persuasive. The art that teaches how to adapt persuasive messages to audiences is rhetoric.

However, by the second, third, and fourth centuries, the problem for the Christian community was that rhetoric had become closely associated with pagan sources and especially with pagan literature. To Christians

> secular learning posed severe problems: 1) Greek and Roman writers presupposed a pantheon of gods, yet Christians believed in the One, true God, 2) the literature of Greece and Rome was characterized by a sort of eager licentiousness, both gods and men sinned lustily and often were portrayed as suffering no ill consequences from their behaviors, 3) the moral "lessons" thus taught often conflicted with the morality embraced and taught by the nascent Christian Church, and 4) the end or telos of mankind's being-in-the-world was, in these pagan sources, at its most noble, mere happiness (Aristotle) and, at its rankest, self-centered pleasure (Epicurus).[9]

The great debate over the role of rhetoric and rhetorical education in Christian teaching spanned several centuries, numerous interlocutors, and multiple theoretical positions. Yet, in the end, St. Augustine, himself a former professor of rhetoric, articulated the emerging consensus when he held that all that is true participates in the Truth and must be reclaimed for the kingdom of God. We are, Augustine instructs, to take the truth as from an "unjust possessor" and reclaim it for the cause of Christ.[10] So understood, rhetoric, along with philosophy and the other liberal arts, came into the service of the Church.

While rhetoric as a unified intellectual discipline disintegrated along with the Roman empire, its vestiges lived on under many guises throughout the Middle Ages, primarily in the arts of letter writing, poetry, and preaching.[11] Virtually all of the important rhetorical works from Augustine's *De doctrina christiana* (completed in 426) through George of Trebizond's *Five Books of Rhetoric*, published around 1433, come from

9. Medhurst, "Between Athens and Jerusalem," 7.

10. Saint Augustine, *On Christian Doctrine*, trans. D.W. Robertson, Jr. (Indianapolis: Bobbs-Merrill, 1958) 54, 75.

11. On the role of rhetoric in the Middle Ages see James J. Murphy, *Rhetoric in the Middle Ages* (Berkeley: University of California Press, 1974); James J. Murphy, ed., *Three Medieval Rhetorical Arts* (Berkeley: University of California Press, 1971).

the pens of Catholic Christians. Of special import to the integration of rhetoric and Christianity are the treatises of Flavius Cassiodorus Senator (*Introduction to Divine and Human Readings*, c. 540–545), Gregory the Great (*Cura Pastoralis*, c. 570), the Venerable Bede (*Ecclesiastical History of the English People*, c. 731), Alcuin (*Disputatio de Rhetorica*, c. 794), Hrabanus Maurus (*De institutione clericorum*, c. 819), Notker Labeo (*Nova rhetorica*, c. 998), Anselm of Besate (*Rhetorimachia*, c. 1010), Hugh of Bologna (*Rationes dictandi prosaice*, c. 1124), and Thomas of Salisbury (*Summa de arte praedicandi*, c. 1210).

The Renaissance brought a renewed interest in the art of rhetoric, and the Reformation and Counterreformation provided sites for rhetorical contestation. Rhetoric was taught at the University of Paris as early as 1215, though it was not highly valued by the Scholastics during the 1200s and 1300s. Even so, rhetoric reemerged as a standard part of the Jesuit *Ratio studiorum* (Program of Study) in 1599 and was developed in interesting ways by such scholars as Cypriano Soares (*De arte rhetorica*, 1619) and Nicolas Caussin, SJ (*De eloquentia sacra et humana*, 1619).

I could go on, but the point should be clear: Throughout the Christian era, Catholics have made major contributions to both the theory and practice of rhetoric and, until quite recently, were at the forefront of rhetorical education. But a survey of the curricula of 18 leading Catholic universities in the United States reveals a disturbing picture: 1) only 10 of the 18 offer any coursework at all in rhetoric, in many cases quite minimal coursework, and 2) only 8 of these 10 make any systematic effort to integrate Christianity with rhetorical instruction.

Current State of Rhetorical Education

Since I have never taught at a Catholic university and cannot speak from personal experience or direct observation, I have done the next best thing: I looked up what these eighteen leading Catholic universities claimed to be teaching in the area of communication by accessing their websites and catalogues. I chose these schools both for their national reputations and, in a few cases, because I knew they had departments or colleges of communication. These schools included: Notre Dame, Georgetown, Fordham, Seattle, Marquette, St. Louis, DePaul, Loyola Marymount, Boston College, Gonzaga, Loyola (Chicago), St. John's, Dayton, Portland, Santa Clara, Catholic University of America, Villanova, and Holy Cross. I make no claim that these 18 schools represent all of what is going on in communication at Catholic universities in America. Neither do I claim that my survey is necessarily complete or wholly accurate. It is always possible that classes which, on the surface, appear unrelated to rhetoric or Catholic Christianity might, as actually taught, have significant components of one or the other. That is impossible to discern from looking at a web page, so follow-up interviews will be necessary to confirm these findings. But I do claim that what follows is, in fact, a representative sample of what Catholic research universities *claim* to be teaching. And I further hold that what starts at the research university eventually finds its way into the curricula of institutions that are primarily oriented toward undergraduate teaching. So what have I found?

Notre Dame, Holy Cross, and Georgetown have no communication department whatsoever. Insofar as I can determine, rhetoric as the theory and practice of discovering the available means of persuasion is not taught in any department at these institutions, although there is one survey of the history of rhetorical theory taught in the English Department at Holy Cross.[12] Instruction in rhetoric appears to be unavailable at these institutions. The other fifteen schools present an interesting mosaic. In my survey, I was looking for two things: 1) the number of courses that were offered in rhetoric, including rhetorical theory, rhetorical history, public address, rhetorical criticism, rhetoric of social movements, rhetoric and media, or any other kind of course where the dominant mode of analysis, without regard for the kind of text or message, was rhetorical, and 2) the number of courses that tried intentionally to speak to the moral, religious, spiritual, or ethical dimension of human existence—this on the theory that any education that proclaims itself Catholic or even generically Christian ought to have a curriculum that reflects, at least in some degree, those theological commitments. And so I was looking for courses whose titles or descriptions included terms such as ethics, morality, social justice, preaching, theology, formation, vocation, and the like.

What I found is that these eighteen schools fell into four basic categories: 1) schools with no communication department or curriculum, 2) schools with a rhetoric curriculum but no moral, ethical, or religious component, 3) schools with a moral, ethical, or religious component but

---

12. The course in the English Department at Holy Cross is taught by Patricia Bizzell, one of the nation's leading rhetorical historians. See Patricia Bizzell and Bruce Herzberg, eds., *The Rhetorical Tradition: Readings from Classical Times to the Present*, 2nd ed. (Boston: Bedford/St. Martin's, 2001).

no rhetoric courses, and 4) schools that balanced rhetorical education with moral, ethical, or religious concerns. In tabular form it breaks out as follows:

No Dept.	Unbalanced/Rhetoric	Unbalanced/Religion	Balanced
Notre Dame	Portland	Fordham	DePaul
Georgetown	Villanova	Santa Clara	Boston Col.
Holy Cross	Loyola Marymount	Gonzaga	St. Louis
	Dayton		Marquette
			Seattle
			Loyola (Chi.)
			St. John's
			Catholic U.

Schools that offer rhetoric courses but none that focus on morality, ethics, or religion include Portland, Villanova, Loyola Marymount, and Dayton. Of these four, only Loyola Marymount and Dayton offer more than a single course, with Marymount offering five different courses ranging from contemporary rhetorical theory to rhetoric of social movements, rhetoric of pop culture, rhetorical methods, and rhetorical criticism. Indeed, in the whole survey only one school offered more rhetoric courses than Loyola Marymount and only one other offered an equal number. So Marymount is doing well in providing a basic rhetorical education to its students. But why are there no courses that implicate rhetoric with anything in the Christian tradition much less the Catholic tradition? While the rhetoric curriculum at Loyola Marymount is strong, there is nothing that distinguishes it from that of its neighbor, the University of Southern California, or from any other secular school in America.

While Loyola Marymount is strong in rhetorical education, the three schools in the third category—Fordham, Santa Clara, and Gonzaga—have the opposite profile. They are strong on courses in the communication curriculum that implicate religion, morality, and ethics, but offer no coursework in rhetoric. Fordham's curriculum is particularly impressive in recognizing the intimate links between communication and Christianity. Fordham offers such courses as Peace, Justice and the Media, Ethical Issues in the Media, Social Ethics in Telecommunications, and Films of Moral Struggle. Clearly there is an intentional effort to relate the specifics of the discipline to the more general concerns of Christian morality. Santa Clara, too, has an impressive array of courses including Communication Ethics, Media and Religion, and Theology of Communication. Again, thought has clearly been given as to how one might integrate the Catholic values of the university with the disciplinary demands of the field. But there is no rhetoric of any sort taught at Santa Clara, either.

The good news in this survey is that eight of the eighteen schools do make a concerted effort to include both rhetoric and religious values in their communication curriculum. In different ways, with different emphases, and to varying degrees, DePaul, Boston College, St. Louis, Marquette, Seattle, Loyola-Chicago, St. John's, and Catholic University adopt a balanced curricular approach that features at least some coursework in both rhetoric and Christian values. Most impressive, because they are both substantial and substantive, are the curricula at DePaul, Boston College, Loyola-Chicago, and Catholic University.

From reading the description of DePaul's communication curriculum one would not necessarily discern much of a concern for the integration of faith and learning, though it does list as one goal "to develop confidence and ability as ethical communicators." But the actual curriculum goes far beyond that rather standard disciplinary piety. Students are offered coursework in Communication, Culture, and Community, where "students can experientially explore the practical, ethical, and moral problems that arise in contemporary community life." They can take coursework in Christian Preaching as Communication, which is "rooted in Catholic tradition but inclusive of the call for all Christians to proclaim the Good News." They can study Ethics in Public Communication as well as Communication Law and Ethics. At the same time, DePaul students can avail themselves of courses such as Cultural and Symbolic Criticism, which is "an introduction to the critical methodologies of rhetorical analysis." They can take courses such as Communication of Resistance and Oppression, which features "rhetorical analysis of the ways in which we can resist the dominant discourse of oppression." They can take courses in the History of Rhetoric and Communication and Rhetorical Constructions of Identity. In short, DePaul's Department of Communication, which, by the way, is heavily oriented toward the media, nevertheless successfully integrates a rhetorical education with specifically Christian concerns.[13]

Much the same thing can be said for the communication curriculum at Boston College, whose opening web page proclaims: "As a Jesuit

13. All quotations are from the DePaul University web page found at <http://communication.depaul.edu/degreeprograms/>.

University, Boston College has as its heritage a 400-year tradition of concern for the integration of the intellectual, moral, and religious development of its students." Here the orientation is very clear and the curriculum that follows is faithful to the proclaimed values. At BC, students can take coursework in Mass Communication Ethics, Communication and Theology, and Ethical Considerations in Mass Communication while at the same time studying the Rhetorical Tradition, Rhetorical Theory, Communication Criticism, and Freedom of Expression. One might hope for even more integration beyond the realm of ethics proper, but at least BC seems to know what it is trying to accomplish.[14]

Likewise, at Loyola-Chicago the curriculum includes courses in Social Justice and Communication, Ethics and Communication, as well as courses in the Rhetorical Foundations of Human Communication, Rhetorical Criticism, and the Rhetoric of Social Change. The courses at Loyola are not as numerous or as deep as those at DePaul and Boston College, but they are, nevertheless, present in such a way as to take seriously the idea of integrating faith and learning.

Most surprising of all is the curriculum at Catholic University of America. The department is called Media Studies and, as the title suggests, focuses largely on the mass media. Yet the approach that is taken to the study of the media is one that is thoroughly rhetorical in orientation. As the initial web page notes:

> The foundation of the Program comprises a carefully designed balance of innovation and tradition. . . . required classes employ methods of analysis from the canons of rhetorical and historical criticism across the humanities.
>
> Our commitment to the liberal arts means that these courses emphasize writing and critical thinking. . . . [T]he Program emphasizes the value of critical distance. Critical distance affords the writer a glimpse of the hidden machinations of political and commercial rhetoric. Students work to disengage themselves from the whorl and blur of media around them, from the constructs and habits that often shield us from the world beyond our own im-media-te experience.[15]

14. All quotations are from the Boston College web page found at <http://www.bc.edu/schools/cas/communication/undergrad/core/>.

15. All quotations come from the Catholic University of America web page found at <http://mediastudies.cua.edu/courses/descriptions.cfm>.

Here, in a Media Studies department, we find the most thoroughly rhetorical orientation of any of the eighteen schools surveyed. And while that orientation is applied primarily to mediated forms of communication—film, television, internet, advertising—students are nonetheless being taught to think rhetorically. Courses in Media and Rhetoric, Media Rhetoric and Aesthetics, Rhetoric of Advertising, Visual Rhetoric, and Rhetoric of Propaganda are offered. There is even one course in American Political Rhetoric. As fine as the offerings are on the rhetorical side, the offerings that integrate media with religion, ethics, or morality are woefully thin, consisting of a single course on Religion and Media. One might hope that at *The* Catholic University of America a somewhat greater effort might be made to integrate faith with learning, especially among a faculty that so clearly understands the value of a rhetorical approach to communication.

The same critique can be leveled at the communication curriculum at St. John's University. In the Department of Speech there are four divisions, one of which is devoted entirely to Public Address. While Catholic University adopts a rhetorical approach to media, St. John's adopts a rhetorical approach to public communication in the form of speeches, debates, discussions, and the like. Students can take course work in American Public Address, Rhetorical Communication Strategies, Foundations of Rhetorical Theory, even one course titled Prosecution and Defense: The Rhetoric of Cicero. St. John's curriculum is thoroughly rhetorical in orientation and more broadly representative of the kind of rhetorical studies traditionally found in American universities. Yet for all its strengths as a rhetorical curriculum the only course that seeks to explore the cross-fertilization of rhetoric and Christian faith is one titled Rhetoric of Religion. One might suppose that any university that teaches rhetoric, whether that university be religious or secular, might have a course in the rhetoric of religion. We had such a course for the fifteen years I taught at Texas A&M University, with three different professors teaching three different iterations of Religious Communication. I taught a course in Early Christian Rhetoric under that rubric. But something seems amiss when avowedly secular schools are offering more coursework that implicates rhetoric and religion than schools with a clearly articulated Christian mission. And this observation leads me to the final part of this research in which I try to imagine what a fully integrated curriculum might look like at a Christian university, whether Catholic or Protestant.

Christian Education and the Communication Curriculum

What would a communication curriculum at a Christian college or university look like if it strove to be both fully rhetorical and faithfully Christian? Clearly we have seen glimpses of what such a curriculum might look like as we've examined these eighteen leading Catholic institutions. But I am not fully satisfied with any of the eighteen, though DePaul and Boston College come closest to the ideal that I want to propose. Such an ideal curriculum would grow naturally out of the following presuppositions:

1. Any comprehensive communication education should have a significant rhetorical component, for it is that component that focuses on choice, judgment, critical standards, interpretation, and decision making.

2. Any communication curriculum at a Christian college or university ought intentionally to integrate the study of rhetoric and communication with the faith commitments of historic Christianity.

3. The requirements of the core curriculum at many Christian institutions of higher learning, laudable as they often are with their courses in philosophy, theology, religion, and Bible, cannot in any way substitute for disciplinary thinking about how to integrate faith and learning.

This last point is where I want to begin. The model of integration that has prevailed at most Catholic universities is one that seeks to teach Catholic thought through required core courses in philosophy and theology. Since all students are required to take these courses, the reasoning goes, all will be exposed to how to think like a Catholic. But there is a difference between learning *what* the Church believes and learning *how* to integrate that faith with one's own discipline. The former can be taught through core courses; the latter cannot, for the simple reason that no core, however rigorous, could possibly teach students how to apply their faith to every conceivable discipline. That task must fall to the disciplines themselves. We need to teach students how to think Christianly about their specific vocation.[16] John Paul II said it best when he wrote in *Ex Corde Ecclesiae* that true learning occurs when "the *moral implications*

---

16. On different models for Christian higher education and the notion of "thinking Christianly," see Duane Litfin, *Conceiving the Christian College* (Grand Rapids: Eerdmans, 2004), esp. chapters 2, 7, and 8.

that are present in each discipline are examined as an integral part of the teaching of that discipline."[17] And that means teaching students to see how their discipline-specific coursework speaks directly to their faith and how that faith, in turn, speaks to their discipline and their vocation. We need, in the words of Michael Baxter and Frederick Bauerschmidt, Christian "institutions of higher learning in which specific philosophical and theological convictions permeate and transform the curricula, departmental structures, faculty membership, and even the specific content of a core of courses."[18] In short, we need faculty members who strive to think Christianly about their subject matter and who actively try to transform such thinking into teaching strategies.

This all begins with the desire to integrate faith and learning.[19] Scholars who are asking faith-related questions in their own research will not be hesitant about bringing those same issues into the classroom. So at the first level we are concerned with who is doing the teaching. Clearly we should prefer to have faithful Christians teaching at all Christian institutions of higher learning. But this is not always the case, especially at Catholic institutions where the percentage of Catholic faculty members continues to decline. The same pattern of decline among members of the sponsoring denomination is found at many Protestant institutions as well, including Baylor.

But faith is not enough. Faculty must also be experts in their respective disciplines. But even that is not enough. They must be faith-filled experts who truly *want* to explore issues of integration of faith and learning. Richard John Neuhaus has observed, "The university is better served by an agnostic who wants the university to be Christian than by a devout believer who does not."[20] And I have no doubt that he is right. In my judgment, those Christians—Catholic and Protestant alike—who

17. John Paul II, *Apostolic Constitution of the Supreme Pontiff John Paul II on Catholic Universities*, August 15, 1990, *Ex Corde Ecclesiae* online at <http://www.Vatican.va/ holy_father/john_paul_ii/apost_constitutions/documents/hf_jp-ii_apc_...>.

18. Michael J. Baxter, CSC and Frederick C. Bauerschmidt, "*Eruditio* without *Religio*? The Dilemma of Catholics in the Academy," *Communio* 22:2 (1995) 284–302. Online at <http://faculty.hcc-nd.edu/RKloska/Personal/Erudito.htm>.

19. I agree with David Lutz when he argues, "What every Christian academic institution needs is not merely faculty members who are Christian in some minimal sense, but scholars who take their Christian faith so seriously that they believe it should be integrated with their scholarship." See David W. Lutz, "Can Notre Dame Be Saved? *First Things* (January 1992) 39.

20. Richard John Neuhaus, "The Christian University: Eleven Theses," 21.

think that there should be no difference between education at a Christian university and education at a secular university are the single greatest threat to Christian higher education in America.

But even if the problem of committed and qualified faculty is solved that still leaves the curriculum as a matter of concern. Were I in a position to construct at a Christian university an ideal communication curriculum with a rhetorical orientation, it would look like this:

Year 1	Year 2
Fall	*Fall*
Introduction to Rhetoric and Communication*	Debate and Argumentation
Public Speaking*	Classical and Christian Rhetorics
Spring	*Spring*
Theology of Communication*	Contemporary Rhetorical Theory
Rhetorical Literature I	Rhetorical Literature II

Year 3	Year 4
Fall	*Fall*
Rhetorical Criticism*	Themes in Christian Communication
Religious Communication	Persuasion
Spring	*Spring*
Media and Morality	Communication Ethics*

(An asterisk indicates a required course)

The first thing to note about this curriculum is that it envisions far more hours than is normally required to obtain an undergraduate degree in communication—42 hours (14 courses of 3 hours each) to be exact. Normally an undergraduate communication major ranges from 30–36 hours, often under the theory that the communication major should be relatively easy to complete so that students can double major in a second, more substantive area such as business or political science. There is, of course, nothing wrong with double majors, but there is something very seriously wrong when communication teachers have so little faith in their own discipline's worth that it must be diluted to accommodate hours in some other field.[21] One of the reasons that the communication major

21. For one Christian college that has not watered down the requirements for a degree in communication see the curriculum at Hope College in Holland, Michigan, where 38

is often thought to be an "easy" field of study is because we have long since ceased to challenge students with the heart of the field, the study of rhetoric. By teaching to what the students appear to "want"—courses in corporate communication, media production, pop culture, and public relations—we fail to discharge our responsibilities as educators to teach what they really "need"—courses that force them to think, to interpret, to evaluate, to judge, to make moral decisions in the face of ambiguity and uncertainty, to read texts, to imbibe values, to participate in the creation of God's world of signs and symbols by speaking and writing and debating and critiquing. That is precisely what my ideal curriculum is intended to accomplish.

While teaching communication skills such as public speaking and debate, the curriculum features rhetorical theory, history, and criticism, and does so from within an explicitly Christian point of view.[22] A student who completed this curriculum would be exposed to public communication skills (Public Speaking, Debate and Argumentation), the theory of rhetoric from both secular and Christian perspectives (Classical and Christian Rhetorics, Theology of Communication, Contemporary Rhetorical Theory), the history of rhetorical practice (Rhetorical Literature I, Rhetorical Literature II), and the criticism of rhetorical messages (Rhetorical Criticism, Media and Morality). Furthermore, courses such as Religious Communication and Christian Themes in Communication could be revolving topic seminars where the content changed from year to year depending on the particular interests and expertise of the professor. At Texas A&M, for example, we taught Early Christian Rhetoric, Religious Discourse and the First Amendment, and Pulpit Oratory all under the rubric of Religious Communication. One could imagine such special topics as Communicating for Social Justice, the Rhetoric of War and Peace, Rhetoric of the Catholic Worker Movement, or the Debate

---

credit hours are required. Unfortunately, Hope, like so many other Christian institutions, has very few communication courses that try to integrate faith and learning. See <http://www.hope.edu>.

22. For an explicitly Catholic approach to the academic study of communication see James M. Farrell, "Rhetoric and the Catholic Imagination," *Rhetoric & Public Affairs* 7 (2004) 499–512. For a Campbellite approach, see Michael W. Casey, "'Come Let Us Reason Together': The Heritage of the Churches of Christ as a Source for Rhetorical Invention," *Rhetoric & Public Affairs* 7 (2004) 487–98. For an approach grounded in the study of literature but more generally applicable to communication see Chris Anderson, *Teaching as Believing: Faith in the University* (Waco, TX: Baylor University Press, 2004).

over *Humanae Vitae* as courses that could be offered under the umbrella of Christian Themes in Communication.

By studying *speakers*, delivering *messages*, through various *media*, in different *situations*, for varying *purposes*, to diverse *audiences*, one can receive an outstanding liberal arts education that, combined with core courses in philosophy, theology, English composition, and the social and natural sciences can lead to the kind of graduates we all want to produce—young men and women who are familiar with the issues and debates, who have studied the arguments on all sides, who have been challenged to think Christianly about their own lives and vocations, who can communicate their ideas clearly and effectively in both oral and written modes, and who are capable of making informed decisions because they have been formed within a tradition of Christian humanism. It is just such a tradition, as John Haughey, S.J., writes, that "draws together into communities of likemindedness those who have learned to envision reality through its classic texts."[23] Learning to envision reality through the study of texts is precisely what a rhetorical education does. We educate in community, we educate for community, because our ultimate goal is communion with God and our fellow man.

Conclusion

I have focused my comments on the field of communication because this is the field I know best. But the principles I have tried to articulate apply across the entire university curriculum. All Christian educators need to strive to think Christianly about their respective disciplines. The challenge, as Baxter and Bauerschmidt note, "will entail exploring seriously how our beliefs can shape the way we write history, analyze data in economics, debate with cynical Nietzscheans in philosophy, or contend with the latest fad of critical theory sweeping through English departments."[24] Every field asks us to see the world whole through its particular lens. But there is only one perspective that truly sees the world for what it is and yet will be, and that is the perspective of God and His Christ. To claim to see the world whole while simultaneously and systematically excluding the One who was, and is, and is to come, is to be not only blind, but foolish. For who besides the fool would try to place himself or herself in the role of the Creator?

23. John C. Haughey, SJ, "Enhancing the Traditions," *Conversations* 22 (Fall 2002) 33.

24. Baxter and Bauerschmidt, "*Erudito* without *religio*?"

"The real task" of Christian higher education, writes Thomas Dillon, "is to steer back to the One who is the font of truth; to go against the stream and be a sign of contradiction in a larger academic community that has, by and large, lost its moorings."[25] As such a sign, the Christian university "must have the courage to speak uncomfortable truths which do not please public opinion."[26] I have revealed only one small truth in this chapter—that there is much room for improvement in the way communication departments at Christian colleges and universities generally, and at Catholic universities in particular, seek to integrate faith with learning. By returning to a rhetoric-based curriculum and intentionally trying to integrate our Christian faith with our teaching and research, and making sure that that integration actually makes it into the curriculum at the department level, we will be far more likely "to produce [educational] communities that are intellectually, spiritually, and morally admirable."[27] And that is a perspective on which Mike Casey and I were in full agreement.

25. Thomas E. Dillon, "From the Desk of the President," *Thomas Aquinas College Newsletter* (Winter 2001), online at: <http://www.thomasaquinas.edu/news/newsletter/2001/winter/fromthedesk.htm>.

26. John Paul II, *Ex Corde Ecclesiae.*

27. George M. Marsden, "The Soul of the American University," *First Things* 88 (December 1998) 47.

14

Solzhenitsyn's Christian Civilization Rhetoric

The Other "Dream" Speech Thirty Years Later

ROBERT STEPHEN REID

"One word of truth shall outweigh the whole world."
—ALEKSANDR SOLZHENITSYN, Nobel Lecture

Aleksandr Solzhenitsyn died on Sunday, August 3, 2008. By all accounts he was one of the literary giants of the twentieth century and certainly a significant player in the era's Cold War politics. Most of the obituaries and tributes have lionized his literary contributions and his role in the politics of the era, but when it came time to comment on the politics of his 1978 Harvard Commencement Address the judgment typically became more reserved. For example, the Associated Press writer Douglas Birch observed that, "Solzhenitsyn was not a storybook hero for his admirers in Europe and the United States. Many, especially in the West, found his political judgments as distressing as his literature was inspiring."[1]

In eulogizing Solzhenitsyn's contributions on a *Morning Edition* broadcast, Martha Wexler hesitated at much the same point as Birch, conveying the surprise still felt by many at the stinging words of his Harvard Commencement Address. Wexler said,

> In 1978 Solzhenitsyn shocked his admirers with the commencement speech he delivered at Harvard University, heard here through an interpreter [An original broadcast is intercut with Solzhenitsyn speaking in Russian and the voice of his English interpreter.]—"How has this unfavorable relation of forces come

about? How did the West decline from its triumphal march to its present debilitation?"—Solzhenitsyn thundered against the West's materialism, its boundless freedom, its reliance on secular law, its spiritual and moral weakness. Many observers said that Solzhenitsyn never got to know America; that he shut himself off from the country like a recluse at his Vermont estate.[2]

It seems that thirty years later we still believe he was wholly insensitive to the country that had hosted his exile.

Of course some commentators responded differently. After reading the Associated Press obituary, NewsBusters.org's managing Editor Ken Shepherd blogged his own frustration with the media's general unwillingness to take Solzhenitsyn's faith commitment as the context of his assessment of the West.[3] Respected Solzhenitsyn scholar, Daniel J. Mahoney, concurred. He wrote,

> The tributes and reflections that have been published on Solzhenitsyn in the Western press since his death have generally been respectful, and many have been evenhanded. But quite a few obituaries and retrospectives have repeated hoary distortions that just won't go away. It has been repeatedly asserted that Solzhenitsyn hated Communism *and* Western democracy equally despite the fact that he repeatedly praised the *civic* experience of the West . . . [T]he legend of Solzhenitsyn's opposition to Democracy—and penchant for authoritarianism—is endlessly recycled in otherwise friendly accounts of his life and legacy.[4]

The epicenter on which this divided assessment rests is Solzhenitsyn's "Commencement Address" at Harvard on June 8, 1978.

Solzhenitsyn's "A World Split Apart" clearly stands with Churchill's 1946 Westminster College "Sinews of Peace" speech as one of the most significant commencement addresses of the 20th century.[5] The choice of Solzhenitsyn to be Harvard's commencement speaker was only publicized a few days before the event, but those who came knew that the speech would transcend the typical commencement genre constraints. Nevertheless, the 22,000 people who gathered that rainy June day to hear this Cold War dissident speak still seemed genuinely surprised that, given such a public stage, he chose to decry the impoverishment of the human spirit he observed in our Western consumer culture.[6] Though some media pundits like Michael Novak and George Will found the Commencement Address to be one of the most important documents of our time,[7] many others dismissed it as "dangerous"[8] and a "gross misunderstanding of Western society."[9] Solzhenitsyn was considered to be a "zealot,"[10] or worse, a "Slavophile."[11] Arthur Schlesinger, Jr. argued that the speech lacked any "clear development."[12] Harvard's Russian historian Richard Pipes agreed finding it "chaotic in structure (it must have been written in fits and starts)."[13] New York Times Columnist James Reston quipped that "for all its brilliant passages, it sounded like the wanderings of a mind split apart."[14]

What are we to make thirty years later of Solzhenitsyn's *moral* critique of the West's Cold War ideological alternative to communism's vision of world domination? Was it an expression of a Christian civilization rhetoric delivered in the wrong forum? Edward Ericson noted that it is his nonliterary letters and speeches of the 1970s that made it fashionable to call Solzhenitsyn a prophet.[15] Does suggesting that he is prophet, even as his critics in the media often do, function as a way of dismissing his critique? In the same prophetic tradition we might also consider Martin Luther King Jr.'s "March on Washington" speech. It can just as readily be termed an expression of a Christian civilization rhetoric as prophetic speech.[16] Yet, unlike the Harvard address, by almost any measure the March on Washington speech is viewed as the *gold standard* of an effective, appropriate, and timely word inviting listeners to re-imagine the potential of our national character. Thus, we might well ask why one speech is accorded the highest praise while the other has received such a mixed if not generally negative response in the media even thirty years later.

In what follows I examine the constructed ethos of Aleksandr Solzhenitsyn's Christian civilization rhetoric in the Harvard Commencement Address with a view toward identifying what Michael Hyde calls "the ethos of an identity that dwells rhetorically" in a speech.[17] To do this I employ the resources of the theory of contemporary Christian discourse I recently articulated which provides a means to consider the coherence of a Christian speaker's *narrative identity*, his or her *moral vision*, and his or her *cultural voice*.[18] My purpose here is to discover whether there is something intrinsic to the way that Solzhenitsyn constructed his ethos that can help us appreciate how it could engender and continue to engender such strong reactions and claims of incoherence.

Solzhenitsyn's Narrative Identity

Solzhenitsyn was raised in a traditional Russian family and was especially influenced by an aunt who loved Russian literature and her Russian

Orthodox faith equally. He traded this worldview in for the Marxist-Leninist alternative during his later schooling, but incarceration in the Gulag caused him to question which ideology should shape his vision of life. His subsequent novels make it quite clear that he believes the totalitarianism inaugurated by the Bolsheviks gave the twentieth century its distinctive character. It is a worldview people must resist, he contends, if the human spirit is to thrive. Edward Ericson and Daniel Mahoney write that he returned to the Christian worldview of his rearing, but that his mature articulation of Christian truths were "deeply informed by his experience in the prison camps" where "he experienced *in extremis* and learned about the heights and depths of the human soul." His faith, they claim, became rooted in this experience and was "severed from every form of sectarianism."[19]

When Solzhenitsyn was released from the prison camp in 1957, he was baptized and received into communion of the Russian Orthodox Church. It was, however, not until 1972 that he made this commitment public when he published an open letter to the leader of the Orthodox Church in Russia in which he confessed that he was scandalized at how the church agreed to innumerable accommodations to the atheistic Soviet state, effectively surrendering the church's influence in the society:[20] "Step by Step we have lost that radiant ethical Christian atmosphere which for a thousand years shaped our mores, our way of life, our beliefs, our folklore, and the very fact that the Russian word for the people—*Krest'iane* [peasants]—was derived from 'Christians.' We are losing the last traces and signs of a Christian people."[21] He saw the abdication of the church as a capitulation of what mattered the most in Russian culture.

Alain Besançon argued that there is a Slavophile tradition, especially a Russian literary tradition in which Solzhenitsyn participates, where the insights arrived at are understood as Christian thought and thereby "stamped with an overall guarantee of truth" which, in turn, creates a "fusion of the national idea with the messianic idea, the identification of Russia with Israel."[22] This tradition that folds the nation's intellectual tradition into a Russian religious philosophy is so all-enveloping that no one who desires to move the Russian intellectual worldview forward can escape it. Besançon noted that, with the exception of the fragile but discontinuous Pushkinian thread, all Russian art, music, and literature have been shaped by its seductions.[23]

This is the Theo-centric worldview he brought to bear in an assessment that juxtaposes the materialist worldviews of the East and West, presenting them as little more than variations on an anthropocentric humanism. This spiritual-humanist contrast is made most apparent in the peroration which provides the clearest statement of his identity as a person of faith:

> We cannot avoid revising the fundamental definitions of human life and human society. Is it true that man is above everything? Is there no Superior Spirit above him? Is it right that man's life and society's activities have to be determined by material expansion in the first place? Is it permissible to promote such expansion to the detriment of our spiritual integrity? If the world has not come to its end, it has approached a major turn in history, equal in importance to the turn from the Middle Ages to the Renaissance. It will exact from us a spiritual upsurge: We shall have to rise to a new height of vision, to a new level of life where our physical nature will not be cursed as in the Middle Ages, but, even more importantly, our spiritual being will not be trampled upon as in the Modern era. This ascension will be similar to climbing onto the next anthropologic stage. No one on earth has any other way left but—upward.

At the citadel of humanist thought in the United States and at the height of the Cold War, when the notion of a mutually assured destruction began to feel more inevitable than just possible, Aleksandr Solzhenitsyn argued that leaders in the West should turn back to a religious worldview to find the courage to make necessary decisions in the game of geo-political brinksmanship being played out between Washington's White House and Moscow's "Old Square."

Apart from the initial audience response, the question is not whether his *narrative identity* in the speech is coherent. He received the Noble Peace Prize for the manner in which his spiritual ethos was construed across the entire corpus of his novels and essays. The question of whether his language is shaped by Slavophile nationalistic longings also misses the point. Virtually all expressions of faith, whether Christian or from any sacred tradition, represent some conception of religion as a frozen controversy tied to a distinctive language of institutional identity or in its fusion of eschatological and nationalistic ideals. The more important question in assessing the coherence of the Christian ethos that dwells rhetorically in the rhetoric of Solzhenitsyn's argument is whether Western listeners were prepared to affirm the possibilities of his Christian civilization rhetoric.

What became apparent is that, rather than experiencing the ring of narrative fidelity in the speech, most of those who gathered that day found the Address to be incoherent. And rather than experiencing good reasons to work for change for belief and action in the world, many were stunned that he would make such condemnatory arguments about the country that hosted his exile.[24] In addition and perhaps of greater significance, they were shocked that in this forum he would imagine believing that moral criteria should matter more than fissionable mass. Did he really have the temerity to repudiate capitalism along with communism as spiritually unworthy of humanity's future? "Good heavens!" went the unspoken response. "Does he seriously expect us to believe that Christian moral convictions should somehow matter when it comes to the very real choices we face with nuclear missiles aimed at our country?"

Yes. He did.

Solzhenitsyn's Moral Vision

In coming to terms with Solzhenitsyn's moral vision in the speech, I have suggested elsewhere that coherent Christian discourse fully shaped by a Christian *ethos* will reveal a *telos* of hope configured in discourse that is rooted in *faith* in the divine Other as well as an assumption that an unconditional *love* flows from the divine Other to the individual and communities of individuals who participate in this storied identity.[25] Solzhenitsyn's *moral vision* is palpable. It arises from a view of suffering that has been at the core of his identity as a survivor of the Gulag. Rather than conceiving the schism in the world as a battle between competing materialistic ideologies, he claims that the split represents a fight of cosmic proportions in which, "the forces of Evil have begun their offensive." The real calamity in the world is the split between those who trust in their own autonomous irreligious humanistic consciousness and those who believe that our collective spiritual life is our most precious possession. In the Eastern and Western worlds of materialism Man has become the measure of all things. We have "lost the concept of a Supreme Complete Entity which used to restrain our passions and our irresponsibility." The result is a West with global calling cards of revolting commercial advertising. He saw no gain in imagining his beloved homeland eventually inundated with media driven publicity, his compatriots made stuporous by TV, and Russian youth bombarded with intolerable music.

Decrying *detente* as a misplaced "belief in eventual convergence" certainly sounded odd in 1978 because it was a moral rather than a political assessment of the Cold War tactics of American foreign policy. At the heart of the speech Solzhenitsyn argued against playing the waiting game of Cold War containment, claiming that it represented a moral loss of will—a loss unworthy of those who truly stand for freedom. His address directly challenged George Kennan's claim that "We can not apply moral criteria to politics." Kennan, the West's leading advocate of the US Cold War *containment* ideology and the architect of the US policy of unilateral disarmament, believed that the only way forward was to develop strategies of negotiation designed to avoid risk. This was foreign policy as a chess game of sly gambits and *intermezzo* moves designed to prolong the possibilities of endgame. It was that policy which eventually saw the Soviet Union crumble under the weight of its own inability to keep up with the West's capacity to outspend the East in a geo-political game of fiscal and technological brinksmanship. Yet in 1978, the idea of bringing about the defeat of communism by way of *convergence*—a belief that the Soviet system would eventually collapse and finally concede victory to a capitalist-consumerist way of life—seemed unworthy to Solzhenitsyn. Instead of accepting the 'bad with the good,' he demanded nothing less than "a spiritual blaze" by those who would defend freedom. The only criteria relevant to assessing the aspiration to be free he concluded would be a moral criteria; "There are," he claimed, "no other criteria."

He argued that the debilitating dream of maintaining the world in status quo at any cost represents a collapse of whatever moral vision America once had. It is, he declares, the symptom of a society which has ceased to develop. "Facing such a danger," he asks, "with such splendid historical values in your past, at such a high level of realization of freedom and of devotion to freedom, how is it possible to lose to such an extent the will to defend oneself?" What is the crisis of a world split apart? His conclusion: "The split in the world is less terrible than the similarity of the disease plaguing its main sections." For Solzhenitsyn life must be more than the search for happiness and the carefree consumption of material goods. It has to be directed in such a way that people come to understand that the earnest duty of one's life is to experience moral growth and leave life "a better human being than one started it."

As Ericson argued, "Solzhenitsyn is ever the writer about moral issues."[26] His Christian vision of life and of the nature man is the subtext that always undergirds and provides the context for all his moral judgments. He writes and speaks with the assumption that he is morally obliged to speak truth on behalf of others—a hard won realization that speech as symbolic action is the greatest resource of prophetic discourse. Baptist theologian Walter Rauschenbusch once argued that religious prophets are simply heralds of the idea "that ethical conduct is the supreme and sufficient religious act."[27] And this is Solzhenitsyn's moral worldview as well; belief can not be responsibly separated from an ethical responsibility to speak and act on behalf of others. In this sense a prophet, perhaps more than anyone else uses symbolic discourse to identify or reify the justice of a *moral vision*. Solzhenitsyn's moral vision, across both his literary as well as his political writings, sustains the humane quality of his discourse and makes of it something that transcends the context that gave rise to it.

Solzhenitsyn's Cultural Voice

There is little question we best understand the Address as an example of the kind of political sermon Perry Miller called a jeremiad.[28] Solzhenitsyn was quite literally revisiting this peculiarly Puritan art form—a form of preaching that had been perfected three centuries earlier for Cambridge audiences by the religious leaders who also happened to be the founders of Harvard University. Thus, what is perhaps more interesting in assessing the response to Solzhenitsyn's speech was the inability of the New Englanders who gathered for the commencement to recognize their own native art form performed once again in their midst. It was a measure of how far removed they were from the vision that had given birth to their own cultural as well as institutional identity.

The jeremiad was born as a fusion of expectations engendered by John Winthrop's original sermon, "A Model of Christian Charity," which envisioned the founding of a Christian colony in New England as a "city on a hill" (a laboratory of visible Christian witness for all Europe) and election day sermons like Samuel Danforth's, "A Brief Recognition of New England's Errand in the Wilderness." Jeremiads begin by cataloguing the iniquities of the day. They presume a causal sequence between physical afflictions experienced by the colonists and their personal iniquities. Thus, personal sins occur and communal afflictions result; when personal repentance occurs, then afflictions subside and communal blessings increase.[29] In jeremiad preaching spiritual failures such as hard-heartedness, sloth, sensuality, lack of next generation zeal, a falling away from primitive affections, formality, hypocrisy, etc., were considered to be the barriers inhibiting the realization of God's blessing on the colony. Miller argued that, "The logic of the [sermon's] narrative is controlled by a precise calculation: defeat must be measured out until the amount of present distress becomes equal to past transgression."[30] But as Sacvan Berkovitch noted, "The Puritan clergy were not simply castigating. For all their catalogues of iniquities, the jeremiads attest to an unswerving faith in the errand; and if anything they grow more fervent, more absolute in their commitment from one generation to the next."[31]

In good jeremiad form Solzhenitsyn began his 'sermon' with the announcement that there is a split or schism in the world more important than the ideological division between East and West; it is the rift in the direction of human destinies captured by the ancient truth that "a kingdom—in this case our earth—divided against itself cannot stand" (Mark 3.25). Once the Biblical text was identified jeremiad sermons typically began to list of the deficits that demonstrate the substance of the divided worldview; in this case Solzhenitsyn provided a list of reasons why the West had failed to live into its promise. Only ego-centric blindness, he stated, could lead the West to assume it should be the cultural "yardstick" of true freedom for other nations. What are America's iniquities? First, he declared there was a decline of courage among its intellectual and ruling elite: "Should one point out that from ancient times declining courage has been considered the beginning of the end?"[32] Second, he argued that the West was obsessed with well-being: "Today, well-being in the life of Western society has begun to reveal its pernicious mask." Third, the West had an over-riding social concern with a legalistic interpretation of freedom. The notion that people in a Western democracy might willingly respond to a call for sacrifice and risk is labeled absurd because of the manner in which legality has replaced morality. "Whenever the tissue of life is woven of legalistic relations," he claimed, "there is an atmosphere of moral mediocrity, paralyzing man's noblest impulses." Fourth, the West's commitment to freedom had become directionless: "It is time, in the West, to defend not so much human rights as human obligations." Fifth, the West had forfeited the "right of people not to know; not to have their divine souls stuffed with gossip, nonsense, vain talk . . . Hastiness and superficiality are the psychic disease of the 20th century and more than anywhere else this disease is reflected in the [Western] press." Finally, the West had permitted the media to fashion "a self-deluding interpretation of the contemporary world situation . . . [that produces] a sort of a petrified armor around people's minds." The promise of the West had turned into a spiritual exhaustion that is unattractive to people who long "for things higher, warmer, and purer."

From this list of deficits, Solzhenitsyn provided an analysis of how the West declined from its original promise to be the world's laboratory of freedom to its present sickness where moral criteria were no longer relevant in social and political matters. He argued that the West's excessive view of individual freedom and individual rights were championed at the cost of society's "sense of responsibility to God." The result was an embrace of a humanistic, anthropocentric materialism, the inheritance of Renaissance and Enlightenment humanism. Because of these intellectual turns in both the East and West, he claimed that it resulted in a diminishment of their most precious possession, their spiritual life, crushed now by a party mob in the East and by a commercial culture in the West. With this indictment, the Address moved to its final appeal where Solzhenitsyn claimed that the watershed we face in history is whether or not we allow our accumulating deficits to traduce our humanity. The only choice left in his eyes was to make a new turn, to ascend to a new more spiritual level of life.

If we ask, 'What is the hoped-for response implicit in the appeal of the Address?' the answer is quite clear. He would wish that his listeners would respond, "You are right! We agree with your assessment of the dreadful error of our ways." In *The Four Voices of Preaching* I identified this as the hoped-for/expected response of the Teaching Voice where the speaker's intention is to explain meaning and argue for a position.[33] Sermons in this cultural voice operate with objectivist assumptions about the nature of reality and call forth faith in an ordered, tradition-centered way of understanding the world. Of course the alternative can always occur. Listeners can respond, "You are wrong! We disagree with your assessment of the error of our ways." And this is largely what happened.

Perry Miller wrote that the dilemma of the jeremiad was that it "Could make sense out of existence as long as adversity was to be overcome, but in the moment of victory it was confused . . . It flourished in dread of success; were reality ever to come up to its expectations, a new convention would be required, and this would presuppose a revolution in mind and in society."[34] Clearly, Solzhenitsyn's Harvard listeners had long since resolved the adversities of New England existence. They had lost any memory of this form of address, concluding that Solzhenitsyn was just confused, or worse, someone who longs to return to a Czarist past. On the other hand, those Western listeners for whom a religious worldview is still vital tend to experience the speech as both a coherent and a provocative assertion that the road to totalitarianism begins with the illusion that humanistic ethics are superior to a moral worldview grounded in the ethics of a religious tradition.[35]

The Coherence of Solzhenitsyn's Prophetic Ethos

In his March on Washington Address, Martin Luther King spoke to a receptive audience of civil rights activists, most of whom were African Americans whose moral vision was nurtured in the black church—a community of the faithful committed to acting on a prophetic moral vision. Solzhenitsyn's audience, on the other hand, was largely secular, ideologically diverse, and highly intellectual. They were independent-thinking Harvard grads, faculty, alums, and other people likely looking to hear a Cold War dissident politically indict the Soviet system. In many ways, Solzhenitsyn's Address eventually found a more favorable response in subsequent years, as Cold War fears waned and the coherence of his prophetic moral assessment of a Western materialistic worldview was appreciated. Both men offered their listeners a dream fueled by Christian civilization rhetoric, Solzhenitsyn speaking a hard "Truth" by way of a Teaching Voice of a failed realization of freedom and King imagining a possible future by way of a Sage Voice that invited listeners to find their way into its variously-imaged dream. The discourse of both men has been viewed as prophetic, but the appellation may have a decidedly different meaning depending on why the critic chooses to describe moral discourse in this manner.

In a considered reflection on the Harvard Address, Sydney Hook, a senior research fellow at the Hoover Institution of War, Revolution, and Peace, differed profoundly with Solzhenitsyn's political assessment of the West save for the assertion that the willingness to risk one's life in the defense of freedom is, in fact, a *moral* stake upon which freedom rests. He rejected both the *cultural voice* that drives Solzhenitsyn's historical assessment that the West is guilty of a failure of moral nerve and he rejected the theological assumption of Solzhenitsyn's *narrative identity* that belief in a Supreme Power is a necessary correlate for acting with integrity and character in human affairs. He did, however, find a deep resonance with the *moral vision* embodied in the speech. He wrote,

> Rarely in modern times—especially in times of relative peace—has one man's voice provoked the Western world to the experience of profound soul-searching. What Aleksandr Solzhenitsyn said . . . has stirred the reflective conscience of the Western world more profoundly than even the eloquent discourses of Franklin Roosevelt and Winston Churchill . . . [The unprecedented response testifies] to the power of his words and to the fundamental character of his challenge to our mode of life, to its basic values, fears, illusions, and to a philosophy of civilization concealed by the apparent absence of any philosophy.[36]

Critics like Hook appear to respond to Solzhenitsyn's *moral identity* as it dwells rhetorically in the Address, but are not always sure what to make of it. They affirm that his argument represents a challenge to Western identity, but resist virtually all of his political analysis and also resist his argument that a tragic de-spiritualized turn of historical events has made the West spiritually incapable of presenting the face of freedom to the rest of the world. Somehow, though, they still hear the prophet. Hook admitted, "Despite my differences with Solzhenitsyn . . . [in his convictions] I regard him as one of the great moral prophets of our time."[37] But Hook then argued that we dare not ground our moral convictions as a nation in the demands of any theological tradition other than pluralism or we deny the human rights of our citizenry.[38] And in making this caveat, Hook reduced Solzhenitsyn to little more than a prophet of courage and, in the process, ends up deifying pluralism as freedom's only pathway forward.

On the other hand, Martin Marty, the eminent Western chronicler of Christianity and *The Protestant Experience in America*, concluded that Solzhenitsyn's critique of the West catches the essence of the matter, "even if he has distorted its pluralism and misrepresented the West through the eyes of a Russian, whose people received the Renaissance and Enlightenment as a brutally swift and violent import or intrusion in the days of Peter the Great."[39] The rhetoric of those who speak as a prophet, Marty maintained, is always characterized by a kind of linguistic totalism without the faintest interest in whether its "language is empirically certifiable in detail."[40] As one who understood that Solzhenitsyn spoke out of a Christian tradition unfamiliar to most Americans, Marty concluded, "I leave to others the details of response to his attack on the ways of capitalism, but I am confident he has gotten to the root of it."[41]

Conclusion

What should be evident from this analysis is that the "ethos that dwells rhetorically" in Solzhenitsyn's Harvard Address is not an incoherent expression of religious identity. Rather, as his defenders have maintained, Solzhenitsyn wanted his words to be heard in the context of what he had been saying in all his writings and essays. His *moral vision* remained consistent across his oeuvre. His *narrative identity* though shaped by a guild of literate Russian reflection is still consonant within a great tradition of Christian thought. His *cultural voice*, which assumed a persuasively determinant orientation toward authority while making its appeal out of a corporately affirmed tradition of truth, revealed his commitment to a consistent tradition of Christian cultural consciousness. It was his audience who no longer shared these assumptions and for that reason his discourse appeared incoherent. They resisted the idea that he had the right or the authority to judge Western culture implied by the *cultural voice* he adopted. They also found the constructed assumptions at the heart of his *narrative identity* too obscure and too Russian for American tastes. If the reactions that appeared in print are any measure, the audience may well have applauded the man more than the speech at its close.[42]

Jewish theologian Abraham Heschel wrote, "The prophet's task is to convey a divine view, yet as a person he *is* a point of view. He speaks from the perspective of God as perceived from the perspective of his own situation . . . The prophet is not only a prophet. He is a poet, preacher, patriot, statesman, social critic, moralist."[43] Identifying Solzhenitsyn's discourse as *prophetic* seems to be the generally agreed upon means to resolve the seeming contradictions of his Harvard Address. For some it clarified and continues to clarify what it means to see our nation operate as a cut flower culture where we have cut ourselves off from the mainstream of any nourishing tradition of values that ground our national identity.[44] For others it served as a term to bracket this discourse as religious and, therefore, something to stir our reflective conscience, but not something to be considered as essential to our national character. And thus it has always been for those who speak and for those "who have ears to hear" such prophetic discourse.

NOTES

1. For the AP obituary see http://www.independent.co.uk/news/world/europe/sol-zhenitsyn-a-life-of-dissent-884590.html.

2. Martha Wexler, "Author Who Chronicled Soviet Abuses Dies At 89," *All Things Considered* (August 3, 2008). The quoted material is transcribed from Wexler's on-air commentary rather than the abbreviated version in print at the website. Retrieved on September 15 at http://www.npr.org/templates/story/story.php?storyId=93250748.

3. Ken Shepherd, "AP Obit for Solzhenitsyn Ignores His Christian Faith," retrieved at *http://newsbusters.org/blogs/ken-shepherd/2008/08/04/ap-obit-solzhenitsyn-ignores-his-christian-faith.*

4. Daniel J. Mahoney, "Hero of a Dark Century," *National Review* (September 1, 2008) 49

5. Winston Churchill's Commencement Address was delivered at the behest of then President Harry Truman at Westminster College, in Fulton, Missouri, on March 5, 1946. The published source of the Harvard Commencement Address is found in *Solzhenitsyn at Harvard: The Address, Twelve Early Responses and Six Later Reflections*, ed. Ronald Berman (Washington, DC: Ethics and Policy Center, 1980) 3–20. It differs, however, in felicity but not substance from the actual speech as delivered (the source cited throughout this essay) found in both audio and authenticated transcript form at http://www.americanrhetoric.com/speeches/winstonchurchillsinewsofpeace.htm.

6. D. M. Thomas noted that The *New York Times* only mentioned that Solzhenitsyn was the Harvard speaker a few days before the event; Thomas, *Aleksandr Solzhenitsyn: A Century in His Life* (New York: St. Martin's, 1998) 460. See also Michael Scammell, *Solzhenitsyn: A Biography* (New York: Norton, 1984) 965.

7. George Will, "Solzhenitsyn's Critics," *Washington Post* (June 1978). Reprinted in *Solzhenitsyn at Harvard*, 33–35; Michael Novak, "On God and Man," in *Solzhenitsyn at Harvard*, 131.

8. "The Obsession of Solzhenitsyn," editorial, *New York Times* (June 13, 1978); reprinted in *Solzhenitsyn at Harvard*, 23.

9. "Mr. Solzhenitsyn as Witness," editorial *Washington Post* (June 11, 1978); reprinted in *Solzhenitsyn at Harvard*, 25.

10. "The Obsession of Solzhenitsyn," *Times/ Solzhenitsyn at Harvard*, 23.

11. Jack Fruchtman, Jr., "A Voice From Russia's Past at Harvard," *Baltimore Sun* (June 18, 1978); reprinted in *Solzhenitsyn at Harvard*, 44.

12. Arthur Schlesinger, Jr., "The Solzhenitsyn We Refuse to See," *Washington Post* (June 25, 1978); reprinted in *Solzhenitsyn at Harvard*, 64.

13. Richard Pipes, "In the Russian Intellectual Tradition," in *Solzhenitsyn at Harvard*, 115.

14. James Reston, "A Russian at Harvard," *The New York Times* (June 11, 1978); reprinted by *Solzhenitsyn at Harvard*, 37.

15. Edward E. Ericson, *Solzhenitsyn: The Moral Vision* (Grand Rapids: Eerdmans, 1980) 178.

16. On King as "prophet," see William M. Ramsay, *Four Modern Prophets: Walter Rauschenbusch, Martin Luther King, Jr., Gustavo Gutiérrez, Rosemary Radford Reuther* (Atlanta: John Knox, 1986); Richard Lischer, *The Preacher King: Martin Luther King Jr. and the Word that Moved America* (New York: Oxford University Press, 1995) 177–84.

17. Michael Hyde, "Introduction: Rhetorically, We Dwell," in *The Ethos of Rhetoric*, ed. Michael Hyde (Columbia: University of South Carolina Press, 2004) xiii.

18. Robert Stephen Reid, "A Rhetoric of Contemporary Christian Discourse," *Journal of Communication and Religion* 31 (November 2008) 109–42. This essay argues for a rhetoric of Christian discourse that also provides for the possibility of a set of critical moves by which the coherence of public expressions of a Christian ethos that dwells rhetorically in discourse can be assessed. Three domains of identity are explored as a narrative rather than doctrinal conception of Christian identity configured in oral and written discourse: a tradition-based reasoning, a narratively-shaped worldview, and a hope engendered identity & ethic of responsibility.

19. Edward E. Ericson Jr. and Daniel J. Mahoney, "Editors' Introduction," in *The Solzhenitsyn Reader* (Wilmington, DE: Intercollegiate Studies Institute, 2006) xvii.

20. Solzhenitsyn demanded that Russian Orthodox Church leaders explain, "By what reasoning could one convince oneself that the calculated *destruction*—one dictated by atheists—of the body and spirit of the Church is the best method of *preserving it*? Preservation, but for *whom*? Certainly not for Christ Preserved, but by *what means*? By *lies*?" Aleksandr Solzhenitsyn, "Lenten Letter: To Patriarch Pimen of Russia," in *Aleksandr Solzhenitsyn: Critical Essays and Documentary Materials*, ed. John B. Dunlop et al. (New York: Collier, 1973) 477.

21. Solzhenitsyn, "Lenten Letter," 552. See also Nils C. Nielson Jr. *Solzhenitsyn's Religion* (New York: Nelson, 1975) 80–94.

22. Alain Besançon, "Solzhenitsyn at Harvard," *Survey: Journal of Soviet and East European Studies* 24 (1979) 136.

23. Ibid., 137.

24. On this criteria for assessing *narrative identity* see Reid, "Rhetoric," 128; cf. Walter Fisher, *Human Communication as Narration: Toward a Philosophy of Reason, Value, and Action* (Columbia: University of South Carolina Press, 1989) 105–23.

25. Reid, "Rhetoric," 132.

26. Ericson, *Solzhenitsyn*, 3.

27. From Walter Rauschenbusch, *Christianity and the Social Crisis* (1907; reprinted, Louisville: Westminster John Knox, 1997) 7.

28. On the Harvard Address as a jeremiad, see Mark Stoda, "Jeremiad at Harvard: Solzhenitsyn and 'The World Split Apart,'" *Western Journal of Communication* 64 (Winter 2000) 28–53. On the genre of the jeremiad, see Perry Miller, *The New England Mind: From Colony to Province* (Cambridge: Harvard University Press, 1953); Sacvan Berkovitch, *The American Jeremiad* (Madison: University of Wisconsin Press, 1978); and Margaret D. Zulick, "The Agon of Jeremiah: On the Dialogic Invention of Prophetic Ethos," *Quarterly Journal of Speech* 78 (1992) 125–48.

29. Miller, *The New England Mind*, 27.

30. Ibid., 32.

31. Berkovitch writes, "The most severe limitation of Miller's view is that it excludes (or denigrates) this pervasive theme of affirmation and exultation" in the jeremiad; *American Jeremiad*, 6.

32. The written translation strengthens a biological-medical metaphor controlling this deficit by adding the word "symptom" to the final pronouncement; *Solzhenitsyn at Harvard*, 6.

33. Robert Stephen Reid, *The Four Voices of Preaching* (Grand Rapids: Brazos, 2006) 53–55.

34. Miller, *The New England Mind*, 33.

35. Cf. Mahoney, "Hero," 50.

36. Sidney Hook, "Solzhenitsyn and Western Freedom," *World Literature Today* 53 (1979) 573. This essay also appears in *Solzhenitsyn at Harvard*, 85–97.

37. Hook, "Solzhenitsyn," 577.

38. Ibid., 576–77.

39. Marty, "On Hearing Solzhenitsyn in Context," *World Literature Today* 53.4 (1979), 579. The italicized reference is to Marty, *Righteous Empire: The Protestant Experience in America* (New York: Dial, 1970).

40. Marty, "Solzhenitsyn in Context," 580.

41. Ibid.

42. Thomas, *Solzhenitsyn*, 462.

43. Abraham J. Heschel, *The Prophets* (New York: Harper and Row, 1962) xiv.

44. On the notion of a "cut-flower culture" Herberg observed, "Cut flowers retain their original beauty and fragrance, but only so long as they retain the vitality that they have drawn from their now-severed roots; after that is exhausted, they wither and die; so with freedom, brotherhood, justice, and personal dignity—the values that form the moral foundation of our civilization. Without the life-giving power of the faith out of which they have sprung, they possess neither meaning nor vitality"; Will Herberg, *Judaism and Modern Man: An Interpretation of Jewish Religion* (New York: Farrar, Straus, & Young, 1951) 91–92.

15

Preaching as Mimesis

*The Rhetoric of the African American Sermon**

GARY S. SELBY

From virtually any perspective—cultural, religious, or historical—the importance of black preaching can scarcely be overstated. Within African American cultural history, black preaching helps to explain what Henry Mitchell describes as the "impressive tenacity" of black Christianity, traditionally nurtured not by "any great missionary activity" but by "independent, clandestine meetings" in which African Americans "adapted their African Traditional Religion . . . into a profoundly creative and authentically Christian faith."[1] From a broader historical perspective, the role of black preaching in contemporary U.S. history, particularly given its contribution to the civil rights movement, is enormous. As Aldon Morris writes, the "central and overpowering force" of the civil rights movement, which forever transformed the U.S. cultural and political landscape, was the black church, providing the movement not only organizational infrastructure and financial resources, but also its "music, trenchant sermons, and challenging oratory."[2] Viewed from a religious perspective, black preaching captures a unique biblical and theological

* This essay is the culmination of a project that Michael Casey encouraged me to undertake when he was book review editor of *Journal of Communication and Religion*, and I am deeply honored to be able to dedicate it to his memory. Its publication is one small indication of the great influence that Professor Casey had on my life and career, an influence for which I am grateful. I also wish to thank Professor Luke Powery for his helpful comments on an earlier version of this essay.

hermeneutic rooted in African American experience, a hermeneutic Cleophus LaRue describes in this way:

> As a result of their historic marginalization, what became most important to blacks in their encounter with Christianity was an intimate relationship with a powerful God, who exhibited throughout scripture a willingness to side with the downtrodden in very concrete and practical ways. The belief that the scriptures consistently showed God acting in this manner in time became a way of construing and using all of scripture. The powerful river of black preaching has its origin in this conceptual framework.[3]

Despite its historical, cultural, and religious significance, however, black preaching has received scant attention from rhetorical scholars. Certainly, African American public discourse, particularly where it has been related to efforts at challenging racial oppression, has received growing attention from scholars in recent decades, with some of these studies acknowledging the roots of much of this discourse in the rhetoric of the black church.[4] Beyond its contribution to social protest, however, black preaching as a significant form of public communication in its own right is remarkably under-theorized in the rhetorical literature, a fact that Gerald Davis attributes to scholars' reactions to what they see as the "high emotionalism" of black preaching, and their tendency to equate this affective component "with lack of sophistication and education."[5]

This essay highlights black preaching not only as a historically, culturally, and religiously important discourse, but also a rhetorically significant one as well. In what follows, I offer a theoretical account of black preaching drawn from a meta-analysis of six important, yet very different, works on black preaching. Three of these, Mitchell's classic *Black Preaching: The Recovery of a Powerful Art*, LaRue's *The Heart of Black Preaching*, and Evans Crawford's *The Hum: Call and Response in African American Preaching*, offer accounts of black preaching from within the tradition itself. The second two, Bruce Rosenberg's *Can These Bones Live?* and Gerald Davis's *I Got the Word in Me and I Can Sing It You Know* provide ethnographies of folk preaching that involve close textual analyses of African American sermons.[6] Theresa L. Fry's *Weary Throats and New Songs* focuses on the preaching women in the African American church and is part ethnography, part theology, and part practical manual for those she calls her "sistah proclaimers."[7] Based on these analyses, I highlight three common elements that characterize black preaching as a unique and significant form of public discourse. The first two, black preaching as oral performance and communal dialogue, are well-attested in the literature. I argue, however, that these two features coalesce into what, I believe, is the tradition's most significant characteristic—that it is mimetic, engaging its participants in imitative, experiential, and, ultimately, transcendent performances of theological content.

Black Preaching and the Problem of Genre

In their volume on African American discourse, Elaine Richardson and Ronald Jackson remind us that this discourse is rich and diverse, comprised of multiple traditions that resist simple categorization. They attempt to capture that diversity in their choice of the term "African American rhetoric(s)" to describe the "study of culturally and discursively developed knowledge-forms, communicative practices and persuasive strategies rooted in the freedom struggles by people of African ancestry in America."[8] African American religious discourse, of course, is similarly rich and varied, with the result that the commonly used phrase "black preaching" can mask variations related to geographical location (northern vs. southern, rural vs. urban or suburban), denominational affiliation (Pentecostal, evangelical, mainline Protestant, or Roman Catholic), or the gender of the preacher, to name a few. In reality, it would be more appropriate to speak of black preaching traditions and to acknowledge that any attempt to address recurring features within these traditions is problematic.

Although they acknowledge such variations—for example, Crawford's observation that the volume with which hearers "talk back" to the preacher varies in different denominational contexts[9]—these authors nevertheless all point to recurring characteristics across these traditions that seem to transcend their differences, leading them to assert that there is, in some sense, a coherent tradition of black preaching. They emphasize a shared biblical and theological hermeneutic grounded in a common "history of oppression and social deprivation," which led blacks to interpret Scripture "from lived experience and a need to experience and witness the possibility of freedom, justice, and God's deliverance."[10] They recognize a distinctive performative quality to black preaching that arises from the central place of orality in African American cultural history. Finally, they highlight features of discourse across these traditions, rooted in "African verbal art,"[11] that were preserved within African

American culture because of its exclusion from "the mainstream of the changing world of White theology and worship."[12] Such elements common to the multiple traditions of African American religious discourse are the focus of this study.

Black Preaching as Oral Performance

Texts on black preaching typically highlight its character as performative, in the sense that oral delivery is central to the process of both the sermon's construction and its impact on the congregation. Davis underscores this feature in his definition of black preaching as a "verbal mold" recognized by African Americans *"in performance."*[13] In other words, only as it is enacted in a particular mode of oral delivery does the African American congregation recognize and respond to the sermon as a successful exemplar of the genre. Fry Brown likewise reflects this understanding in her use of "singing" as a metaphor to describe both the sermon and the struggle of women to find their voices within African American religious traditions. For Crawford, central to a sermon's success in bringing an audience to the response of celebration, the "Glory Hallelujah," are features of oral performance—"timing, pauses, inflection, pace, and the other musical qualities of speech to engage all that the listener is in the act of proclamation." He thus shifts the focus of sermon development away from "the more common homiletical concepts—outline, development, exposition, structure, and so forth"—toward a "musical understanding of the way sermons are *heard* and the oral response they awaken in listeners, who, in turn, are *heard* by the preacher and one another." Preaching is a "sonic experience with musical qualities."[14]

This performative character is rooted in African American cultural history and theology. Black preaching emerged from a profoundly oral culture within which blacks "listened to scriptures and retold the story in the manner of their own African cultural heritage." As Mitchell writes, "To a people who were not oriented to print, the gospel was preached most often from combined memory and narrative improvisation, in the common tongue, with all of its freshness and relevance." Closely aligned with the Bible's status as oral tradition is a particular theological tradition that sees scripture not as a repository of abstract theological ideas but rather, as the living voice of the ancestors. "A Black preacher is more likely to say 'Didn't he say it!' as one quoting a beloved parent. The preacher would not be so pompous about what 'the word of God declares!' or 'my

Bible says.'" This hermeneutic mirrors the "Hebrew oral tradition, which spoke of the deity as the 'God of Abraham, Isaac, and Jacob.' God was best understood by means of the talk and walk of the ancestors: the lived life and spoken word of parents, grandparents, and great-grandparents."[15]

LaRue likewise emphasizes the theological grounding from which arise the more obvious and "ancillary characteristics of language, emotion, authority, and celebration." The power of black preaching, he argues, grows out of

> what blacks believe about God's proactive intervention and involvement in their experiences. As a result of their historical marginalization and struggle, what became most important to blacks in their encounters with Euro-American Christianity was not dogma or abstract theological reflection, but an intimate relationship with a powerful God who demonstrated throughout scripture a propensity to side with the downtrodden.[16]

This theological orientation underscores Rosenberg's distinction between what informants in his study termed "manuscript" versus "spiritual" preachers, the latter speaking more extemporaneously. "Spiritual" preaching occurs when

> prepared, written texts are (partially or wholly) abandoned by the preachers, who consequently break away from the prose of the printed source and into the rhythm with which they are more comfortable; the resulting demonstration is of the spontaneous creation of metrical utterances. When the preacher departs from a prose text for the sake of metrical consistency, the sermon becomes "spiritual" (as the preachers themselves call it), or "oral" or "spontaneous."[17]

Although hearers expect the preacher to be "properly prepared to receive God's gift and that this preparation be done well in advance of the preaching event" they nevertheless "want the Word God gives preachers on the spot."[18]

Discussions of oral performance in black preaching emphasize the tonal variations that give the sermon its musical quality. Rosenberg highlights this characteristic in its more extreme form in what he called the "chanted sermon," a conflation of prose preaching and the traditional Negro spiritual that "embodies the emotional power of music and the (ostensibly) rational power of the spoken word."[19] In his discussion of the stylistic features of sermon delivery, Mitchell likewise asserts that "the most common or stereotypical is the use of a musical tone or chant in preaching. Among initiates it is variously referred to as 'moaning,' 'whooping,' 'tuning,' 'zooning,' or any one of several other more localized terms, each with a slightly different shade of meaning."[20] Based on an acoustical analysis of sound patterns recorded African American sermons, Davis argues, "articulated sound, as distinguished from articulated words, carries a semantic affect in the context of African-American narrative performance." He adds,

> "Sound" manifested during an African-American sermon is not "noise." Community-determined ideas and values are communicated in the coded sound channels of the sermon event. And the concurrent coding and decoding processes which characterize preacher and congregational oral-aural interaction during sermon segments have philosophical and aesthetic dimensions. This nonarticulated but full voicing is as significant to a congregation's interpretation of the preached sermon as the articulated word.[21]

Although they vary in the features they emphasize, these examples underscore that black preaching's unique and powerful communication is constituted as much from its form of oral delivery as its content.

Moreover, these dimensions of oral performance play a crucial part in actually transmitting the sermon's theological content. Mitchell, for example, notes the "slow rate of delivery" which he sees as a hallmark of black preaching, as well as the "stammer or hesitation" which builds "suspense and increasing interest in the message to be delivered"; these features, he argues, portray "the preacher as one who seems to be groping for the truth, struggling to hear what is coming from above."[22] In his close analysis of the constant tension between sacred biblical content and secular application in African American sermons, Davis finds a dramatic shift in the form of delivery. Whereas the secular portion employed a "staccato style," the "sacred portion of the formula takes a more even contoured oral style"; this stylistic pattern, he concluded, provides the preacher with a way of "supporting and identifying the sacred/secular polarities in his sermon formulas."[23] Crawford likewise captures this connection between theology and orality in an especially poignant description of a particular performative feature of black preaching, the strategic pause, which is

> more than a break in the delivery that is used by skillful speakers. I see it as a metaphor of spiritual formation, as an acknowledg-

ment by preachers that they must not cram the air so full of their words that they obscure the vast and silent mystery from which true speech arises. Sermon pause represents not only a rest from the sound of the preacher's voice, but an opening in the preacher's consciousness through which the musicality of the sermon resonates with the living truth.[24]

In other words, theological convictions are not simply conveyed through the meanings of the sermon's verbal content; rather, they are powerfully embodied in the sermon's nonverbal features—in rhythm and tone and pause, in gesture and mien.

Of course, all public communication is performative to some degree, depending for its success on elements related to the oral transmission of the message. Viewed through the lens of the classical canons of rhetoric, however, public discourse in the tradition of Western rationalism typically exalts invention and, secondarily, arrangement and style, reducing delivery to something of an afterthought. Most rhetorical critical studies ignore performative elements altogether. Black preaching, by contrast, places delivery at the center, reconfiguring the traditional canons of rhetoric by subsuming invention, arrangement and style within the act of delivery. Rosenberg describes this reality:

> Everything is in flux: the congregation and its moods, the rhythms, diction, syntax, and the emotions of the preacher, and the message for the day. A skillful preacher will take all, or nearly all, of these considerations into account, however unconsciously, and will mold the sermon accordingly. The end result should be the movement of the Spirit of God in the church.[25]

This is not to say that black preaching ignores content, that the black preacher is not "prepared" prior to the preaching moment, or that the preacher is free to develop the sermon in any way that he or she chooses.[26] Indeed, Davis emphasizes, the sermon's content presents a highly conventional blend of scriptural content and secular application, the deviation from which will doom a sermon to failure.[27] In tension with preparation and the need to conform to conventional forms, however, is a spontaneity that several have compared to jazz improvisation:

> What of the spontaneity so universally accepted as Black culture's greatest trait? The riff or improvisation on the melody so characteristic of the Black jazz instrumentalist or vocalist is Black spontaneity at its best . . . No real jazz musician ever riffs on the theme

until the diatonic scale, the instrument, and the theme have been mastered. When musicians do their thing, creating and playing "from the bottom of the soul," they have already practiced the basics for years. To be sure, they are creating in Black fashion, and they are in dialogue with the Black audience, which is comparable to the Black-preaching audience. But the least-informed Black jazz buff can feel the difference if the artist has not done the proper preparation and practice.[28]

What makes the sermon "work," then, is not so much the cogency of an argument or an idea that the audience judges, but the preacher's successful performance of that idea or argument. Put another way, while in some preaching traditions "content reigned supreme" and print became "lord over plot and even proclamation itself,"[29] in black preaching, the sermon comes into being in that moment when theological content comes alive in the preacher's voice and body.

Black Preaching as Communal Dialogue

Writers from within and outside the tradition of black preaching emphasize the sermon as a communal event, one that results from a process of co-creation involving both preacher and congregation. As Crawford puts it, "The minister preaches as much *for* the congregation as *to* it," so that "sermon delivery is a creative and inclusive moment where the preacher embodies for the whole congregation or group of hearers their celebrative gifts."[30] Of course, rhetorical theorists have emphasized the central role of the audience in the communicative event at least since the days of Aristotle, who wrote that persuasive arguments are always "persuasive *in reference to someone*."[31] In that tradition the audience holds a central place in the rhetor's development of the speech, a place reflected in Perelman and Olbrechts-Tyteca's dictum: "The essential consideration for the speaker who has set himself the task of persuading concrete individuals is that his construction of the audience should be adequate to the occasion."[32] As their observation suggests, however, members of the audience are conceived as objects of the strategic action of the rhetor, who considers their beliefs, preferences, and values and develops persuasive appeals accordingly.

In contrast, the sermon event is a partnership between preacher and audience in the black preaching tradition. This tradition is as much of how to hear and respond to the sermon as it is about composition and delivery.[33] Davis captures this communal nature when he describes preaching as a "shared responsibility" in which performer and the audience together shape the sermon in accord with the "well-defined set of compacts" that define the genre:

> During a performance, when both "performer" and "audience" are actively locked into a dynamic exchange, the audience compels the performer to acknowledge the most appropriate characteristics of the genre system—the "ideal" in terms of that particular performance environment—before permitting the performer sufficient latitude for the individuation of his genius and style.

The congregation, as an "aesthetic community," is as much the source out of which the sermon arises as is the preacher's own processes of invention.[34]

The nature of black preaching as a communal experience is reflected in the process through which preachers have been traditionally called and "trained." As Rosenberg observes, the process begins in childhood, where children "sit in church and learn the stories of the Bible, the popular sermon topics, the melody and rhythm of gospel songs (and, more important, the melody and rhythm of the pastor's chanted sermons), and, however unconsciously, many of the phrases that will later become formulas." From there, the young preacher might apprentice under an established preacher, developing his or her skill and building up a repertoire, to the point where the preacher has "become an active part of the tradition," mastering "certain aspects of language and certain rhythms that are sure to elicit a predictable response."[35] Traditionally, that process of apprenticeship means mastering the sermons of other preachers who have been part of the black church's oral tradition, such sermons as "The Eagle Stirreth Up Its Nest" or "Dry Bones in the Valley." Value comes not from the insights drawn from the preacher's personal encounter with the text but from the faithful and skillful performance of homiletic scripts already present in the cultural tradition.

The communal nature of preaching is most obvious in the particular kinds of audience responses for which black preaching is famous. One such example is the practice that occurs early in the sermon in which the preacher "lines up" the congregation, developing the "atmosphere" in which the sermon is to be preached. As Rosenberg explains, it is not as though the preacher browbeats the congregation into a predicable response.

> Rather, the term is intended to identify that portion of a con-
> gregation's energies that are voluntarily yielded to the preacher
> for the duration of the sermon. It is the preacher's task and duty
> to charge the preaching environment with dynamic energies and
> in so doing to induce the congregation to focus oral and aural
> mechanisms on the content and structure of the sermon perfor-
> mance. Preacher and congregation are locked into an aesthetic
> environment dependent on the continual transmission of mes-
> sages between the units of the performing community for the
> successful realization of the performance.[36]

Mitchell likewise emphasizes the element of dialogue between preacher and congregation, consisting of the

> well-known cries, "Amen!" "Praise the Lord!" "Well!" "Have
> Mercy!" "Sho'nough!" and a hundred other spontaneous audible
> responses. It also includes facial expressions, swaying bodies,
> nodding heads, raised hands, foot patting, shouting, tears, and
> (in recent years) hand clapping. Whatever the form, the commu-
> nication is real. It may even include coaching. When some folks
> feel it's time to celebrate they may without hesitation cry, "Come
> on up!" If it appears that a preacher's strength is waning, one may
> cry, "Help him, Lord." . . . And the coaching . . . may make a
> variety of candid appeals for support: "Are you praying with me?"
> "You're getting mighty quiet out there." "Can I get a witness?"
> "Amen, lights!" (since the people aren't saying anything).

Strategic, rhythmic pauses which follow predictable code words function as invitations for the audience to respond, a pattern that invites what is perhaps the most well-known element of the African American sermon performance, the call and response pattern: "When a Black preacher quotes the centurion (Matt 27:54), it is almost obligatory that a pause fol-low the first 'truly,' to provide the congregation time to repeat the word. In fact, this may be done several times before the quotation . . . is completed with 'this was the Son of God.'"[37] As Davis concludes, "Both preacher and congregation share in the encoding and deciphering of sermon element. When this complex, concurrent activity is most intense, the only suitable responses are sound or word-absent phrases—those 'moans,' 'cries,' and 'shouts.'"[38]

For women in many African American communities, of course, the notion of embodying the community's voice has been problematic, as they have struggled to find both legitimacy and authenticity within traditions that long prohibited women from preaching and where models of public proclamation were predominantly male. Nevertheless, Fry Brown emphasizes that preaching for her "sistah proclaimers" is no less dialogical, since "the call of God through the preacher to the people of faith and the response channeled back to God through the preacher is the essence of the preaching moment." For women preachers that dialogical character evidences itself in recurring features that transcend the sex of the preacher, as in the traditional "call and response" pattern:

> In a communicative cycle, one speaks and another listens and responds. The original speaker then counters the original listener's rejoinder, and the pattern is established. The timing, rate, and volume of the exchange depends on both the speaker and the listener.

In particular, she notes a variety of recurring prompts in the sermons of the black women, such as "Do you hear me?" "Stay with me!" and "Can I get a witness?" As with their male counterparts, these prompts in the voices of her "sistahs," which invite the audience to join in the performance, are "part of the oral tradition . . . Some catch you off guard. Some are planned. Some are identified with particular preachers, denominations, or worship styles." In any case, these verbal features of the African American sermon event bring the audience into the performance so that, "like steps to a dance, the movement flows naturally."[39]

In this way, black preaching anticipates the attempts of contemporary communication theorists to reconfigure the traditional roles of rhetor and audience. For example, Foss and Griffin offer what they term "invitational rhetoric" as a "nonhierarchical, nonjudgmental, nonadversarial" process that emphasizes dialogue over control and manipulation:

> Invitational rhetoric is an invitation to understanding as a means to create a relationship rooted in equality, immanent value, and self-determination. Invitational rhetoric constitutes an invitation to enter the rhetor's world and see it as the rhetor does . . . Ideally, audience members accept the invitation offered by the rhetor by listening to and trying to understand the invitation offered by the rhetor's perspective and then presenting their own. When this happens, rhetor and audience alike contribute to the thinking about an issue.[40]

This reconfiguration is also reflected in the conception of the audience as an "interpretive community" comprised not simply of passive recipients to meanings intended by the rhetor and encoded within discourse, but as active participants in the process of creating meaning through communal processes of interpretation.[41]

Black preaching, however, represents a more dramatic departure from traditional rhetoric than even these proposals suggest. The African American sermon is a communal performance, a reflexive form of communication through which the congregation articulates its theology back to itself, re-presenting and celebrating its most deeply held values and beliefs even as it anticipates the voice of God. The content derives not simply from the preacher's personal insight and creativity, but from the forms and topoi, even entire sermons, that comprise the community's cultural tradition. The "audience" socializes the preacher into its values, equips the preacher with themes and modes of discourse, calls the preacher into his or her vocation and then guides the preacher in the articulation of that message. The preacher is simply the voice through which the community speaks to itself, affirming its identity as the people of God.

Black Preaching as Mimesis

Arising out of its performative and communal nature is perhaps the most significant characteristic of black preaching: it is mimetic. It offers the participating community not simply a persuasive argument but an imitative experience of its theological content.

The distinction between mimesis and persuasion goes back at least to the writings of Aristotle, who conceived of rhetoric and poetics as distinct modes of expression and representation. Aristotle argued that the defining characteristic of all poetic arts from epic, tragedy, and comedy to "flute-playing and lyre-playing," was that they are "modes of imitation." For example, "Rhythm alone, without harmony, is the means of the dancer's imitations; for even he, by the rhythms of his attitudes, may represent men's characters, as well as what they do and suffer."[†] With this observation Aristotle captured the distinction between explanation and representation that lies at the heart of rhetoric's division from poetics. Wilbur Howell explains, "Faced with the problem of doing something about a crisis in their society, the poet and the orator respond in different

---

† Aristotle *Poetics* 1447a.

ways. The poet deals with the problem by telling a story or by presenting a dramatic action."[42]

Central to the mimetic process is the poet's use of language to create a state of consciousness in which the audience experiences in their imaginations and emotions what would normally only be experienced in "real life." For example, "the usual way to feel or to become heroic has nothing to do with music; but music can be contrived in such a way that it has this effect." Similarly, the events portrayed in a tragedy are not literally taking place, but their dramatic depiction evokes the kinds of emotions that the audience would feel if they were actually happening. As Woodruff puts it, "The script has the same effect on you that the actions would have had, if you had believed they were taking place. In this way the poet's mimesis is aimed at producing a result that is normally achieved by other means."[43]

Although they do not use the word mimesis, each of these works examined in the present study underscores this quality as a central feature of black preaching. LaRue notes that behind all of the particular rhetorical elements of the sermon lies the aim of "bringing into view" the "things of God."[44] Davis similarly emphasizes this element in what he sees as the downplaying of doctrinal explanation over explicit, secular illustration: "The environment of the sermon is the world of experience in which people live and love, hate and believe."[45] Mitchell argues that the sermon's goal is fundamentally to create a highly personal identification with the biblical text: "The Black preacher is not in favor of pat, easy, legalistic, or literalistic answers. The unspoken but intuitive goal is an *experience* of the Word, which plants the Word deep in human consciousness." In the African American sermon, "the Black experience is lifted up and celebrated, and the hearers enter vicariously into the story, making it his or her own personal story."[46]

Mitchell particularly underscores the mimetic dimension of black preaching by highlighting celebration—"the one aspect of the sermon that most nearly deserves to be called typically Black"[47]—as both a discreet part of the sermon as well as the sermon's overall goal. Mitchell explains,

> The preacher accelerates the rhythm, and the accentual stresses become distributed through the line as in singing . . . Often a tonal center emerges. Preachers gradually increase rhythm and vocal intensity . . . At some self-determined emotional climax

they will break off, reverting in their concluding remarks to nor-
mal, or near-normal conversational prose.[48]

This moment provides an "ecstatic reinforcement" of the sermon's theme,
significant because "people relate to and remember what they celebrate,
and it influences their behavior." Mitchell admits the danger of "irrelevant
celebration" insisting that "there simply must be a biblical lesson and behavioral objective that justifies stirring people's feelings." Nevertheless,
he claims,

> The emotional is most essential; it may not be omitted. If there
> is no impact in emotive consciousness, then the sermon has
> not influenced people where it counts most: in behaviors that
> are emotional, such as love and hate, fear and trust. The Black
> pulpit tradition is still so important because it has unashamedly
> addressed the whole person—the cognitive, intuitive, and emo-
> tive. People have survived still-unbelievable horrors only because
> their feelings of trust were regularly nourished from pulpit and
> fireside.

Thus, he concludes, "If the sermon is remembered, . . . it will be because
the text was etched by ecstasy on the heart of the hearer."[49]

Black preaching achieves this mimetic function, in part, through
its performative character. The traditional African American biblical
hermeneutic viewed the Bible as oral tradition, looking to scripture not
for a set of propositions to be argued but as a living story that mediated
the presence of God. The kind of preaching that grew out of this hermeneutic sought to place hearers in the story, combining "imagination with
role playing and spontaneous dramatization" in a way that would "reach,
hold, and lift the Black audience."[50] Through its particular conventions
of language and sound, its tonal quality, its use of rhythm and meter,
and the nonverbal vocalizations uttered by preacher and audience, the
sermon performance ushers the congregation into the "sacred present," a
moment that imaginatively transcends the boundaries of time and space.
Drawing on Eliade's definition of the sacred, Levine notes that this moment extends "the world spatially upward so that communication with the
other world becomes possible, and . . . [extends] it temporally backward
so that the paradigmatic acts of the gods and mythical ancestors can be
continually re-enacted and indefinitely recoverable."[51] In that moment,
the Gospel has become truly a living word "vicariously experienced in
worship, rather than simply heard in theory."[52]

The communal nature of black preaching also contributes to its mimetic character. As public discourse was described in the Western rhetorical tradition, the rhetor's initial task was to win over the skeptical audience, assumed to be resistant to the rhetor's efforts as a matter of course. Black preaching offers its own analogous activity in the process, noted above, of "lining up the congregation." As these writers emphasize, however, the African American congregation comes not resisting the preacher but fully anticipating a powerful experience of the Holy Spirit; the preacher's role is not to win a skeptical audience over, but simply to arouse and awaken the congregation so that they can fully participate in the performance.

The black sermon's distinctive formal dimensions further serve to engage the audience at an experiential level. As Burke emphasizes, elements of form or structure in an artistic work—such things as crescendo, balance, repetition, and series—all work to awaken "an attitude of collaborative expectancy in us." He adds,

> Imagine a passage built about a set of oppositions ("we do this, but they on the other hand do that; we stay here, but they go there; we look up, but they look down," etc.). Once you grasp the trend of the form, it invites participation regardless of the subject matter. Formally, you will find yourself swinging along with the succession of antitheses, even though you may not agree with the proposition being presented in this form.[53]

Form draws the audience into participation in the rhetorical act—and prepares the audience to give assent to its content. The conventional elements of the African American sermon, especially the preacher's use of such features as repetition, rhythm, pause, and so forth, create this kind of engagement. In black preaching, however, that participation is not simply auditory and cerebral, with passive hearers drawn into a message through the formal elements in the sermon's language and structure. For the African American audience, participation is material and embodied. Through such features as the call and response, the voicing of "Amen," "Well," and "Praise the Lord," the nonarticulated moans, the swaying bodies and nodding heads, the audience joins with the preacher in creating the message event.

In this way, black preaching does far more than explain or argue in an effort to win the audience's assent to particular theological propositions. Instead, preacher and congregation together use language, sound and movement to create a shared mimetic experience of those propositions. Whereas in many Western homiletic and rhetorical traditions the audience stands removed from the sermon's content, hearing *about* it and rationally evaluating it from "the outside," the black sermon places hearers subjectively "in" the content, so that they imaginatively experience its veracity. The black congregation does not intellectualize theological abstractions. In black preaching, rather, theological truth becomes "virtual reality."

Conclusion

This essay illuminates the rhetorical character of black preaching as described by writers within the tradition and from outside observers. This analysis lays groundwork for explanation of the tradition's enduring and nurturing qualities. As a communal performance, black preaching engages the entire community in the creation of the sermon event. Using conventional forms and familiar vocal inflections, enacted in the choreography of African American spirituality, drawing upon the topoi of the African American theological traditions, the black sermon brings the community's unique Christian story to life. As mimetic celebration, the African American sermon provides a visceral experience of the new heaven and the new earth, for a people who have historically lived with oppression and injustice on this earth. Its distinctive and enduring power "lies in the soul of black Christian experience, . . . in the way that African Americans have come, in the refining fires of history, to understand the character of God."[54]

Although its precise forms are unique to the black church, its preaching tradition has much to offer the broader homiletic conversation. Crawford expresses that possibility:

> My hope is that even while I draw from the particular riches of the black church, preachers of other cultures and traditions can find here a way of renewing their own homiletical musicality. To learn in this way from the black church is to participate in the spiritual depths of racial reconciliation.[55]

At the very least, it infuses preaching with the sense of risk and passion that characterize the messages of the biblical prophets. The black preacher is "caught up in sharing the Word. Black preachers have to let go. They feel what they are preaching about: freedom, sorrow, fear, rage, and joy.

They must make no pretense of objectivity. You can't be objective when God lays hands on you."[56] Wherever there is a tendency for the sermon to be a highly scripted and controlled event, black preaching casts the sermon as a leap of faith and it positions the audience as a community gathered in the expectation of hearing the living voice of God.

As a communicative event, African American preaching also highlights the creation of transcendent experience as a crucial dimension of religious rhetoric. To be sure, it is possible for experience to become a substitute for theological reflection or for the disciplines of Christian spirituality, a danger recognized by no one more clearly than LaRue, who downplays the outward trappings of the African American sermon in favor of explicating its underlying theology and biblical hermeneutic. Nevertheless, black preaching, as mimetic performance, reminds us that the aims of Christian rhetoric—inspiring hope, promoting a biblical worldview, and encouraging actions that befit a profession of faith— have never been achieved exclusively through doctrinal explanation or argument. Celebrative and emotional religious experiences that integrate exegesis and poetry, exposition and choreography, providing imaginative glimpses of the world to come, are all essential qualities. Mitchell captures this understanding of the role of language in a description of a hypothetical sermon on Hebrews 12:1–2, the famous text that envisions the Christian life as a long-distance race, run in the midst of a great cloud of witnesses. The sermon follows the logic of the text, moving from the vision of the great cloud of witnesses to the laying aside of every weight, to running with patience the marathon race, to anticipating joy at the finish line. What places the sermon squarely within the African American preaching tradition is the way the preacher helps the hearers experience the text:

> The Black preacher will be very biblical but also very vivid, and the hearers will see themselves actually warming up and stripping down and running . . . It might not be quite so proper and dignified as some might desire, but it will have "gut" impact and give power to the Gospel. Children will listen attentively, and some menfolk will be more interested than usual. Years later, someone will say, "I can *see* that old preacher now, as he took us out on the track and got us ready for the race."

The result for the congregation, he concludes, will be a word from God "better retained in memory and also better placed in practice."[57]

NOTES

1. Henry H. Mitchell, *Black Preaching: The Recovery of a Powerful Art* (Nashville: Abingdon, 1990) 13.

2. Morris, *Origins of the Civil Rights Movement* (New York: Free Press, 1984) xiii, xii.

3. Cleophus J. LaRue, *The Heart of Black Preaching* (Louisville: Westminster John Knox Press, 2000) 114–15.

4. See Keith D. Miller, "Epistemology of a Drum Major," *Rhetoric Society Quarterly* 18 (1988) 225–36; *Voice of Deliverance: The Language of Martin Luther King and its Sources* (New York: Free Press, 1992). Particularly helpful is Miller's observation that black preaching is rooted in a typological view of the history, which treats "Biblical figures and events as types recurring throughout human existence, up to the present moment" (*Voice of Deliverance*, 21). The rhetorical dimensions of black preaching highlighted in the present essay grow out of this typological view of history. See also Gary S. Selby, *Martin Luther King and the Rhetoric of Freedom: The Exodus in America's Struggle for Civil Rights* (Waco: Baylor University Press, 2008); Kirt H. Wilson, "Interpreting the Discursive Field of the Montgomery Bus Boycott: Martin Luther King Jr.'s Holt Street Address," *Rhetoric & Public Affairs* 8 (2005) 299–326; and the essays in Carolyn Calloway–Thomas and John Louis Lucaites, ed., *Martin Luther King, Jr. And the Sermonic Power of Public Discourse* (Tuscaloosa: University of Alabama Press, 2005).

5. Gerald L. Davis, *I Got the Word in Me and I Can Sing It, You Know: A Study of the Performed African-American Sermon* (Philadelphia: University of Pennsylvania Press, 1985) 40–41. Reid, Bullock, and Fleer offer a brief but incisive theoretical treatment of black preaching in their examination of developments in contemporary homiletic thought. See Robert Reid, Jeffry Bullock, and David Fleer, "Preaching as the Creation of an Experience: The Not-So-Rational Revolution of the New Homiletic," *Journal of Communication & Religion* 18 (1995) 1–9.

6. Bruce A. Rosenberg, *Can These Bones Live? The Art of the American Folk Preacher*, rev. ed. (Urbana: University of Chicago Press, 1988; orig. pub. 1970); Evans E. Crawford, *The Hum: Call and Response in African American Preaching* (Nashville: Abingdon, 1995). It should be noted that whereas Davis focuses on African American preaching, Rosenberg broadens his focus to "folk preaching," although he includes among his artifacts a number of African American sermons.

7. Theresa L. Fry Brown, *Weary Throats and New Songs: Black Women Proclaiming God's Word* (Nashville: Abingdon, 2003).

8. Elaine B. Richardson and Ronald L. Jackson II, *African American Rhetoric(s): Interdisciplinary Perspectives* (Carbondale: Southern Illinois University Press, 2004) xiii. An excellent starting point for exploring the study of African American rhetoric generally is Keith Gilyard's "Introduction: Aspects of African American Rhetoric as a Field" in the same volume (1–20).

9. Crawford, *The Hum*, 56.

10. Fry Brown, *Weary Throats and New Songs*, 91.

11. A. Duku Anokye, "A Case for Orality in the Classroom," *Clearing House* 70 (May-June) 229–31. Available on-line: http://vnweb.hwwilsonweb.com.lib. pepperdine.edu/hww/results/results_single_fulltext.jhtml;hwwilsonid=MVYQNH13CLX2NQA3DILSFGOAD UNGIIV0.

12. Mitchell, *Black Preaching*, 19.

13. Davis, *I Got the Word*, 46, emphasis added.

14. Crawford, *The Hum*, 16–17.

15. Mitchell, *Black Preaching*, 20, 57–58.

16. LaRue, *The Heart of Black Preaching*, 2.

17. Rosenberg, *Can These Bones Live?* 12.

18. Mitchell, *Black Preaching*, 125.

19. Rosenberg, *Can These Bones Live?* 23.

20. Mitchell, *Black Preaching*, 89.

21. Davis, *I Got the Word*, 7, 95.

22. Mitchell, *Black Preaching*, 84, 97–98.

23. Davis, *I Got the Word*, 79.

24. Crawford, *The Hum*, 17.

25. Rosenberg, *Can These Bones Live?* 65.

26. On the issue of preparation, see Mitchell, *Black Preaching*, 124.

27. Davis, *I Got the Word*, 104–6.

28. Mitchell, *Black Preaching*, 124–25. Rosenberg makes an almost identical observation (Rosenberg, *Can These Bones Live?* 32).

29. Crawford, *The Hum*, 66.

30. Ibid., 43, 71.

31. Aristotle *Art of Rhetoric* 1.2 (emphasis added).

32. Chaim Perelman and Lucie Olbrechts-Tyteca, *The New Rhetoric: A Treatise on Argumentation*, trans. John Wilkenson and Purcell Weaver (Notre Dame: University of Notre Dame Press, 1960) 19.

33. See Mitchell, *Black Preaching*, 23.

34. Davis, *I Got the Word*, 30, 26, 31.

35. Rosenberg, *Can These Bones Live?* 31–32.

36. Ibid., 17.

37. Mitchell, *Black Preaching*, 100, 92.

38. Davis, *I Got the Word*, 66.

39. Fry Brown, *Weary Throats and New Songs*, 9, 166, 168.

40. Sonja K. Foss and Cindy L. Griffin, "Beyond Persuasion: A Proposal for an Invitational Rhetoric," *Communication Monographs* 62 (1995) 5.

41. One of the earliest conceptualizations of interpretive communities is Janice Radway's *Reading the Romance*, which located the production of meaning in the interpretive practices of readers rather than within textual structures, although she emphasized that the reader's social context limits the range of interpretation. As she put it, "What the theoretical possibilities of an infinite number of readings, in fact, there are patterns or regularities to what viewers and readers bring to texts in large part because they acquire specific cultural competencies as a consequence of their particular social location." Janice Radway, *Reading the Romance: Women, Patriarchy, and Popular Literature*, 2nd ed. (Chapel Hill: University of North Carolina Press, 1991) 8. For a recent treatment of the interpretive community as a tool for analyzing actual message effects, see Daniel A. Stout, "Secularization and the Religious Audience: A Study of Mormons and Las Vegas Media," *Mass Communication and Society*, 7 (2004) 61–75.

42. Wilbur Samuel Howell, *Poetics, Rhetoric, and Logic: Studies in the Basic Disciplines of Criticism* (Ithaca, NY: Cornell University Press, 1975) 56–57.

43. Paul Woodruff, "Aristotle on *Mimēsis*," in *Essays on Aristotle's Poetics*, edited by Amélie Oksenberg Rorty (Princeton, NJ: Princeton University Press, 1992) 91–93.

44. LaRue, *The Heart of Black Preaching*, 115.

45. Davis, *I Got the Word*, 104.

46. Mitchell, *Black Preaching*, 59, 67.

47. Ibid., 119. Although the term "celebration" may appear to oversimplify black preaching as naively carefree, a view that belies its roots in oppression and suffering, Mitchell uses it more in a dramatic sense, to denote a process through which preacher and congregation enact and experience the sermon's theological content. Du Bois's designation of this element of the sermon as the "frenzy," not altogether positive in its connotation either, nevertheless captured its character as a transcendent, "extra-rational" experience— as the point when, Lischer notes, "the *experience* of God replaces *talk about* God." See Richard Lischer, *The Preacher King: Martin Luther King, Jr., and the Word that Moved America* (New York: Oxford, 1995) 138–39.

48. Rosenberg, *Can These Bones Live?* 128.

49. Mitchell, *Black Preaching*, 119, 120–22.

50. Ibid., 93.

51. Lawrence W. Levine, *Black Culture and Black Consciousness* (New York: Oxford University Press, 1977) 30–32.

52. Mitchell, *Black Preaching*, 83.

53. Kenneth Burke, *A Rhetoric of Motives* (Berkeley: University Press, 1969) 58.

54. LaRue, *The Heart of Black Preaching*, 1.

55. Crawford, *The Hum*, 22.

56. Mitchell, *Black Preaching*, 95–96.

57. Ibid., 117.

PART III

Pacifism, Just War, and Areas of Related Inquiry

16

Keeping Alive the Narratives of War and Peace

LEE C. CAMP

If memory serves me correctly, I had never given a great deal of thought to questions of war, peacemaking, and violence until my professor Doug Foster assigned to me certain readings from Mike Casey.[1] When I read Mike's story-telling about the generations past, I was both intrigued and puzzled. Voice after voice had cried out for a peaceable church to bear faithful witness to the peaceable Kingdom. Why had I, raised in a church that took seriously "restoration of New Testament Christianity," never heard these arguments? Why was church polity more important than modern mechanized war, when the Hebrew prophets proclaimed so much about the coming of peace to accompany the coming of the Messiah? Why did we give lip service to the unity of the church, a trans-national identity, while being acquiescent to the State that calls us to kill members of the church in other nations? *And*—a question with which Mike and Richard Hughes and Leonard Allen and other informed voices on the American Restoration Movement have grappled at length—and *why* did the stance on the issue of peacemaking among the leaders of our movement change with apparently so little resistance?

On this latter question, Mike contended that one missing element in the witness to peace in Churches of Christ was our story-telling. Mike

1. In preparing this essay, I found the reading Doug Foster had assigned: it was a lecture Casey had presented to the Christian Scholars' Conference at David Lipscomb University, July 19, 1991, titled "The Courage of Conscience: The Conscientious Objectors of World War II and the Churches of Christ."

put it this way: in Churches of Christ, the stories of conscientious objectors of earlier generations have simply been ignored and forgotten. Their memories not kept alive, other forces and stories fashion our interpretive lenses. As we grew wealthier, we became more conservative, militaristic, and "American." We thus read the Bible differently, all the while claiming our interpretations to be "objective."[2] In contrast, the Anabaptist churches have collections of stories that help keep alive the witness to peace. The recounting of those stories develops a shared consciousness of the calling to non-violent discipleship.[3]

Observations such as these gave rise to another lesson taught me by Doug Foster, through the reading of Mike Casey: the history of ideas is important, if only because they allow you to understand oneself and one's own community better. The reasons *why* we think certain ways are most often *not* located in mere "objective" rationality, but in the social and historical setting in which those ideas are birthed and articulated. This is not to say that we must yield to a simple historicism, or to a behaviorist model of psychology. But it *is* to say that reading history is important because it allows us to understand why we carry around some of the ideas we have in the present.

Much can be learned from a careful, systematic comparison and contrast between the doctrine of Christian non-violence on the one hand, and the Christian Just War tradition on the other. Such analyses are terribly important. In my mind, the teaching of Jesus and the New Testament requires the practice and embrace of non-violent Christian love. But so far as I know, Mike never undertook such a systematic treatment of the issue.

Thus he never argued me into pacifism. Mike was more interested in telling stories of those who had grappled with the question, and thought that this was an indispensably important part of helping us make sense of who we are, or, more troubling for him, who we have not been:

2. He makes this point—a classic example of H. Richard Niebuhr's "sect to denomination" shift—in the lecture mentioned in fn. 1. See also Michael W. Casey, "Churches of Christ and World War II Civilian Public Service: A Pacifist Remnant," in Theron F. Schlabach and Richard T. Hughes, *Proclaim Peace: Christian Pacifism from Unexpected Quarters* (Chicago: University of Illinois Press, 1997) 110, where he discusses the contrast with the historic peace churches.

3 Thieleman J. van Braught, *The Martyrs' Mirror*, trans. Joseph F. Sohm (1660; reprinted, Scottdale, PA: Herald, 1938) being the most obvious example; but a casual perusal of Herald Press' offerings shows a large number of resources, both fiction and non-fiction, which recount such stories.

The story of the transformation of the Churches of Christ from a tradition of peace to one of pro-war civil religion has significant theological and sociological ramifications . . . . While many decry the 'identity crisis' and the change in the Churches of Christ, the irony is that many of the decriers have contributed significantly to change that has already taken place. They have buried and forgotten many 'lost stories' that point to a road not taken. My ongoing task is to try to recover and preserve some of these lost stories as many of us rethink who we are and what we are up to as a religious tradition.[4]

I soon found myself intrigued with his stories of "our" conscientious objectors, who also served their time in the war years, but in a way that they believed consistent with the way of Jesus. For example, I heard Mike tell with relish the story of Corbett Bishop, a disciple of Jesus who pioneered non-violent activist techniques later employed in the Civil Rights movement, this Corbett Bishop who came from an Alabama Church of Christ. Bishop had been imprisoned for his war resistance and subsequently went on hunger strike. When the authorities insisted that he eat and drink, he refused. The authorities put a feeding tube down his nose, and when a cock roach fell into the feeding solution, Bishop's passive resistance continued unabated. Rather than simply reaching up and pinching the tube to stop the roach, he allowed it to continue down the tube into his stomach. Whatever one makes of Bishop's tale, one does not forget it, and one is left asking questions one would not otherwise.[5]

Thus Mike's work was certainly as important as systematic theological or biblical work. In his story-telling, he helped us realize that when the question *does* arise in our churches over the legitimacy of Christian participation in warfare, the answers may have little to do with the honest intellectual differences between the Just Warriors and the Pacifists. The embrace of war in our churches may have little to do with having honestly grappled with New Testament texts and the requisite ethical questions. Instead, it seems other stories, commitments, and powers are at work. The story-tellers, it turns out, may have much more to do with our ethical and moral sensitivities than our careful academicians. This is no excuse for lazy thinking. It is simply an observation that, in our so-called post-modern days, even the academicians have been making judgments.

4. Casey, "Courage of Conscience," 1–2.

5. Mike presented a lecture on Bishop at Lipscomb some few years prior to his death. He also tells this story in the much earlier essay, "Courage of Conscience," 7ff.

To summarize, what has become almost a common-place in our day, but something I think Mike began to teach me: what we take as "common sense" or "objectively true" may be greatly indebted to the stories we tell. That is, our interpretation of facts or artifacts is much dependent upon the stories that we have been told, and the stories we tell. In that light, and in honor of Mike's great interest in the issue of Christian pacifism and war-making, I recount here two research visits of my own; and I share stories I carried with me into those visits, and stories I've garnered since those visits; and in doing so, I seek to illustrate the manner in which these stories affect the way in which "objective facts" may be interpreted. Along the way, I shall ask how these facts and stories may, in turn, inform our own understanding of Christians, violence, and peacemaking.

A Cowboy Museum

The recollection of a child-hood memory drew me back to the National Cowboy and Western Heritage museum in Oklahoma City. My family had toured the museum on a family vacation "out west" probably some thirty years ago. I remembered only this one image from the museum: the larger-than-life sculpture by famed artist James Earle Fraser entitled *The End of the Trail*. The sculpture displays an utterly dejected and defeated Cherokee warrior upon his mighty horse of war, the magnificent horse, too, in a posture of defeat, consequent to the White Man's coming. Fraser's work memorializes Andrew Jackson's forced relocation of the Cherokee westward.

Along with my vague childhood memory of the sculpture, was another recollection: my father's sense of sadness, and his few words of lamentation uttered in response to this monument to injustice. I had had, as I recall it, enough grammar schooling to understand that the Cherokee and Creek were tribes from regions now called Alabama. Geography and names and historical monuments reminded me, as a boy, that my people were the newcomers to this place. I was raised in the hills around Talladega, Alabama. Talladega was the name of a Creek Indian village, and in our county was Mount Cheaha, the highest geographical point in the state; "Cheaha," according to some sources, means "high place" in the Creek language. So this sculpture said to me, even as a child, something like this: other people once lived in the Alabama hills you love, other people once walked amid the long-leaf pines, other people once loved the red clay of the place you call home. The *beginning* of *The End of the*

Trail began in the region I called home, and I was not quite so sure how to process that.

So, I wanted to see that sculpture again. It did seem to me, in this most recent visit, that the Cowboy Museum depicted Native American culture in a compelling and beautiful manner. Nevertheless these artifacts sat uneasily alongside the celebration of cowboy culture. After all, Dee Brown teaches us that all the "great myths of the American West"—"tales of fur traders, mountain men, steamboat pilots, gold seekers, gamblers, gunmen, cavalry men, cowboys, harlots, missionaries, school marms, and homesteaders"—arose out of the very same forces by which "the culture and civilization of the American Indian was destroyed."[6] But I found in the museum no placard that says, "look at the violence of it all; look at the manner in which Protestant Christianity supported and gave warrant for the conquest of this land; look at the injustice waged, all in the name of progress, manifest destiny and the will of God." The museum simply seems to assume that Native American artifacts can sit quietly alongside the display of firearms, the magnificent display of Colts and Winchesters, the display of "how the west was won."

I contend thus that we need not only stories of the conscientious objectors which Mike recovered for us, but also story tellers—in our churches—like Dee Brown or Howard Zinn. We need stories that give us pause about the American imperialist project in which we find ourselves. We might even need, for example, our Sunday School teachers to tell stories like The Pequot War. This was one of the earliest American Christian incidents of grave violence, setting the early context that would in time lead to Fraser's *End of the Trail*. The Puritans, recently arrived from England, soon found themselves in competition for land with the original inhabitants of the land. The Puritans, in short order, had their own tales to tell that justified in their minds, the vengeful war: the death of John Oldham, killed by Indians. John Gallop came upon the scene of the murder, and in response to the murder of Oldham, killed a dozen or so Indians.[7] After taking one Indian captive, binding him with ropes, another was taken captive and bound similarly. Ill-at-ease due to the stories he had heard of Indians being capable of untying themselves when kept

6. Dee Brown, *Bury My Heart at Wounded Knee: An Indian History of the American West* (New York: Holt, Rinehart & Winston, 1970) xv.

7. Here my story-telling follows Richard Drinnon, *Facing West: The Metaphysics of Indian-Hating and Empire Building* (Norman, OK: University of Oklahoma Press, 1997) 35ff.

together in captivity, Gallop took the latter captive and, still bound, threw him into the sea.

But the death of some dozen or so in retribution for the one was apparently not vengeance enough. Thus, Captain John Underhill declared that "the blood of the innocent called for vengeance." Underhill set out from Boston in August of 1636 under the leadership of Captain John Endicott to deliver such vengeance. Landing at Block Island, Endicott and his men hunted for two days, for Indians to either capture or kill. According to the surviving eyewitness account, they did not kill all the men on the Island only because "the Indians being retired into swamps, so as we could not find them. We burnt and spoiled both houses and corn in great abundance; but they kept themselves in obscurity." Thus on day one of their foray, the Englishmen busied themselves "burning and spoiling the island," continuing such destruction the second day. Historian Richard Drinnon continues, "in all they burned the wigwams of two villages, threw Indian mats on and burned 'great heaps of pleasant corn shelled,' 'destroyed some of their dogs instead of men,' and staved in canoes."[8] Endicott continued on his way from Block Island to confront the Pequots the next day. When they offered to parley unarmed, Captain Endicott preferred to "bid them battle." The Pequots would not engage the battle, so Endicott spent that day, again, "burning and spoiling the country." Sailing that night to Narragansett Bay, the Indians again would not engage the battle, so the English "burnt and spoiled what we could light on."[9]

When Captain John Mason subsequently took up the War against the Pequots, he believed his work mandated by God: "the Lord was as it were pleased to say unto us, The Land of Canaan will I give unto thee

8. John Underhill, *Newes from America . . . Containing a True Relation of Their War-like Proceedings These Two Years Last Past* (London: 1638), cited in Drinnon, *Facing West*, 36.

9. Underhill, cited in Drinnon, *Facing West*, 36ff. Drinnon goes on to incisively note: "of course, rules eager to make war can made do with almost any first victim, so long as his death will infect everyone with the feeling of being threatened and provide basis for belief that 'the enemy,' broadly defined, is responsible. It this minimal foundation be laid, every other reason for his death may be ignored or suppressed, as Elias Canetti observed, save one, the victim's 'membership of the group to which one belongs oneself'" (38). Drinnon notes that the apparently innocent beginning to the war was, in fact even less innocent than it appears: surely the death of a dozen Indians killed by Gallop could satisfy the thirst for vengeance for Oldham's death? Apparently not. How civilized, we might note, was Moses' limiting injunction of an eye-for-an-eye and a tooth-for-a-tooth compared to Ancient Near Eastern thirst for blood, or (some of) the early Puritans thirst for blood.

though but few and Strangers in it." Similarly, the Reverend Thomas Hooker had prophesied that the Pequots should be so defeated "that they should be Bread for us."[10] So Mason and his fellow soldiers launched a surprise attack against the Pequot's fort on June 5, 1637, before dawn. The men, women, and children still slept, and the soldiers began to burn the fort. Drinnon recounts: "the stench of frying flesh, the flames, and the heat drove the English outside the walls." John Underhill, fighting along with Mason, recounted that many of the Pequots "were burnt in the fort, both men, women, and children. Others [who were] forced out . . . our soldiers received and entertained with the point of the sword. Down fell men, women, and children."[11] So the war against the Pequots quickly moved from burning corn and wigwams, to the burning of four hundred men, women and children in the space of one hour.

Mason and Underhill rejoiced, convinced that their merciless triumph was the work of God, indeed that God "had fitted the hearts of men for the service." Underhill was later asked by some, "why should you be so furious?" He referred them to the scriptures: "When a people is grown to such a height of blood, and sin against God and man, and all the confederates in the action, there he hath no respect to persons, but harrows them, and saws them, and puts them to the sword, and the most terriblest death that may be." In other words, Underhill summarized: "We had sufficient light from the word of God for our proceedings."[12]

A few weeks later, Captain Israel Stoughton arrived with more militiamen, and captured a hundred Pequot refugees, who were hiding in a swamp. According to one Puritan observer some twenty of those captured were taken by John Gallop to "feed the fishes with them," that

10. Cited in Drinnon, *Facing West*, 42.

11. Ibid., 42.

12. Ibid., 43. The point here is not that the native Americans never indulged their blood lust. It seems a rather all-too-common human practice, to give way to the lust for violence. Rather, the point is that the stories told placed the blood-lust all on the side of the "enemie." In fact, in the case of the Pequots, Drinnon's account is telling on this point: it appears that the "systematic ferocity of the Europeans" far outweighed that of their opponents. In fact, the Narragansett, allied with the Englishmen against the Pequots, came to Underhill after the battle and "cried Mach it, mach it; that is, It is naught, it is naught, because it is too furious, and slays too many men" (ibid., citing Underhill). In Underhill's professional estimation as an English soldier, the Indians fought "more for pastime, than to conquer and subdue enemies" (ibid.). In other words: in this case, the ferocious and systematic war-making of the Christian Europeans far outweighed the "hobby" of Indian war-making.

is, to throw the still bound captives into the sea. Stoughton hunted down other Pequot families whom the pursuers knew could travel only slowly because of their children. Drinnon recounts that "three hundred of the quarry were literally run to ground. Many of those killed were tramped into the mud or buried in swamp mire."[13]

Reflecting upon the Pequot War, Captain John Mason concluded: "Thus was God pleased to smite our enemies, and to give us their Land for an Inheritance."[14] Mason received fame and fortune, appointed major general of the Connecticut militia. In ceremonial fashion, Reverend Hooker gave Mason a staff "like an ancient Prophet addressing himself to the Military Officer," reported an observer. The staff was given to Mason as "the Principal Ensign of Martial Power, to lead the Armies and Fight the Battles of the Lord and of his People," reported Thomas Prince.[15]

Were we to tell such stories in our churches, then we may begin to realize that more is at stake than simply an abstract, intellectual debate between the advocates of non-violent enemy love on the one hand, and the advocates of the Just War tradition (JWT) on the other. In my own experience in the tradition that Mike and I shared, my experience has been this: when actually confronted with Mike's stories of conscientious objectors, these are often quickly dismissed. The dismissal typically follows the assertion that war is regrettable, but there comes a time when it is justified and necessary. That is, the dismissal of the story of CO's flows from a purported adherence to the Just War Tradition (JWT).

But, as already indicated, I doubt this is what is really happening. In my teaching ethics courses, my agenda includes teaching the criteria of the JWT. When I ask my students how many of them have ever heard a sermon or a Sunday school class on the criteria, ten years of undergraduate teaching in a Christian university has yielded virtually zero responses. If our preachers do not teach the criteria, if our Sunday School classes do not teach us the criteria, and if we do not know the criteria, how can we say we hold such beliefs?[16]

---

13. Ibid., 45.

14. Ibid., 46.

15. Ibid., 47.

16. So, for example: if in the case of the most recent Iraq War, (most) honest adherents to the Just War tradition agreed (in this case) with the Pacifists, that the war in Iraq was illegitimate, what other commitments or convictions were at work? Mike's brother Shaun circulated a brief statement opposing the war, which was signed by numerous Christian ethicists who subscribed both to the Just War tradition and Christian pacifism. See

In his classic work *Christian Attitudes Toward War & Peace*,[17] Roland Bainton specified another mode of thought on war historically employed in the Christian tradition: the "Holy War" or "Crusade." The Holy War or Crusade model stereo-typically proceeds with a charismatic leader who speaks on behalf of God or the good to wage battle against the enemies of God and the good. This model differs from the JWT in several respects. The Holy War model does not, for example, employ purportedly objective criteria for determining when to go to war. That is, instead of seeing a given war, as the JWT would require, as a limited engagement with clearly defined objectives to deal with a specifiable injustice, the Holy War model will tend toward waging war on behalf of a more encompassing "goodness" or "God" led by a leader who has a purported mandate from God, such as Joshua or Mohammad. As a second instance, the Holy War model does not typically subscribe to the restraints required by the JWT, such as the prohibition of attacks against civilians, or the requirement to submit to international law.

Ethicists typically count the Holy War model as illegitimate for Christians today. Holy War was the practice of the Joshuas of a by-gone era; was the practice of medieval popes and Crusaders, but is not a legitimate practice for Christians today. But if the coming of the White Christian Man to America tells us anything, it is that Holy War and Manifest Destiny and a Crusade on behalf of the purported New Israel are inextricably linked with the American Christian experience. We would be naïve to think that such an ethos does not affect us, still, at the beginning of the twenty-first century.

As John Howard Yoder suggested, Bainton's typology was too simplistic. There are, in fact, many more modes of thought on war than simply Pacifism, Just War, and Holy War: Reinhold Niebuhr's "Christian realism," Machiavellian "political realism," Rambo-like machismo, and nationalist self-interest.[18] Thus all sorts of rhetoric and justifications and rationalizations may be at work in any given Christian community's acceptance (most always) or rejection (almost never) of any given war. But without the lenses to see or to *name* these other commitments and

---

"100 Leading Christian Ethicists Oppose Iraq War," online at http://www.sojo.net/index.cfm?action=action.ethicists_statement.

17. Bainton, *Christian Attitudes Toward War & Peace: A Historical Survey and Critical Re-Evaluation* (Nashville: Abingdon, 1960).

18. John Howard Yoder, *Nevertheless: Varieties of Religious Pacifism*, rev. and exp. ed. (Scottdale, PA: Herald, 1992) 151ff.

convictions, and without stories to tell to help us name these other commitments and convictions, we may simply be unaware of their presence.

Telling a story like that of the Pequot War immediately brings these other commitments and convictions to the foreground: we do not find here any serious engagement with the JWT, with its rigorous and systematic and demanding criteria. Some other set of convictions and commitments is at work. John Mason and Israel Stoughton and Reverend Hooker are not taking seriously the tradition of Justifiable War—there is an altogether different sort of logic at work. We might thus begin to ask ourselves: when we have discussions in our church communities over war-making, are we really having an honest debate between the substantive and serious commitments of the Just War Tradition (JWT) on the one side, and Christian non-violence on the other?

Perhaps this is the best place to surface what I suspect would be a very serious immediate objection to the argument thus far—especially in response to my suggestion that we should be telling stories like that of the Pequot War in Sunday School. "Church is no place to be telling such political stories," someone might say. But such an objection employs the label "political" selectively, and thus unfairly. In my experience at least, prayers in our churches for the American military is *not* seen as "political," while talk of non-violence *is* "political." Talk of select contemporary moral issues, especially regarding sexuality, is *not* seen as "political," while talk of "justice" is looked upon with suspicion. In fact, all these issues are both "political" *and* "spiritual." No doubt, telling Mike's stories of conscientious objectors or Drinnon's story of the Pequot War is a political act. But if rightly understood, we will see that preaching is a political act, too. Unless we subscribe to the second- and third-century heresies of Neo-Platonism, which sharply divided the "spiritual" from the "physical," we cannot but understand the proclamation of the Kingdom of God and the confession that Jesus is Lord as fundamentally political.[19]

But that's no reason not to proclaim it and confess it in church. Once this is established, the next question is whether our political story-telling rightly forms us into a people better able to embody the ways of God's Kingdom. The question becomes whether our practice of preaching is rightly formed politically, or not; it becomes a question of whether the

---

19. There are numerous works these days that help debunk the false dualisms of "spiritual" versus "political." See for example, Rodney Clapp, *A Peculiar People: The Church as Culture in a Post-Christian Society* (Downers Grove, IL: InterVarsity, 1996).

mission of the church has been coopted by nation-state and empire, or not. John Borelli, in a fascinating reflection upon eighteen years of work in inter-religious work under the oversight of the U.S. Conference of Catholic Bishops, notes that "the word 'mission' functions in the same way among Muslims as the word 'jihad' does among Christians. Both are beautiful words, but in their use or perceptions, there are implications of violence which are difficult to avoid."[20] While the American Christian might be quite willing to point out the violent political realities of *jihad*, the violent political implications of *mission* have tended to be overlooked.

The National Memorial

After visiting the Cowboy Museum, I made my first visit to the National Memorial: the scene of the greatest domestic terror attack that ever occurred in U.S. history. On April 19, 1995, Timothy McVeigh drove a Ryder Rental Truck packed with several tons of explosives directly in front of the north entrance to the Murrah Federal Building in Oklahoma City. On that pleasant spring morning, the truck exploded, shearing off the northern half of the building, killing 168 people, 19 of whom were children. The carnage was beyond comprehension. Now at the former site of the Murrah Building is a grassy lawn, protected by a low fence, the lawn bounded by pine trees, and on the lawn, a single chair for every victim of that horrid day, large chairs for the adults, smaller chairs for the children and babies. Now where that street once lay, along which the rental truck was driven, is a reflecting pool, bounded on east and west by great gates.

I was deeply moved and troubled and wept there in that place. But one item particularly caught my attention, and surprised me. In the memorial museum, a small computer kiosk provides research on American domestic terrorism, and reports that the idea for bombing the Murrah building apparently first arose among a group in Arkansas, among a charismatic Christian commune called the Covenant, the Sword, and the Army of the Lord. Kerry Noble, one of the evangelists and pastors in the CSA, tells his story at length in *Tabernacle of Hate: Why They Bombed Oklahoma City*. He tells the tale of an apparently sincere people, who cared about scripture, worship, and discipleship, who sold possessions

20. John Borelli, "Christian-Muslim Relations in the United States: Reflections for the Future After Two Decades of Experience," *Muslim World* 94 (July 2004) 327.

and gave up social stability to establish a community they believed honored God. But coopted by paranoia, and becoming willing to employ violence in the name of righteousness, they formed the conviction that they were playing an important role in the inevitable war that would bring about the purification of America.[21]

Similarly, McVeigh and accomplice Terry Nichols were deeply indoctrinated in the American militia movement and the far-right wing ideology that supported it. While it is not exactly clear who had contacts with whom, and who knew what, what does seem clear is that the bombing of the Murrah Federal Building arose out of a broad cultural matrix of a convoluted Christian faith that was mixed with racial hatred, fear of communism, and a willingness to employ grave violence all for the sake of a righteous "Christian" nation.[22]

A classic case study of such logic is the Posse Comitatus. In his book *The Terrorist Next Door,* Daniel Levitas gives a history of the radical right, starting with Posse member Reverend Gale. Gale's 1982 broadcast typifies the Posse's matrix of Christian faith and patriotism. Regarding an official who violates the Constitution as Gale saw it, the good white Christian citizens should "take him to the most populated intersection of the township and at noon hang him by the neck [then] take the body down at dark and that will be an example to those other officials who are supposed to be your servants that they are going to abide by the Constitution . . ."[23]

Similar is the tragic story of Gordon Kahl, a farmer caught up in his own hatred of the U.S. Federal Government. Kahl believed the U.S. Government had denied its responsibility to honor the law and lordship of Jesus. "These enemies of Christ . . . threw our Constitution and our

21. Kerry Noble, *Tabernacle of Hate: Why They Bombed Oklahoma City* (Prescott, ON: Voyageur, 1998).

22. See for example, Daniel Levitas, *The Terrorist Next Door: The Militia Movement and the Radical Right* (New York: Dunne, 2002). Levitas says: "Gale's Posse manifesto fed and nurtured the American militia movement—including, in part, the ideology that motivated the Oklahoma City bombing orchestrated by Terry Nichols and Timothy McVeigh in 1995" (300).

23. Levitas, *Terrorist,* 1. "Arise and fight!" Gale said at another time. "If a Jew comes near you, run a sword through him" (cited in ibid., 2). Gale, along with numerous other right-wing groups like the CSA, adhered to the doctrine of Christian Identity, which claims that Anglo-Saxon Christians were the chosen people of God. The Identity doctrine follows an earlier teaching called British Israelism, in which the ten lost tribes of Israel purportedly made their way to Britain. Jews were children of the devil, while non-white races were "mud people," and thus all "race-mixing" violated, proclaimed Gale and other Identity adherents, God's law.

Christian Common Law (which is none other than the Laws of God as set forth in the Scriptures) into the garbage can." The "enemies" have "two objectives in their goal of ruling the world. Destroy Christianity and the white race." Thus, maintained Kahl, "we are engaged in a struggle to the death between the people of the Kingdom of God, and the Kingdom of Satan."[24] Kahl killed two federal agents in a shoot-out himself. He was later killed in another shoot-out, in which he shot a local law enforcement officer. He died when federal agents poured diesel fuel down a roof vent and set afire the house in which he was hiding out.

Angered by Kahl's death, others attempted in late 1983 to blow up a natural gas pipeline in Arkansas with dynamite—but only dented it. The leader of that attempt, Richard Wayne Snell, would rob pawn shops, and give the proceeds to the CSA. Snell, also legitimating his crimes based upon his strained interpretation of Christian faith, believed that most owners of pawn shops were Jews and "deserved to die." So a week and a half following the failed pipeline incident, Snell robbed a pawnshop and murdered the owner William Stumpp, who was not Jewish but an Episcopalian. In 1984, and in cold blood, Snell killed an African-American state trooper, Louis Bryant. Some twelve years after the murder of Stumpp, Snell was executed on April 19, a date bearing significance in right-wing circles: this was the day of the burning of the Branch Davidian compound at Waco, Texas; it was the date of Snell's execution; and twelve hours prior to Snell's execution, McVeigh bombed the Murrah Federal Building.[25]

Conclusion

American Restorationist that I am, I found particularly interesting a display in the Cowboy Museum, a life-sized model of a stereo-typical nineteenth-century western town. At one end of Main Street sat the "Christian Church." In many ways, this was one of the driving questions behind Mike's work: how did we, in the Stone-Campbell tradition, with such a vociferous witness to peace in the nineteenth and early twentieth centuries, become Main Street Christians?

And indeed, the danger of telling Main Street Christians the sorts of tales I've told here is the temptation simply to discount them. "We are more advanced than those early Puritans and we would never treat

24. James Corcoran, *Bitter Harvest: Gordon Kahl and the Posse Comitatus: Murder in the Heartland* (New York: Viking, 1990) 152–53.

25. Ibid., 5–6, 205–6.

a native population in such a manner. We are more educated than these far-right Arkansas woodsmen, and we would never be like the mass murderer Timothy McVeigh." I found fascinating, though, the definition of "terrorism" provided by the U.S. Federal Government, posted at the National Memorial: "pre-meditated, politically motivated violence perpetrated against non-combatant targets by sub-national groups or clandestine agents, usually intended to influence an audience." [26] By defining terrorism as "sub-national," does the federal government thus exempt itself? And by our use of "we," do we thereby exempt ourselves from any soul searching?

This was the question raised in an essay attributed to Timothy McVeigh prior to his execution by the State. McVeigh was a decorated U.S. Army veteran of the first Iraq War, and characterized U.S. foreign policy as deeply hypocritical. The U.S. claims, says the essay, that "Iraq has no right to stockpile chemical or biological weapons ('weapons of mass destruction')." Yet, it continues, the U.S. is precisely the country that set the precedent for the use of such weapons. We see the pictures of the Kurds, killed by Saddam's chemical weapons, but why are these pictures never set alongside pictures of women and children killed in Hiroshima and Nagasaki, the essay asks.[27]

This making exceptions for "us"—assuming that we are the good guys, and the enemy not—has a long history, as Andrew Bacevich notes in his recent book *The Limits of Power: The End of American Exceptionalism*.[28] Bacevich is a conservative Catholic, a political conservative, a professor of history and international relations, and a retired Army colonel. But his conservatism finds primary expression in distrust of human institutions wielding power. He thus distrusts "American Exceptionalism," which claims that America has a special mandate by God to make things turn out right, and is thus granted an exception to do the things others are not. American Exceptionalism began, claims Bacevich, with the earliest arrival of Europeans on these shores, and continues not merely unabated

26. Cited in display at National Memorial, Title II U.S. Code, Section 265F(d).

27. Timothy McVeigh, "Essay on Hypocrisy," distributed by Media Bypass / Alternative Media, Inc. Accessed online at: http://www.outpost-of-freedom.com/mcveigh/okcaug98 .htm. I say "attributed to Timothy McVeigh" because, other than online sources, some of which dispute McVeigh wrote the essay, I have not been able to confirm authorship. But the incisive question remains attributed to McVeigh.

28. Andrew Bacevich, *The Limits of Power: The End of American Exceptionalism* (New York: Holt, 2008).

to this day, but increasingly militant, arrogant, and presumptuous, especially in the last forty years.

This sort of conservatism, of course, is very different than a Main Street Christian Church, which assumes that American interests equates with Christian interests. "The difference between you and me," a rather annoyed Christian and former military intelligence officer once said to me, "is that you see a difference between America and Christianity, and I don't." For my part, at least, I do not know whether I would have ever begun to countenance such questions and tensions apart from Mike's sort of story-telling. He taught me to read, listen to, and tell different sorts of stories than this false sort of conservatism.

And I give thanks for that.

17

A Contemporary Case for Selective Conscientious Objection

SHAUN A. CASEY

My brother Michael's scholarly career examined an impressive array of subjects. Current and future scholars will grapple with his groundbreaking work on a number of intellectual fronts. However, pacifism and conscientious objection ranked near the top of his concerns. There are no doubt historical and personal reasons for this, given his coming of age during the Vietnam War. My purpose in this essay is to honor his memory, his scholarship, and his desire to recover conversation on the morality of war. My task is to outline a moral case for why the United States government should recognize and honor the status of selective conscientious objectors. My task is not to argue that Michael would have completely endorsed the case I make. While I do not believe he would have opposed my view, in fact I suspect he would have welcomed it, he would likely have thought a stronger case could be made for a more consistent conscientious objection position. By combining moral and historical analysis I will make a case for selective conscientious objection.

My essay will proceed in four steps. First, I will define selective conscientious objection in the context of the just war ethic and in distinction from conscientious objection. Second, I will offer a brief history of selective conscientious objection drawing on the work of Leroy Walters. Third, I will examine one historical case study, drawn from the era of the Vietnam War in which the U.S. government gave some, perhaps even significant, attention to the question of whether or not the government should recognize the right to selective conscientious objection. This case will include examining the analysis of two of the theological voices of the twentieth century primarily responsible for the recovery of the just war ethic, Paul Ramsey and John Courtney Murray. Finally, I will outline my own constructive case for why the United States should recognize and honor selective conscientious objection on the part of its citizens.

The proper beginning point is to establish the difference between conscientious objection and selective conscientious objection. The current Selective Service Act contains this paragraph labeled "Conscientious Objectors":

> Nothing contained in this title (sections 451 to 471a of this Appendix) shall be construed to require any person subject to combatant training and service in the armed forces of the United States who, by reason of religious training and belief, is conscientiously opposed to participation in war in any form. As used in this subsection, the term "religious training and belief" does not include essentially political, sociological, or philosophical views, or a merely personal moral code. Any person claiming exemption from combatant training and service because of such conscientious objections whose claim is sustained by the local board shall, if he is inducted into the armed forces under this title (said sections), be assigned to noncombatant service as defined by the President, or shall if he is found to be conscientiously opposed to participation in such noncombatant service, in lieu of such induction, be ordered by his local board, subject to such regulations as the President may prescribe to perform for a period equal to the period prescribed in section 4(b) (section 454(b) of this Appendix) such civilian work contributing to the maintenance of the national health, safety, or interest as the Director may deem appropriate and any such person who knowingly fails or neglects to obey any such order from his local board shall be deemed, for the purposes of section 12 of this title (section 462 of this Appendix), to have knowingly failed or neglected to perform a duty required of him under this title (said sections). The Director shall be responsible for finding civilian work for persons exempted from training and service under this subsection and for the placement of such persons in appropriate civilian work contributing to the maintenance of the national health, safety, or interest.[1]

1. Compilation of the Military Selective Service Act (50 U.S.C. App. 451 et seq.) Sec. 456 (j) p. 26. Online: http://www.sss.gov/PDFs/MSSA-2003.pdf.

So current U.S. law states that should the draft be initiated, men who by reason of religious training or belief are opposed to participation in war in any form, shall not be compelled to participate directly in the armed forces. This is the current legal form of conscientious objection. While there may be other theologically or philosophically derived definitions of conscientious objection for my purposes we will use the current legal definition throughout this essay.

In contrast, selective conscientious objection is simply the right of individuals to dissent from a country's specific use of force, not based upon a moral rejection of war in any form, but based on a judgment against a specific case of war in which one judges one's participation in the war as immoral because the specific war is immoral. Current American law recognizes the standing of the opponents of all war but not the standing of those who oppose specific conflicts. Thus the pacifist is afforded alternatives to military service in all cases while proponents of the just war ethic have no recourse when called to serve in a war they deem unjust.

LeRoy Walters, writing near the end of the Vietnam War, gives a valuable summary of the history of selective conscientious objection within the long and vast trajectory of the just war ethic. A brief summary of his findings is a useful exercise on the way to establishing a contemporary case for the recognition of the right of selective conscientious objection.[2] Walters looks at three major questions related to selective conscientious objection as they are assessed by major just war thinkers: What is the citizen's presumptive duty, to obey a summons to participate in warfare or abstain from participation? Under what circumstances, if any, is selective conscientious objection morally justified? Should governments make legal provision for conscientious objectors to particular wars?

Walters found the answer to the first question was a fairly strong consensus among the major thinkers that while the prince was permitted to go to war as a last resort, given the prima facie duty to abstain from war, there was not an analogous duty for the subject to avoid military action. The prince's decision to go to war had sufficient moral weight to reverse any presumption against the resort to war on the part of the subject. The majority view was that a prince's call to arms created a prima facie duty

2. LeRoy Walters, "A Historical Perspective on Selective Conscientious Objection," *Journal of the American Academy of Religion* 41 (1973) 201–11. This article is more easily found in Richard Miller, ed., *War in the Twentieth Century* (Louisville: Westminster John Knox, 1992). All citations will be from the Miller collection.

on the part of the subject to obey and take up arms. The burden of proof rested with the selective objector.[3]

Yet there was a minority strain found in the work of Hugo Grotius who implied that participants in actions that potentially involve the taking of human life should investigate the circumstances before participating in these actions. He argued further that if a prince could not give clear explanations for the cause of a war he might discover that his skeptical soldiers might be less than enthusiastic for the war. In doubtful cases of war Grotius argued that disobedience is a lesser evil than the slaughter of innocents. Walters concludes that while the majority position in the tradition was that the citizen's presumptive duty was to obey the prince's call to war, Grotius's dissent provided an expanded theoretical basis for selective conscientious objection.[4]

Walter's second question regarding the theoretical justification for selective conscientious objection in the tradition concentrates on the natural law position on the question of disobedience to political authority. What began in the tradition as a simple moral doctrine allowing civil disobedience by a citizen to an unjust command from a prince in the work of Aquinas evolved into a position by Vitoria and Grotius that regarded selective conscientious objection as a moral duty if the citizen regarded the cause of a war to be unjust. Walters concludes that among these theorists there was general agreement that no citizen was obligated to participate in a war that was clearly unjust. Further, the subject had a moral duty not to take part in a clearly unjust war and a citizen's sincere conviction that a particular war was unjust obligated him to abstain from military participation.[5]

In response to the third question about provisions a state should make with respect to selective objectors only Grotius considered this question. It is worth keeping in mind here that the historical context of the sixteenth and seventeenth centuries meant that almost all soldiers were volunteers who fought as professionals in standing national armies or were mercenaries. Thus the question was less acute than in historical contexts where a military draft might be the norm. Nevertheless Grotius argued that administrative procedures be established to insure that no

---

3. Ibid., 217. Augustine and Aquinas were the major theoretical architects of this position.

4. Ibid., 220.

5. Ibid., 223.

citizens, either pacifist or selective objector, be compelled to participate in a war that violated their consciences. He proposed levying a special tax on them.

Walters concludes his historical survey by noting that while the tradition as a whole did not heartily endorse selective objection there are strains that provide positive moral warrants to such a position. He concludes:

> Finally, the contemporary interpreter must seek to apply an ancient tradition to a situation characterized by post-monarchical forms of government, military conscription in wartime, and highly-sophisticated weapons of destruction. In short, it is difficult, but possible, to reconstruct what the major just-war theorists said about selective conscientious objection within their varied historical contexts. What their views mean for our own attempt to think through an ethic of war and peace is much less clear.[6]

The next step in this essay is to examine a case from the Vietnam era in which the U.S. government formally took up the last question Walters examined. On July 2, 1966, President Lyndon Johnson issued Executive Order 11289 establishing a National Advisory Commission on Selective Service, chaired by Burke Marshall, a former assistant attorney general who headed the civil rights division of the Department of Justice in the Kennedy administration and who was a vice president and general counsel of IBM at the time of his appointment to the commission. The Marshall Commission as it came to be known was charged with considering the past, present, and future functioning of selective military service and to make recommendations to the president regarding methods of classifying and selecting registrants for military service including grounds for deferment and exemption as well procedures for appeal. Perhaps the most interesting member of the commission was John Courtney Murray, SJ, the leading Roman Catholic advocate of the just war ethic of that era. Murray's presence meant that selective conscientious objection would be on the docket for this commission.

In its initial summary of findings the Commission's report (*In Pursuit of Equity: Who Serves When Not All Serve?*) stated that the commission took up, but ultimately rejected, a proposal to recognize selective conscientious objectors. It revealed that this position found support in the Commission but a majority opposed it. While the report did not list the

---

6. Ibid., 225.

supporters and detractors by name, the main body of the report devoted space to describing the contours of the debate within the Commission.[7] At the beginning of the growing discontent with the conduct of the Vietnam War, we have a fleeting and rare glimpse into one corner of the U.S. government's deliberation over the desirability and feasibility of adopting some form of recognition of selective conscientious objection during a wartime draft.

The part of the report dealing with matters related to conscientious objection begins with the observation that Congress "considered it to be both wise and right as a matter of legislative policy, not to impose military service on those who feel that they cannot in conscience participate in the killing of other men."[8] The then current statute gave three criteria for this status. First, the objection must be based on religious training and belief. Second, it must be conscientious, meaning it is a sincerely held belief that is binding in conscience. Third, the objection must be against war in any form. The state then recognizes two types of conscientious objectors, those who are opposed to combatant service but would accept noncombatant service and those who are opposed to both combatant and noncombatant service. This second group is required to perform two years of civilian work contributing "to the maintenance of national health, safety, or interest," in place of military induction.

The report stated that while conscientious objectors represent one of the smallest groups in the Selective Service System, recently the issue had begun to assume far greater importance as a result of opposition on the part of some to American involvement in Vietnam. "Much of this opposition is felt—and expressed—with particular sharpness in the student community."[9]

The increasing political pressures of the day found a way to seep into the six-month deliberations of the Commission. It is tantalizingly frustrating to see the members of the Commission struggling to resist the call to endorse selective conscientious objection without having access to their full debate. But the report did give an extraordinary account of how it disposed of the formal proposal advanced by a minority of members who recommended selective conscientious objection.

7. *In Pursuit of Equity: Who Serves When Not All Serve? Report of the National Advisory Commission on Selective Service* (Washington, DC: U.S. Government Printing Office, 1967) 9.

8. Ibid., 48.

9. Ibid.

Two proposals were made by Commission members regarding conscientious objection. The first proposal was that the current statute be amended to eliminate the requirement that conscientious objection be lodged against war in all forms. The report states that proponents of this position made the following assertions. First, while the statute recognizes the position of absolute pacifism and even though this view has a time honored place in U.S. society it is a sectarian position and does not represent the moral consensus of the American people with regard to the use of force. Although it should continue to be honored in the Selective Service Act, "it should not be accorded its present place of privilege as the legal doctrine which alone controls the issue of conscientious objection."

Second, the classical doctrine on war widely held in the Christian community has been based on the moral premise that not all uses of military force are inherently immoral. The morality of war is no more than a marginal morality, in view of the destruction, suffering, and death that war always entails. The tradition does maintain that certain uses of force for certain circumstances can be morally justified. War may be just and it may unjust.

Third:

> Although the decision to make war is the prerogative of duly constituted government, responsible to its people, and constitutes a presumption for the citizen in favor of the legitimacy of the war, the citizen still is personally responsible for his own moral judgments on matters of public policy. He may not abdicate his own conscience into the hands of government. In making his moral judgment on the legitimacy of war he must assess the political and military factors in the case, but the judgment itself is to be a moral judgment. In particular cases, therefore, it can happen that the conscientious moral judgment of the citizen is in conflict with the judgments made by government, either with regard to the justice of the nation's cause or with regard to the measure and mode in which military force is to be employed in defense of the nation's vital interests. In such cases the citizen should not be compelled by government to act against his conscience by being forced to bear arms. Government, however, may legitimately require of citizens some manner of alternative service, either in a noncombatant or in a civilian capacity, as a duty of citizenship.[10]

10. Ibid.

These members proposed to amend the statute to recognize this ethic. There were two additional features. The objector must state his case before a competent panel whose purpose would not be to judge if the applicant was right in his analysis, but whether the views were "truly held" as required for regular conscientious objectors. This feature was seen as lifting the moral discourse in society. Potential draftees would be required to reflect on the issue of war and peace with the guidance of their mentors and thus form their consciences early in adulthood. The second additional feature was that the alternative service requirement be stringently enforced.[11]

Anyone familiar with Murray's writings on the just war tradition will immediately see his fingerprints all over this proposal. He takes the categories Walters outlined in his historical survey mentioned above and fashions a modern proposal calling for the formal legal recognition of selective conscientious objection by the U.S. government.

A second, similar proposal was also made by some Commission members. It called for public recognition that there may be moral validity to conscientious objection to particular wars. Measures should be taken to effectively distinguish between two groups among current students. There were responsible students who felt they were caught in a dilemma between their duty to country and the exigencies of personal integrity and conscience. This group deserved serious consideration. "There is also a handful of irresponsible individuals whose opposition to particular wars is simply part of a broader revolt against organized society. This group should be deprived of an issue which gives them an opportunity of seeming to represent all opposition." The policy proposals flowing from this viewpoint were to preserve the current recognition of absolute pacifism and to create a category for selective objection. The latter would require noncombatant military work under conditions of hardship and even hazard, perhaps for a longer period.

A majority of the Commission voted to retain the current requirement that conscientious objection must be based on moral opposition to war in all forms. The report set out five responses to the cases of the minority in which they reject the premises and the proposals for selective conscientious objection. The first response rather ineptly said it was one thing to recognize moral opposition to all killing of people under any circumstances while it was another to accord special status to a person who

11. Ibid., 48–49.

believes he is responding to a moral imperative which tells him he can kill under some circumstances and not others. This response completely misses the fact that almost all legal codes in the West, if not everywhere, already do precisely this. The right to use lethal force in self-defense is recognized in many cases while premeditated murder is not. This first response also claimed that "classical Christian doctrine" on just and unjust war was interpreted in different fashions by different denominations and the Commission could not pass judgment on them. And yet the proposal from the minority was not that the government should assess the accuracy of the moral just war case, but to have competent assessors measure the case for its basic sufficiency and that it was truly held. These are the same standards for evaluating regular conscientious objector claims.

The second response was that "selective pacifism" was essentially a political question of support or nonsupport of a war and it cannot be judged in terms of moral imperatives. The majority believed political opposition to a particular war should be expressed through recognized democratic processes and should make no special claim to a right of exemption from democratic decisions. This view completely misunderstood the historical point that the just war ethic and selective objection based upon it is a venerable historical moral position.

The majority argued third, that legal recognition of "selective pacifism" could open the doors to a general theory of selective disobedience to law, which could quickly tear down the fabric of government. They argued that a distinction between a person conscientiously opposed to participation in a particular war and one consciously opposed to payment of a particular tax was dim. This is, of course, a form of the all too common slippery slope logical fallacy. If this threat were real, would not the legal recognition of pacifist conscientious objection lead to outright anarchy? The proponents of selective conscientious objection argued for some form of commensurate alternative public service. Tax avoiders and law avoiders would not on analogy be able to avoid legal penalty and consequences.

Fourth, the majority was unable to see the morality of a proposition which would permit the "selective pacifist" to avoid combat service by performing noncombatant service in support of a war which he had theoretically concluded to be unjust. But that is precisely what the Selective Service Act already allowed for absolute pacifists who were willing to do noncombatant alternative service instead of fighting. If that position was moral then certainly alternative service by a selective conscientious objector can be seen as moral, too.

Finally, the majority believed that a legal recognition of selective objection could be disruptive to the morale and effectiveness of the Armed Forces. Here we may be getting to the real crux of the matter for the presidential appointees operating in the context of an increasingly unpopular war. This objection is worth quoting directly:

> A determination of the justness or unjustness of any war could only be made within the context of that war itself. Forcing upon the individual the necessity of making that distinction—which would be the practical effect of taking away the Government's obligation of making it for him—could put a burden heretofore unknown on the man in uniform and even on the brink of combat, with results that could well be disastrous to him, to his unit, and to the entire military tradition. No such problem arises for the conscientious objector, even in uniform, who bases his moral stand on killing in all forms, simply because he is never trained for nor assigned to combat duty.[12]

These sentences exude a fear regarding the moral compass of ordinary soldiers. Soldiers do in fact possess the right, even the duty, to resist illegal orders in combat. This is viewed as something they are honor bound to exercise. The fear expressed here is that they might actually exercise a similar moral judgment about the overall enterprise of the war and reject their country's call if they deem the war unjust. How would that be a bad thing, morally, for a democracy? I believe, as Walters argues above from the perspective of the just war ethic, that soldiers do not surrender their moral agency to a government proxy when they join the military. They are still morally culpable for what they do in war and no government can change that moral fact. A democratic polity should provide citizens a way to exercise their moral agency precisely in cases of particular wars that they deem to be unjust.

It is true that any recognition of selective conscientious objection would place administrative demands on the military. But I dispute that the threat this might pose is as grand as the majority of the Commissioners believed. And if, indeed, a sizable section of the military sought release from duty before or during a specific conflict, then the very legitimacy of that war would be called into question and that is not an inherently bad thing for a democracy.

12. Ibid., 51.

So while the Commission, which reported to President Johnson in February 1967, did not endorse selective conscientious objection it did have at least a moderately robust discussion of the subject and it chronicled the outlines of its debate in its public report.[13]

Six months after the Commission issued its report, and barely ten weeks before his untimely death, Murray gave an address at Western Maryland College entitled "Selective Conscientious Objection" in which he reflects on his experience as a commissioner and the ongoing struggle to win legal recognition for selective conscientious objection.[14] While acknowledging from the outset the complexity and subtlety of the implications of the topic he believed it was incumbent upon intellectuals to continue to press the case even against the background of the rejection of this thesis by the majority of the Commission and the ongoing firestorm over the war itself. He believed that the argument was raised chiefly by academics—students, seminarians, and professors, and that they were a socially significant group. While many aspects of the debate had been mishandled—presumably referring to student agitation, he praised the student community nonetheless for having raised this profound moral issue that had been neglected for too long.[15]

Murray proceeded to argue that the case for selective conscientious objection should be separated from debate over Vietnam. He confessed that while he could make the case for recognizing this moral option he was also fully prepared to make the case justifying the presence and action of the American military in South Vietnam. (This was precisely the same position his counterpart Paul Ramsey held). He described the intellectual's role as being provocative and to make the moral case for selective conscientious objection was to be provocative. He believed that

13. The composition of the twenty-member commission probably precluded any proposals embracing selective conscientious objection from gaining a majority endorsement. In addition to chairman Marshall and Murray the membership included establishment figures such as Yale University President Kingman Brewster; Morgan Guaranty Bank President Thomas Gates, Jr.; former CIA Director John McCone; former LBJ aide George Reedy; retired Marine General David Monroe Shoup; Judge Frank Szymanski of Michigan; and Warren Woodward, Vice President of American Airlines. Interestingly, a very young Vernon Jordan, Jr., project director of the Voter Education Project of the Southern Regional Council, was also a member.

14. This address was first published as a pamphlet "Selective Conscientious Objection" by Our Sunday Visitor (Huntinton, IN: Our Sunday Visitor). And online: http://woodstock .georgetown..edu/library/Murray/1967L.htm.

15. Ibid., 89.

he was witnessing a political over-reaction to the moral case. He alluded to the House and Senate hearings on the revision of the Selective Service Act when conscientious objection was brought up as evidence of the political reaction.

The focus of the balance of the address was not to argue the moral case. Rather it was to address the practical question about how to get the moral validity of this position understood and how to get it legally recognized. Murray took credit for the suggestion to the Commission that an applicant for selective conscientious objector status plead his case before a competent panel of judges. One side effect would be the elevation of the level of moral discourse around war, as the minority case argued in the Commission report.

Murray believed that the main reasons the political community did not accept the argument for selective conscientious objection were practical. He cited two examples: the enormous difficulty of administering a statute that would provide for selective conscientious objection and the perennial problem of what he called erroneous conscience. That is, an applicant might advance arguments that were empirically mistaken and demonstrably false. What should a tribunal then do?

Murray argued that in Seeger, the recent Supreme Court case, the court had ruled that regular conscientious objectors were not required to demonstrate their objections to be the truth, but that the objections were truly held. Thus Murray believed that the right to selective objection had to be extended to possibly erroneous consciences or it could not be granted at all. On the other hand he acknowledged that the political community could not be blamed for fearing that if the right to selective objection is acknowledged in such terms, it might possibly lead to the breakdown of society, anarchy, and paralysis of public policy.[16]

He concluded that the proponents of selective objection had to understand the reality of this fear and not abuse such a right should it be granted. Society would defend itself against such a threat as he added ominously:

> The solution can only be the cultivation of political discretion throughout the populace, not least in the student and academic community. A manifold work of moral and political intelligence is called for. No political society can be founded on the principle that absolute rights are to be accorded to the individual con-

16. Ibid., 97.

science, and to all individual consciences, even when they are in error. This is rank individualism and to hold it would reveal a misunderstanding of the very nature of the political community. On the other hand, the political community is bound to respect consciences. But the fulfillment of this obligation supposes that the consciences of the citizens are themselves formed and in-formed. Therefore, the final question may be whether there is abroad in the land a sufficient measure of moral and political discretion, in such wise that the Congress could, under safeguard of the national security, acknowledge the right of discretionary armed service.[17]

This was vintage Murray, arguing simultaneously for a strong moral position that demanded commitment and discipline on the part of its advocates and for a robust public political deliberation to enshrine the practical fruit of the moral discourse in societal norms and legislation. At the same time he realistically drew a map of the practical concerns that stood in the way of realizing selective conscientious objection.

During this same time frame Protestant theologian and ethicist Paul Ramsey assessed the Commission's report and made a positive case for selective conscientious objection. In 1968 Ramsey published *The Just War: Force and Political Responsibility*, which was a collection of essays he had written since the publication of his 1961 work *War and Christian Conscience: How Shall Modern War Be Conducted Justly?* The later collection included the essay, "Selective Conscientious Objection," which provided his analysis of the Commission report and his own defense of selective conscientious objection.

Ramsey paid close attention to the objections, listed above, that the majority of the Commission registered. He believed they should be engaged, but he was not particularly optimistic that the Christian churches of his day were up to the task. He argued that they had a twofold burden in replying to the majority. First, there had to be a moral political view to underwrite the warrants for objecting to particular wars. Ramsey believed the just war ethic was capable of providing this. Second, there had to be a moral consensus in the country governing the use of force. Ramsey was not hopeful that either of these conditions might be obtained in the country or by the churches.[18]

17. Ibid., 97–98.

18. Ramsey, *The Just War: Force and Political Responsibility* (New York: Scribners, 1968) 94.

He argued that the growing pluralism of the nation made it much more difficult to hold to any consensus on the moral use of force. In Christian churches he decried a movement away from the use of historically derived moral principles toward various faddish trends. This was, of course, a familiar refrain in Ramsey's work throughout his later career. Nevertheless he soldiered on and outlined a constructive proposal for selective conscientious objection.

His proposal was to base selective conscientious objection on the *jus in bello* criteria of the just war ethic. These are the two criteria that govern the morality of the conduct in war. They are discrimination or noncombatant immunity, which prohibits the direct targeting of noncombatants, and proportionality of means, which argues for using only the force sufficient to accomplish tactical objectives. Ramsey called these criteria deonotological.

Ramsey believed that given the messy moral pluralism of the country it was impossible to render consensus on the content of the *jus ad bellum* criteria of the just war ethic. These are the criteria that govern the resort to war: just cause, public declaration of war, right intention, last resort, reasonable chance of success, and proportionality of ends. Ramsey called these the consequentialist or teleological criteria.

While it would be hard for an applicant for selective conscientious objection to make a convincing case based upon the *jus ad bellum* criteria since people of good will could disagree on these, it would be possible for an applicant to state that the war in question was being prosecuted in such a way that violated the two *jus in bello* criteria and thus it was a violation of their moral standards. In effect Ramsey was splitting the just war ethic in half in hope that this might satisfy the skeptics who were not predisposed to accept selective conscientious objection. I find this truncation strategy to be highly unsatisfying.

So where are we left at this moment in history? Should we recognize the right to objection to particular wars? If so, how might such a system be administered? Time does not permit a full-blown answer to these important questions. Rather I will close with a set of tentative conclusions.

First, the Marshall Commission is a cautionary tale. Resistance to selective conscientious objection was real and powerful in the Vietnam era. On the one hand it is remarkable that Murray and his fellow minority members on the commission got a hearing at all. On the other hand it may well have been Lyndon Johnson's political genius at work that allowed them into the formal government discussion in order to dismiss them and undermine their arguments in the larger society. ("Keep your friends close and your enemies closer.")

While the majority response was hardly consistent or air tight, it did identify government fear in creating a wider avenue for more citizens to formally express their outrage at the conduct of the war. Their response was primarily of fear: if we allow selective conscientious objection it would become harder for the government to fight the war. My belief is that if the American public withdraws its moral support for such a war as Vietnam, the government needs to respond and allow its citizens to reject participation in such conflicts.

Second, since we have an all-volunteer military why should we worry about selective conscientious objection? The short answer is that since we are conducting wars in two countries at this writing, an escalation in one, say Afghanistan, or the outbreak of major hostilities elsewhere in the world might easily trigger a draft given the severe stress on our current forces. Our military is in many ways currently broken and it will not be possible to sustain higher troop levels than we currently have without a draft. Combine that possibility with the fact that the current war in Iraq is unjust in my opinion and the possibility that the war in Afghanistan might be able to pass muster morally in terms of the just war ethic, and it is a real possibility that citizens might face induction into the armed services where not all the conflicts can pass moral muster. Those are reasons to worry about selective conscientious objection.

Third, adherents of the just war ethic can have moral objections to a particular war that are as deeply held as pacifists who oppose all war do and they can give as eloquent and convincing a case for that belief as an opponent of all war. The adjudication of conscientious objection applications has been and will continue to be complicated. The processing of selective objection cases will be complex, too, but that is no excuse for not granting citizens the right of redress. Governments at all levels in our country administer a dizzying array of administrative law courts that adjudicate complex legal and societal questions. It is simply not true to say that it would be impossible to structure a system that would be able to process these cases.

Finally, while I do not have the space here to fully argue my case, the just war ethic provides a robust moral framework for citizens to form their consciences with respect to particular wars and it provides a moral idiom and moral criteria with which they can argue for selective objection.[19] This would allow the government to develop standards by which the various claims for selective objection could be evaluated.

In the case of the Iraq War we have seen the nightmare of an unjust war being prosecuted with a large majority of the country now in opposition to that effort. Had there been a draft citizens would have had no legal recourse to protect themselves from this moral danger of fighting an unjust war. A liberal democracy owes its citizens more than that.

Now is the time to work to establish a legal mechanism for selective conscientious objection as part of our Selective Service legislation.

19. For a primer on the just war ethic, see Nicholas Fotion, *War and Ethics: A New Just War Theory* (New York: Continuum, 2008).

18

Why the World Needs Christian Leaders Committed to Peacemaking[1]

RICHARD T. HUGHES

One way to address the question, "Why does the world need Christian leaders committed to peace making?" is to ask that question in light of Samuel P. Huntington's magisterial volume, *The Clash of Civilizations and the Remaking of World Order*. By now, the two fundamental premises that drive this volume are familiar ones—that "clashes of civilization are the greatest threat to world peace," and that "religion is a central defining characteristic of civilizations."[2] This means, quite simply, that religious leaders of the future will play an enormous role in preserving—or threatening—the peace of the world.

Albert Einstein explained what is really at stake in the question of war and peace when he offered this sobering assessment: "I do not know with what weapons World War III will be fought, but World War IV will be fought with sticks and stones."

But how can religious leaders, of all people, help to lead the world in ways of peace?

In his book-length response to Samuel Huntington—*The Dignity of Difference: How to Avoid the Clash of Civilizations*—Jonathan Sacks offers an important first step. Each religion, Sacks argues, must abandon the illusion that it and it alone embodies universal truth. Instead, he writes, "We need to search—each faith in its own way—for a way of living with, and acknowledging the integrity of, those who are not of our faith. Can we make space for difference? Can we hear the voice of God in a language, a sensibility, a culture not our own? Can we see the presence of God in the face of a stranger?"[3] In other words, he asks, can we make room for "the dignity of difference?"

That is a first step, but there is a second step as well. And as I outline this second step—which is the substance of this chapter—I want to speak clearly and explicitly as a Christian whose chief concern is for Christian leaders of the future.

It's common knowledge that from the fourth century forward, Christian leaders have often been fervent advocates of violence and war. That fact is no less true today than it was during the twelfth and thirteenth centuries when Christian leaders advocated crusades against what they called the "Muslim infidels," or during the seventeenth century when Protestant and Catholic leaders alike summoned the faithful to slaughter their religious competitors.

More recently, at the outset of the war in Iraq, the pastor of the First Baptist Church in Atlanta told his congregation that "we should offer to serve the war effort in any way possible. . . . God battles with people who oppose him, and fight against him and his followers." Others, including Franklin Graham, son of Billy Graham, and Marvin Olasky, editor of the *World* magazine, suggested that the war would open up a whole new field for converting Muslims to the Christian faith. Still others, like Tim LaHaye, co-author of the best-selling *Left Behind* series of end-times books, suggested that by virtue of the war, Iraq would become "a focal point of end-times events."[4]

With preaching like that, it's hardly surprising to learn that when the war was still being planned, "some 69 percent of conservative Christians favor[ed] military action against Baghdad, 10 percentage points more than the U.S. adult population as a whole." And by April of 2003, a month after the United States launched its preemptive strike against Iraq, the decision to invade that nation drew support from an astounding 87 percent of all white evangelical Christians.[5]

At the root of the militarism that has dominated so much Christian teaching and Christian leadership is the easy and facile confusion of the purposes of the Christian faith with the purposes of the American state, leading many to assume that the United States is, in fact, a Christian nation. A single example of this sort of confusion will suffice: Julia Ward Howe's "The Battle Hymn of the Republic," published in the *Atlantic Monthly* in 1862.

The first stanza of that majestic hymn equated "the glory of the coming of the Lord" with the cause of the Republic in America's Civil War. It then suggested that in the guns of the Union Army, God himself "hath loosed the fateful lightning of His terrible swift sword." Indeed, Howe concluded, in the midst of that war, "His truth is marching on."

The third stanza spoke of a "fiery gospel writ in burnished rows of steel," thereby suggesting some connection between the gospel of Christ and the nation's military agenda.

But the fifth stanza did the most to confuse America's civic faith with the Christian religion, for it directly linked the work of Christ with the work of the Union Army, and the cross of Christ with the cause of temporal freedom.

> In the beauty of the lilies Christ was born across the sea;
> With a glory in His bosom that transfigures you and me;
> As He died to make men holy, let us die to make men free,
> While God is marching on.[6]

Over the years, millions of Christians have sung that song, fully convinced that they were singing a Christian hymn, or at least a hymn that was in keeping with the central themes of the Christian gospel. They could make that assumption because they firmly believed that the United States was, indeed, a Christian nation.

The notion of Christian America remains firmly entrenched in the American psyche. Indeed, the sociologist Christian Smith reports that "not only conservative Protestants but the majority of Americans believe that America was founded as a Christian nation."[7]

Obviously, there is a sense—and, in fact, a profound sense—in which America is a Christian nation. After all, some 76 percent of the American people claim to be Christian in one form or another. But the Christian character of the United States is comparable to the Christian character of the Roman Empire following Constantine, or the Christian character of the Holy Roman Empire in the sixteenth century. Christian trappings abound, but if one compares, for example, the Christian dimensions of the Holy Roman Empire with the teachings of Jesus, the differences are stunning.

Jesus counseled peace, but the Empire practiced violence. Jesus counseled humility, but the Empire engaged in a ruthless pursuit of power. Jesus counseled concern for the poor, but the Empire practiced exaltation of the rich. Jesus counseled modesty, but the Empire practiced extravagance. Jesus counseled simple living, but the Empire encouraged luxurious living for those with the means to embrace that way of life. And while Jesus counseled forgiveness and love for one's enemies, the Empire practiced vengeance.

Like that ancient Empire, the United States abounds in Christian trappings. Still, the United States is an empire that embraces virtually all the values that have been common to empires for centuries on end. It seeks peace through violence, exalts the rich over the poor, prefers power to humility, places vengeance above forgiveness, extravagance above modesty, and luxury above simplicity. In a word, it rejects the values of Jesus, though many Americans wish to claim that the United States is a Christian nation.

The surest way to get a handle on all of this is to compare the notion of "Christian America" with the only phrase in the New Testament that even comes close to suggesting the idea of a Christian nation. That phrase is "the kingdom of God." And when we make that comparison, we quickly discover that the notion of "Christian America," on the one hand, and the notion of the kingdom of God, on the other, are polar opposites.

There is no theme about which Jesus spoke with greater regularity than the notion of the kingdom of God. That phrase, or its equivalent, appears in the New Testament well over a hundred times, and it is impossible to understand the message of Jesus without grasping the meaning of that idea.

In almost every instance where that phrase appears, it is closely linked to two important themes. The first of those themes is compassionate concern for the poor, the dispossessed, those in prison, the maimed, the lame, the blind, and all those who suffer at the hands of the world's elites. In other words, the kingdom of God is where the powerless are empowered, where the hungry are fed, where the sick are healed, where the poor are sustained, and where those who find themselves marginalized by the rulers of this world are finally exalted.

The second of those themes consistently condemns those nations that amass their wealth and power on the backs of the poor and the dispossessed. Sharing in that condemnation are all the empires of the earth, including the politicians, businesspeople, religious leaders, and others who serve the imperial cause.

In other words, when Jesus uses the phrase, the kingdom of God, the context is almost always a struggle between the reign or rule of God on behalf of the poor and the dispossessed, on the one hand, and the empires of this world that serve powerful and privileged elites, on the other. The New Testament, in fact, consistently views the empire as the arch-villain in the biblical drama. At the same time, there is no more important—nor a more pervasive—theme in the New Testament text than its message regarding God's concern for the powerless and the poor.

These are precisely the conclusions of some of the best and most recent New Testament scholarship—the work, for example, of John Dominic Crossan, Warren Carter, Richard Horsley, Barbara Rossing, and others.[8] And Walter Brueggemann, a noted scholar of the Hebrew Bible, has suggested that the struggle between the people of God and the empire is an equally pervasive theme in that text as well. The people of God, Brueggemann notes, are called to acts of mercy, while the empire inevitably devotes itself to an infinite expansion of land, wealth, and power.[9]

I want to suggest that if there is any hope that Christian leaders of the future might become agents of peace instead of agents of war, they must abandon both the idea and the rhetoric of Christian America and embrace instead both the idea and the rhetoric of the kingdom of God.

Jesus spells out the relation of the kingdom of God to peace and non-violence especially in the fifth through ninth beatitudes, found in Matthew, chapter five. All five of those beatitudes counsel mercy, peace-making, and nonviolence. "Blessed are the merciful," Jesus says in the fifth of these statements, "for they shall obtain mercy." And then in the sixth, "Blessed are the peacemakers, for they shall be called the sons of God."

The sixth, eighth, and ninth beatitudes continue the themes of peacemaking and nonviolence since they pronounce blessings both on the pure in heart and on those who suffer persecution for righteousness' sake. Here is the way those beatitudes read.

Blessed are the pure in heart, for they shall see God.

Blessed are those who are persecuted for righteousness' sake, for theirs is the kingdom of heaven.

Blessed are you when men revile you and persecute you and utter all kinds of evil against you falsely on my account. Rejoice and be glad for your reward is great in heaven, for so men persecuted the prophets who were before you.

Why do I suggest that these three beatitudes go together? Because those who are pure in heart are those who reject the impulse to hate when faced with oppression and persecution. And in the context of the Roman Empire, the poor were faced with oppression every day.

The fact is, later in the Sermon on the Mount, in his most explicit and radical teaching on peacemaking and nonviolence, Jesus enlarges on the beatitudes that focus on these themes when he counsels love for one's enemies. Here are his words as reported in the Gospel of Matthew.

> You have heard that it was said, "An eye for an eye and a tooth for a tooth." But I say to you, Do not resist one who is evil. But if any one strikes you on the right cheek, turn to him the other also; and if any one would sue you and take your coat, let him have your cloak as well; and if any one forces you to go one mile, go with him two miles. Give to him who begs from you, and do not refuse him who would borrow from you.
>
> You have heard that it was said, "You shall love your neighbor and hate your enemy." But I say to you, Love your enemies and pray for those who persecute you, so that you may be sons of your Father who is in heaven. (Matt 5:38–45)

It is difficult for Americans, so accustomed to violence and retribution, to imagine that Jesus could possibly have meant these teachings in any literal sense. Yet, this theme of peacemaking and nonviolence is constant throughout the Christians' New Testament. In fact, there is no theme more central to what Christians call their "gospel" (good news), since the gospel focuses on the Christian claim that Jesus refused to resist those who sought to kill him but instead gave his life for the sake of others.

According to Matthew, just hours before he was crucified, one of his disciples, in an obvious attempt to defend Jesus, drew a sword and "struck the slave of the high priest, and cut off his ear." But Matthew reports that Jesus said to his disciples,

> Put your sword back into its place; for all who take the sword will perish by the sword. Do you think that I cannot appeal to my Father, and he will at once send me more than twelve legions of angels? (Matt 26:51–54)

John's gospel reports that during the course of his trial, Jesus said to Pilate, "My kingship is not of this world; if my kingship were of this world, my servants would fight . . . ; but my kingship is not of this world." Indeed, it was not, for Jesus consistently claimed that he represented not the kingdoms of this world, but an altogether different kingdom that he called "the kingdom of God." And this kingdom was one of peacemaking and nonviolence.

After Jesus' death, his followers kept this very same vision alive. Here, for example, is the apostle Paul, in the Epistle to the Romans.

> Bless those who persecute you; bless and do not curse them . . . Repay no one evil for evil, but take thought for what is noble in the sight of all. If possible, so far as it depends upon you, live peaceably with all. Beloved, never avenge yourselves, but leave it to the wrath of God; for it is written, "Vengeance is mine, I will repay, says the Lord." No, "if your enemy is hungry, feed him; if he is thirsty, give him drink; for by so doing you will heap burning coals upon his head." Do not be overcome by evil, but overcome evil with good. (12:14–21)

The truth is that for the most part, the early Christians conformed their lives to Jesus' teachings regarding peacemaking and nonviolence for the first three hundred years of the Christian movement. The testimony from two Christian leaders during that period makes this point clear. Tertullian (ca 155–230), for example, claimed that Jesus' command to love one's enemies is the "principal precept" of the Christian religion. In that light, he asked, "If we are enjoined to love our enemies, whom have we to hate? If injured we are forbidden to retaliate. Who then can suffer injury at our hands?"

Again, Cyprian (c. 200–258) summarized the heart of the Christian faith like this: "That you should not curse; that you should not seek again your goods when taken from you; when buffeted you should turn the other cheek; and forgive not seven times but seventy times seven . . . That you should love your enemies and pray for your adversaries and persecutors."

If the rejection of vengeance and the commitment to peacemaking and nonviolence was such a central part of the Christian religion for its first three hundred years, it's fair to ask, what happened? Why do most American Christians—and most Christians around the world, for that matter—view Jesus' teachings on nonviolence as noble ideals but finally unrealistic and unworkable?

There are doubtless many answers to those questions, but any answer would have to begin with the radical changes that transformed the Christian religion in the fourth century—first under the Roman Emperor Constantine (272–337) and then under the Emperor Theodosius the Great (347–395). Prior to Constantine, Rome had officially outlawed the Christian religion, and for one to convert to the Christian faith might well cost one's life. In 313, however, Constantine legalized Christianity for the first time in its history. Then, in 391, Theodosius made Christianity the only legal religion in the Roman Empire.

These decisions were far-reaching, for they created for the first time in Christian history the marriage of church and state, a marriage in which the state agreed to protect and honor the church, while the church would honor the state and its rulers by encouraging the faithful to conform to the rulers' decrees. Inevitably, those decrees included the command to participate in the Empire's wars.

Under the circumstances, it's hardly surprising that Christian theologians now found ways for Christians to serve the Empire by taking up the Empire's sword. The first Christian theologian to work out a systematic justification for this radical change was Augustine (354–430) whose just war theory stated that Christians *could* participate in warfare—and Christian emperors *could* declare and wage war—but only with certain safeguards and constraints. A just war, for example, would be a defensive war, would be fought for a just cause, would be fought with good intentions, and would avoid the killing of non-combatants.

Standing at the heart of just war theory are the assumptions that war is inevitable and that the biblical vision of peacemaking and nonviolence is finally illusory and impractical in this violent world.

Ironically, no one has made that case any more strongly than Samuel Huntington who cites approvingly the Venetian nationalist demagogue in Michael Didbin's novel, *Dead Lagoon*. "There can be no true friends without true enemies," the Venetian says. "Unless we hate what we are not, we cannot love what we are. These are the old truths we are painfully rediscovering after a century and more of sentimental cant." In response to this affirmation, Samuel Huntington comments, "The unfortunate truth in these old truths cannot be ignored by statesmen and scholars. For people seeking identity and reinventing ethnicity, enemies are essential."[10]

Maybe so, but if there is any chance that Christian leaders might lead us toward peace and not toward war and conflict, those are precisely the assumptions they must challenge. Put another way, so long as Christian leaders assume that the imperial vision is both normative and true to life, and so long as they assume that the biblical vision of the kingdom of God is finally unworkable and irrelevant, there is no chance that they will offer leadership any different from the standard imperial leadership that has driven the world for centuries.

The truth is, Christian leaders of tomorrow must embrace a new paradigm for thinking about war and peace—a paradigm that is at the very same time an ancient paradigm, embraced both by Jesus and the early church.

Let me offer just one example of what that paradigm might mean. David Lipscomb was a religious leader in the American South from the Civil War through the early twentieth century. After the Civil War, he reflected on his own role during that conflict. "In the beginning of the late strife that so fearfully desolated our country," he recalled, "much was said about 'our enemies.' I protested constantly that I had not a single enemy, and was not an enemy to a single man North of the Ohio River."[11]

Lipscomb's statement stands in stark contrast with Samuel P. Huntington's assumption that "there can be no true friends without true enemies" and that, when all is said and done, "enemies are essential."

And when, in 1896, the United States employed the Monroe Doctrine to threaten war against Great Britain, Lipscomb offered leadership on other grounds. He wrote, "When the leading lights among politicians begin to advocate war in defense of the Monroe doctrine, it is high time . . . to commence preaching peace on earth and good will among men in defense of the doctrine of the Sermon on the Mount."[12]

There are some who will no doubt object that what I have said in this presentation is far too visionary to be workable. But religious leaders are not called to embrace and sanction imperial assumptions. They are called, instead, to offer a vision grounded in their religious traditions. And deep in the Christian tradition there lies a powerful vision for peace on earth and good will among all humankind.

Tragically, this vision has rarely been tried, even by those who wear the mantle of the Christian religion and claim to represent the Prince of Peace. But the hour has now grown late, and wars and the threat of wars now threaten the very existence of the planet. We have no more time to waste.

So now is the time for Christian leaders to claim a vision that, for the most part, they have been too timid to claim for the past 1,700 years. Now is the time for Christian leaders to proclaim the heart of the Christian gospel. Now is the time for Christian leaders to reject the values of an imperial culture and to embrace instead the values of the kingdom of God.

These are momentous tasks, but these are the tasks to which all Christian leaders are finally called. And these are the tasks they must embrace if we hope to avoid catastrophe in these extraordinarily perilous times.

NOTES

1. This essay is a revision of my speech published in *Vital Speeches of the Day* 73 (December 2008) 536–40 and printed in this volume with permission. The speech was presented October 1, 2007, at the Installment of Robert M. Randolph, First Chaplain at Massachusetts Institute of Technology, Cambridge, MA. It was also presented at the "Preaching Peace" conference at Messiah College, August 13, 2008.

2. Samuel P. Huntington, *The Clash of Civilizations and the Remaking of World Order* (New York: Simon & Schuster, 1996) 42, 47.

3. Jonathan Sacks, *The Dignity of Difference: How to Avoid the Clash of Civilizations* (New York: Continuum, 2003) 5.

4. Ibid.

5. Jim Lobe, "Conservative Christians Biggest Backers against Iraq, Poll Shows," *Common Dreams News Center*, www.commondreams.org, October 10, 2002; and Charles Marsh, "Wayward Christian Soldiers," *New York Times* (January 20, 2006).

6. For the text of "The Battle Hymn of the Republic," along with an analysis, see David Hackett Fischer, *Liberty and Freedom: A Visual History of America's Founding Ideas* (Oxford: Oxford University Press, 2005) 331–32.

7. Christian Smith, *Christian America: What Evangelicals Really Want* (Berkeley: University of California Press, 2000) 199.

8. See, for example, Warren Carter, *Matthew and Empire: Initial Explorations* (Harrisburg, PA: Trinity, 2001), and *What Are They Saying About Matthew's Sermon on the Mount?* (New York: Paulist, 1994). See also Richard A. Horsley, *Jesus and Empire: The Kingdom of God and the New World Disorder* (Minneapolis: Fortress, 2003); Horsley, *Religion and Empire: People, Power, and the Life of the Spirit* (Minneapolis: Fortress, 2003); and Richard A. Horsley and Neil Asher Silberman, *The Message and the Kingdom: How Jesus and Paul Ignited a Revolution and Transformed the Ancient World* (Minneapolis: Fortress, 1997). See also Barbara R. Rossing, *The Rapture Exposed: The Message of Hope in the Book of Revelation* (New York: Basic Books, 2004).

9. Walter Brueggemann, "Alien Witnesses: How God's People Challenge Empire," *Christian Century* 124 (March 6, 2007) 28–32.

10. Huntington, *Clash of Civilizations*, 20.

11. David Lipscomb, "Babylon," *Gospel Advocate* 23 (2 June 1881) 340.

12. Lipscomb, "From the Papers," *Gospel Advocate* 38 (9 January 1896) 17.

Index of Names

Lincoln, Abraham, 205
Lipscomb, David, vi, xxi, 3, 6, 11–15,
18, 20, 54–55, 58, 61, 64, 67–69,
105, 124–25, 127, 129–39, 269,
271, 308–9
Lischer, Richard, 244, 266
Litfin, Duane, 225
Longman, Tremper, 151, 156
Lopus, Jane S., 191
Lucaites, John Louis, 264
Luther, Martin, 79
Lutz, David, 226

MacClenny, W. E., 90, 92
Mahoney, Daniel J., 232, 234, 244–45
Mansfield, Lee P., 68
Marsden, George M., 52, 166, 230
Marshall, Burke, 288, 294, 297
Marshall, Donald G., 158
Marshall, R., 93
Marshall, I. Howard, 87
Marty, Martin, 53, 242–43, 246
Mason, Captain John, 274–76, 278
Massa, Mark S., 37
Mathes, James M., 105
Matlon, Ronald J., 168
Maxwell, Nan L., 191
McAllister, Lester J., xii, xiii
McClintock, John, 75
McClung, John, 95, 110
McCone, John, 294
McCorkle, J. P., 112
McCoy, Charles S., 74
McCracken, Victor, 99
McGarvey, J. W., 36–53
McGary, Austin, 55, 58, 61, 135
McKane, William, 150
McKay, Heather A., 157
McKenzie, Alyce, 144
McKenzie, R., 162
McLoughlin, William G., 9
McQuiddy, J. C., 39, 128, 130
McVeigh, Timothy, 279–82
Mead, Stith, 93
Meade, George Herbert, 174

Medhurst, Martin J., vi, viii, 213–30,
214
Meeks, Wayne A., 216
Melton, Johnny, 57
Meynet, Roland, 195
Millard, David, 101
Miller, Keith D., 264
Miller, Perry, 238–40, 245
Miller, Richard, 286
Miller, William E., 191
Milligan, Robert, 72–74, 79–80
Milne, Robert, 108–11
Mitchell, Henry, 247, 250–52, 256,
259–60, 263–65
Mitchill, Samuel L., 96
Moore, John H., 4
Moore, W. T., 21, 23–25
Morgan, Thomas McBride, 113–14
Morris, A. M., 59
Morris, Aldon, 247
Morro, W. C., 47
Moser, K. C., 70–71
Moss, R. H., 111–12, 122
Mueller, John, 191
Murphy, James J., 218
Murray, John Courtney, 285, 288,
294–97
Mutuma, Mushambi, xiii

Nance, Clement, v, 89–105
Nelson, Michael, 180, 192
Neth, John W., 93
Neuhaus, Richard John, 213, 226
Newman, Robert P., xi
Nichol, C. R., 126, 128–29
Nichols, Terry, 280
Niebuhr, Reinhold, 277
Niebuhr, H. Richard, 270
Nielson, Nils C., Jr., 245
Noble, Kerry, 279–80
Notker Labeo, 219
Notte, Frederick, 98
Novak, Michael, 232, 244

O'Beirne, H. F., 5
O'Hare, Kate Richards, xix